I MY NEEDLE PLY WITH SKILL

Maine Schoolgirl Needlework of the Federal Era

I MY NEEDLE PLY WITH SKILL

Maine Schoolgirl Needlework of the Federal Era

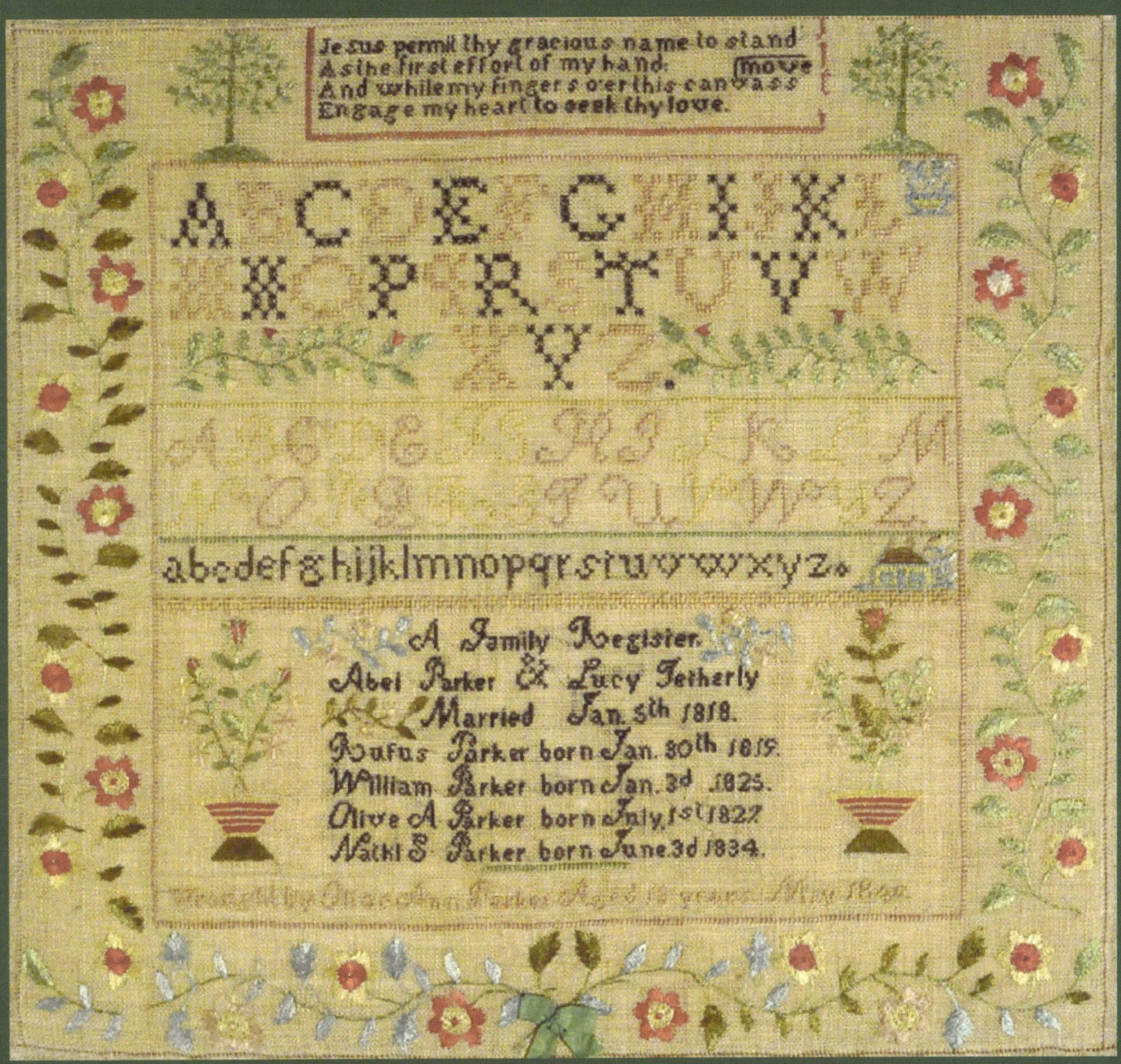

Leslie L. Rounds

Saco Museum
Saco, Maine

Published by Virtualbookworm.com Publishing Inc.
P.O. Box 9949
College Station, TX 77842
www.VirtualBookworm.com

This catalogue was published in conjunction with the exhibition *I My Needle Ply with Skill: Maine Schoolgirl Needlework of the Federal Era*, organized by the Dyer Library and Saco Museum and presented at the Saco Museum January 12 through March 2, 2013. The exhibition and catalogue were generously supported by a grant from the Coby Foundation.

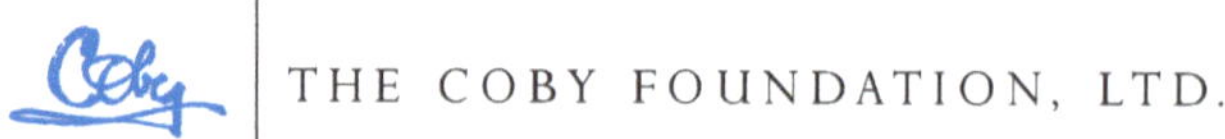

The exhibition was funded in part by a grant from the Maine Arts Commission, an independent state agency supported by the National Endowment for the Arts and the Maine Humanities Council, a private nonprofit organization affiliated with the National Endowment for the Humanities.

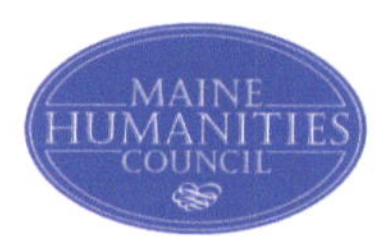

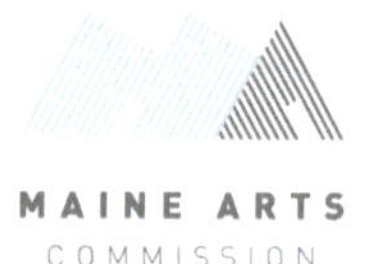

Written by Leslie L. Rounds
Book design by Susan Dudley Gold, Custom Communications, Inc.
Typography & Setup by Custom Communications, Inc.
Printed by www.virtualbookworm.com Publishing

Library of Congress Control Number:

ISBN-13: 978-1-62137-187-8

Photo Credits: Thank you to the following people for providing photos for this catalogue:
Cover: Family register sampler stitched by Olive Ann Parker of Eliot, Maine, in 1840.
Collection of the Dyer Library and Saco Museum.
Opposite page 1: Family register sampler of Martha, Ann, or Louisa Hawks of
Windham, Maine, stitched circa 1820. Collection of Julie Lindberg.
Contents, chapter openers, and back cover: left to right, top, Dan and Marty Campanelli, Dyer Library/Saco Museum, Dyer Library/Saco Museum, Maine Historical Society; left to right, bottom:
Sue and Dexter Perry, Julie Lindberg, Glee Krueger, Dyer Library/Saco Museum;
pp. 22, 72, and 124: Glee and Ralph Krueger; pp. 23, 30, 32, 46, 47, 50, 51, 58, 103, 116, 117, and 118: Maine Historical Society; p. 34: Sue and Dexter Pond; pp. 39, 43, 138, 140, and 141: Dan and Marty Campanelli; pp. 44, 96, and 98–100: Portland Museum of Art; pp. 45, 106, and 137: M. Finkel and Daughter; p. 48: Maine Maritime Museum; pp. 54, 58, 120, and 124: Mike Fredericks and the Maine State Museum; pp. 56 and 104: Pook & Pook Auction; pp. 64, 91, 92, and 97: Julie Lindberg; pp. 71, 78, and 132: Historic New England; pp. 74 and 122: Bret Thomas, Colonial Photography, Williamsburg, Virginia; p. 94: Mrs. Nancy Mairs; p. 113: Boothbay Historical Society; p. 121: Mr. and Mrs. Daniel Scheid and daughter; p. 125: Lynne Anderson; p. 136: Stephen and Carol Huber. All remaining photos except of the works of Burton W. Pearl taken by Fotografix, Saco, Maine.

A final word about photography concerns the many pieces of needlework owned by Dr. Burton Pearl. These were originally photographed by the author, inexpertly, for research purposes, with the intention of obtaining professional photographs if and when the pieces were lent for the exhibition. When the loan became impossible, a series of events followed that resulted in never obtaining better photographs. Although several of the images do not do full justice to the lovely nature of these samplers, Dr. Pearl consented to their inclusion in this publication because many of the pieces provide key documentation for schools and styles of needlework that no other pieces were able to offer.

1 3 5 6 4 2

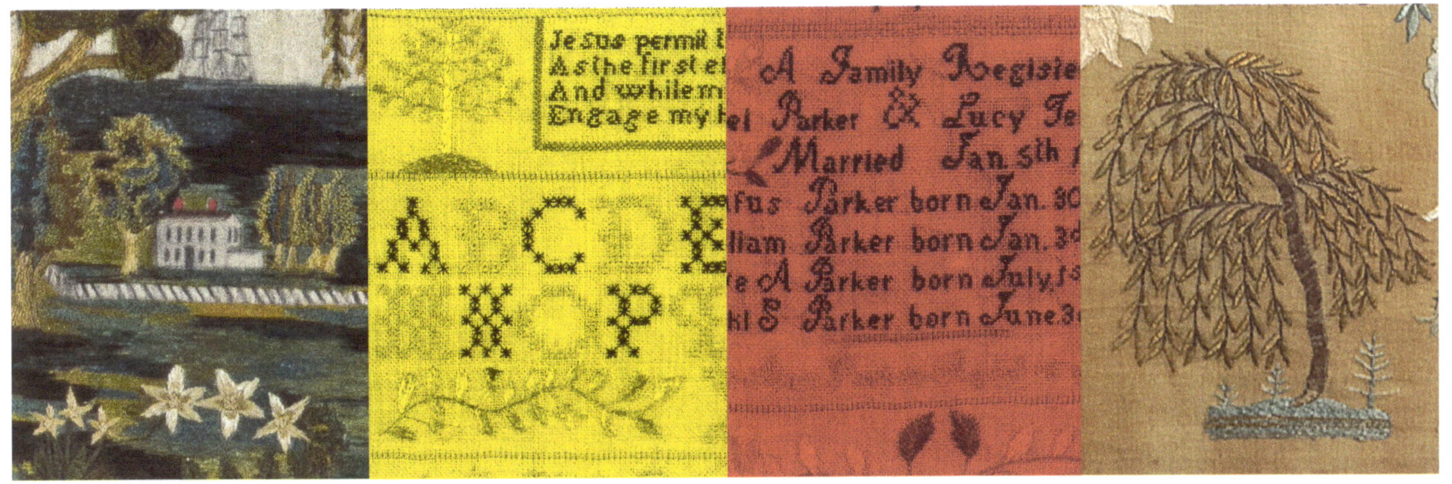

CONTENTS

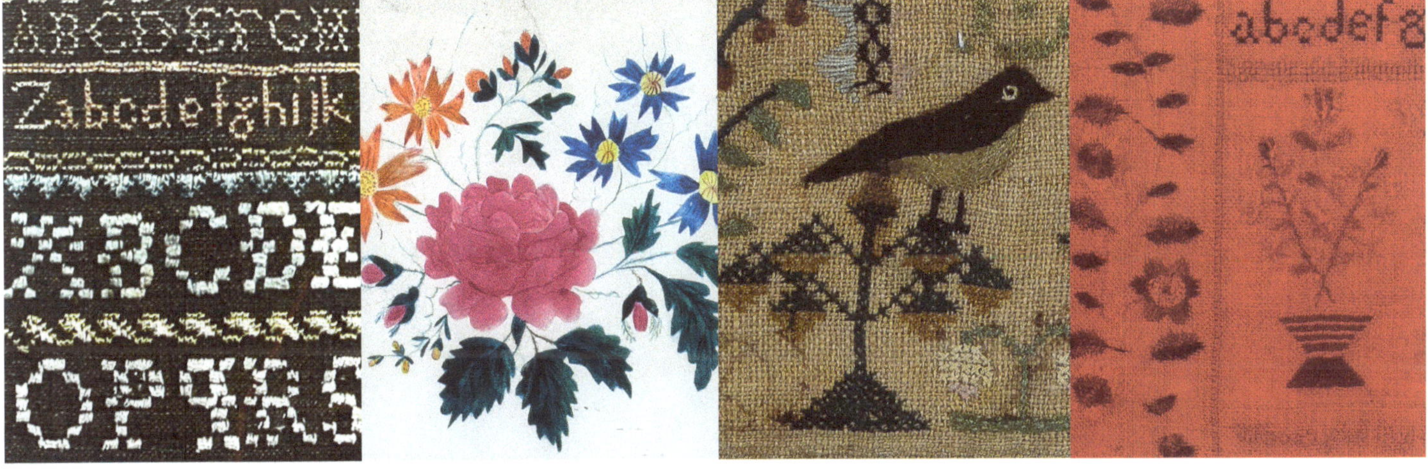

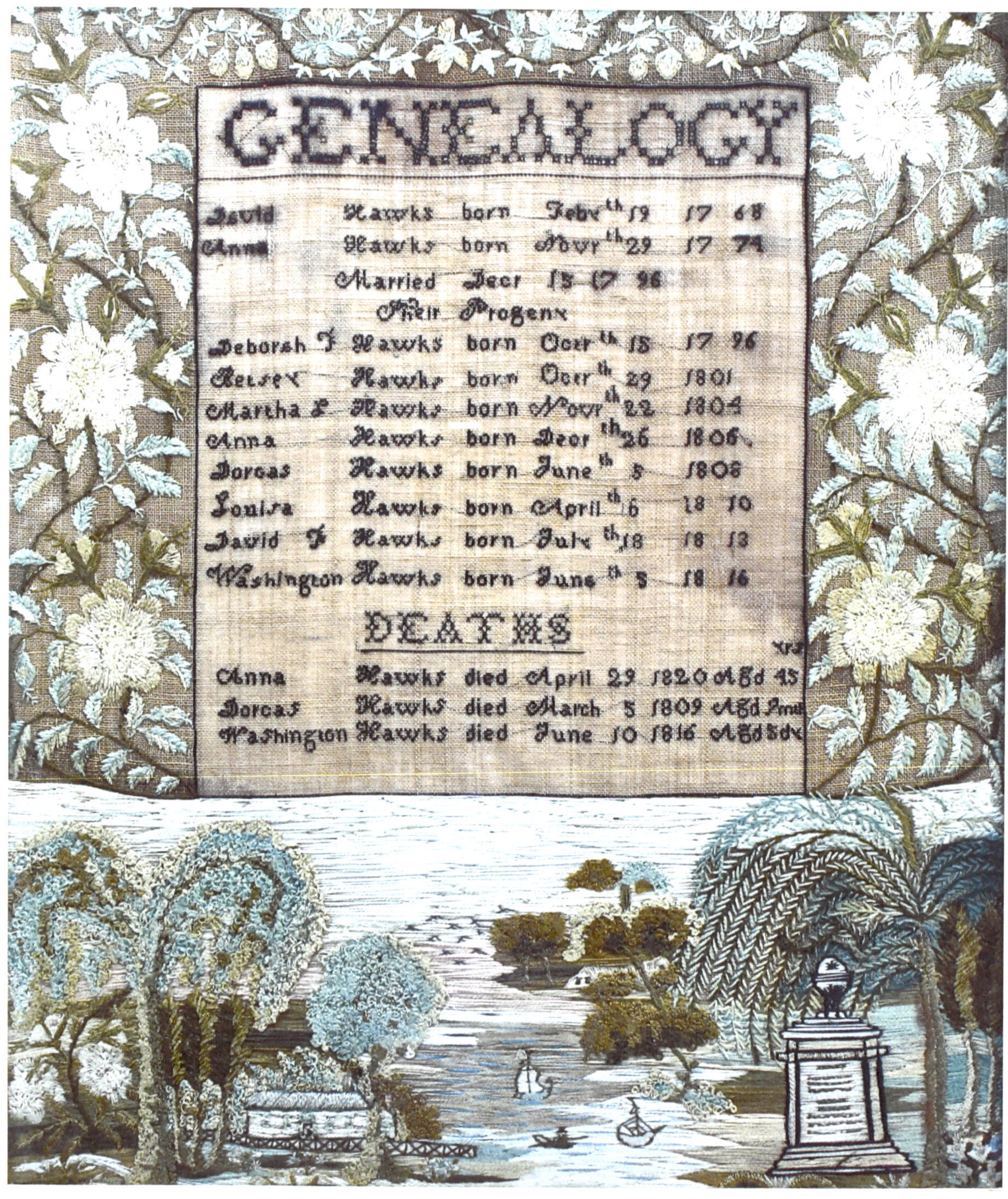
GENEALOGY
David Hawks born Febr th 19 17 68
Anna Hawks born Novr th 29 17 74
Married Decr 15 17 96
Their Progeny
Deborah T Hawks born Octr th 15 17 96
Betsey Hawks born Octr th 29 1801
Martha L Hawks born Novr th 22 1804
Anna Hawks born Decr th 26 1806
Dorcas Hawks born June th 5 1808
Louisa Hawks born April th 6 18 10
David T Hawks born July th 18 18 13
Washington Hawks born June th 5 18 16
DEATHS
Anna Hawks died April 29 1820 Agd 45 yrs
Dorcas Hawks died March 5 1809 Agd
Washington Hawks died June 10 1816 Agd

ACKNOWLEDGMENTS

First, I want to dedicate this book to my husband, Emory Rounds, my parents, Robert and Barbara Lambert, and my children, Emory, Kate, Chris, Erin, and Megan, and thank them all for their loving support and encouragement.

Many people have contributed to this effort. I will endeavor to thank as many as possible, but forgive me if I inadvertently omit anyone.

Thank you to the Coby Foundation, the Maine Arts Commission, and the Maine Humanities Council for your marvelous support.

For providing much needed advice when it was essential to have it, thank you to Glee Krueger, Lynne Anderson, Laura Fecych Sprague, Amy Finkel, Julie Lindberg, Patricia Nguyen, Stephen and Carol Huber, Charles Burden, Bill Gemmill, and Tara Vose Raiselis.

For assistance with research on the sampler makers and their teachers, thank you to Marie O'Brien, Donna-Belle and James Garvin, Mary Dawn, Doug Cruger, Fred Clark, Kitty Chadbourne, Randall Bennett, and innumerable family genealogists who generously responded to my queries, and especially to Camille Smalley and Jill Jakeman for cleverly discovering some very-hard-to-find ladies.

Thank you to all of the museums, historical societies, and private collectors who made access to their collections and knowledge so easy, especially to Dan and Marty Campanelli, Mr. and Mrs. Richard Larkin, and Sue and Dexter Pond for all their wonderful hospitality.

Thank you to Betty Ring, Ethel Stanwood Bolton, Eva Johnston Coe, and Glee Krueger (again!) for the wisdom and inspiration offered by their groundbreaking research.

Thank you to the Board of Trustees of the Dyer Library and Saco Museum for their enthusiastic encouragement.

Finally, thank you to the sampler makers, who persevered in stitching these works long after the fun must have gone out of it, and to their teachers, who guided and inspired them. They created a lasting body of lovely work that moves me beyond my power to express it.

—Leslie L. Rounds

INTRODUCTION

In December of 1805, Deborah Gordon, Lydia Dutch and Eliza "Betsey" Clapp gathered in Rachel Hall Neal's Portland rooms to master the intricacies of both plain and fancy needlework, to acquire a ladylike skill with pen and brush, and to advance their writing, reading, and ciphering abilities. They represented a new and critical change in the shape of America. Unlike the more wealthy girls of Maine (part of Massachusetts until 1820), who had attended boarding schools in distant Boston in the last quarter of the 18th century, these young women were the daughters of striving merchants, craftsmen, and tradesmen. The fine finish of advanced education for young women was no longer just the purview of the upper class that had developed in America over the past century. It was now both available to and desired by a burgeoning middle class. In Maine, in response to that emerging trend, numerous new female academies were opening, especially in Portland, but even in smaller ports and mountain villages, in the early years of the nineteenth century. The fine quality of needlework that was created in Maine academies rivaled that of major metropolitan areas of New England.

The female academies of the Federal era provided instruction not only in sampler making, but also in academic subjects and other needle arts, lending a genteel veneer to a large population of young women who previously had not had access to these refinements. Just a few decades later, even girls who could not attend the female academies could purchase, with the money they made through mill employment, some of the trappings of elegance they offered. The increasing difficulty of distinguishing between classes led Sarah Hale, editor of *Godey's Lady's Book* to bemoan:

> O the times! O the manners! Alas! How very sadly the world has changed! The time when the lady could be distinguished from the no-lady by her dress, as far as the eye could reach; but now you might stand in the same room, and judging by their outward appearance, you could not tell "which was which."[1]

This change in the class structure of American society had one of its roots in that first generation of the new republic's schoolgirls and their attendance at female academies.

Rachel Hall Neal herself reflected the developing middle class and its new, very democratic determination to acquire the physical trappings as well as the polite manners and behavior of the sophisticated upper class. Widowed in 1793 at twenty-five, almost immediately after giving birth to twins, Neal typically would have faced either a life of dependent near-poverty or a quick remarriage. Instead, she summoned the energy to open her own school, a business that she successfully operated and that provided gainful employment for both her and, eventually, her daughter for the next thirty-plus years.

In planning this book and its accompanying exhibition, it quickly became clear that the only possible way to document the existence of many teachers and female academies would be to examine as much needlework as possible and to watch for stylistic trends. When looking at many samplers and categorizing them by the towns where they were stitched; the dates they were made; the motifs, styles of alphabet, layouts and borders used; and the family relationships of the makers, connections emerge that cannot be observed from a smaller grouping. Preparation for *I My Needle Ply With Skill* has provided the opportunity to locate and study an unprecedentedly large group of Maine schoolgirl needlework; more than two hundred pieces were examined. These came from a variety of sources, including the collections of museums, historical societies and individuals; the records shared by sampler dealers; photographs in previous publications; auction records; and websites. Research for this work depended heavily on the in-depth work of previous scholars, including Ethel Stanwood Bolton and Eva Johnston Coe, Betty Ring, and Glee Krueger. This endeavor has brought to light many previously unknown connections and has raised interesting new areas of inquiry for future scholarship.

Often, the biographical information on the samplers themselves provided tantalizing clues that suggest connections among the young women, or between them and their teachers. Since women were not named on the U.S. Federal Census until 1850, that resource proved useful only for learning about the sampler makers' later lives. Local vital records, town histories, printed family genealogies, cemetery records, period newspapers, family historians, and the information the girls themselves stitched onto their needlework were the most significant sources for biographical information. All sampler researchers probably yearn for the same thing: rediscovery of a sampler that matches a body of work, conclusively identifies the maker, offers her genealogical details, and includes the name of her teacher. These are rare. In their absence, we can only draw speculative—though often compelling—conclusions. Consequently, this publication will frequently rely on the words *may*, *might*, and *probably*. As new pieces of needlework emerge, more connections will be discovered and tenuous ones proven either correct or mistaken.

I My Needle Ply With Skill begins with a section entitled *Industry Taught in Early Days: Massachusetts Beginnings*, exploring how Maine's emerging sophistication of material culture led residents to choose Boston as a center of education for young women. In 1783, Elizabeth Cutts wrote home to Saco, Maine, from Eleanor Druitt's female academy in Boston. Cutts was planning to make a coat-of-arms for her parents, a fashionable endeavor at Boston female academies serving American gentry of the era. Once completed, her rather ostentatious needlework (p. 18) was surely given place of pride in the Cutts mansion.[2] It signified not only Elizabeth's refined needle skills, but also the Cutts family's eminent and apparently deserved position in society, given their well-bred background as evidenced by having a coat-of-arms. A significant investment was made in the lavish materials: silk, gold, and silver threads; a hand-painted églomisé mat; and a custom-made frame. None of this, of course, presented any obstacle to Elizabeth's wealthy merchant father. The family carefully preserved this treasure, along with her schoolgirl letters home, until the objects were donated to the York Institute Museum (now Saco Museum) in the nineteenth century by one of its founders. Ironically, Elizabeth stitched the wrong coat-of-arms. Somehow, she worked the Milward family arms instead of the one of the Cutts family.[3] Presumably, the Cutts family displayed it, unaware that it was incorrect.

Some well-to-do Mainers continued to send their daughters to Boston schools throughout the early years of the nineteenth century. This practice was partly a result of the strong family connections many recently-arrived Maine residents had to that area, but it was also probably encouraged by the schooling choices of friends and neighbors and by the certain aspirational appeal of choosing distant academies over (perceived) less sophisticated local ones. Even so, some Boston-area schools failed to satisfy. When Eliza Southgate wrote home in 1797 to her father, a well-to-do doctor in Scarborough, Maine, with complaints about her school in Medford, Massachusetts (four beds to a room, two girls to a bed and chocolate served both breakfast and supper), it didn't take him long to choose another, possibly more expensive school for her.[4] By February, she was cheerfully writing home from Mrs. Rowson's school in Boston. A couple of years later, her next-youngest sister, Octavia, continued the new family tradition of attending Mrs. Rowson's, rather than one of the (by then) more readily available and well-established Portland schools.

The financing for a good Boston education was less fully in place for Dorcas Storer of Saco, but a distant academy was chosen anyway, perhaps partly because at least one elder sister had attended there. In a 1790 letter (in the collection of the Brick Store

Museum of Kennebunk), Eleanor Druitt wrote to Hannah Storer, Dorcas's older sister, reassuring her that she would keep Dorcas on at her academy at a reduced rate on the hope that the girls' missing father, Seth Storer, a mariner, would reappear and make good on the delinquent account. Storer's career at sea and access to some of the advantages of gentility had initially made the Boston boarding-school education of his daughters affordable and advantageous. Further, his good friends, Thomas Cutts and the Reverend John Fairfield, had both sent their numerous daughters to Boston for their educations. Wouldn't Storer want to be seen as capable of doing the same, even if it was a greater financial stretch for him?

Another reason the late eighteenth-century daughters of Southgate, Cutts, Storer, Fairfield, and many others went south for education is that there was little homegrown competition at the time. This began to change around 1800, and the second part of this project, *Industrious Ingenuity: The Rise of Urban Sophistication in Maine and Portland's Evolving Embroidery Style*, is devoted to exploring the rise of Portland-area female academies and their proprietary styles of needlework during this era. An attempt has been made to divide Portland needlework into groups by shared design elements and to assign those groups to teachers whenever possible. This teacher-assignment should lead to a greater recognition and a broader dialogue among dealers and collectors about Portland teachers and their bodies of work.

The first known school for young women in the growing town of Portland—the cultural and mercantile center of Maine at the time—was that of Virgin Islands transplant Sarah Jenkins Price.[5] Price had operated a female academy in St. Kitts after the early death of her husband. When her daughter Mary wed Portland sea captain William Campbell in 1762, he moved Sarah and her son to Portland along with his fifteen-year-old bride. In 1776, Campbell was lost at sea, and Price is supposed to have opened her school around the time of his death. Her academy operated until at least 1810, with little or no competition in early years.

Portland's other early schools also included that of the previously mentioned Rachel Wilson Hall Neal, which opened in 1794 and continued until well into at least the 1830s, when it was primarily run by her daughter, Rachel Neal. In about 1803, the Mrs. Dawes Academy opened when Elizabeth Bailey Dawes, the widow of the Reverend Ebenezer Dawes, left her position as preceptress (a historical term for the teacher/principal of a school) of the Derby Academy in Hingham, Massachusetts, and relocated to Portland. By all accounts a talented woman,[6] Dawes already had thirty-one students by the summer of 1804, when she proposed to hire an assistant and increase the size of her school to forty (see p. 26). Her success was short-lived: in April 1805, she chose the certainty of financial stability for herself and her two sons over the rewards of entrepreneurial efforts by marrying an older widower from Massachusetts and relocating to Brookline. Love might not have been a motivating factor in her choice, as suggested by the words of a man who knew the couple: "In old age, Mr. Lucas married a celebrated preceptress of the Hingham Academy; but, with all her accomplishments she failed to render him happy."[7]

Sally Perry also operated a Portland school from about 1805 until her marriage in the summer of 1807. Around the time that Sally's school opened, another of the longest-running schools, that of the Misses Martin, opened in Portland and continued in operation until about 1832, when a sizeable inheritance permitted the hardworking sisters to retire. Probably later in the same decade that the Martins' school opened, or early in the next, the Misses Mayo—Martha Merchant Mayo and her daughters—opened a school that lasted for many years. Although the school wasn't advertised until 1817, evidence of the family's financial need suggests that it had been in operation prior to that time. Simeon Mayo had by 1810 stopped being able to support his wife and six daughters, probably due to alcoholism,[8] and according to the 1810 federal census he no longer lived with his wife and children. Mrs. Mayo may have founded her school around this time in order to provide necessary income for herself and her family.

The Misses Martin's School for Young Ladies presents particular challenges and opportunities for scholars of Maine schoolgirl embroidery. Thanks to the recent research efforts of Laura Fecych Sprague, much is known of their school.[9] It opened near the end of 1803 in the Martin family home in North Yarmouth, Maine, but relocated to the larger mercantile and population center of Portland almost immediately. The school was operated by parents William and Elizabeth Martin, immigrants from England; several of their adult children were deeply involved and later fully took over operation of the academy. Catherine and William Clark Martin managed the day-to-day operations, and Elizabeth and Penelope taught the students. Edward H. Elwell, a Portland historian who knew the Martins, observed that they were "cultivated English ladies and brought with them the customs and traditions of their own teaching at home. English branches were taught, a little French, music, painting and many kinds of fancy work, lacemaking, and filigree, also geography with the use of globes."[10]

Perhaps around the time when the school closed in about 1832, the Martins published a list of 582 girls who had attended there.[11] The hometowns of most are noted, as well as spouses' names for about half of the girls; those who were already known to be deceased have asterisks after their names. This remarkable record ought to make it possible to establish a body of work for the academy, and indeed Sprague identifies work in a variety of media by girls from the Misses Martin's School. But to date, only a few *samplers* can be connected to the documented students. Deborah Gordon's name appears on the list, but this is not the Deborah Gordon who stitched the 1804 sampler illustrated on page 28; it is instead her niece.[12] Betsey Clap "of Bath" is named, and while she is the same girl as the sampler maker, she made her known 1805 sampler prior to attending Misses Martin's school; she didn't reside in Bath until after the death of both her parents in Portland late in 1810 .[13] Narcissa Stone of Brunswick is on the list, but her sampler (p. 98) is very like the ones worked by her sisters (pp. 99–100), and therefore it probably originated at the Brunswick school operated by Catherine Palmer Putnam from 1808 to 1829, fully covering the period of the Stone samplers, where Narcissa herself was assistant for many years. Narcissa Lyman, too, appears on the list. Her linsey-woolsey work with frequent use of trefoil and heart motifs (p. 62) is strongly suggestive of farther southern Maine or coastal New Hampshire (where she was born and resided) rather than of Portland works of the era, making it more likely to have been stitched prior to her attendance at the Martins' school. Eliza Elden of Buxton is named, but her sampler (p. 89) features a quirky, unsophisticated style and probably originated in a rural school. Finally, the currently unlocated sampler worked by Priscilla Purinton of Harpswell in 1805 was described this way in *American Samplers*: "5 alphabets Eyelet, stem, satin, and cross stitch Strawberry-vine border outside and sawtooth design inside Strawberry-vine cross border at bottom Also at bottom large tree with birds on several branches, and under tree are sheep, dog, man and woman in Colonial dress shaking hands In center is a large basket filled with flowers, and on the right side a large bush with a bird on top and a cage hanging from a branch Various cross borders."[14] This description, especially the inclusion of small human figures, makes Purinton's sampler unlike any other known Portland works; whether it therefore represents the true style of the Martins' school or a work from elsewhere is unknown.

It is surprising that so few samplers made by the Misses Martin's young ladies have come to light. Given the large number of identified students that attended there, this may indicate that sampler making was simply not taught. Perhaps the studies at the Misses Martin's were only in more advanced needle arts, such as silk embroidery. The silk embroideries that have been definitively linked to the Misses Martin's instruction (as shown in Betty Ring's "Samplers and Silk Embroideries of Portland, Maine," *The Magazine Antiques*, September, 1988, pp. 516–517) are richly embroidered but somewhat idiosyncratically designed compared to other schools' efforts. They are enough like each other that, if more come to light, it ought to be relatively easy to connect them. This remains an intriguing field for future research.

The crowded Portland field was joined by one academy after another in the Federal era, some short-lived and others operating for long spans. Long-running ones included those of the Paine sisters Charlotte, Sarah and possibly Phebe—daughters of a physician—who ran a Portland school from about 1821 to 1839; the Dupee sisters, Sarah and Abba (granddaughters of famous Boston mathematical instrument-maker John Dupee), who ran a school from about 1811 until perhaps as late as 1820; Elizabeth Hussey, whose school lasted from about 1810 to 1827, known through limited advertising and named only on the 1818 rose-bordered genealogical sampler of Ann Matilda Greely, (in a private collection); and Mary Rea, who operated a school connected to a known body of work that opened around 1822 and lasted until not long before her death in 1846. Silk embroideries (and one known genealogical sampler attributed to Hannah Harding Smith) from Rea's school feature willowy-armed figures (awkwardly done when compared to those from the Mayo school), realistic depictions of buildings with little or no concern for perspective, and often, like some from the Martins' school and some from the Mayos', clusters of oversized flowers in the foreground.

Some schools are well documented through newspaper advertisements, family histories of students, and listings in city directories. Other schools, like Clarissa Dela's, are only known because their names appear on single samplers made at their academies. Mrs. Abigail Fellows's school, which operated from at least 1807 to about 1820, when she died on a visit to family in Havana, Cuba, is only known because it is mentioned in a nineteenth-century biography of Henry Wadsworth Longfellow; she was his first teacher.[15] The listing in *American Samplers* for a sampler by Mary Jane Barker states that she attended "Mme. Niel's school . . . hand-in-hand" with her young neighbor, Henry Wadsworth Longfellow, according to her descendant.[16] The "Mme. Niel" referred to must be Rachel Hall Neal, who as previously noted operated a Portland school at the time; however, a substantial body of Longfellow scholarship shows that neither Henry nor his sisters were ever students of the Neal's, making that attribution very questionable. It is more probable that Mary Jane Barker and her twin sister Flavilla made their identical samplers (p. 35) at the school of Mrs. Fellows, where we know Longfellow to have attended.

Portland-made samplers have come to be identified with an iconic rose border. The earliest example is the sampler stitched by Dorcas Shaw (1803, p. 26), which may have been made under the tutelage of Elizabeth Dawes, her distant relative, during the brief tenure of her school.[17] It includes a simple queen-stitch rose border accompanied by alphabets and the maker's name and date, but it is not genealogical like so many Portland samplers that came later. Both Shaw's sampler and a similar one done by Eliza Harden (p. 27) feature a black-filled name cartouche with a sawtooth edge around it. A remarkably similar cartouche also appears in a small group of samplers worked a few years later in Leominster, Massachusetts.[18] The intriguing connection, if any, between these two groups remains undiscovered.

A closely related group of samplers, dating from 1804 to 1820, includes both the queen-stitch rose border (later satin-stitched) and a genealogical format. The first is the previously noted 1804 sampler by Deborah Gordon (p. 28), which was very likely stitched at Rachel Hall Neal's school, given that this particular Deborah Gordon is not one of the listed students for the Misses Martin's School for Young Ladies, and that Neal's school is the only other one that spans the years of the now-identified body of work.[19] From the precise dates of completion stitched into the samplers themselves, we know that Deborah finished her sampler only a couple of weeks prior to those of Lydia Dutch (p. 31) and Eliza Clapp, (sold by Carol and Stephen Huber, location unknown) which were also made at the same school[20] and feature a nearly identical border and also a view of a village at the bottom. It's wonderful to imagine these three girls, perhaps sitting side by side in the pale winter light of a window, hard at work on their stitchery.

Possibly influenced by the work of the Neal students, in 1807, Mary Lewis also completed a genealogical sampler with a queen-stitch border and a village scene, but under the direction of a different teacher, Sally Perry, intended as a wedding gift for her and providing the information about her identity (page 34). Perry is responsible for the design of least three other works; the samplers of Nabby Horton, illustrated in *The Magazine Antiques*, September, 1988, p. 513; Mary Fernald, for sale at Antique Associates at West Townsend Inc., Massachusetts; and Eleanor Douglass, taken to Hawaii by her daughter in the mid-nineteenth century, illustrated in *Father Bond of Kohala*, 1927, by Ethel M. Damon. Its location is unknown.

The style of these samplers seems to have become fixed in imaginations of Portland teachers. While the queen-stitch roses gradually evolved over two decades into a strikingly realistic and lovely satin-stitch version, the general format remained the same among known Portland samplers, with only small variations evidencing the different design ideas of various instructors. Since many of the students who attended Portland's female academies were local, it's quite likely that parents or students saw work of other girls and asked teachers to include genealogical information or a village scene in the designs they drew. Just as possibly, teachers saw the work from other schools and then chose to include admired design elements in what they offered. This active "cross-pollination" in the village-like atmosphere of Portland no doubt led many teachers to offer somewhat similar patterns to their students. Only by viewing and comparing many Portland samplers can scholars begin to distinguish defining stylistic differences among schools, an opportunity that research for this project has presented.

While research for this book and exhibition has brought to light many new Maine samplers for documentation, creating new connections and rediscovery of previously unidentified teachers, the same cannot be said for silk embroideries. The reasons for this are at least threefold. One is that silk embroideries—works that were stitched with silk thread on a silk ground and generally embellished with paint—remain much scarcer than samplers. Many schools simply did not teach this advanced and challenging art form. Secondly, silk is much less durable than the linen ground of most samplers; when painted it often becomes even more fragile, so that fewer of these works have survived.[21] Finally, silk embroideries were much more likely to go unsigned and undated. These unattributed works, unless very similar to known ones, usually cannot even be assigned to a particular state or region, severely limiting opportunities for scholarship.

Beginning about 1820, much later than in other states, sumptuous ornamental silk thread and paint on silk works were designed and created in Portland. The needlework came from several schools. Betty Ring surmised that one very likely source was one of Martha Mayo's daughters, Martha. Ring believed that she might have been the designer of the numerous pieces of Portland needlework that feature cherubs with neck ruffs[22] (but probably not the one or two that have less attractive cherubs *without* ruffs).[23] Martha married in 1827 and moved away; no cherub works appear to have been made after she left. Thickly bordered genealogical samplers also apparently originated with the ruffed cherub designer, since they include the iconic little angelic figure.[24] Several of these have been identified, including one made by one of the daughters of Stephen Knight (p. 46). In this group of about five samplers, students usually failed to name themselves or the date of completion on the works. The borders are so dense as to draw the eye away from the genealogical information in the center, which generally names "Progeny." There is usually a pair of darkly rendered willows at the bottom. Two of this group—one stitched in about 1828 or later, documenting the family of Jacob Chase, born in Amesbury, Massachusetts, and one worked by Elizabeth Haskins in 1833—demonstrate an amateurish design compared to earlier works. They also lack the typical cherub, probably lending credence to the idea that Martha Mayo was the artist for the earlier ones, but not these related examples.

With their high level of detail and the sophistication of their compositions, the silk works reflect the growing influence of the fine arts tradition in Portland at this time. Indeed, Betty Ring pointed out that the landscape painter Charles Codman, shortly after arriving in Portland in 1822 from an apprenticeship in Boston, advertised that he would draw for ladies' needlework.[25] One of Codman's most enthusiastic promoters was America's first art critic, John Neal, who also relocated to his native Portland about 1827.[26] Intriguingly, Neal was the son of Rachel Hall Neal, one of the twins she had given birth to back in 1793.[27] Could he have met Codman because the young artist was already working with his mother and her students?[28] While there are several extant letters between John Neal and his mother and sister,[29] they all predate Codman's residence in Portland and thus cannot provide that crucial link. The degree to which John Neal's mother and sister, then, engendered the alliance of these two major figures in Maine's art history remains undetermined.

While female academies have been documented throughout the state, the largest and best known body of work is associated with Portland, most likely because of the sheer volume of needlework that was created in the numerous competing schools there. It appears that many of the other schools across the state served only very small groups of girls at a time or were short-lived, resulting in minimal numbers of samplers that would then have to survive the severe winnowing of the next two hundred years. Still, Portland was not the only place in Maine where girls could receive instruction, and the third section of this volume, *How Letters Great and Small Are Wrought: Individual Creativity and Portland's Influence on Rural Academies,* includes a wide range of schoolgirl embroidery from across the state.

The population in Maine began at the southern coast and migrated both inland and "downeast" toward Canada, accompanied by growing refinement as new settlements became established communities. The styles of needlework, too, sometimes traveled along analogous paths. In some of the smaller towns, a flavor of the Portland sampler trickled over into local designs: rose borders remained popular, and genealogical information was often included. As late as 1846, Sarah Cheney worked her genealogical sampler (p. 138) in far downeast Eastport, yet, except for the modern background of Penelope canvas (a double mesh needlepoint canvas), it could easily be mistaken for the work of three decades and hundreds of miles distant.

The Cony Female Academy, founded in Augusta in 1815, has the next-largest body of work after the Portland schools. An attractive rose-bordered genealogical sampler style emerged there that is both visually appealing and quite different from the iconic Portland style. (An added bonus is that many Cony samplers name the school.) The Cony Female Academy was founded by the Honorable Daniel Cony, who was the father of at least four grown daughters (one of whom appears on the list of students of the Misses Martin's School for Young Ladies in Portland) and wanted to find a way to provide young women with a quality education closer to home. In 1815, he noted in a letter to prospective trustees, "The importance of female education has for a number of years been a subject of my most serious and anxious solicitude."[30] Between 1815 and 1820, Miss Hannah B. Aldrich, "an approved and experienced preceptress,"[31] ran the school. She then married Pitt Dillingham, and a Miss Bancroft replaced her. In 1823, Aldrich (now Mrs. Dillingham) returned for a year, and then Miss S. A. Farnham of Boston was hired for 1824, Miss Harriet Green in 1825–27, and then in 1828 Mrs. Dillingham came back once again and was assisted by her sister, Miss Mary Aldrich. In spite of these changes in instructors, the overall style of sampler work remained relatively constant, perhaps because Mrs. Dillingham was never far away, even when not actively teaching there.

The size and professionalism of the Cony Academy notwithstanding, the contrast between the larger, more sophisticated coastal communities and smaller inland ones was often sharp. In *A Midwife's Tale*, historian Laurel Thatcher Ulrich documented the remoteness of Hallowell, Maine—just outside of Augusta—describing how midwife Martha Ballard had to ford rivers on horseback to attend births at outlying farms.[32] Meanwhile, Eliza Southgate, back from her Boston schooling and on one of her frequent visits away from home, was describing to her mother (with just a touch of ironic humor) the social conditions of 1800 Wiscasset, a wealthy coastal village: "I am informed, they are so monstrous smart as to take no notice of any lady that can condescend to wear a calico gown; therefore, dear mother, to insure me a favorable reception, pray send my spotted muslin by the next mail."[33] Though inland towns faced disadvantages, soon they, too, recognized the democratic obligation to provide their citizenry with at least a fundamental education. This led to the founding of schools and educational opportunities much closer to rural homes, providing the hope of gentility to the daughters of families who could not afford a boarding-school education. Good-sized coeducational academies opened in Fryeburg in 1792, in Gorham in 1803, in Bridgton in 1808, and in Saco in 1811, among other locations. Some schools hired preceptresses and offered schooling in the female arts. Others, reflecting new thinking about women and their educational potential, had no instruction in stitchery, painting or other "refinements," and instead offered a more purely academic curriculum.

These much bigger schools often had between thirty and fifty pupils, both day students and boarders; however, many women also continued to operate small schools in rural villages. Mrs. Rhoda Remington, whose school was the well-documented primary competition for the more famous school of Mary Balch in Providence, Rhode Island, in the early years of the new century,[34] relocated to Hallowell, Maine, and operated an apparently small but actively advertised school there from about 1810 to 1815, when she married and moved to Massachusetts.[35] This was in the same primitively undeveloped town where Martha Ballard had delivered babies almost up until her death in 1812,[36] a sharp divide in contemporaneous lifestyles. "Edee" (Edith) Richardson Pease ran a school in Chesterville, a tiny town that, nonetheless, was large enough to provide business for her. She is known only because she was named on a sampler stitched by her student, Rosetta Stoddard (p. 124). The existence of these schools can often only be proven by small, unique bodies of work that are all connected to a particular geographic area. Generally (but not always), the styles were more modest and lacked the artistic quality associated with the larger schools. The large group of samplers that names Bethel, Maine (pp. 126–131), offers an example of this.

Traditional female academies flourished in Maine long after most died out elsewhere. "Ornamental" topics of instruction in the female arts continued well into the nineteenth century in Maine. Most of the academies that persisted had been founded earlier in the century. Typically, however, as that generation of talented female instructors became aged and infirm, the schools closed their doors. From that point on, young women were primarily taught in new public schools, in somewhat more academic subjects designed to prepare them best for what was still viewed as their almost certain career choice: motherhood and skilled family management.

Fine needlework, like the more elaborate samplers and silk embroideries included in this exhibition, was the culminating achievement of a comprehensive education in the needle arts. But it all began with basic sewing skills, which were, as Eliza Mayo told a prospective client: "so essential for a lady to be perfected in before she takes up ornamental needlework."[37] Having acquired these skills, later in the century women often did not lay down their needles when they no longer needed to keep them in motion stitching family clothing and other essentials. Instead, there was a new flowering of home arts. The final part of the exhibition, *The Various Texture of the Twining Thread: Where Did All That Creativity*

Lead?, examines the wide range of women's creativity that followed the Federal era. For many (if not most) young women, schoolgirl needlework was only the beginning of a lifetime of creativity with needle and thread. Many nineteenth-century women, in spite of notable hardship, continued to decorate their lives with the beautiful though often utilitarian textiles they made.

With machine-sewn, factory-made clothing, first for men and children and then for women, starting to flood into stores, the need to be a skilled seamstress diminished and then largely disappeared; good needle skills were no longer critical for women. There were, for example, eighty percent fewer dressmaking establishments in Philadelphia in 1880 than there had been in 1860: so much ready-made clothing was now available that women no longer needed either to have their family's clothing custom-made or to make it themselves.[38] This represented, over the course of the lifetimes of the Federal-era sampler makers, a drastic reduction in one of the most time-consuming chores they faced in their daily lives. The skills with needle and thread that young women of that era had so studiously acquired instead found a new manifestation in personal and highly decorative work that straddled functionality and artistic expression. Yarn-sewn and then hooked rugs emerged and were proudly exhibited at fairs alongside homemade needle lace; knitted, crocheted, tatted, and embroidered objects for home and attire; and most evident of all, lovely, intricate young children's clothing on which attention was often lavished beyond any proportion to necessity or practicality. As these women matured, and their daily environment transformed from the schoolroom to their own parlors, their handiwork, too, evolved to embrace new desires to handsomely outfit their beloved children and elegantly furnish their cherished homes.

This talented and educated generation of sampler-makers of the Federal era went on to create a lasting, although sadly almost always anonymous, record of their continued existence. Haunting today's flea markets and antique stalls, their beautifully wrought works are a powerful reminder that we are all compelled to leave a proof of our existence. A sampler verse that first appeared on a 1785 needlework captures that effort: "When this you see, remember me/ And bear me in your mind/What others say when I'm away/Speak of me as you find."[39]

NOTES

1. Sarah Hale quoted in Benita Eisler, *The Lowell Offering: Writings by New England Women* (New York: W.W. Norton & Company, 1977), 184.

2. Born in 1736 into a well-to-do Kittery family, Thomas Cutts relocated to Saco in 1758, where he invested in numerous successful business ventures, including purchasing vast tracts of land, successful shipping, founding of a bank, and building a nail factory. He constructed a mansion on a Saco River island and was probably Saco's wealthiest resident during his lifetime. Elizabeth's letter is partially transcribed in Laura Fecych Sprague et al., *Agreeable Situations: Society, Commerce, and Art in Southern Maine, 1780–1830* (Boston: Northeastern University Press, 1988), 240.

3. This amusing bit of trivia was discovered by Betty Ring. John Guillam's *A Display of Heraldry* was the usual resource for illustrations of coats-of-arms. The Milward arms appeared on the same page as the Cutts design, perhaps leading to some confusion. Betty Ring, *Girlhood Embroidery American Samplers and Pictorial Needlework 1650–1850* (New York: Alfred A. Knopf, 1997), 72.

4. Eliza Southgate was the third child of Robert Southgate and Mary King. Her engaging letters span the years from her period of education in Boston until just before her death from tuberculosis at the age of twenty-five. Sadly, all but one of her siblings died in very young adulthood. Eliza Southgate Bowne, *Letters of Eliza Southgate, Mrs. Walter Bowne* (Lexington, Ky.: Library of Congress reprint of original edition, 2011), letter of May 12, 1797.

5. Bhima MacDonald Sturtevant, "Portland's First Teacher Sara Jenkins Price," Maine Women Writers Collection, University of New England.

6. A genealogical record of the Kingman family states, "She was a lady of very many personal accomplishments." Bradford Kingman, *The Kingman memorial: genealogical memoirs of the descendants of Henry and Joanna Kingman of Weymouth, Mass., U.S.A. : together with a brief history of the family in England, 1635–1898* (Washington, D.C.: Library of Congress Photoduplication Service, 1984), 72. After she married her third husband, she crafted a yarn-sewn rug (a precursor to the hooked rug) and won first place at a western Massachusetts fair. The rug is in the collection of Historic Deerfield.

7. This comment was written by Zachariah O. Whitman in the first volume of *History of the Military Company of the Massachusetts Now Called the Ancient and Honorable Artillery Company of Massachusetts, 1637–1888.* Whether he personally knew Lucas or not is unknown. A second volume, like the first mostly consisting of brief biographies of men who belonged to the organization, has an expanded biography of Lucas that states that Dawes was preceptress of the Hingham Academy from 1796 to 1804, dates also noted by Betty Ring. Roberts, Oliver Ayer Roberts, *History of the Military Company of the Massachusetts Now Called the Ancient and Honorable Artillery Company of Massachusetts, 1637–1888, Volume 2* (Boston: Alfred Mudge & Son, 1897), 211. Ring's notes are not yet available for researchers, making it currently impossible to check on her source for the dates, but it was likely to have been Thomas Tracy Bouve et al., *History of the Town of Hingham, Massachusetts, in Three Volumes,* Volume 1, Part 2 (Hingham: Town of Hingham), 141.

8. William Willis, *The History of Portland from 1632 to 1864* (Portland: Bailey & Noyes, 1865), 486.

9. Laura Fecych Sprague, "Schoolgirl Art From the

Misses Martin's School for Young Ladies in Portland, Maine," *Antiques and Fine Art*, September 2011, 48.

10. Edward H. Elwell, *The Schools of Portland* (Portland: William M. Marks, 1888), 33.

11. The list may have been created through reference to the account books of the academy; it's difficult to imagine it being constructed from memory. Since William Martin Sr. was an experienced businessman, it seems reasonable that he would have followed typical record-keeping methods of the period, so that ledgers would have been maintained, providing a ready and no doubt comprehensive resource for whomever created the list.

12. This is proven both by the names of the niece Deborah's sisters on the list and her spouse's name, which also appears on the Misses Martin's list.

13. She appears to be one of the females in her father's household on the 1810 United States Federal Census.

14. Ethel Stanwood Bolton and Eva Johnston Coe, *American Samplers* (Boston: Thomas Todd Company, 1921), 211.

15. Samuel Longfellow, *Henry Wadsworth Longfellow* (Cambridge: John Wilson & Son, 1886), 16.

16. Bolton and Coe, *American Samplers*, 125.

17. Dorcas Shaw was a cousin-in-law of Ebenezer Dawes—not a close relationship! The sampler is otherwise attributed to Dawes by the date it was made.

18. The black cartouche of the Leominster samplers is described in Mary Jaene Edmonds, *Samplers & Sampler Makers: An American Schoolgirl Art 1770–1850* (New York: Rizzoli International Publications, Los Angeles County Museum of Art, 1991), 59.

19. Sarah Jenkins Price may also have taught after 1810, but by 1820 she was ninety years old, infirm, and residing with her also-unwell daughter, Mary; their ill health makes it unlikely that they were still teaching.

20. The attribution of these three works to the same school is based upon their marked common elements. Some are virtually identical. Known samplers in this style, all now attributed to Neal's school, include those by Deborah Gordon, Elizabeth Mountfort, Mary Merrill, Lydia Dutch, Eliza Tukey (all in private collections), Amelia Lowell (Baxter House Museum, Gorham, Maine), Mary Richards (Smithsonian Cooper-Hewitt, National Design Museum), Joanna Poole, Mary A. Twombly (both at Maine Historical Society), Eliza Clapp, Betsy Wheelwright (both in private collections and kindly brought to my attention by Stephen and Carol Huber), Sarah Jordan (sold by Skinner, Inc. November 5, 2011) and Martha Wilder (whereabouts unknown but readily available on the internet as a poster).

21. The 1921 publication of *American Samplers* by the Colonial Dames of American no doubt encouraged the public to begin to regard samplers as worthy of preservation and collection. That recognition of silk embroidery seemed to come much later, perhaps another detrimental factor that limits the number of remaining works.

22. Ring, *Girlhood Embroidery*, 254. However, a few related silk embroideries—or perhaps painted works—have recently emerged that have identical monuments, sharing charming perspective problems on a rear "foot," but *no* cherubs. See http://americangardenhistory.blogspot.com/2009/11/garden-urns-in-early-america.html.

23. The elaborate genealogical sampler of (probably) Janet Carruthers (Maine Historical Society, p. 47) features an awkward ruff-less cherub on a monument. This piece has many stylistic elements that differ from

the genealogical samplers with ruffed cherubs, including a much more attractive border with roses that are stitched concentrically, a painted and embroidered landscape, and boats and buildings that more closely resemble those of the Mary A. Reed silk embroidery (p. 45) and others. These have been attributed to the school of Mary Rea.

24. For example, samplers by Fanny Whitney (Winterthur), Mary D. Chase, Elizabeth Haskins (both in private collections; Chase (sold by Sotheby's, 2011); Haskins (sold at James D. Julia, 2012), a Bryant daughter, and a Knight daughter (both at Maine Historical Society).

25. Betty Ring, "Samplers and Silk Embroideries of Portland, Maine," *The Magazine Antiques*, September 1988, 519. An overview of Codman's life and career is provided in Jessica Nicoll, *Charles Codman: The Landscape of Art and Culture in 19th-century America* (Portland, Maine: Portland Museum of Art); the advertisement cited is reproduced on p. 21.

26. John Neal, *Wandering Recollections of a Somewhat Busy Life* (Boston: Roberts Brothers, 1869), 323, 329.

27. Neal, *Recollections*, 14.

28. John Neal, as early as 1835, claimed to have "discovered" Codman eight years earlier by his talent from a series of landscapes painted on the walls of the Elm Tavern in Portland. According to Neal, even Codman was unaware of his own talent, a rather surprising conclusion since Codman had already been working as an artist in Portland for five years. This story of discovering Codman would certainly have seemed more impressive than if Neal had met the artist through his mother. Nicoll, *Codman*, 31.

29. In the collections of the Maine Historical Society, Portland.

30. James W. North, *History of Augusta* (Augusta, Me.: Clapp and North, 1870), 422.

31. North, *Augusta*, 423. Aldrich was born and raised in Mendon, Massachusetts. Perhaps future research will reveal where she had previously taught. Since she is surely responsible for the Cony sampler style, discovering her teaching roots might make a valuable connection to another group of samplers.

32. Laurel Thatcher Ulrich, *A Midwife's Tale* (New York: Random House, 1990), 5.

33. Southgate, *Letters*, July 1, 1800.

34. Betty Ring, *Let Virtue Be a Guide to Thee* (Providence, R.I.: Rhode Island Historical Society,1983), 107.

35. The vital records of Charlestown, Massachusetts, show that she married Jedediah Lakeman and relocated to that city.

36. Ulrich, *A Midwife's Tale*, 341.

37. Letter from Eliza Mayo to Nancy Stone of Brunswick, March 9, 1827, Collection of the Portland Museum of Art.

38. Joan Severa, *Dressed for the Photographer* (Kent, Oh.: Kent State University Press, 1995), 293.

39. Bolton and Coe, *American Samplers*, 256.

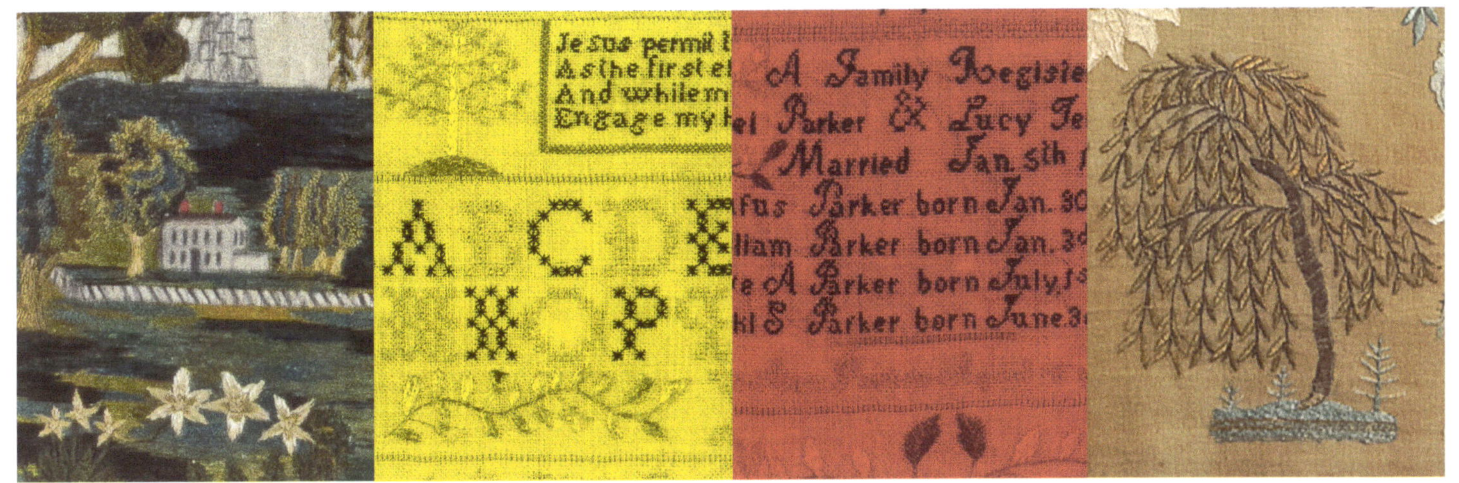

Part One

Industry Taught in Early Days:
Massachusetts Beginnings

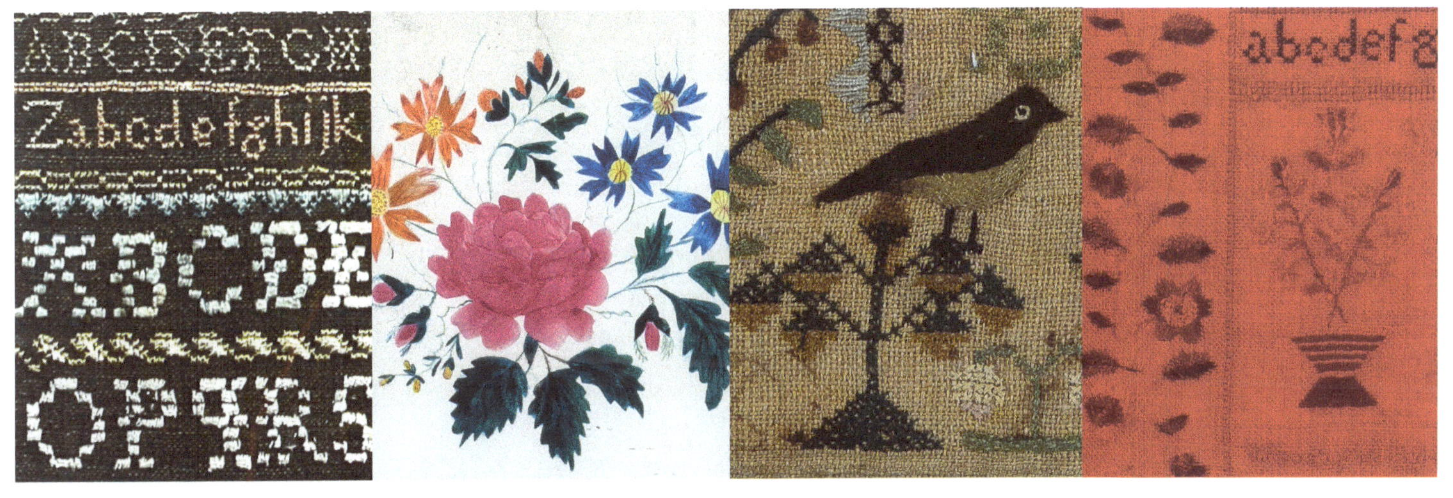

Eunice Cutts (1782–1853)
Marking sampler, 1792
Worked at unknown school
Silk thread on linen
Cross, Algerian eye, satin, stem, running, rococo and chain stitches
14 ½ x 8 ½
Collection of the Dyer Library and Saco Museum

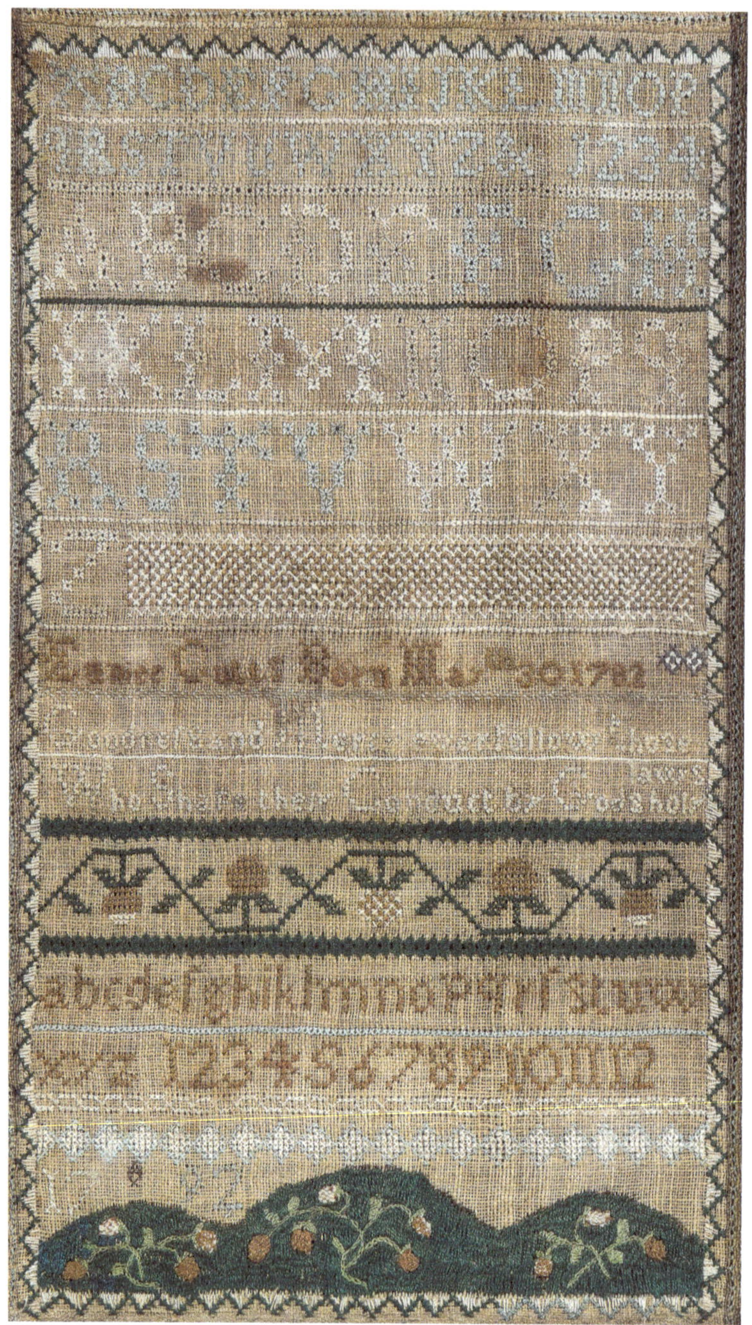

Eunice Cutts was born May 30, 1782, into one of Saco's wealthiest families of the period; she was the youngest of the seven children of Colonel Thomas and Elizabeth Scamman Cutts. He was a merchant and land speculator, and well-to-do enough to commission artist John Brewster Jr. to paint full-length portraits of himself and his wife (in the collection of the Saco Museum). Eunice and at least two of her older sisters received a boarding-school education in Boston, attending the female academy of Eleanor Druitt. Since Eunice was only ten when she made her sampler, it may have been completed in Saco before she attended Druitt's academy. The distinctive three-hilled ground across the bottom of her marking sampler, with its stylized strawberries, also appears on a sampler worked by Abigail Brown in Leicester, Massachusetts, in 1825, in a private collection. Perhaps a teacher there had also once been taught by whoever instructed Eunice. Cutts married Boston physician Samuel Nye in 1803; she may have met him while at boarding school. Between 1806 and 1824, she gave birth to nine children and died in Saco on October 26, 1853, having outlived her husband, all of her siblings, and four of her children.

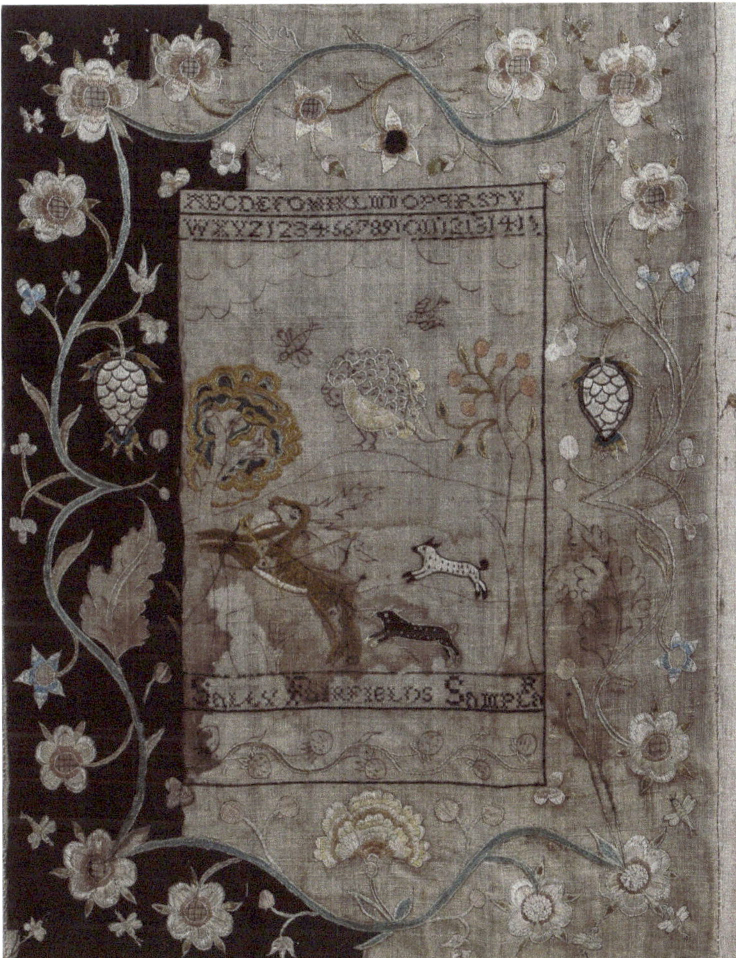

Sally Fairfield
Sampler, circa 1782
Possibly worked at the academy of Eleanor Druitt, Boston
Silk thread on linen
Satin, cross, split, and outline stitches, and French knots
22 x 16
Collection of the Brick Store Museum

Sally Fairfield was one of the six children of the Reverend John Fairfield of Saco, Maine, a well-known figure in Saco history. John was born in Boston and retained strong connections there throughout his long life, but his five daughters and one son were all born in Saco. He married Mary Goodwin Cutts, the widow of Foxwell Cutts, shortly after being ordained in Saco in 1761. As his daughters reached an age when a more sophisticated education was called for, Fairfield naturally chose the Boston area. Some circumstantial evidence through Fairfield's diaries indicates that Sally, baptized July 23, 1769, may have been taught by Mrs. Eleanor Druitt: other Saco residents (good friends of John's as proven by his diaries) were contemporaneously sending their daughters to her academy, including the offspring of Colonel Thomas Cutts and the daughters of Seth Storer. At least four documented samplers bear a strong resemblance to Sally's unfinished work, including those of Grace Welsh, Sukey Makepeace, and Abigail Means, described (and one photographed) in *American Samplers*, 1921, and a near-identical 1781 sampler by Betsey Bentley that sold at Thomaston Place Auction Galleries in Maine in 2009. Fairfield genealogist Wynn Cowan Fairfield noted that Sally's sisters, Betsey and Mary, both stitched coats of arms while at boarding school. The locations of these are currently unknown, but since not all Boston-area schools offered instruction in coats of arms, that further limits the possible schools the Fairfield daughters may have attended.

Sally Fairfield grew up in Saco and married Daniel Cleaves of Biddeford on April 28, 1795. They were parents to at least three daughters born between 1801 and 1806 and a son, William, born about 1797. On July 7, 1801, the Reverend John Fairfield noted in his diary that he had had a visitor: "He informs me that my grand Child Wm Cleaves about 4 years old fell from his father's wharf in Saco into the river & was drowned tho perhaps taken out alive on Tuesday last but died immediately & was buried the next day." Sally outlived her husband by eighteen years, dying at age 66 in 1835.

Elizabeth Cutts (1766–1810)
Coat of Arms, 1783
Worked at the academy of
Eleanor Druitt, Boston
Silk and metallic threads
and spangles on silk
Satin, padded satin, and
outline stitches
20 x 20
Collection of the Dyer Library
and Saco Museum

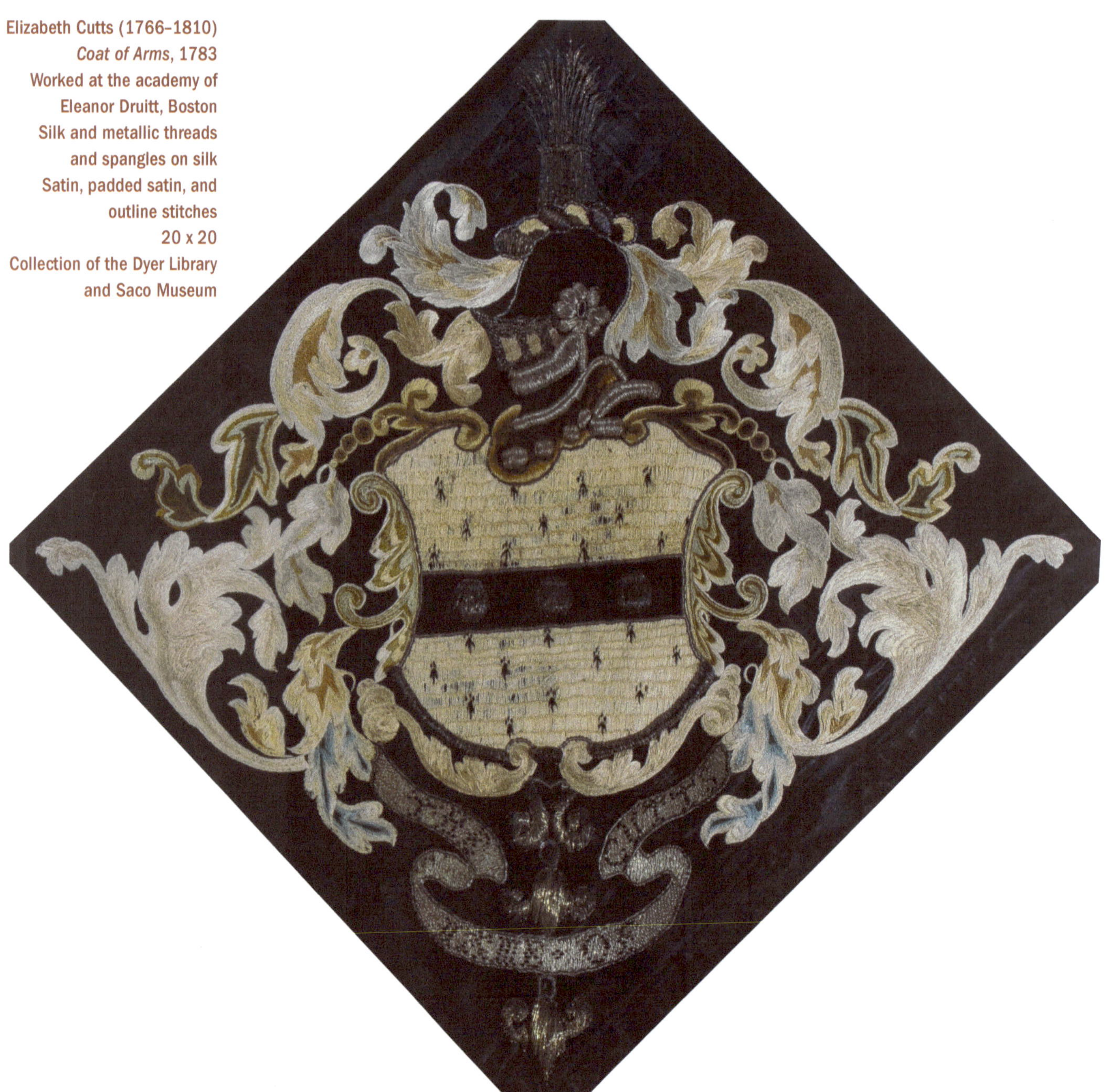

Elizabeth Cutts was the third eldest of the eight children of Colonel Thomas and Elizabeth Scamman Cutts of Saco. Their daughter Elizabeth, like her youngest sister Eunice (and most probably her other sisters), was sent to the female academy of Eleanor Druitt in Boston. She wrote home from there on April 22, 1783, seeking more information about the appropriate coat of arms for the Cutts family, since the heraldry book included two. She promised "as my utmost abilities shall be exerted to please Mama and yourself sir in the making." Whatever advice she might have received didn't apparently help; she stitched the heraldic device of the Milward family instead. Her coat of arms is very similar to several other known ones, as documented by Betty Ring in *Girlhood Embroidery*. Among those is one stitched at about the same time by her younger sister Sarah for the Scamman family of their mother, in a private collection. Elizabeth married her cousin, Richard Foxwell Curtis Cutts, in 1785. They settled in Berwick, where they became the parents of ten children, including sampler maker Elizabeth Cutts, whose linsey-woolsey work has been reproduced in several publications. When Elizabeth died in 1810, the youngest of her children was just one year old.

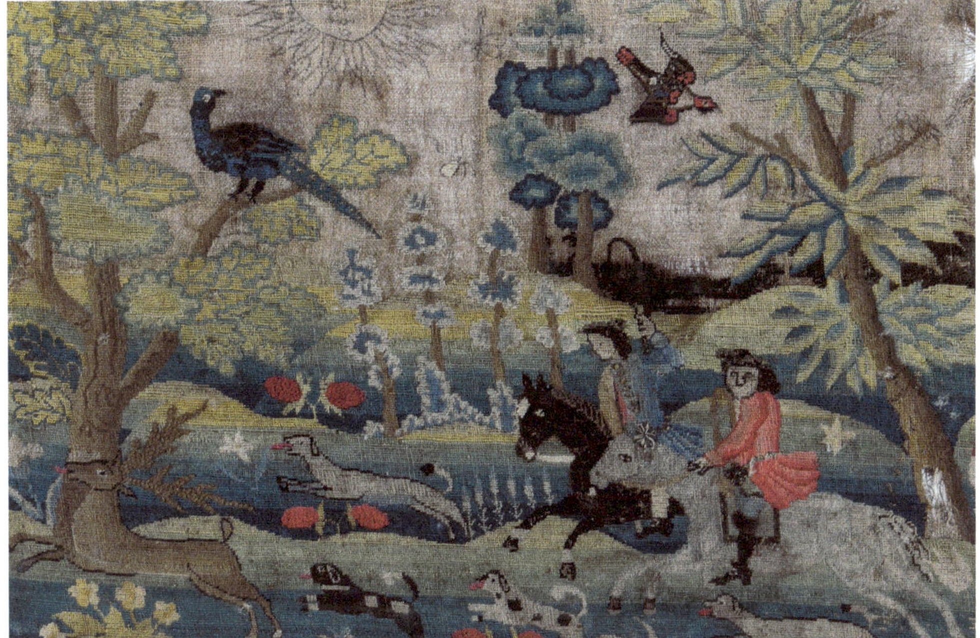

Alice or Rebecca Burton
(dates unknown)
Needlepoint, circa 1750-70
Probably worked in Boston,
school unknown
Wool on canvas
Tent stitch
12 x 16
Collection of the Baxter
House Museum

Maker unidentified
Practice embroidery, circa
1775-1800
Worked in unknown location
Silk thread on linen
Satin and outline stitches and
cut and drawn thread work
14 ½ x 12 ½
Collection of Leslie Rounds

While **Alice and Rebecca Burton** *may* not have been Maine girls, this piece is included here both to demonstrate the breadth of Boston instruction and to provide a photograph of it for researchers who may not be familiar with this diminutive piece. Alice and Rebecca were daughters of Benjamin Burton and Alice Lewis. Some of their siblings, including their brother Benjamin, who participated in the Boston Tea Party in 1773, were born in the Thomaston, Maine, area. A source described Alice and Rebecca as having been reared and died in Boston but offers no evidence of this. Given their likely birthdates, circa 1740–1760, when their parents were apparently residing in Maine, it is more probable that they were born in Maine, but schooled in Boston.

How did youthful needleworkers achieve such perfection in their work? At least in some cases, they practiced their stitchery. Pieces that demonstrate that effort are rare since they must have been saved infrequently. The anonymous stitcher of this practice work carefully hemmed it before beginning, but then worked some of the stitches from the front and others from the back, creating an interesting needlework that was no doubt never meant to be displayed.

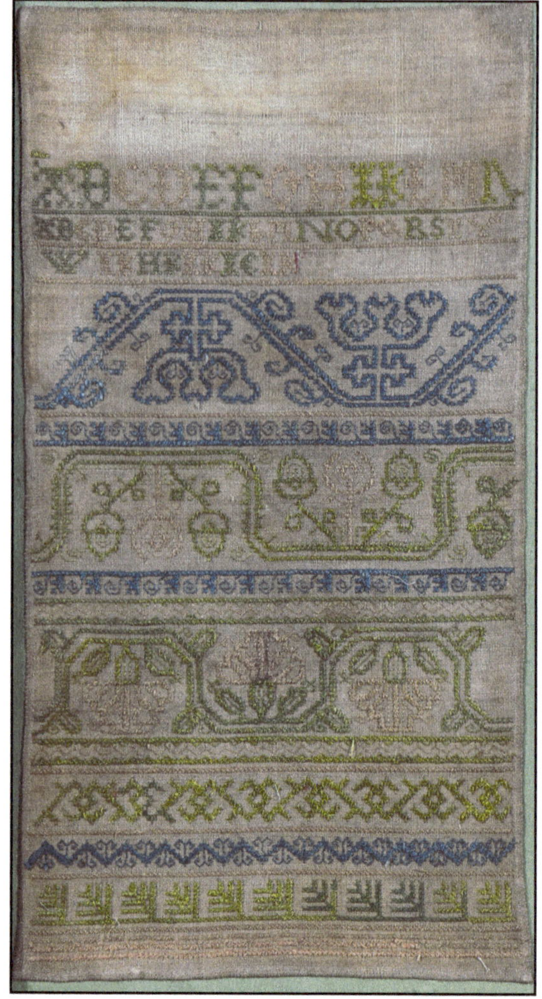

Right: Maker unidentified
Band Sampler, circa 1725–1750
Worked in an unknown school
Silk thread on linen
Cross, straight, and
Algerian eye stitches
16 ½ x 8 ¾
Collection of Leslie Rounds

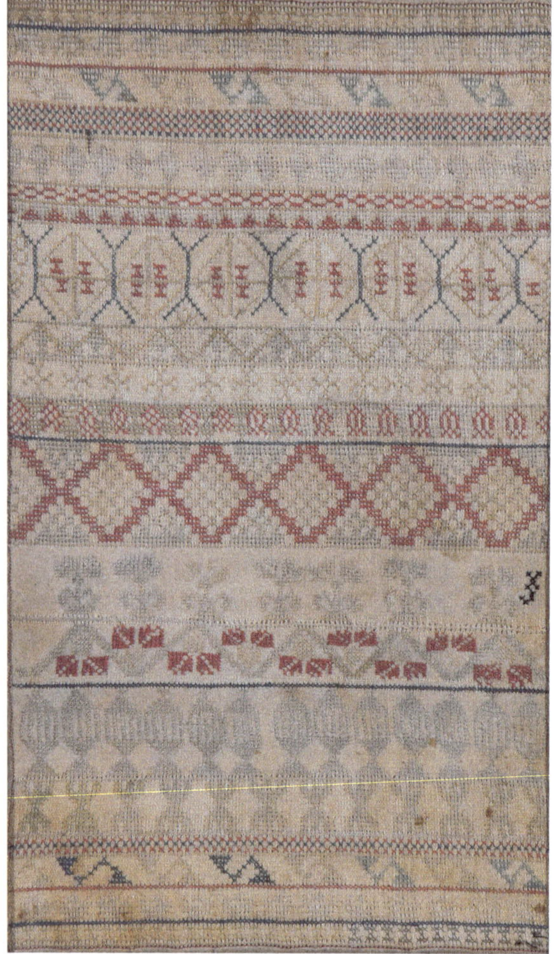

Left: Maker unidentified
Band Sampler, circa 1750–1775
Worked in an unknown school
Silk thread on linen
Cross stitch
15 ¾ x 8 ½
Collection of Leslie Rounds

Most of the oldest schoolgirl embroideries are in the form of **band samplers**. Typically, these were worked on long, narrow pieces of linen on which bands of various decorative patterns were stitched, presumably both to provide practice for novice stitchers and to preserve the designs for future reference. During the eighteenth century, the shape of band samplers gradually grew shorter. The green and blue band sampler on the top was likely made earlier than the similarly anonymous piece illustrated on the bottom. The bands of the lower piece are of a narrower width and notably different from the more typically seen bands of the top piece. There are also many mistakes in the lower one, as the maker seemed to experiment with the style of some bands. At the beginning of the eighth band from the top, there appears to be a numeral eight. At the far right of the thirteenth band, the small black figure may represent an initial, possibly of the maker. This piece was very likely made in New England. In *A Gallery of American Samplers*, page 8, Glee Krueger noted of American needlework of the eighteenth century, "Some is superb, but much lacks the discipline and polish of the English or Continental examples."

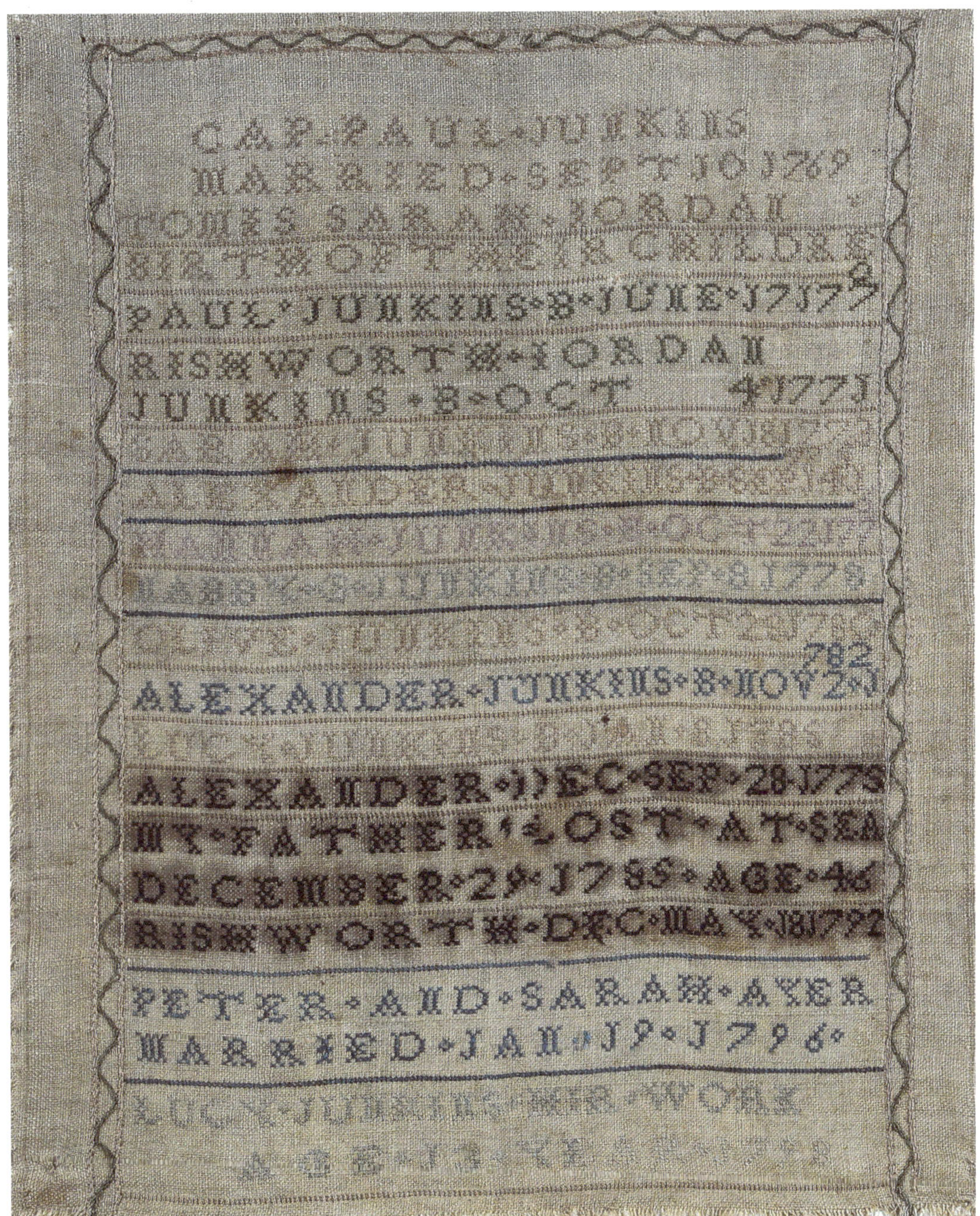

Lucy Junkins (1785–1861)
Family register sampler, 1798
Made in an unknown school, probably in Saco, Maine
Silk thread on linen
Cross, queen, and straight stitches
23 x 18 ½
Collection of the Museums of Old York

Compared to only slightly later family registers, this example by **Lucy Junkins** is notably plain. Typical of the majority of all samplers, it is an example of the maker's mastery of alphabets and embroidery stitches, but not intended (as others would be) as a work of artistic merit. Lucy Junkins's father, Paul Junkins, was a sea captain who had been born in 1739. He married Sarah Jordan of Saco, and, as Lucy notes on her sampler, he was lost at sea in December of 1785, leaving her mother a widow with ten children, the eldest just sixteen years old. Just about the time that Lucy worked her sampler, her mother remarried and moved to Buxton. Lucy married Samuel Paine of Gorham, Maine, in 1804. He was, for many years, a farmer and beloved deacon of the First Congregational Church in Gorham. They adopted two daughters. Lucy died January 18, 1861.

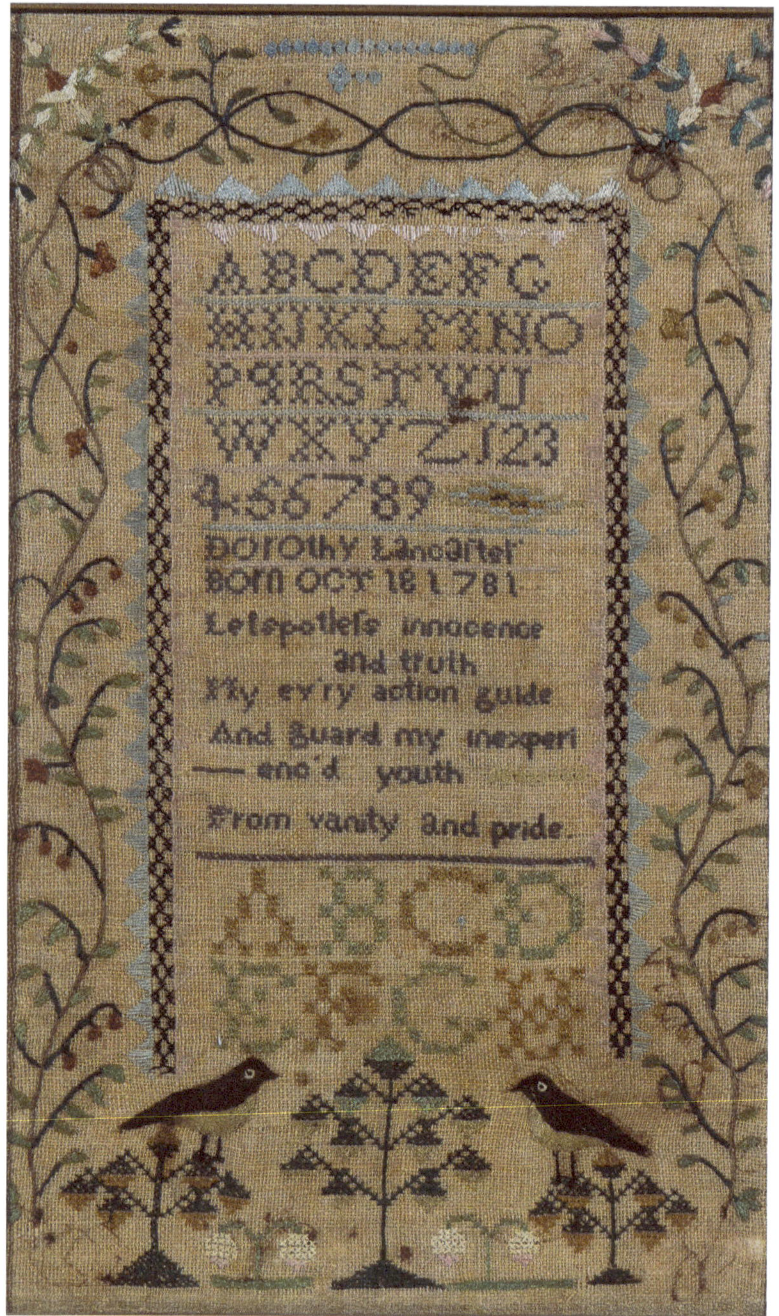

Dorothy Lancaster
(1781–1806)
Marking sampler, circa 1795
Probably worked in either Scarborough or Portland, Maine
Silk thread on linen
Cross, satin, queen, and straight stitches, and French knots
23 x 15
Collection of Glee Krueger

Dorothy Lancaster was born October 18, 1781 in Scarborough, Maine, the sixth of the eight children of Thomas Lancaster of Rowley, Massachusetts, and Lydia Jones Lancaster of Beverly, Massachusetts. For fifty-six years, her father served as pastor of the First Parish Church in Scarborough. Like two of her brothers, Dorothy died young, on April 29, 1806. Dorothy's sampler has the rather long and narrow configuration that was typical of eighteenth-century samplers. Curiously, however, in 1806, Sally Fogg of Scarborough made a very similar sampler with identical birds and other motifs at the bottom, but hers, eighteen inches long and only eight inches wide, was much longer and narrower. Fogg's sampler was sold at auction by Skinner Auctioneers and Appraisers in 2010, and its current whereabouts are unknown. In *Grandfather Tales of Scarborough*, 1925, Augustus F. Moulton related information passed down to him by his grandfather, Ezra Carter, who moved to Scarborough in about 1800. Ezra noted that Maria Libby, Lucy Hunnewell, and Statira Staples all kept schools in Scarborough in the Federal era.

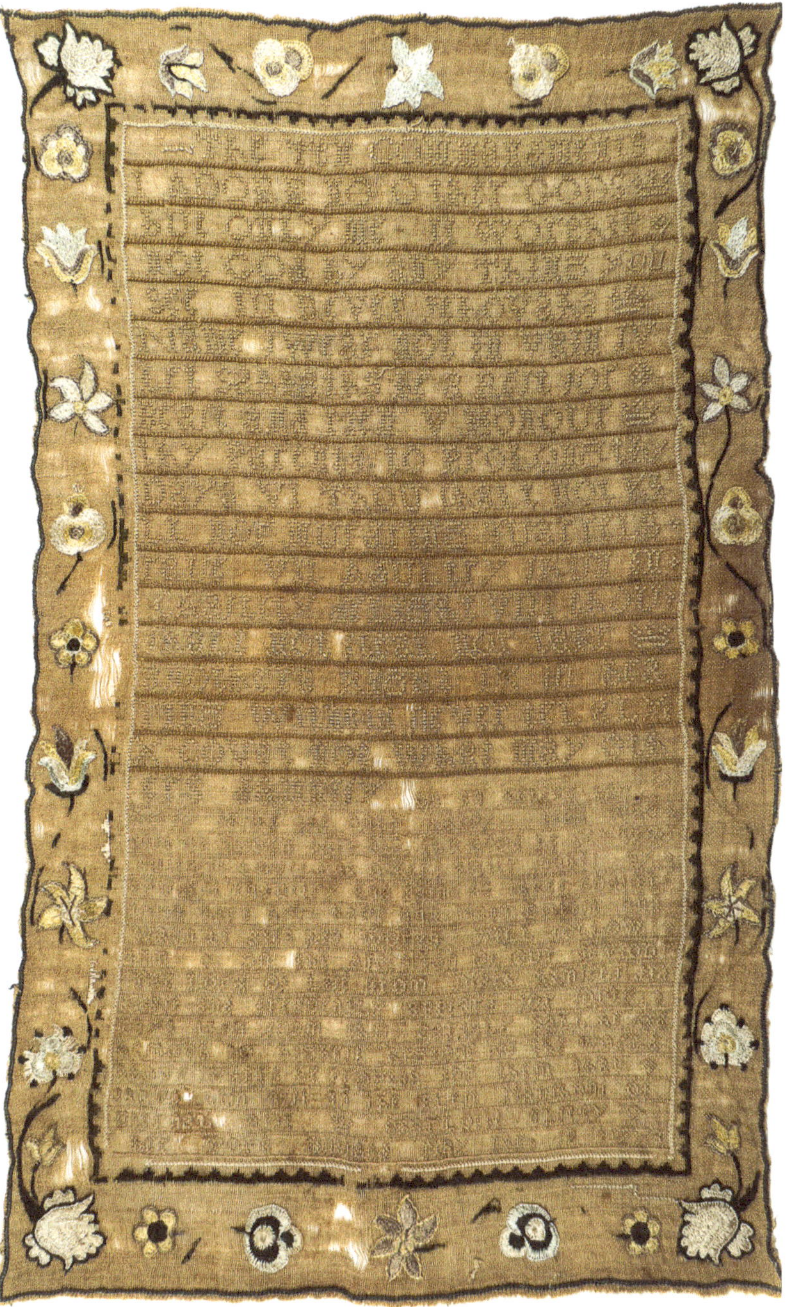

Charlotte Ilsley (1763–1892)
Marking sampler, 1773
Probably worked either in the Boston, Massachusetts, area or in Portland, Maine
Silk thread on linen
Cross, satin, and outline stitches
21 x 14
Collection of the Maine Historical Society

Charlotte Ilsley's sampler beautifully demonstrates the transition that was occurring in the design of samplers around the last quarter of the eighteenth century. Like the unfinished work of Sally Fairfield, her lustrous, ornamental, satin-stitched border makes her work differ sharply from the traditional and much plainer band samplers (p. 20) that had been in style previously. But, like earlier pieces, Charlotte's sampler is long and narrow, with row after row of text substituting for decorative bands, enhancing the verticality of the work.

Charlotte, born January 25, 1763, was the fifth of the eleven children of Enoch Ilsley and Mary Parker of Portland, Maine. She married wealthy merchant Stephen McLellan, but died shortly thereafter, on September 23, 1802. Five months later, Stephen married her younger sister, Hannah, and they became the parents of sampler maker Mary Ann McLellan (p. 44).

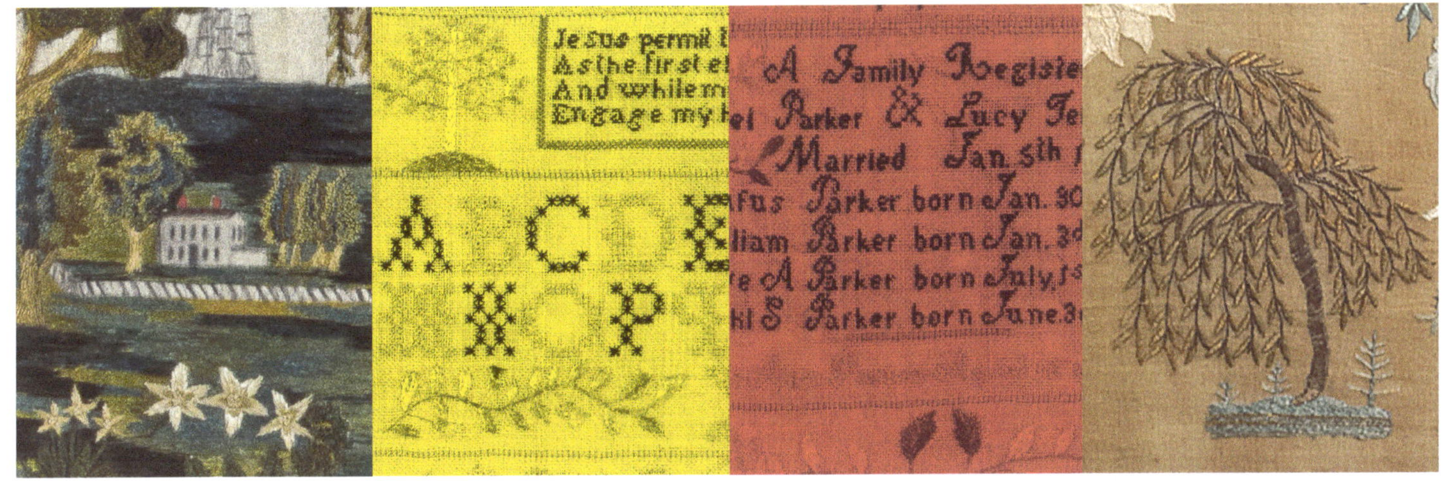

Part Two

Industrious Ingenuity:

The Rise of Urban Sophistication in Maine and Portland's Evolving Embroidery Style

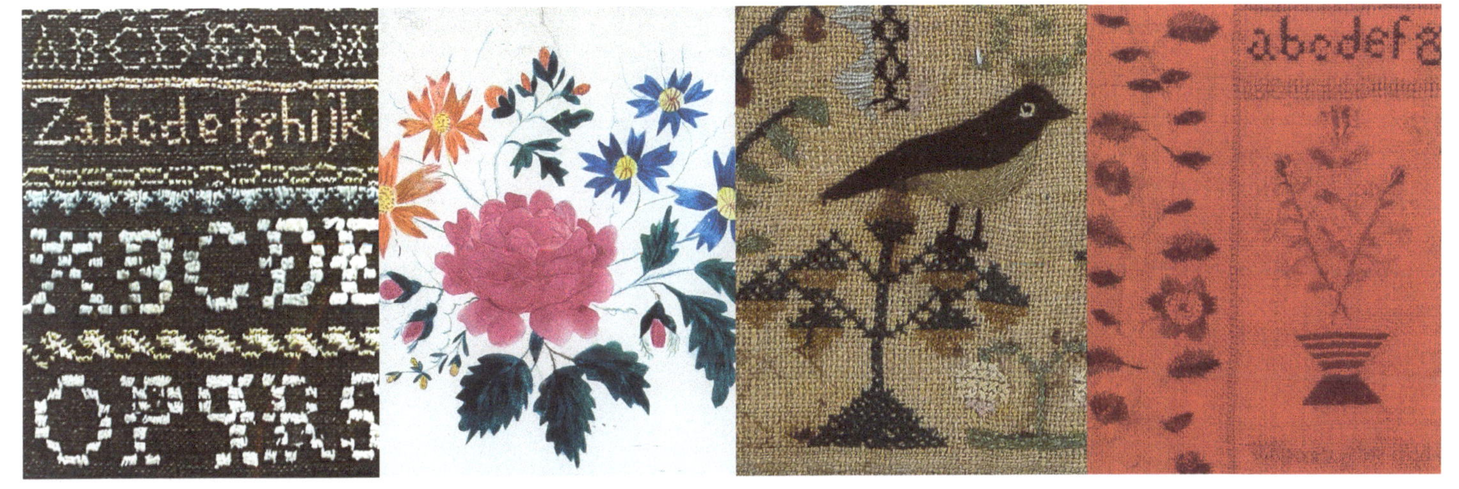

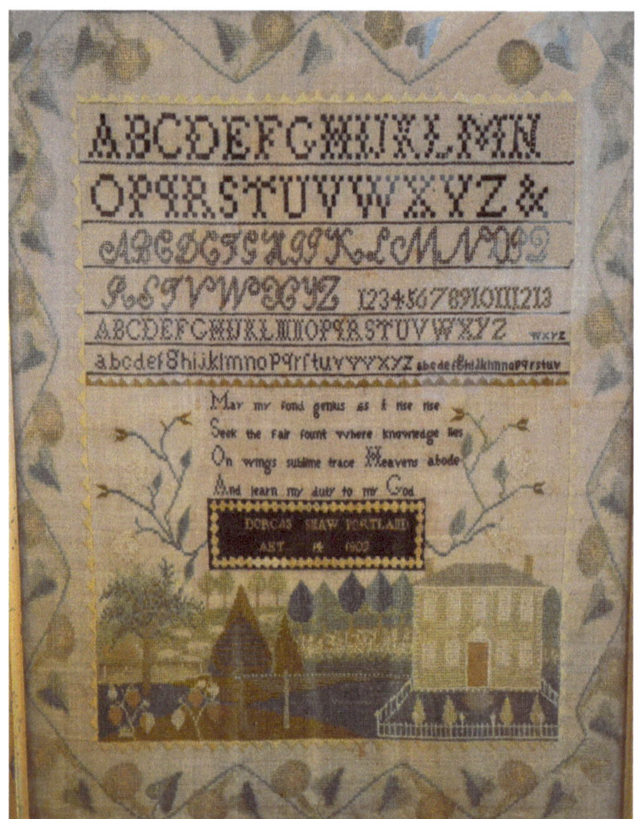

Dorcas Shaw
(1788–1879)
Marking sampler, 1803
Possibly worked at the school of Elizabeth Dawes, Portland
Silk thread on linen
Cross, satin, four-sided, and outline stitches
21 x 15 ¾
Collection of Burton W. Pearl

Dorcas Shaw, a second cousin of Elizabeth Dawes's husband, was the daughter of Eliab Shaw and Sarah Savage; she was born September 17, 1788, in Augusta. Dorcas married Samuel Marshall in Augusta on August 5, 1810. After living in Augusta for several years, Marshall and his family moved to the somewhat better farming area of Corinth, Maine, where they would remain for the rest of their lives. They were parents to at least three sons, two of whom died in young adulthood, and two daughters. After Samuel died in 1867, Dorcas moved in with her eldest son, Enoch, a farmer, and remained with him, his wife, and her daughter, Hannah, until she died February 21, 1879 at the age of 90.

On August 18, 1804 this advertisement appeared in the *Portland Gazette*:

Mrs. Dawes Academy

The subscribers to Mrs. Dawes Academy, which is now full, having been informed that some gentlemen have expressed a wish to put their daughters under her instruction, contemplate employing an Assistant; in which case the number of her Pupils will be increased to forty being nine more than now attend—Such gentlemen therefore, whether in town or country, as wish to embrace the opportunity, will please apply without delay to Samuel Freeman Hugh McLellan Daniel Tucker, Committee

Mrs. Dawes was born Elizabeth Bailey on August 29, 1767 in Hanover, Massachusetts. On June 25, 1789, she married the Reverend Ebenezer Dawes. He died only months after the birth of their second son in 1791. Elizabeth became preceptress of the Derby Academy in Hingham. Silk embroideries stitched there in 1796 are among the earliest made in America. Although a history of Hingham reported that she left the school in 1804, since her academy was already well established in Portland by that summer, it's very likely she arrived here somewhat earlier. Elizabeth probably chose Portland because both an uncle and one of her brothers had already moved to southern Maine, and her husband also had family in the area. In April 1805, Elizabeth became the second wife of widower John Lucas, an older merchant (born 1738) from Brookline, Massachusetts. He died in 1812 and she married for a third time, to Dr. William Williams of Deerfield, Massachusetts, in 1822. Widowed in 1829, Elizabeth died in Deerfield on February 17, 1844.

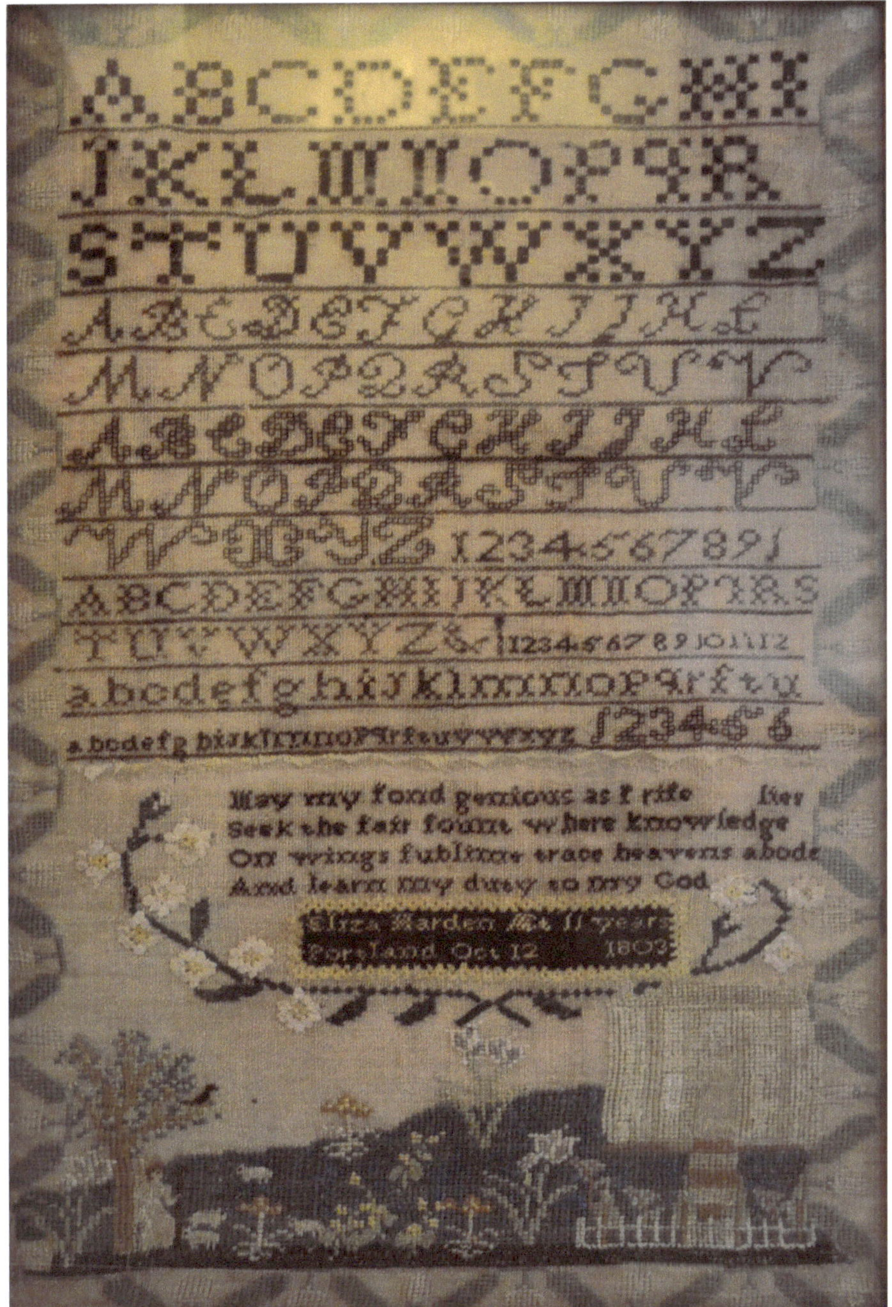

Eliza Harden (1792–?)
Marking sampler, 1803
Possibly worked at the school of Elizabeth Dawes, Portland
Silk thread on linen
Cross, outline, and four-sided stitches
23 x 16
Collection of Burton W. Pearl

Eliza Harden stitched her sampler under the instruction of the same teacher as Dorcas Shaw. If Elizabeth Dawes was not their instructor, a second possibility is Miss Turner, who advertised in Portland's *Eastern Argus* newspaper on February 24, 1804, that she would be continuing her school "from the first of April next solely for teaching Embroidery, working muslin, Marking, Drawing, Grammar, Reading and Geography." She said she would be able to accommodate six to eight boarding students. Miss Turner might have been Harriot C. Turner, whose intentions of marriage to Joseph McLellan Jr. were posted in Portland on October 24, 1813. No further advertisements appeared for her after the typical four-week run of this advertisement, implying that her school, like Elizabeth Dawes's academy, was only open briefly. Eliza Harden was the eldest child of William Harden of Portland and his wife, Betsey Fowler, who was from Ipswich, Massachusetts. She was born on August 14, 1792. Her parents would go on to have three sons and a second daughter. Eliza married Joseph Smith in Portland on December 30, 1817. They might be the Joseph and Eliza Smith who were farming in Hollis as noted on the 1850 and 1860 U.S. Federal Census, and who had at least two children.

Deborah Gordon (1786–1810)
Family register sampler, 1804
Probably worked at the school of Rachel Hall Neal, Portland
Silk thread on linen
Cross, satin, queen, and outline stitches
30 ½ x 17
Collection of Mr. and Mrs. Richard Larkin

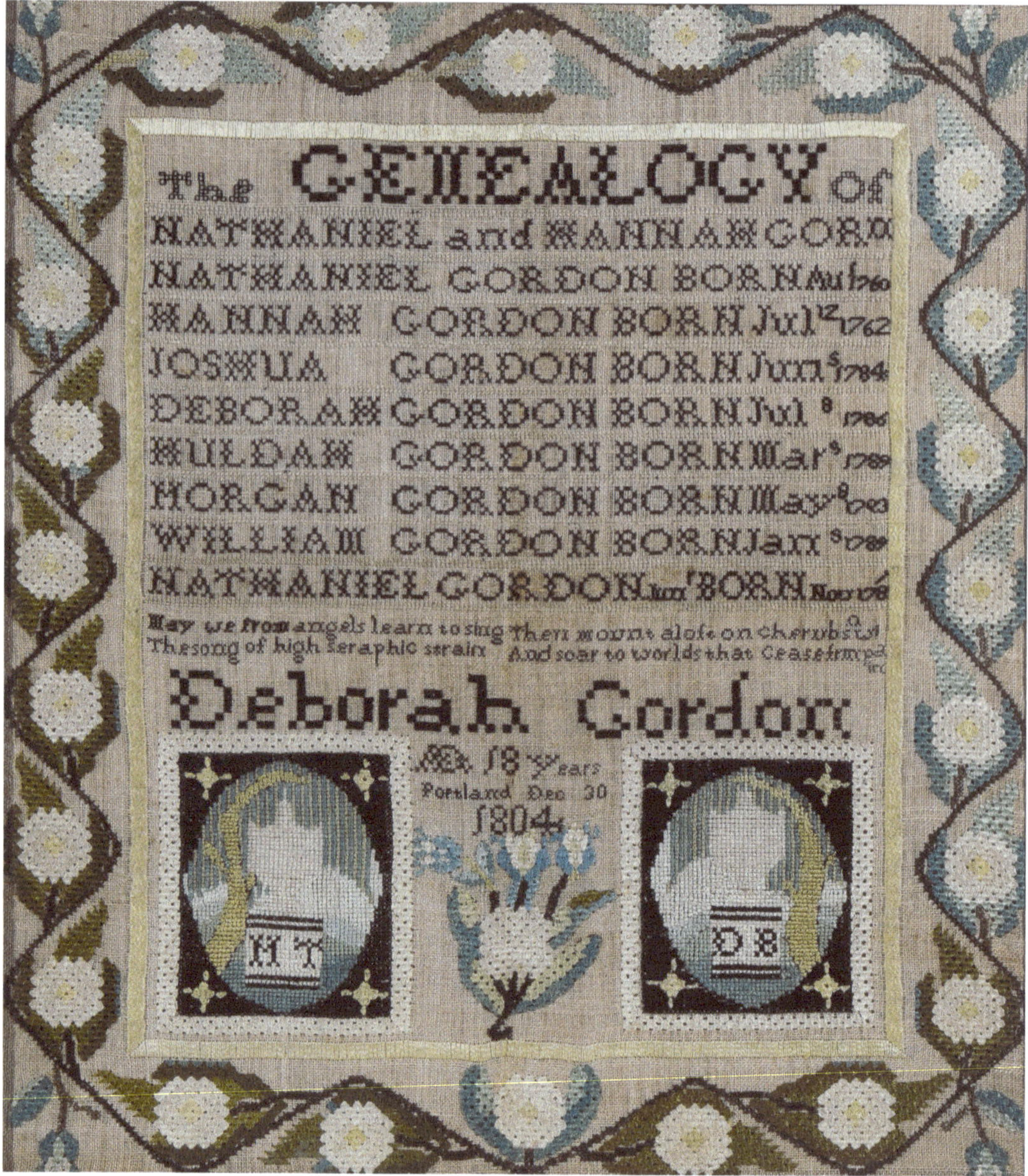

Deborah Gordon's genealogical sampler currently represents the earliest known one from a rather large group of Portland-made work. She is also the oldest sampler maker in the group, having stitched her iconic work at the age of eighteen. It may well be that she attended school at the same time as her younger sister Huldah, who would have been a more typical age. (Work by Huldah has not come to light.) Deborah's mother, Hannah Fisher Gordon, died in 1808, after which Nathaniel remarried. Since her father is listed as having died in St. Bartholomew's in Barbados (in 1817), he may have been involved in shipping, perhaps a sea captain like his son, Joshua. In early 1810, Deborah married Peter Thacher of Gorham. Peter's mother, Aphia Mayo, was Simeon Mayo's sister and therefore also the aunt of the Misses Mayo, who later ran a Portland academy. On December 10, 1810, only about nine months after her marriage, Deborah died. Her husband died several months later. They are both buried in the family tomb in Gorham. Many of Peter's family members of that generation died of consumption (tuberculosis) which was rampant and highly lethal in nineteenth-century America, especially among young adults. Given that Deborah's death came about nine months after her marriage, another possible cause for her demise might have been a complication of pregnancy. Deborah's nieces Margaret, Susan, Huldah, and her namesake, Deborah Gordon, all daughters of her eldest brother, Joshua, attended the Misses Martin's School for Young Ladies as day students.

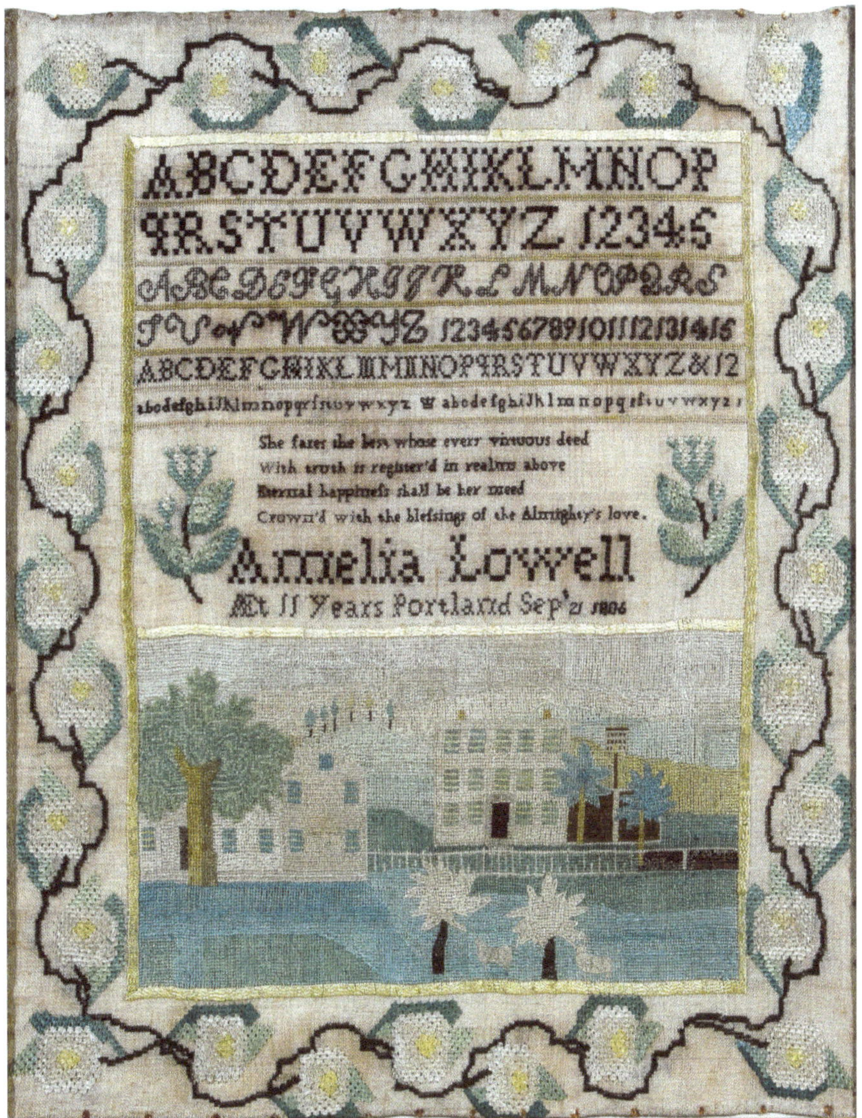

Amelia Lowell
(circa 1796–1871)
Marking sampler, 1806
Probably worked at the school of Rachel Hall Neal, Portland
Silk thread on linen
Cross, queen, satin, and outline stitches
28 x 16 ½
Collection of the Baxter House Museum

Amelia Lowell, born about 1796, completed her sampler September 21, 1806 in the same school that was attended by Lydia Dutch, Martha Wilder, Joanna Poole, and Mary Richards. She is probably the Amelia Lowell who married Joseph Libby in Portland on November 2, 1821. He was disabled during his youth, taught penmanship, and became the Libby of Lunt & Libby, Grocers of Portland; unfortunately, he died less than a year after their marriage. In 1825, Amelia became the second wife of Simeon Hall. Simeon was the son of Daniel Hall and Lorana Winslow and the younger brother of Rachel Winslow Hall Neal, who operated a Portland female academy for many years and was probably Amelia's teacher. At the time of Simeon and Amelia's marriage, he had seven children still living at home. At least two more children followed. Simeon, a lumber dealer, died at the age of eighty-eight in 1870. Amelia died June 21, 1871 and was buried next to Simeon in Portland.

Amelia Lowell's sampler fits into the largest group of related Portland samplers, created during the years 1804 to at least 1820. There are only three Portland schools that are known to span this full period of time: the Misses Martin's school and the schools of widow Rachel Hall Neal and of Sarah Jenkins Price. However, the Misses Martins published a possibly somewhat incomplete list of their students and none of these sampler makers appear on it. Also, by 1820, Price was ninety years old and probably not actively teaching, leaving Rachel Hall Neal as the likely teacher. The autobiography of Elizabeth Oakes Smith names Neal as her teacher; perhaps a needlework by this nineteenth-century lyceum speaker will come to light to definitely confirm or disprove Neal as the teacher of the group.

Joanna Poole (1794–1864)
Family register sampler, 1807
Probably worked at the school of Rachel Hall Neal, Portland
Silk thread on linen
Cross, queen, satin, and outline stitches
24 x 30 framed
Collection of the Maine Historical Society

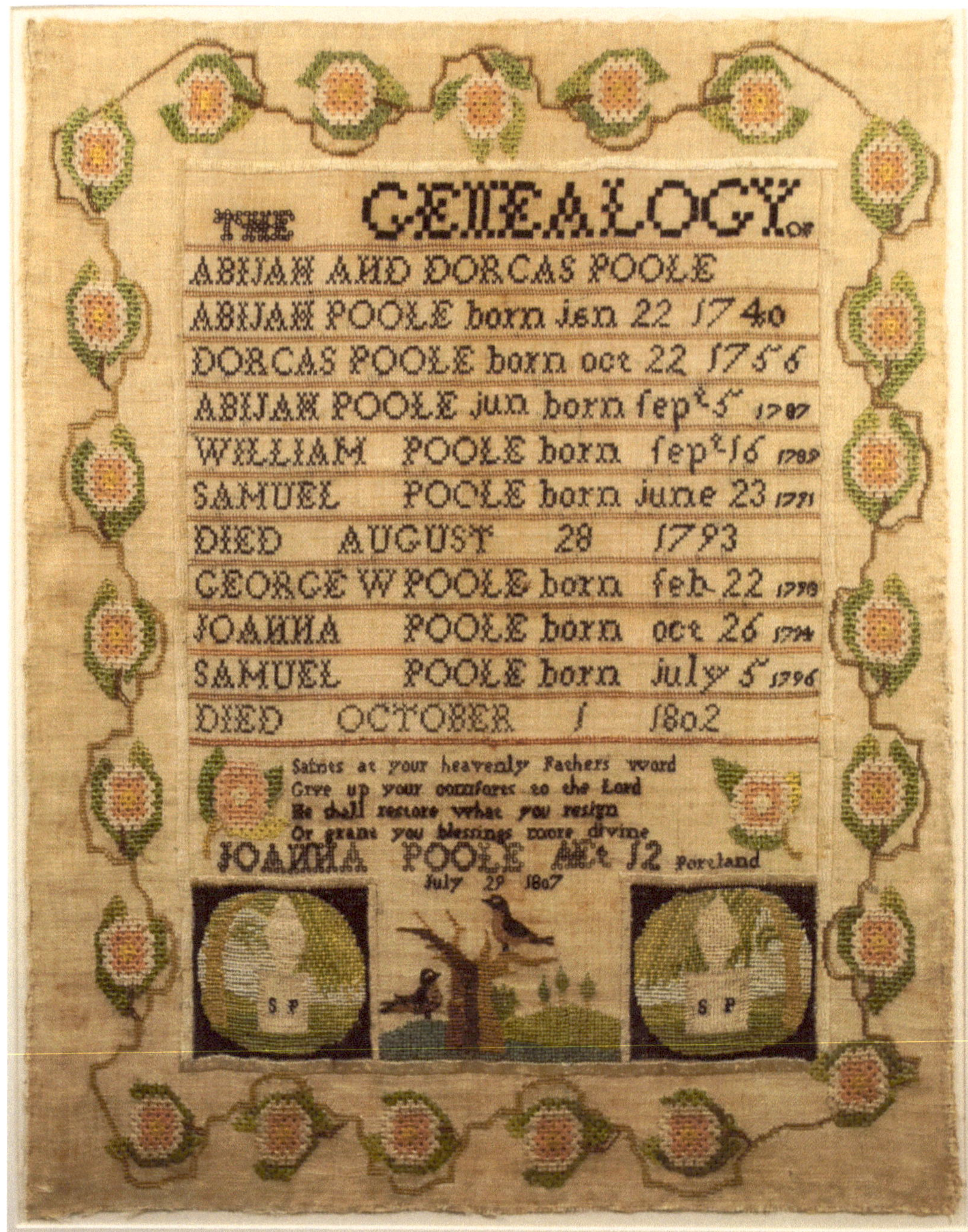

When **Joanna Poole** stitched her sampler in 1807, she charmingly created backwards Ns in her name. She carefully noted the births of her parents Dorcas Bagley and Abijah Poole (a Revolutionary War officer and later a Portland bricklayer), who were married in Portland on November 10, 1786, as well as the births of her five brothers and the deaths in early childhood of both Samuels. If she had waited only a few more months, she would have also recorded the death of William, who died in December 1807. George lived only until 1821. Joanna never married. In 1850, she was living with her widower brother, Abijah, a sail maker, and two of his children. By 1860, he had also died, and Joanna resided in Portland with her nephew William and his wife. She died August 15, 1864, of tuberculosis. Joanna's sampler is very similar to one worked two years earlier by Martha Wilder and belongs to a group of needlework that share several characteristics: queen-stitched rose borders with stylized triangular leaves (which later evolved into attractive satin-stitched roses and leaves), the use of "Aet" with the maker's age, inclusion of the precise date when the work was completed, and queen-stitched floral sprigs on both sides of the girl's boldly spelled-out name.

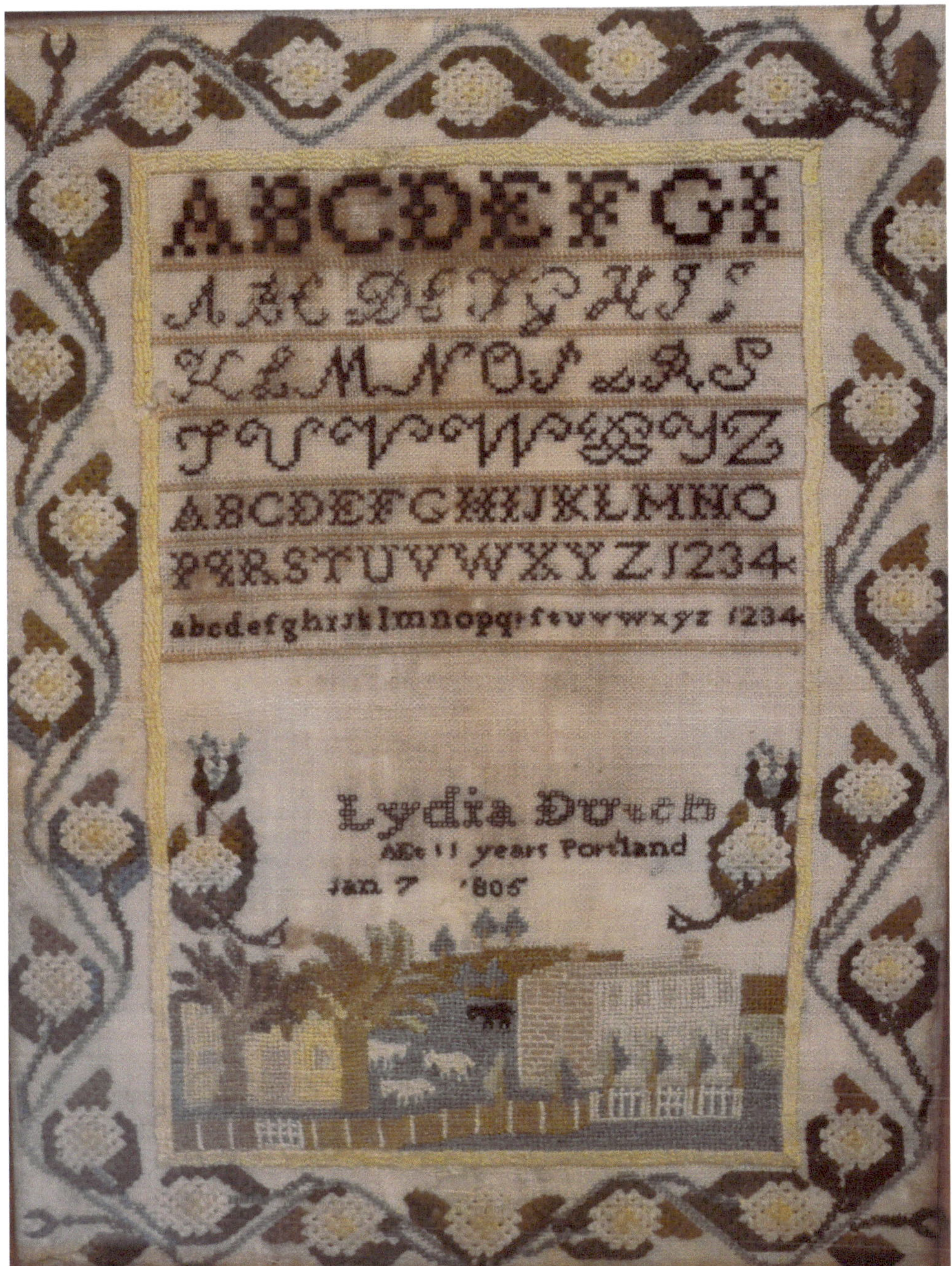

Lydia Dutch (1793–1864)
Marking sampler, 1805
Probably worked at the school of Rachel Hall Neal, Portland
Silk thread on linen
Cross, queen, satin, and outline stitches
16 x 12
Collection of Burton W. Pearl

Lydia Dutch, who worked one of a large group of related Portland samplers, listed her age as eleven in 1805. She is likely the daughter of Captain John Dutch and Mary Calef of Ipswich, Massachusetts. Captain John was a very busy privateer during the Revolutionary War and appears to have been active in the shipping of Maine lumber after the war ended. John's three adult sisters relocated to Kennebunk, Maine, and John eventually settled in Portland. Lydia was the twelfth and youngest child of the family. On August 29, 1824, she married William Hackett of Kennebunk, a successful merchant. They were the parents of at least three children. Lydia died September 8, 1848.

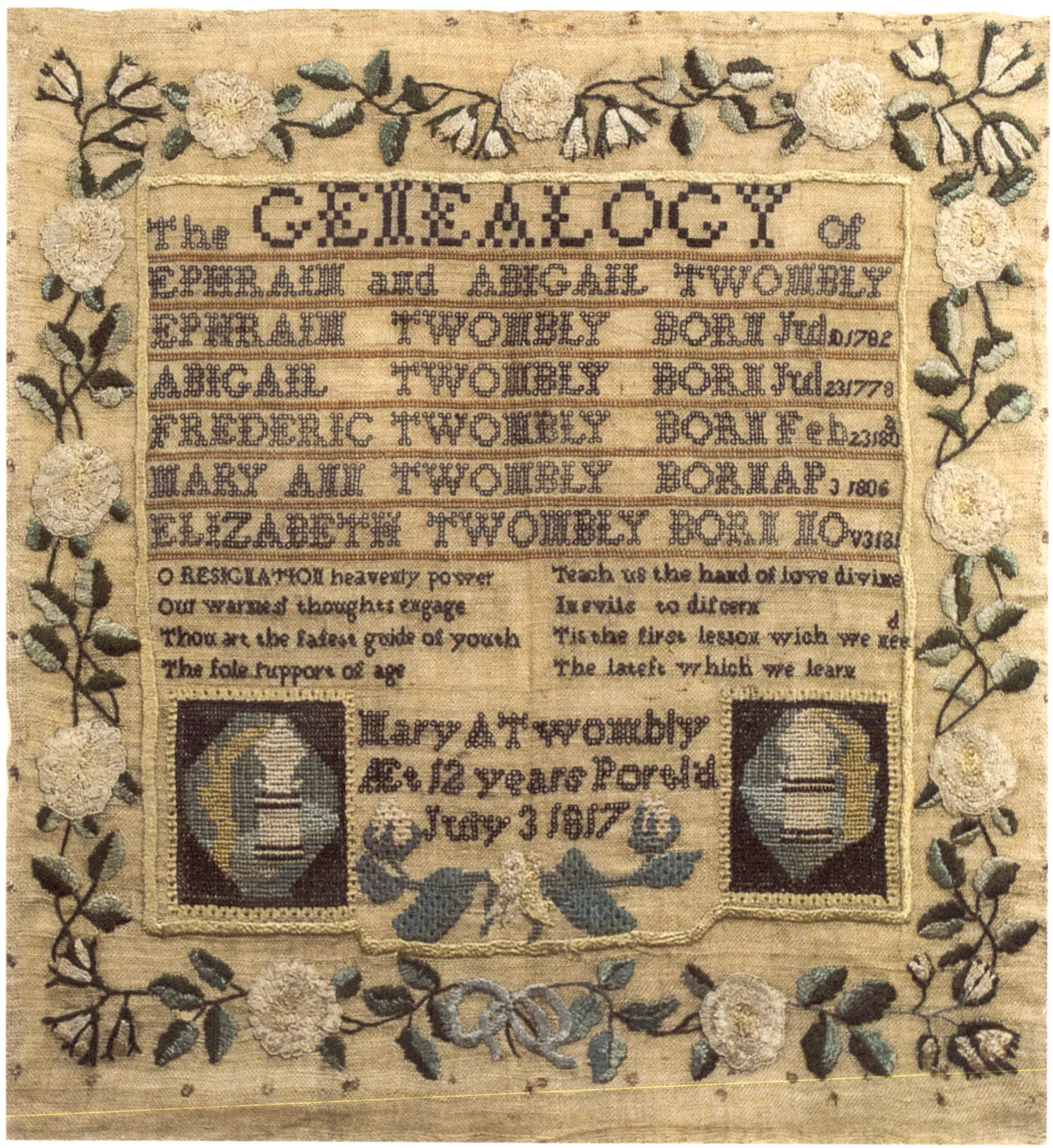

Mary A. Twombly
(1805–1850)
Family register sampler, 1817
Probably worked at the school of Rachel Hall Neal, Portland
Silk thread on linen
Cross, queen, satin, and outline stitches
21 x 20 framed
Collection of the Maine Historical Society

Mary Ann Twombly was one of the four children of Ephraim Twombly, a farmer who seems to have divided his time between Portland and Berwick, and Abigail Sampson, who were married in Portland, Maine, in 1801. Mary Ann worked her sampler in the same school as several other girls in the exhibition, likely that of Rachel Hall Neal. Where Mary Ann and her sister and two brothers were born is unknown; they don't appear on Portland vital records. Ephraim died between 1830 and 1834, Elizabeth married in 1835, and afterward Abigail ran the household that consisted of herself, her two sons and Mary Ann. Mary Ann died of consumption (tuberculosis), unmarried, on May 20, 1845. Her brother Leonard is variously listed as having never married, or as having married Eliza Cressey of Gorham. Neither of her brothers had children.

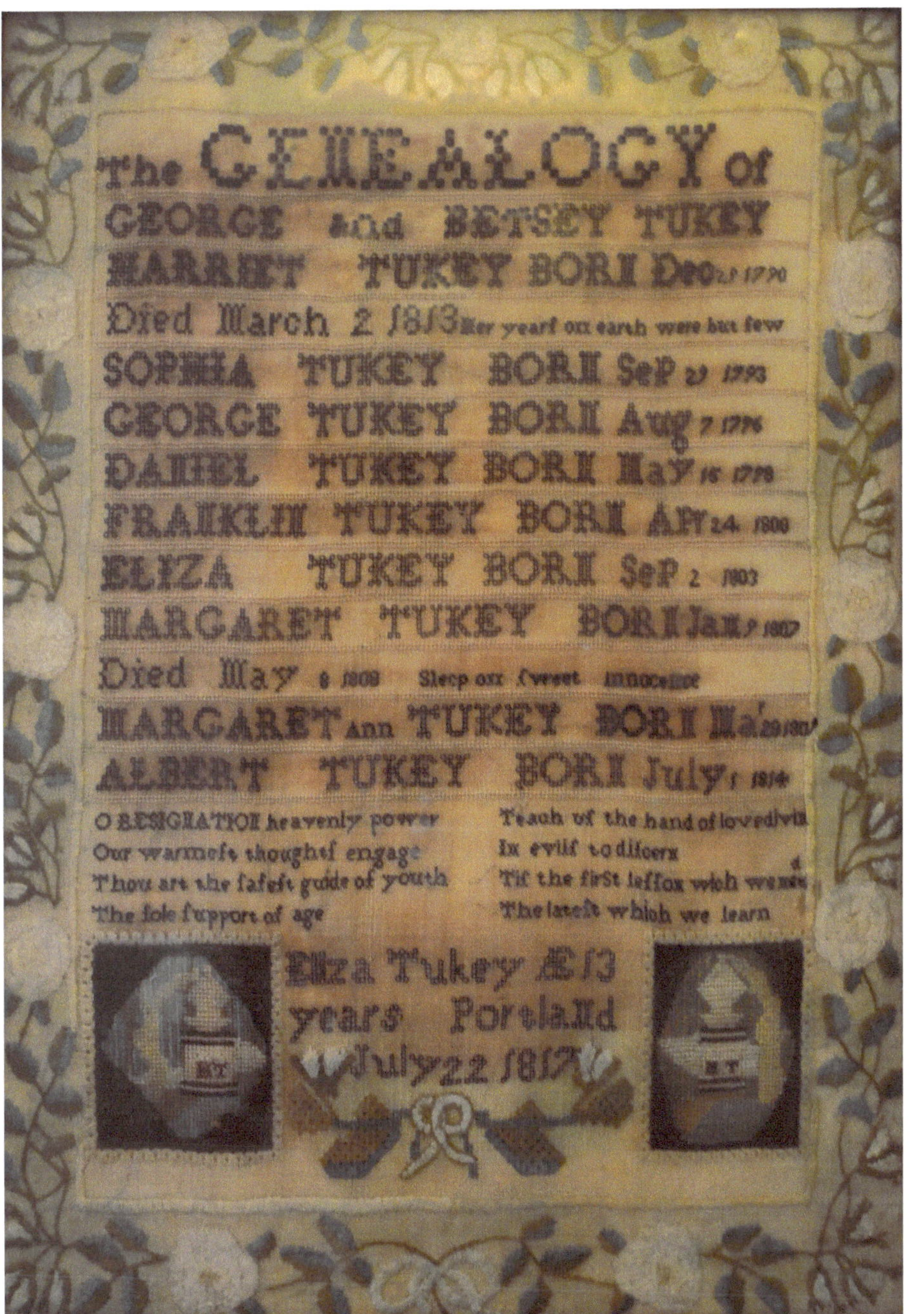

Eliza Tukey (1803–?)
Family register sampler, 1817
Probably worked at the school
of Rachel Hall Neal, Portland
Silk thread on linen
Cross, satin, queen, and
outline stitches
20 ¾ x 14 ½
Collection of Burton W. Pearl

George Tukey, son of John Tukey and Abigail Sweetser, married Betsey Snow on September 12, 1790. **Eliza Tukey** was the sixth of their nine children, born in Portland. Tukey's Bridge, a rather famous Portland landmark that is now part of the infrastructure of I-295, was named for her uncle, Lemuel Tukey. No further records have been found for Eliza. Her sisters, Harriet, Margaret (who died as an infant), and the second Margaret (who lived on, unmarried, until 1905), are all buried in the family plot in Portland. Since Eliza is not buried there, she may have married and after her death been interred with her husband and his family.

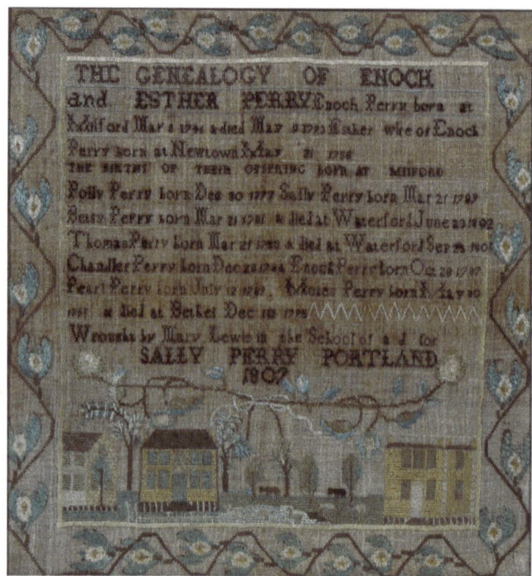

Left: Mary Lewis (1797–?)
Family register sampler, 1807
Worked at the school of Sally Perry, Portland
Silk thread on linen
Cross, satin, and queen stitches
28 x 16
Collection of Sue and Dexter Pond in memory of Grace Lyman Stammers

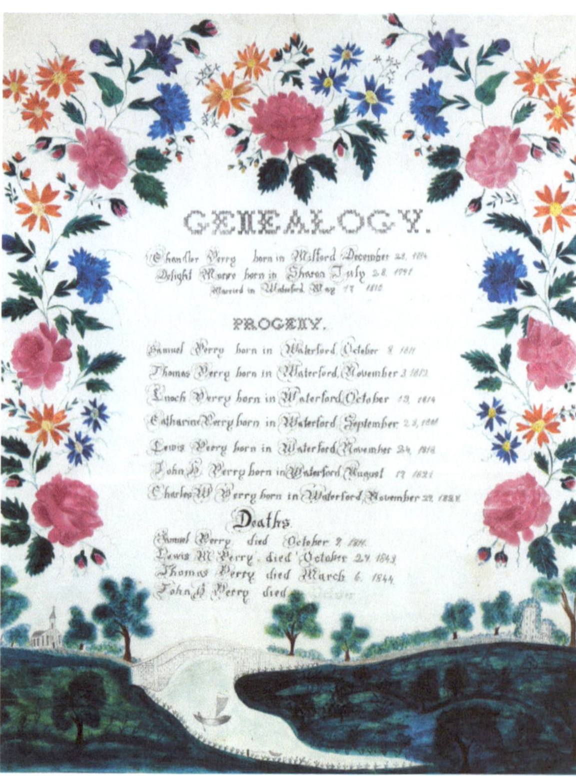

Right: Catharine Perry (1816-?)
Family register, circa 1835
Worked at an unknown school, possibly in Portland, Maine
Watercolor and ink on paper
23 x 18 ½
Collection of Sue and Dexter Pond in memory of Grace Lyman Stammers

Mary Lewis stitched a very unusual genealogical sampler in the school of Sally Perry. Rather than provide information about her own family, as was typical, she chose instead to tell the story of her teacher's family, and then she gave the resultant sampler to Sally Perry as a gift. Nothing is known of Mary Lewis, since she provided no information to help identify her. She may have been the daughter of Ansel Lewis and Comfort Manchester of Portland, born October 29, 1797, who married Job Thomes on November 10, 1812.

Sally Perry was the second of the eight children of Enoch Perry and Esther Bartlett. Enoch and Esther relocated from Milford, Massachusetts, to Oxford County, Maine (sometime shortly after the 1790 census but before his death in 1793), leaving Esther with eight small children and no obvious way to support them. Three died very young. By 1805, Sally, just sixteen years old, had relocated to Portland and opened a school. Four nearly identical samplers can be linked to her instruction, all demonstrating the style now becoming popular in Portland but with Perry's unique touches: genealogical information enclosed in a queen-stitch rose border, a village scene at the bottom, and a pair of crossed floral sprigs tied with bow. One of these, stitched by Nabby Horton, was illustrated in *The Magazine Antiques*, September, 1988, p. 513. On August 11, 1807, Sally Perry became the second wife of an established Portland pottery maker, Benjamin Dodge. Sally was the mother of six children, two of whom died in very early childhood. She died in Portland on August 19, 1846. One of the other samplers from her school, made by Eleanor Douglass, was eventually taken to Hawaii by her daughter when she moved there as the wife of a young missionary in the mid-nineteenth century. A photo of the sampler appeared in a biography of her husband in the 1920s. Its location is unknown. Eleanor's father, Robert Douglass, married Sally Perry's sister Polly in 1805 after the death of Eleanor's mother.

A generation later, **Catharine Perry**, the daughter of Sally's brother, Chandler Perry, and his wife, Delight Morse, of Waterford, Maine, painted a family register. It includes a mimicking of queen stitch to spell out the title, "Genealogy" at the top, the word "Married" underlined, and the use of the word "Progeny" prior to the naming of the offspring. While the floral border is very similar to ones painted on other works from Mary Rea's school, the handwritten genealogy in not typical, since other known works from her school featured printed text. It was probably created in the early 1830s; although it includes two dates from the early 1840s, they seem to have been added later. Catharine appeared on the U.S. Federal Census, living with her parents, through 1860. After that, no further records for her were discovered.

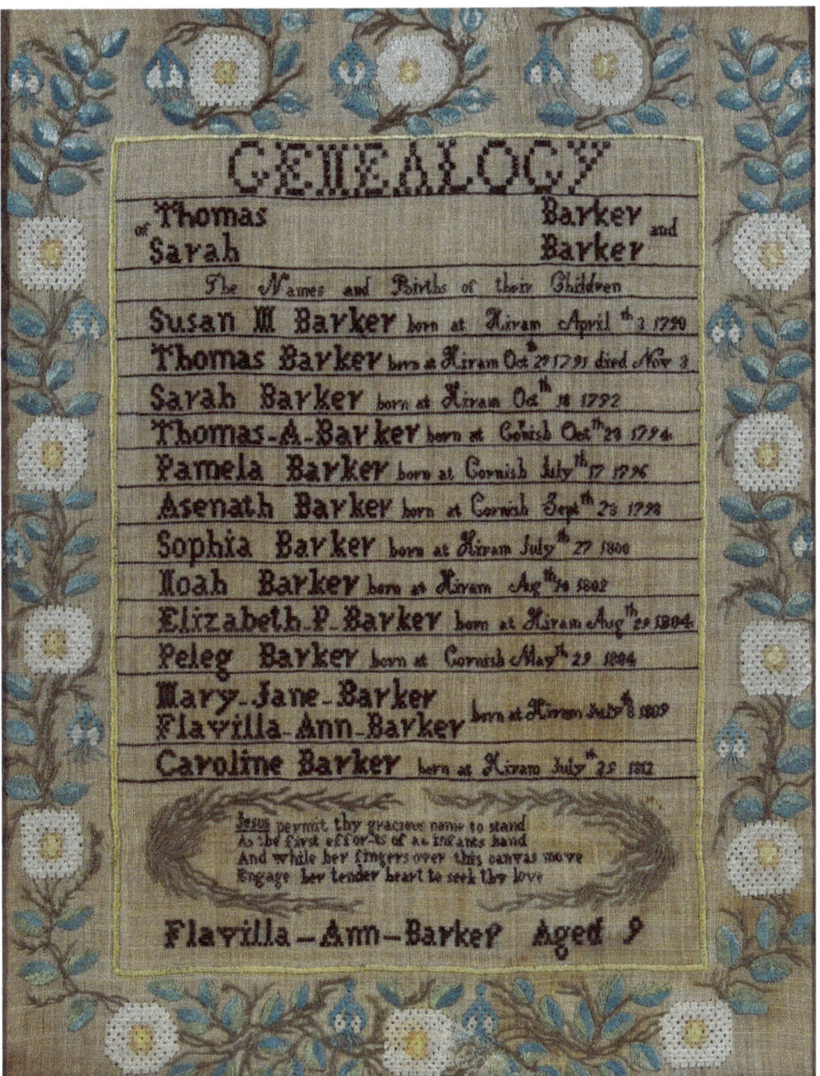

Flavilla Ann Barker
(1809–1882)
Family register sampler, 1818
Probably worked at the school of Abigail Fellows, Portland
Silk thread on linen
Cross, queen, satin, and stem stitches
20 ½ x 16 ½
Collection of the Androscoggin Historical Society

Flavilla Ann Barker and her twin sister, Mary Jane, stitched identical samplers, probably under the instruction of Abigail Fellows. Mary Jane's sampler was described by an aged descendant in *American Samplers* in 1921. It continued to pass down through the family but was eventually sold at auction in 2000 by Butterfields in San Francisco. Thomas Barker, the twins' father, operated a "public"—or tavern—on Congress Street in Portland for many years. His wife, Sarah Ayer, was from Hiram, Maine, and may have returned home for the births of their children. Mary Jane married Timothy Eastman at the age of sixteen. After she died in 1858, Timothy married her sister Sophia. Flavilla married James Mason Williams of Taunton, Massachusetts. She was the mother of two sons and a daughter, two of whom died in early adulthood. Flavilla died on January 15, 1882, and is buried alongside her husband and two of her children in Taunton.

Abigail Fellows operated a school in Portland from about 1806 until 1820, when she probably died during a visit to Havana, Cuba. She was most likely the second wife of Nathaniel Fellows of Boston, who married her sometime after the death of his first wife in 1782. Nathaniel died in Havana in May 1806. Two nineteenth-century sources identify her as running a Portland school; she is reported to have been the first teacher of Henry Wadsworth Longfellow (1807–1882). The Barker twins' samplers are attributed to her school because a Barker descendant recalled that they had been made at the school that the girls attended with Longfellow as young children (*American Samplers*, p. 125). That descendant identified the school as that of "Mme. Niel," but Longfellow never attended Mrs. Neal's school. Therefore, it is more likely that all three children attended Abigail Fellows's school together.

Nancy Cushing (1802–?)
Family register sampler, 1818
Probably worked in Portland (school unknown)
Silk thread on linen
Cross, satin, queen, and outline stitches and French knots
29 ½ x 18
Collection of Newburyport Historical Society

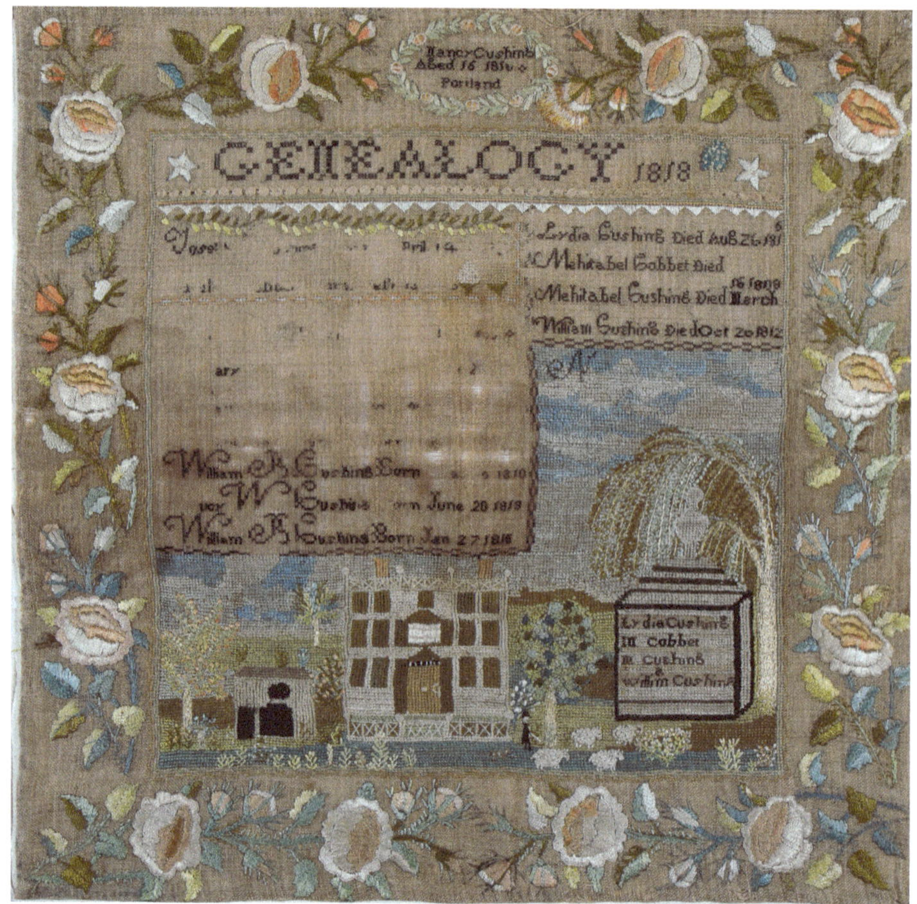

Nancy Cushing's remarkably lovely and artful sampler is one of a group of at least four nearly identical works that were made in Portland around 1818. They feature a unique stepped format, a wreath around the maker's name, stars, a scene across the bottom, an attractive naturalistic rose border, and ample genealogical information. Unfortunately, Nancy's sampler has suffered significant stitch loss, making it difficult to be certain about her identity. She is very likely the daughter of Joseph Cushing, who was born in Massachusetts and may have married first Mehitabel Corbett—whom Nancy listed on this work—and second, her younger sister Sally Corbett on May 16, 1802, in Boston. That would make Sally the mother of most of the children on the sampler, including Mehitabel, Lydia, two Williams, and Nancy. Joseph was a sparmaker in Portland. The deaths of Mehitabel and William Cushing, children of Joseph, were noted in Portland newspapers, as was the marriage of his daughter Mehitabel in 1819. What became of Nancy is unknown.

The best example of this sampler style is the Sophia Dyer work owned by the Metropolitan Museum of Art in New York; another fine example, stitched by Dorcas Berry and previously owned by Betty Ring, was included at the Sotheby's auction in New York, January 2012. The sampler of Charlotte Perkins, 1819, sold by Skinner Auctioneers and Appraisers in June 2004, probably also belongs to this group, although it does not exhibit the same stepped layout. Charlotte's mother was the widow of Ezekiel Cushing. While it is hard to determine the precise connection between Charlotte Perkins and Nancy Cushing, the Portland-area families of both included McCobbs as well as Cushings. The sampler of Mary Ann Morton, 1820 (pictured in Glee Krueger's *A Gallery of American Samplers*, p. 58), shows stylistic similarities, with a leafy vine around her name cartouche, a completely filled-in scene across the bottom, and the identical method of stitching the roses using a buttonhole stitch for the outside edge. Sophia Dyer and Mary Ann Morton were second cousins. Although the source of these samplers is unknown, it was almost certainly not the school of the Misses Mayo. A sampler that names their school, stitched by Lucy Harris in 1817 (*The Magazine Antiques*, September, 1988, p. 515) shows none of the same delicate artistry.

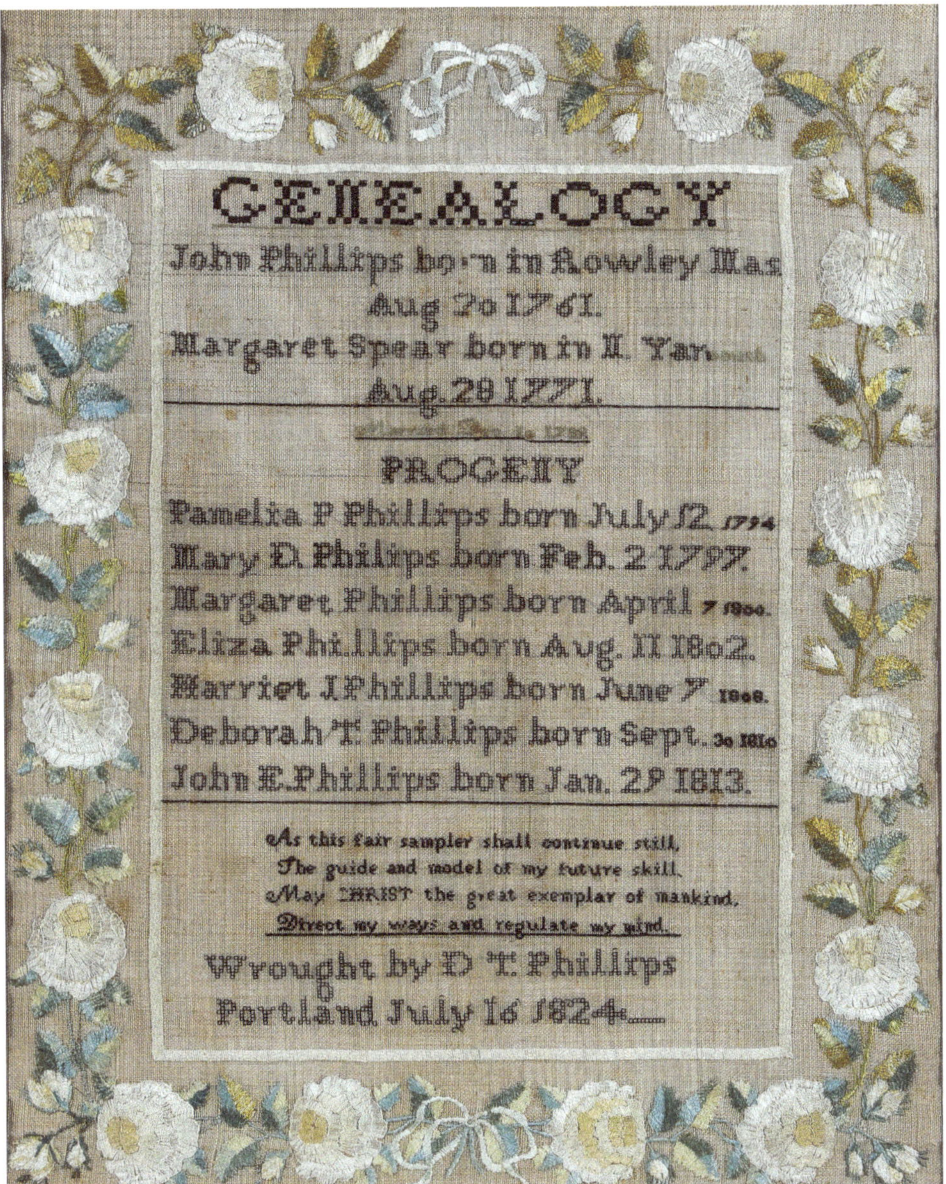

Deborah T. Phillips
(1810–1885)
Family register sampler, 1824
Probably worked in Portland
(school unknown)
Silk thread on linen
Cross, satin, and
outline stitches
28 x 18 ½
Collection of Virginia Moody

Deborah Phillips was the youngest daughter of the seven children of John and Margaret Spear Phillips, all born in Portland. The rose-bordered 1817 sampler by Deborah's elder sister, Harriet Jane Phillips, was described in *American Samplers* as featuring three alphabets and a house with tall trees. Its present location is unknown. The 1815 sampler of Mary Owen, sold by M. Finkel and Daughter, has a well-developed rose border, a house with tall trees, and a single alphabet, and may relate to Harriet's work. The use of the word "Progeny" on the sampler with the word "Married" underlined appears on nearly all the known genealogical samplers that emerged contemporaneously from the school of the Misses Mayo—but those works are much bolder than Deborah's piece, and hers lacks the typical cherub. The gold satin-stitch band and signature section, which names Portland and provides a precise date of completion, more closely resemble the works in the group attributed to the Neal school. An unfinished or badly damaged 1817 sampler by a daughter of Joseph Owen and Sarah Thombs (possibly a sister of the Mary Owen named above), which can be found at www.antiquesamplers.org, has a similar border, gold band, and underlined "Married" and may also represent a related work. On June 30, 1842, Deborah became the second wife of botanical physician Moses Lunt shortly after his first wife died. Deborah was probably the mother of the youngest child of that family, Caroline. Moses disappeared from the records between 1850 and 1860. After that time, Deborah kept her own home but took in boarders. She died March 2, 1885.

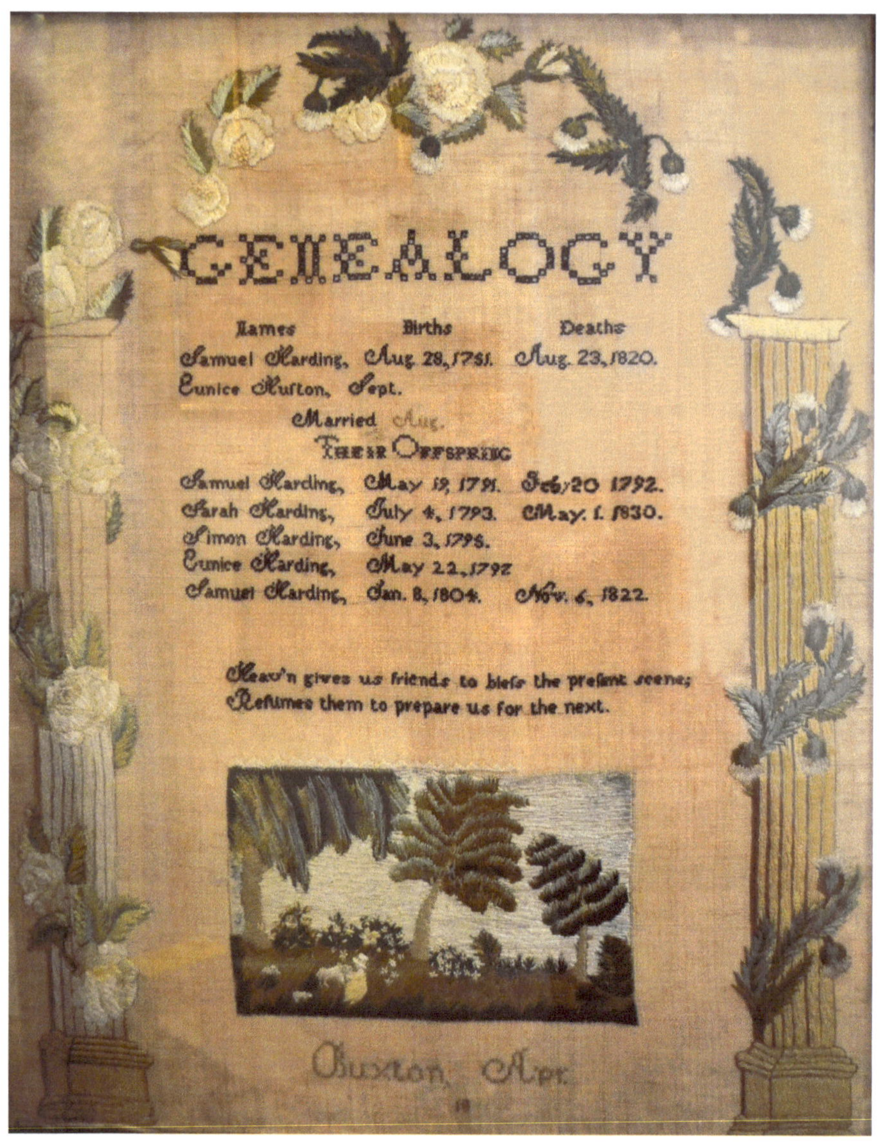

Sarah or Eunice Harding
(1793–1830, 1797–1849)
Family register sampler,
circa 1804–1830
Possibly worked in Portland
(school unknown)
Silk thread on linen
Cross, satin, straight, and
outline stitches
21 ½ x 17 ½
Collection of Burton W. Pearl

This attractive work was stitched by either **Sarah or Eunice Harding**. While it is not at all unusual to find samplers with the date that would reveal the maker's age picked out (evidence that very young talent, once a source of pride, would in later years be cancelled by vanity), that does not seem to be the case in the Harding girl's work. More likely, she waited to find out her mother's birthdate and the date of her parents' marriage—some of the last details she needed to add before completing her sampler. Once she had set the work aside, she seems not to have had the opportunity to complete it, although someone may later have added some death dates. The maker's mother, Eunice Huston Harding, was the third wife of Samuel Harding Sr. Both of them, like many of the Harding family, were from Eastham, Massachusetts. A sizeable contingent of the family relocated to southern Maine in the late eighteenth century and are represented with other samplers in this exhibition. Both Mrs. Eunice Harding and her son, Simon, died in 1825. Daughter Eunice became the second wife of Robert Wentworth of Buxton in 1832. He was a clockmaker and, after a serious accident, operated a foundry. They were the parents of four children, one of whom was killed at the battle of Spotsylvania Courthouse during the Civil War. Eunice died in Buxton on April 19, 1849. Sarah probably never married and died in 1830. While this elaborate embroidery names the girls' small hometown of Buxton, it seems more likely to have originated in a Portland boarding school, which would account for the maker not having ready access to the correct dates. The roses, full-blown and glorious on the left and top, appear withered and then dead on the right column, creating vivid but unusual symbolism.

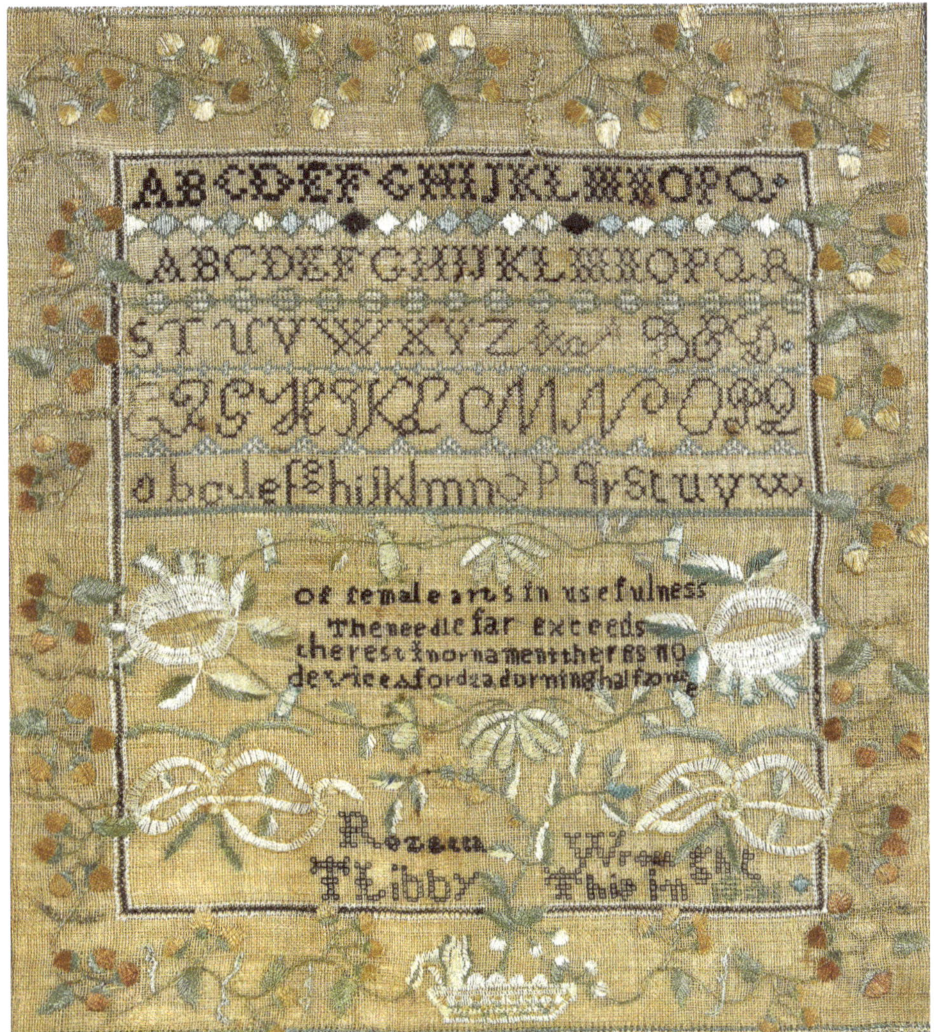

Rosetta Libby (1815-1887)
Marking sampler, circa 1830
Possibly worked in the school of the Misses Charlotte and Sarah Paine, Portland, or in the Gorham Academy, Gorham, Maine
Silk thread on linen
Cross, satin, and outline stitches
28 ½ x 16 ½
Collection of Dan and Marty Campanelli

Rosetta Libby was born in Limerick, Maine, on September 20, 1815, the eldest child of Parmenio and Eunice Jewell Libby, making her a distant relative of several other sampler makers in the exhibition: Mary L. Skillings and Louisa Otis, who stitched nearly identical samplers, and the unnamed makers of the Bullfinch-Harding silk embroidery and of the Samuel and Eunice Harding genealogy (pp. 43, 38). Parmenio, a blacksmith, later became a deacon of the Congregational Church in nearby Limington, also the hometown of Louisa Otis. After Rosetta's mother died in 1820, her father remarried. His second wife also died, and he married for a third time in 1831. On September 3, 1843, Rosetta married Moses Blake in Limington and gave birth to six children, two of whom died in childhood. Rosetta died April 14, 1887 after consuming poison, just ten months after the death of her husband.

The long-lasting school where Rosetta, Mary and Louisa made their samplers is unknown. The three samplers show considerable artistry and share many distinctive features. If they were made in Portland, only three schools span the necessary years: the Misses Martin's (but none of the girls appear on their list of students), Rachel Hall Neal's, and the school of Charlotte and Sarah Paine. Two interesting connections make the school of the Misses Paine a more likely choice. Their father, Dr. James Paine, had practiced medicine in Limerick, and his brother married into the same Harding family that the Libbys were connected to. However it was noted of the Paine school, "The terms were high and only the daughters of the wealthy could obtain admission" (*The Schools of Portland*, 1888, p. 34). None of these three sampler makers appeared to come from significant wealth. Additionally, the samplers are not stylistically similar to the dominant Portland fashion in needlework, making it just as likely that the school was located in an area closer to the girls' homes, perhaps in Gorham, where the Gorham Academy was operating and educating girls throughout the necessary timespan.

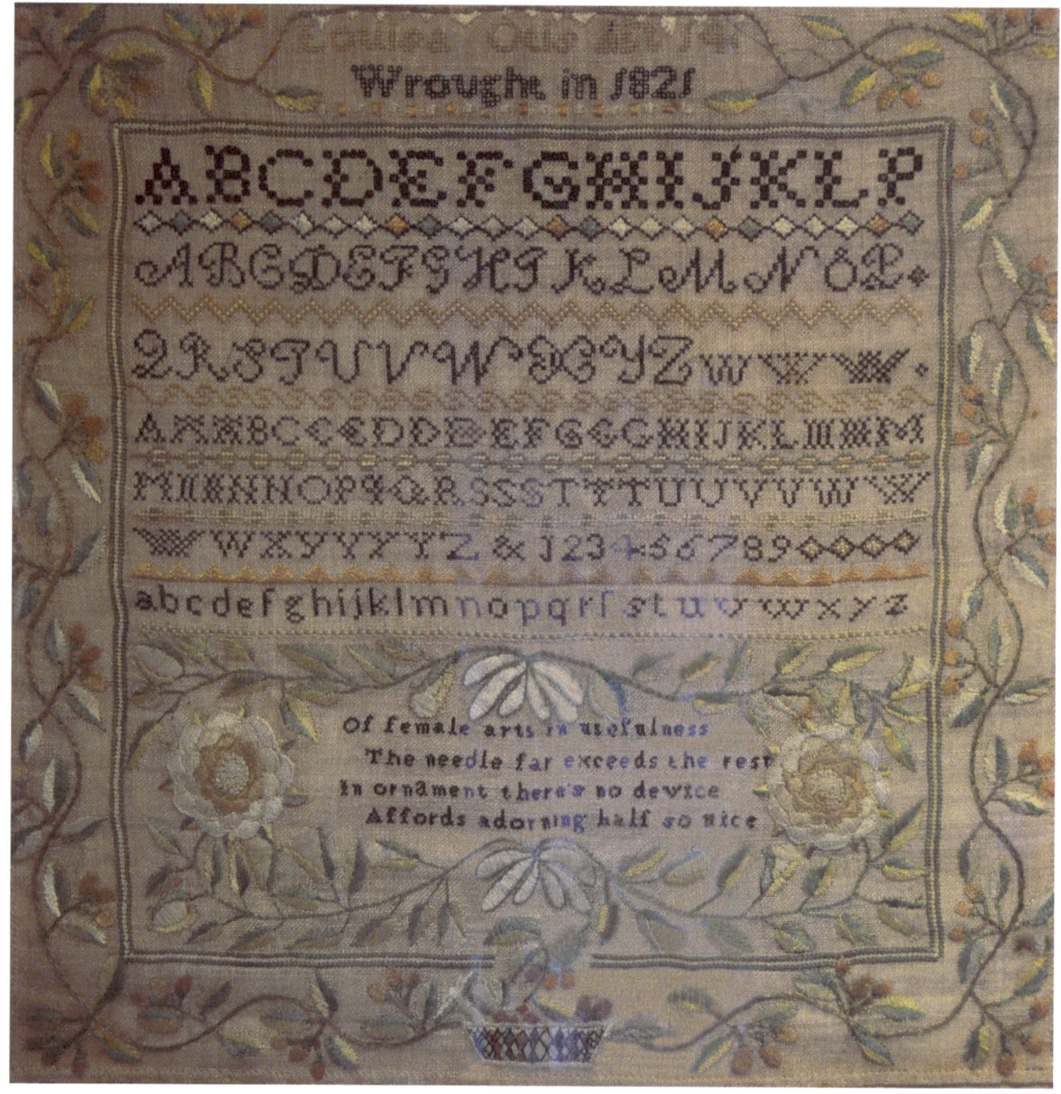

Louisa Otis (1807–?)
Marking sampler, 1821
Possibly worked in the school of the Misses Charlotte and Sarah Paine, Portland, or in the Gorham Academy, Gorham, Maine
Cross, satin, and outline stitches
17 ½ x 17 ½
Collection of Burton W. Pearl

The location where **Louisa Otis** stitched her lovely sampler is unknown. Since her family and the families of Rosetta Libby and Mary L. Skillings, who made very similar works, were all from the general vicinity of Gorham, it's possible that the Gorham Academy, which opened in 1803, may have been the source. Another possibility would be the Portland school of the Paine sisters, since they had a strong family connection to that area, as well. Louisa Otis was the youngest of the three children of Captain David Otis, a farmer, and Anna Small Libby, born on April 7, 1807, in Limington. In 1829, Louisa married William Paine of nearby Standish. On the 1860 census, William is listed as a "teacher of music," as is their eldest daughter of the four children that still resided at home. William died at the age of 102 in 1898; no record has been found for Louisa's death.

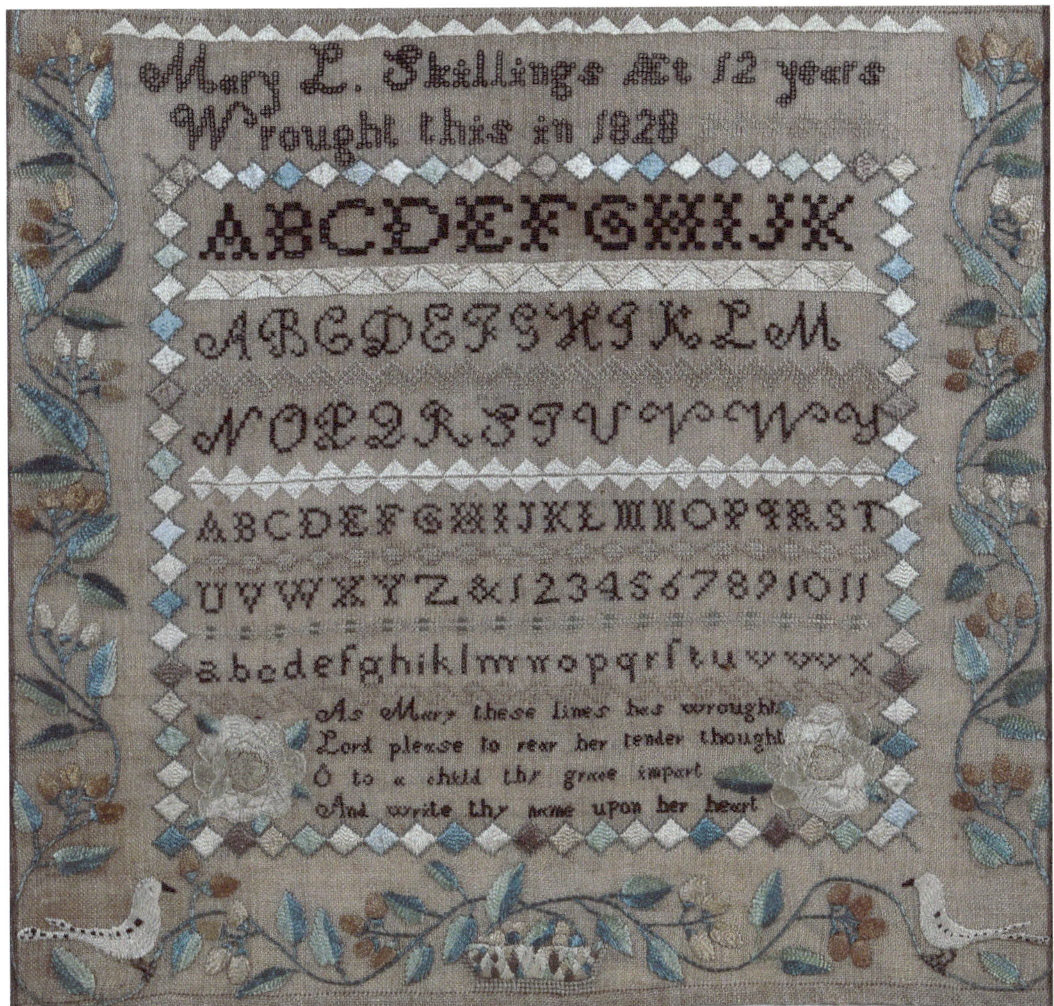

Mary L. Skillings
(1816–1857)
Marking sampler, 1828
Possibly worked in the school of the Misses Charlotte and Sarah Paine, Portland, or in the Gorham Academy, Gorham, Maine
Silk thread on linen
Cross, satin, and outline stitches
28 x 16
Collection of the Baxter House Museum

Mary Skillings was just twelve years old when she completed her masterful sampler in 1828, so similar to those worked by Rosetta Libby and Louisa Otis, her distant relatives, who both grew up in nearby towns. Mary was born May 10, 1816, the fifth of the eleven children of Joseph and Susan Clark Skillings, of whom at least four died in childhood. In 1850, Mary was one of the three offspring, including her younger sister and brother, still residing at home with her father on the original Skillings farmstead in West Gorham, Maine. Her father died in 1853, and on September 11, 1857, Mary died as well.

Sarah Ann Bonney
(1822–1898)
Family register sampler,
circa 1832
Worked at Miss Hall's Infant School, Portland
Silk thread on linen
Cross, stem, satin, four-sided, Algerian eye, and chain stitches
20 ½ x 17 ¾
Collection of the Pejepscot Historical Society

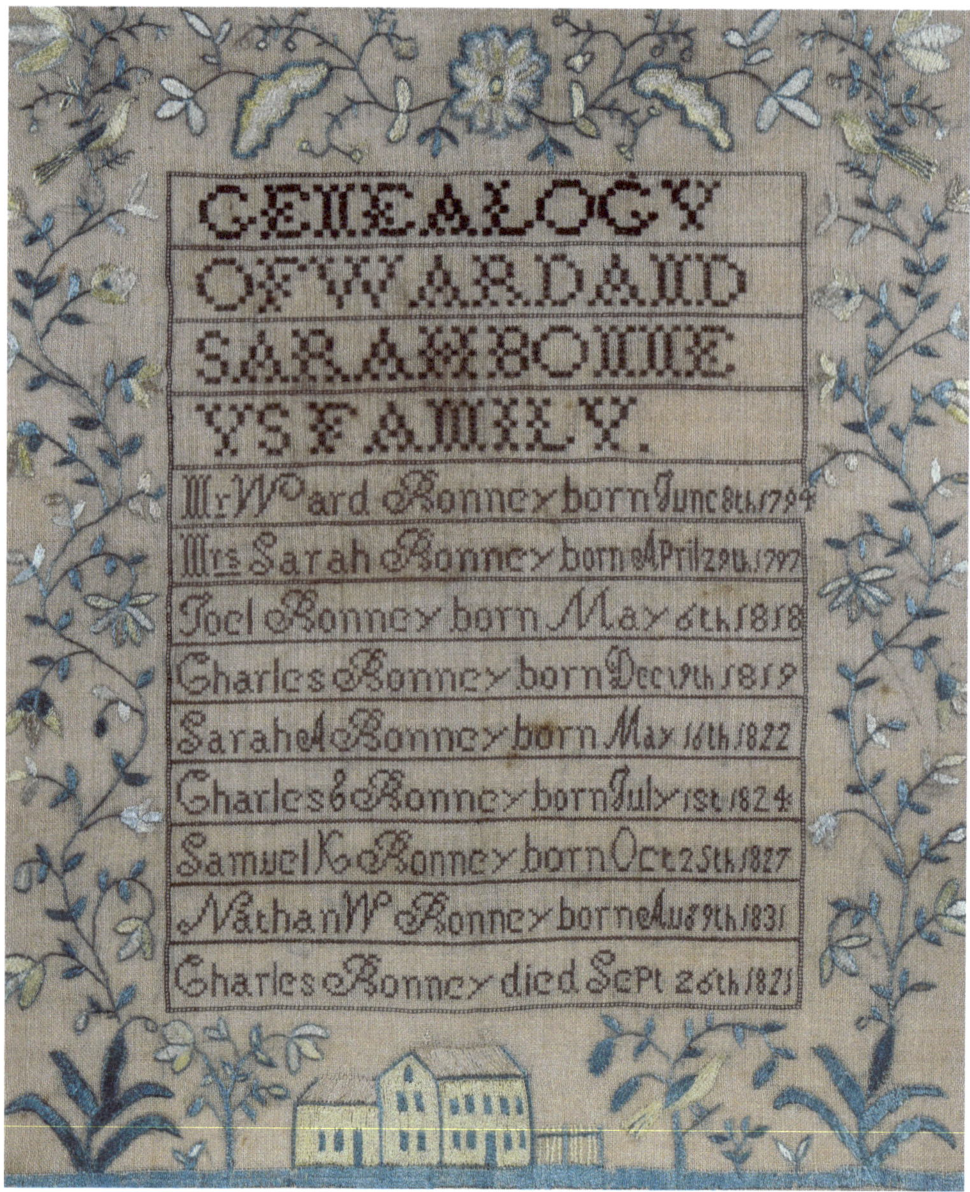

Sarah Bonney was the only daughter among the six children of Ward and Sarah Stanford Bonney, who were married in Portland in 1817. Ward was a merchant in Portland, but by 1835 he operated a mail route in Androscoggin County, where the family had probably moved by that time. Sarah Ann Bonney married John Crawford, a teamster, in Durham, Maine, in 1842. They relocated shortly after their marriage to Brunswick where they appear to have had only limited financial success. They were the parents of seven children, including a set of twins. John died in 1888 and Sarah in 1898.

Sarah Ann stitched her sampler at Miss Hall's Infant School in Portland, information that was noted on the back of the frame by one of her daughters. The style of this family register sampler, while attractive, is quite different from others associated with Portland in the Federal era. Miss Hall might have been connected to one of two Portland households that were headed by Hall women, as noted in the 1834 city directory—those of Susan Hall and Martha Hall, both listed as widows. The same directory suggests a third possibility: A.D. Hall and Harriet Purinton were operating a "millinery and fancy goods" shop on Middle Street. A. D. Hall was Abba (or sometimes Abigail) D. Hall, who was born in Stoddard, New Hampshire, in 1808 and was the daughter of Ellis Hall and Sally Pitcher. Harriet may be the same woman who married Moses G. Dow on October 7, 1834, in Portland, and possibly the daughter of widow Dianna Purinton, who is also listed in the 1834 directory. Hall and Purinton's shop is not listed in city directories after that time.

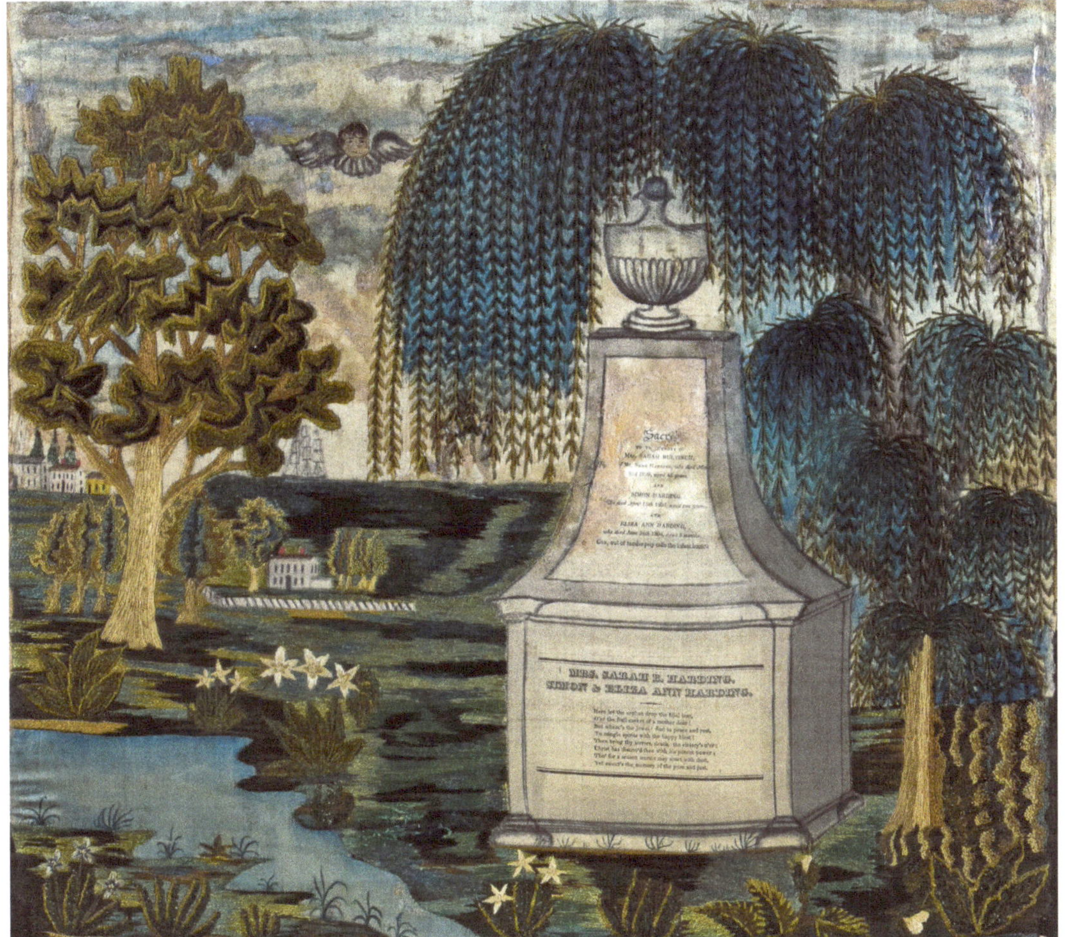

Harding (dates and maker unknown)
Silk mourning embroidery, circa 1825
Worked at the school of the Misses Mayo, Portland
Silk thread on silk over linen
Satin stitch
18 x 21 ½
Collection of Dan and Marty Campanelli

Stitched at the school of the Misses Mayo, as evidenced by the presence of the easily recognized cherub, this mourning embroidery memorializes Sarah Bullfinch **Harding** and her young daughter, Eliza. Noah, Sarah's husband, was the son of Simon and Elizabeth Cressey Harding, born in Gorham, Maine, in 1777. For a period of time around 1800, Noah relocated to Boston, where he was recorded as being engaged in retail commerce and where he married Sarah Bullfinch in 1802; she was about eleven years his senior. They moved to Portland, where little five-month-old Eliza died in 1804, two-year-old Simon in 1805, and Sarah in 1809. Noah and the elder Sarah may have been the parents of at least one other daughter, possibly also named Eliza, born after the first Eliza's death. Seven months after Sarah's death, Noah married Hannah Watts of Boston. Later census records indicate that they were the parents of at least one daughter, another Sarah, who was born about 1814 and with whom Hannah later resided, as noted on the 1860 and 1870 censuses. The maker of this embroidery is unknown: the 1820 census lists a female aged ten to fifteen and another aged sixteen to twenty-five in the household, neither of which, oddly, fits daughter Sarah. Although seemingly complete, this piece was never removed from the stretcher on which it was stitched, providing an interesting look at how silk embroideries were worked.

Mary Ann McLellan
(1803–1831)
Family register sampler, 1807
Probably worked in Portland, school unknown
Silk thread on linen
Cross, satin, straight, and queen stitches
24 x 17
Collection of the Portland Museum of Art, Museum purchase, 1981, 1063

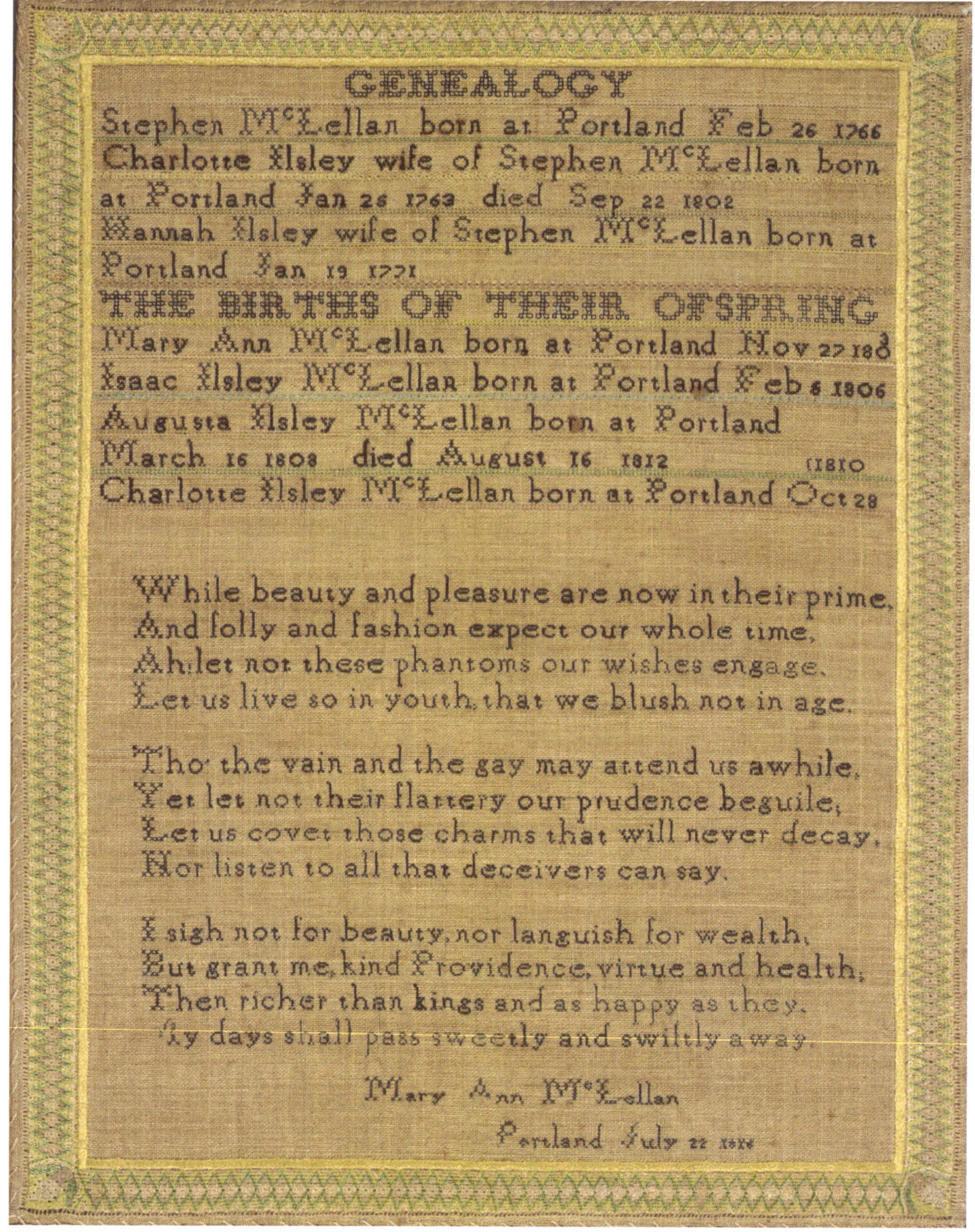

Mary Ann McLellan was born on November 27, 1803 into what was at the time the most prominent family in Portland, Maine. Her parents were Stephen and Hannah Ilsley McLellan. A generation before, the McLellans had arrived in America nearly destitute but by 1800 had acquired vast wealth through mercantile and shipping businesses. Shortly after Stephen's marriage on February 22, 1803 to the younger sister, Hannah Ilsley, of his five-months-dead first wife, he began construction of a prominent mansion directly across the street from a nearly identical one just completed by his equally wealthy brother, Hugh McLellan, who had been listed as a sponsor of Elizabeth Dawes academy in 1804 advertisements. But less than five years later, a trade embargo had destroyed the family business and consumed the wealth. The McLellans were forced to sell their mansions. Asa Clapp, the father of another Portland sampler maker, bought Hugh's home for his son. Mary Ann died July 26, 1831 at the age of just twenty-seven. Her sampler, while not in any way iconic of Portland work, is nonetheless attractive and meticulously planned. Her instructor is unknown. Dawes' academy closed in April of 1805, so that was not the source.

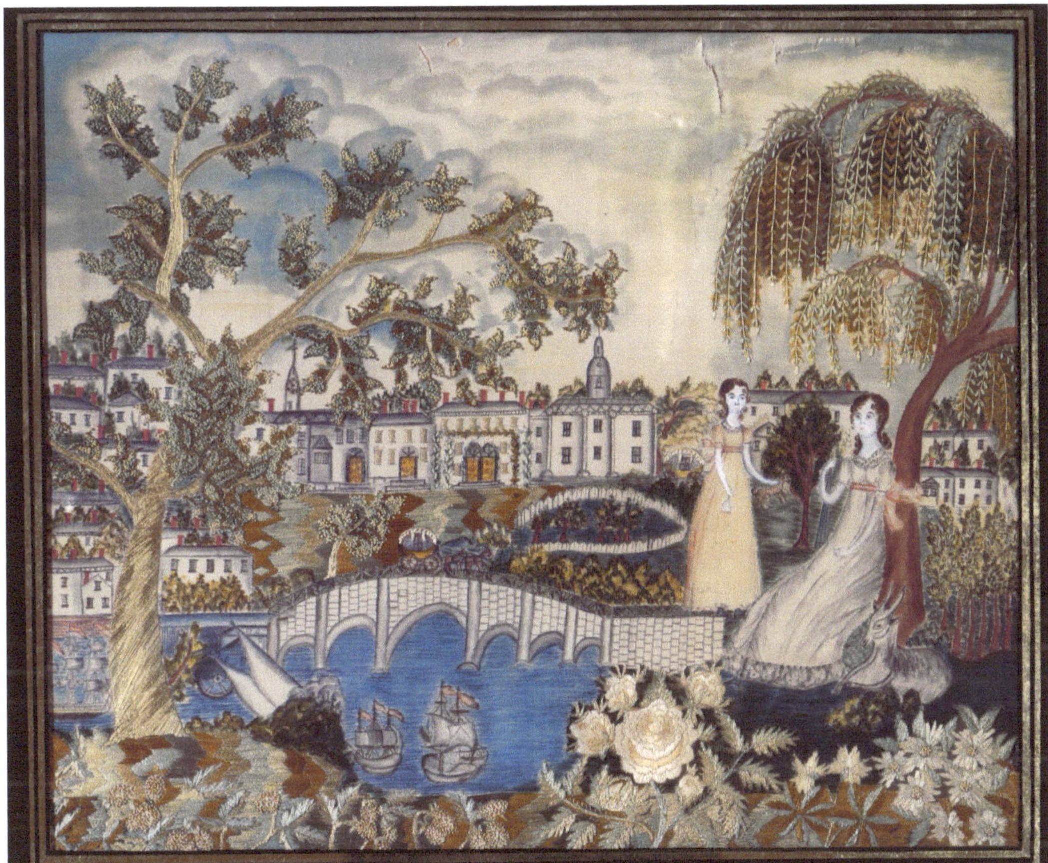

Mary Reed (1806–?)
Silk embroidery, 1824
Probably worked at the school of Mary Rea, Portland
Silk thread, chenille, pencil, and paint on silk
Satin stitch and French knots
20 x 23 ½
Collection of Burton W. Pearl

Mary Ann Reed most likely worked her artful silk and painted embroidery at the school of Mary Rea. There are several characteristics that seem to appear in most of the works identified with her school. Buildings in the background display considerable detail, but perspective is awkwardly handled; the buildings face in a variety of directions. Willow trees are delightfully depicted, but deciduous trees have clusters of green and brown leafy sections that are less realistic. Perhaps the most charming distinction, however, is the "willowy" arms of the people. Arms are elongated and seem almost boneless. Most of these works feature a large flower in the foreground. Although at least two other Portland female academies also included these flowers, Mary Rea's were drawn and stitched in a more naturalistic way.

Mary Reed was the ninth of the ten children of Jonathan and Dorothy Blake Reed of Westbrook, Maine (just west of Portland). In 1828, she married Dr. Cornelius Brackett of Westbrook. They were the parents of two sons born in 1832 and 1837, both of whom died in young adulthood, after Mary was widowed in 1839. Mary Rea was born in Windham, Maine, and evidently taught both there and in Portland. For more on Rea, see pp. 96–97.

Eunice or Eleanor Knight
(1806–1892/1808–?)
Family register sampler,
circa 1825
Probably worked at the school
of the Misses Mayo, Portland
Silk thread, chenille, pencil,
and paint on linen
Cross, satin, four-sided, and
outline stitches
24 x 18 framed
Collection of the Maine
Historical Society

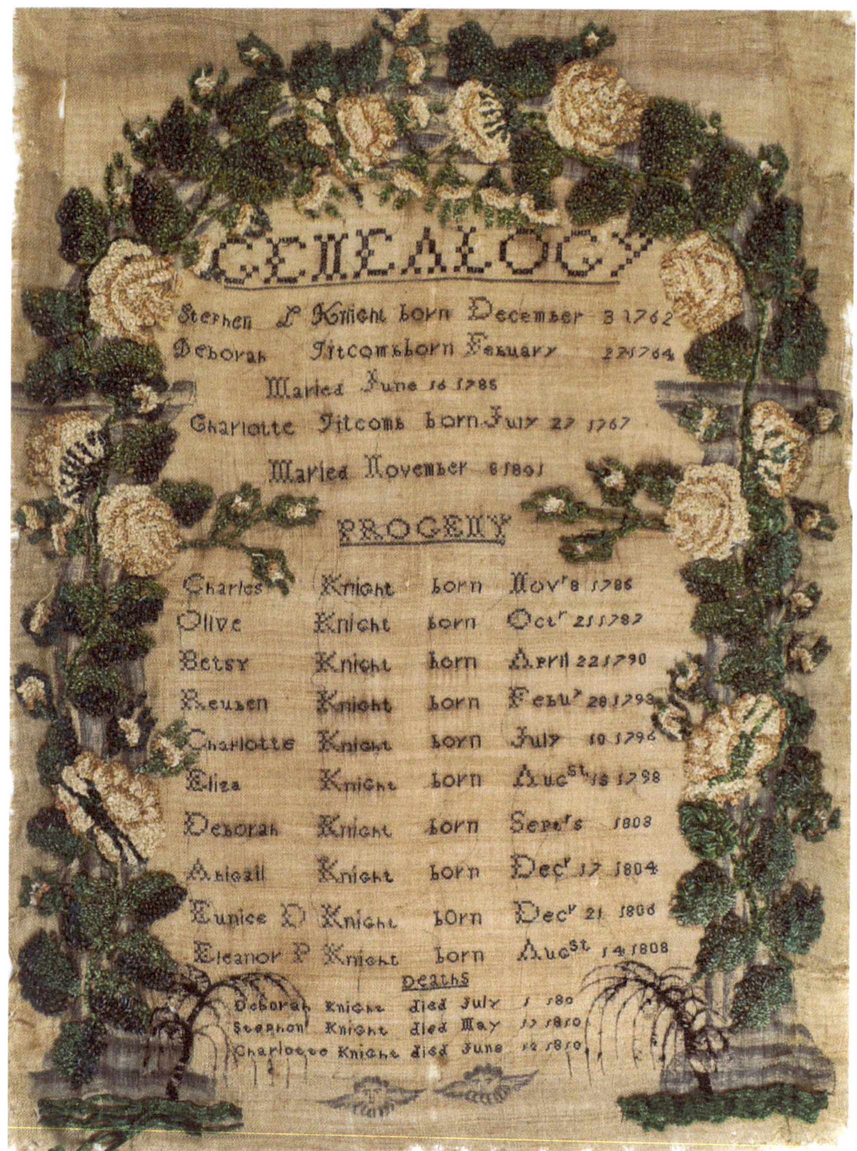

Unfortunately for collectors and researchers, not all girls "signed" their samplers. This sampler is attributed to one of the younger girls in the **Knight family**, because the hallmarks of its design didn't emerge until after about 1820, when some of the elder sisters were unlikely to have still been making samplers. By then, Olive, Charlotte, and Eliza were all married. Betsy seems to have never married and lived for many years with her next-youngest brother, Reuben, who was a glazier. There are no further records for Deborah, Abigail, or Eleanor. Eunice never married and spent the last decade or more of her life in the Home for Aged Women in Portland. She died on March 24, 1892. One or rarely a pair of winged cherubs appear on a large group of Portland needlework, both highly decorative embroidered and painted samplers like this one, and on attractive silk embroideries, as well. They were almost certainly made at the school of the Misses Mayo and generally include several common features: an elaborate floral border that often includes columns, the word "Genealogy" at the top, the underlined word "Married" after the parents' names, the use of the word "Progeny" to describe the children, and the inclusion of a cherub, prior to about 1826. The family register sampler of Lucy Harris, stitched in 1817, and somewhat rudimentary compared to later works, includes many of these features and named the school of the Misses Mayo. It was illustrated on page 515 of the September, 1988 issue of *The Magazine Antiques* in Betty Ring's "Samplers and Silk Embroideries of Portland, Maine."

Recently, the badly damaged graves of Stephen and Deborah Titcomb Knight, parents of this sampler maker, were rediscovered by an Eagle Scout in an unmaintained cemetery in Falmouth that he has now restored.

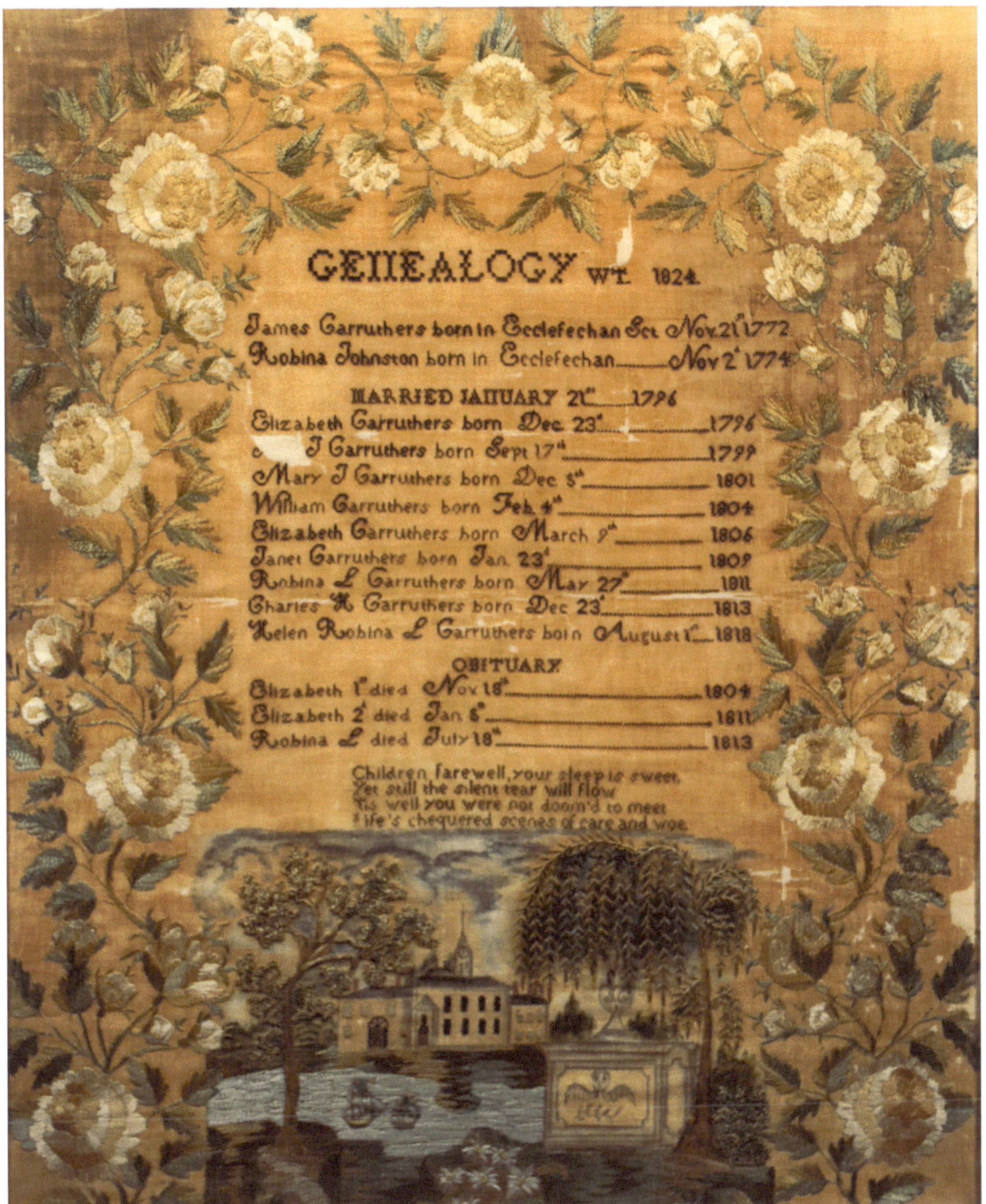

Janet Carruthers (1809–1838)
Family register sampler, 1824
Probably worked at the school of Mary Rea
Silk thread, pencil, and paint on linen
Cross, satin, and outline stitches
25 x 22 framed
Collection of the Maine Historical Society

The maker of this attractive painted and embroidered family register sampler very modestly didn't sign her work. Some Portland teachers seemed to particularly emphasize the importance of identifying the maker—which is a key feature for collectors—but Mary Rea, in whose school this piece was probably worked, did not. The Reverend Mr. Carruthers is said to have arrived in America from Scotland in 1813, which would mean that most of his children were born, and some died, there. His daughters Elizabeth and Rubina died before the sampler was made in 1824. Mary would have been rather old to be the sampler maker and Helen too young, so it's very likely that **Janet Carruthers** stitched this intricate work. Both she and her sister Helen died in young adulthood, Janet on December 1, 1838, and Helen in 1842. By the time of his death in 1857, of the Reverend's large family, only his sons survived. While many of the works from the Misses Mayo's school included penciled cherubs, the one on the Carruthers family register lacks the typical neck ruff of the Mayo cherubs and actually seems intended more to mark the monument than to serve as an artistic signature. However, the teacher for this sampler would surely have been aware of the Mayos' common use of the cherub to mark their pieces; this may constitute a sly nod at a competing school. The satin-stitched scene at the bottom of this work closely resembles the scene on Cordelia Knight's primarily painted family register (p. 50).

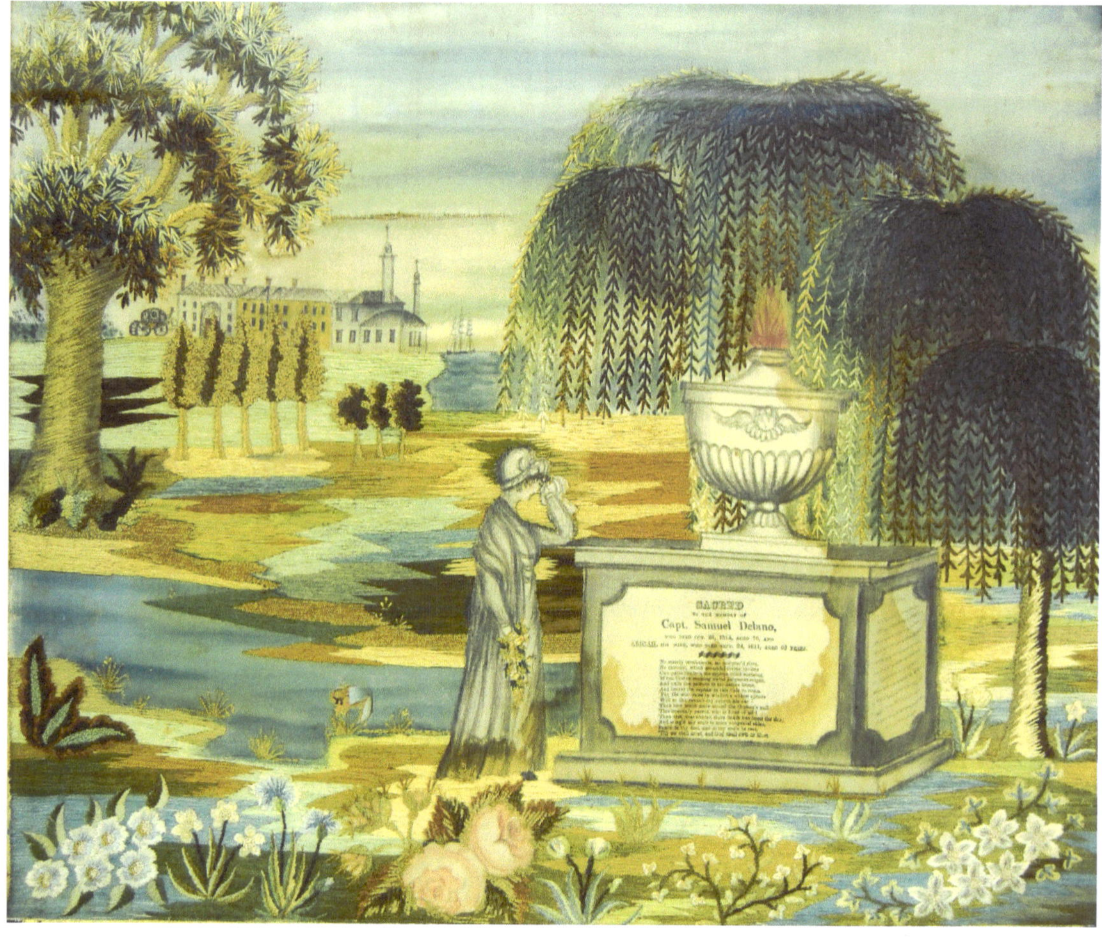

Elizabeth or Abigail Moody
(1809–1838, 1811–1847)
Silk embroidery, circa 1825
Probably worked at the school of the Misses Mayo, Portland, Maine
Silk thread, ink, pencil, and paint on silk
Satin, outline, and lazy daisy stitches
18 x 22
Collection of the Maine Maritime Museum

The Maine Maritime Museum owns two silk embroideries that are nearly identical; both feature a single female mourner leaning disconsolately against a large memorial that is topped with an urn bearing a hand drawn cherub. Since one of the pair is badly damaged, it is not included in the exhibition. It was dedicated to Broadstreet Moody, who died in 1820 at the age of forty-two, and his two young daughters. Broadstreet was the husband of Elizabeth Delano Moody. This silk memorial is dedicated to her parents. The single mourner in each probably represents Elizabeth, although just as commonly, embroideries from this group would depict as mourners all of the surviving members of the immediate family. When Broadstreet died, he had three surviving children: Elizabeth, born in Bath, Maine, on October 9, 1809; Abigail Minott born May 31, 1811; and a son, Broadstreet Delano, born March 18, 1817. Most likely, either **Elizabeth or Abigail Moody** stitched this attractive embroidery. It's possible that the second silk embroidery may have been made by the other sister. Elizabeth died unmarried, June 6, 1838, and Abigail, also unmarried, died January 17, 1847. Both were outlived by their mother, who died in 1859.

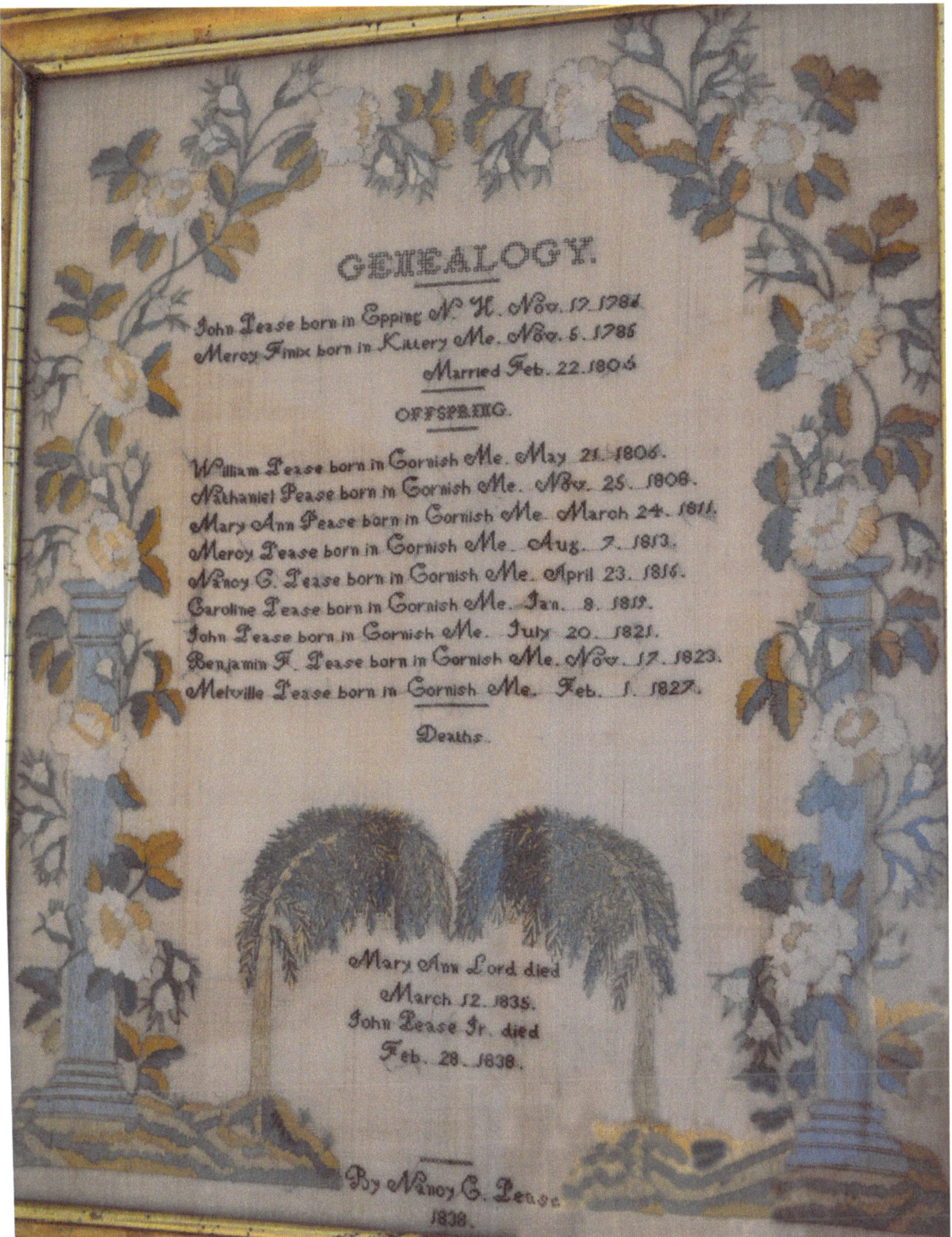

Nancy C. Pease (1816–1887)
Family register sampler, 1838
Worked in an unknown Portland school
Silk thread on linen
Cross, straight, satin, chain, and four-sided stitches
20 ½ x 17 ½
Collection of Burton W. Pearl

Nancy C. Pease was born in the small town of Cornish, Maine, located near the foothills of the White Mountains. Her father, John Pease, was a farmer of no great wealth who married Mercy Finix (likely Phoenix). Nancy married James Libby Small, also a farmer of no particular affluence, and they raised a daughter and two sons. Nancy died June 23, 1887 in Cornish. Her husband lived on until 1898. Nancy's sister Mary Ann, whose death is noted on the sampler, married Henry Lord in 1833. Mary Ann's daughter, Armine P. Lord, was living with the Pease family in 1850. Nancy's sampler raises a conundrum. Her father doesn't seem wealthy enough to have sent her to Portland for schooling, but her sampler is virtually identical to one stitched by Sarah A. Skillin in Portland in 1835 which is in the collection of the National Museum of American History, Smithsonian Institution, and that was pictured in *Family Record* by Gloria Seaman Allen, D.A.R. Museum, 1989, p. 67.

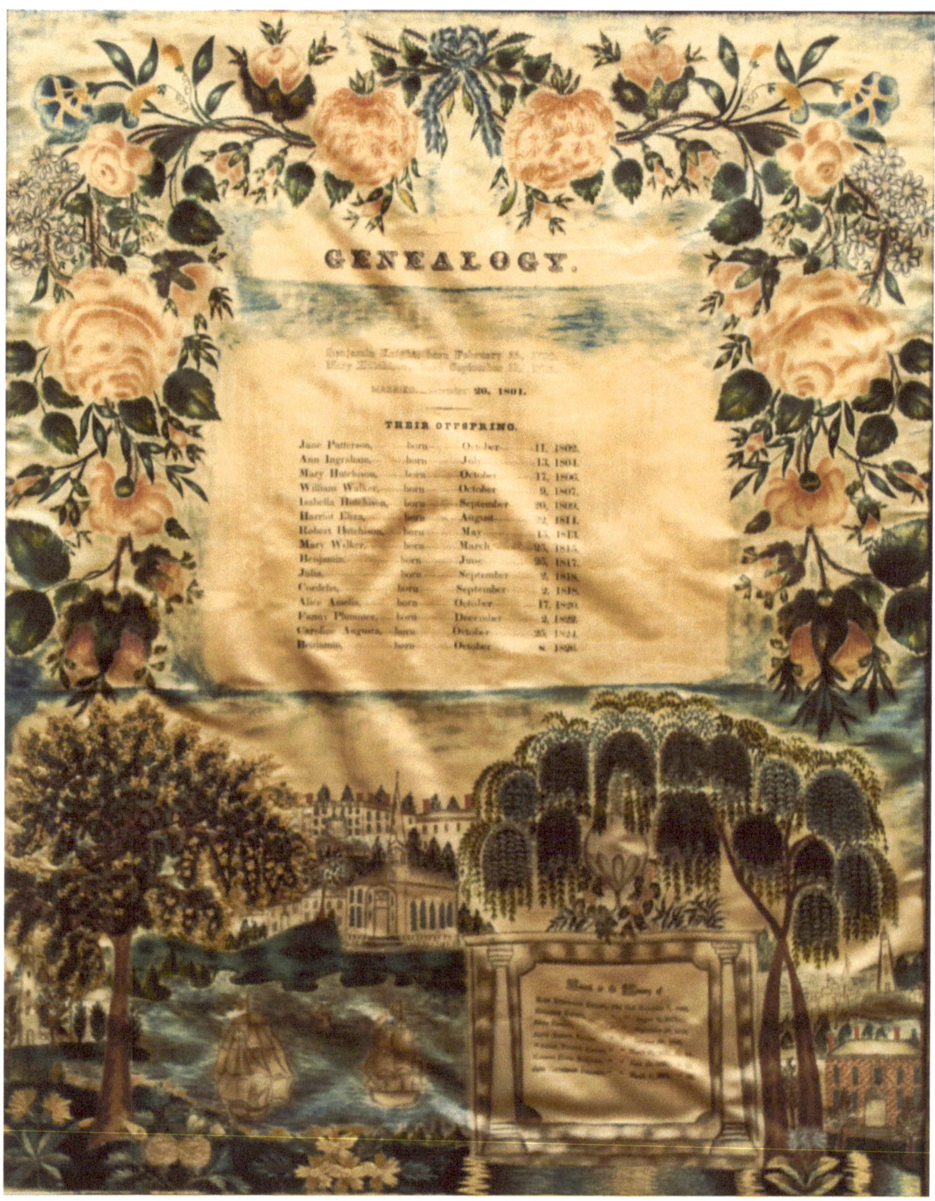

Cordelia Knight (1818–1853)
Family register sampler, 1835
Probably worked in the school of Mary Rea, Portland
Silk thread, pencil, and paint on linen
Cross, satin, and outline stitches
23 ½ x 17 ½
Collection of the Maine Historical Society

Cordelia Knight's sampler represents an interesting crossroads among Portland's lavish silk mourning embroideries, family register samplers, and schoolgirl painting—another important branch offered by many female academies. While her work retains a basic similarity to some of the most elaborate genealogical samplers, paint has become the primary medium. Cordelia's father was a well-to-do Portland merchant but notably unfortunate with his children. This sampler includes a memorial to seven of the fifteen children of Benjamin and Mary Hutchinson Knight, both of whom also outlived their daughter, Cordelia. In 1844, Cordelia married Elijah Adams, a sail maker, and died in 1853, probably in childbirth with her fourth child, Delia, who survived. The sampler was passed down in the family of her eldest daughter, Ella. It was made in the school of Mary Rea where Cordelia's sister, Harriet, also attended and worked a mourning embroidery (pictured in *The Magazine Antiques*, September 1988, p. 521).

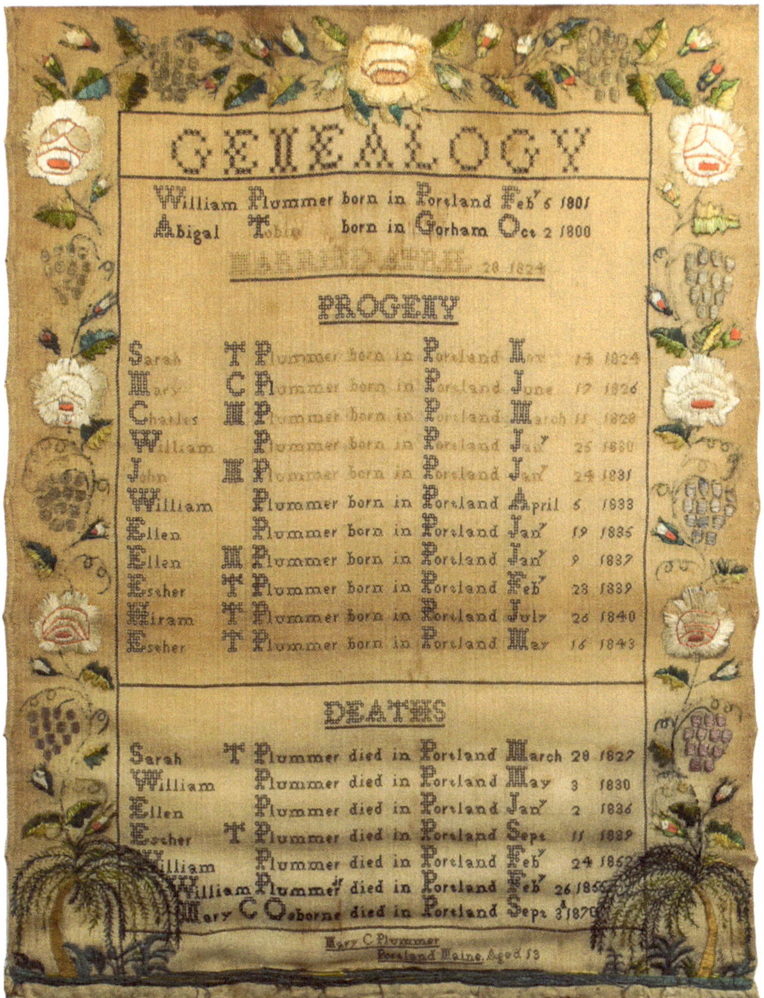

Mary C. Plummer
(1826–1870)
Family register sampler, 1839
Probably worked at the school of the Misses Mayo, Portland
Silk thread and paint on linen
Cross, satin, and outline stitches
28 x 17 ½
Collection of the Maine Historical Society

Mary Crockett Plummer was born June 17, 1826, to William Plummer of Portland and his wife, Abigail Tobin, who was from Gorham, Maine. Mary carefully stitched the names of her ten brothers and sisters, of whom she was the second eldest, on her elaborate family register sampler. William joined the blacksmithing business of his father, which gradually evolved during his lifetime into a vibrantly successful plumbing, heating, and gas pipe fitting company. He would be joined later in the business by one of his sons, who became a major figure in the construction of the Portland Water Company and who, with a second brother, was largely responsible for the Portland and Rochester Railroad. Seven deaths are recorded on the sampler; the last of these is of Mary herself, on September 3, 1870. In 1846, she married Thomas Osborne, variously listed as a trader or a mariner. She gave birth to two sons, and a namesake daughter who died in infancy. Neither Mary nor Thomas was listed on the 1870 census; Mary died later that year. If Mary was buried in Portland, her grave is unmarked; her infant, Mary, appears to be buried alone.

Mary's sampler was likely worked in the school of the Misses Mayo. Earlier works from the school almost always featured a drawn-in cherub with a ruff at its neck. After 1827, when one of the sisters, Martha Mayo, married and stopped teaching, no more cherubs appeared. It's uncertain when the school was opened. Martha Merchant was living in Portland with her husband, Simeon Mayo, and their six daughters according to the 1800 census. By 1810, Simeon was living separately. The first advertisement for the school appeared in 1817, but given Martha Mayo's presumably difficult economic situation, the school may have opened a few years earlier. The related Mary Bryant sampler, in the collection of the Maine Historical Society, may date from as early as 1819 (its latest recorded date); a related silk embroidery by Harriet Whitney (with cherub) identified by Betty Ring dates from 1822 (pictured in *The Magazine Antiques*, September, 1988, p. 519). Another related work of 1822 is the sampler of Almira W. Lincoln, 1822, currently (2012) listed for sale at www.houseoftheferret.com.

Charity Noyes Merrill
(1796–1876)
Silk mourning embroidery,
circa 1810
Probably worked at an unknown Portland school
Silk thread and watercolor paint on silk
Satin stitch
13 x 11 ½
Collection of Dan and Marty Campanelli

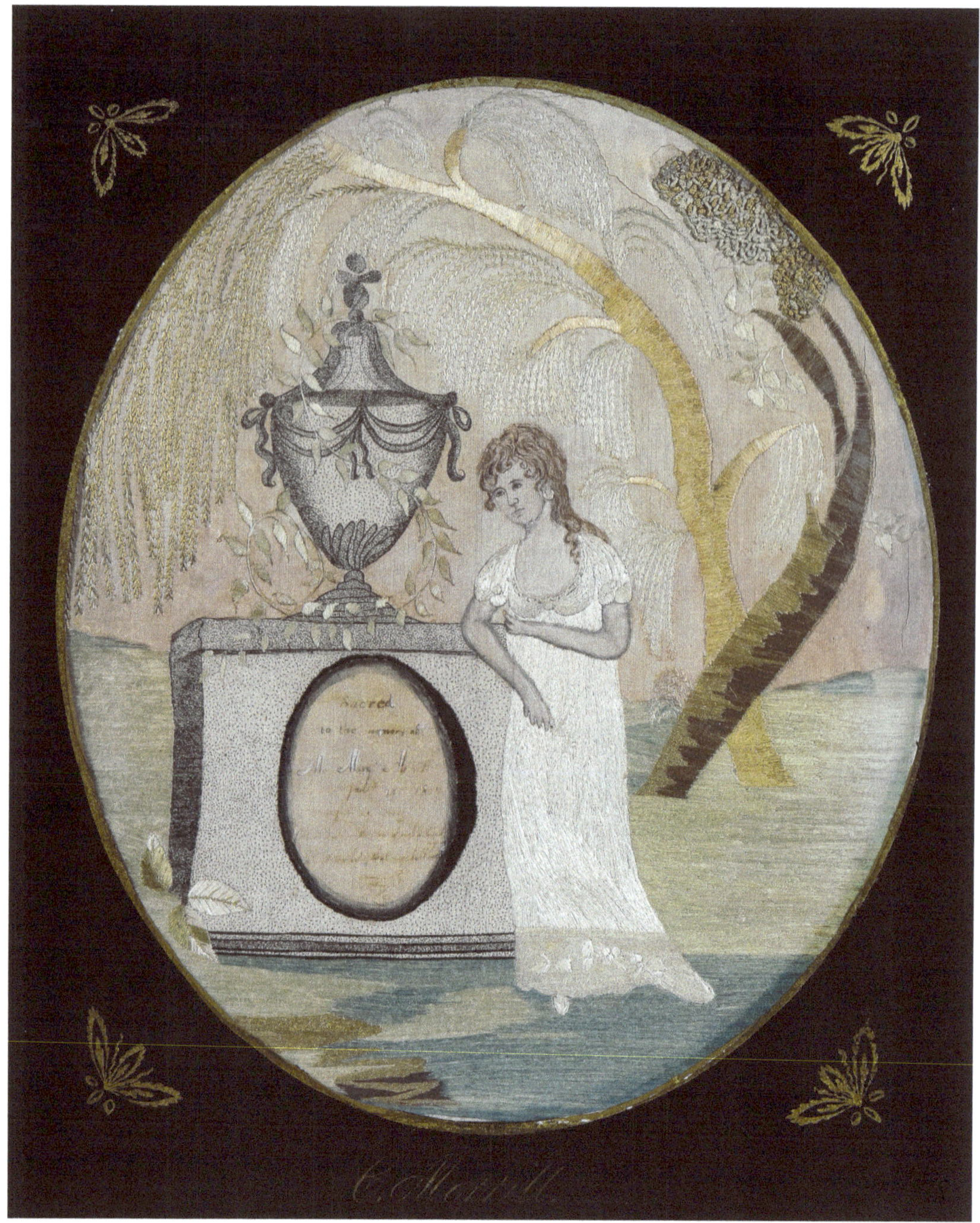

Can we sustain the loss of such a friend/Without the hope that we shall meet again? This is the verse that the embroiderer, likely **Charity Noyes Merrill**, chose to memorialize her elder sister, Mary, who had died January 29, 1807, at the age of twenty-one years. They were two of the children of James Merrill and his first cousin, Salome Merrill, of Falmouth, Maine (which was, until 1786 when Portland became a separate town, the name of the whole metropolitan area). Charity married Jeremiah Merrill, a carpenter and farmer, her second cousin. Her sister Asenath married Jeremiah's brother Giles, but she died very young. It's difficult to imagine the complicated relationships between members of this family. Adding another level of connection were frequent marriages between Merrill and Noyes family members, as well. There is no record of Charity having children. Jeremiah died in 1865 and Charity probably died on April 18, 1876. Charity's delicate silk mourning embroidery is evidently one-of-a-kind, with its tracery of vines, needle stippling, attractively drawn female figure and finely worked willow branches. Most of Portland's known mourning embroideries bear later dates than the likely one for this piece, around 1810 to 1815, when Charity was a teenager.

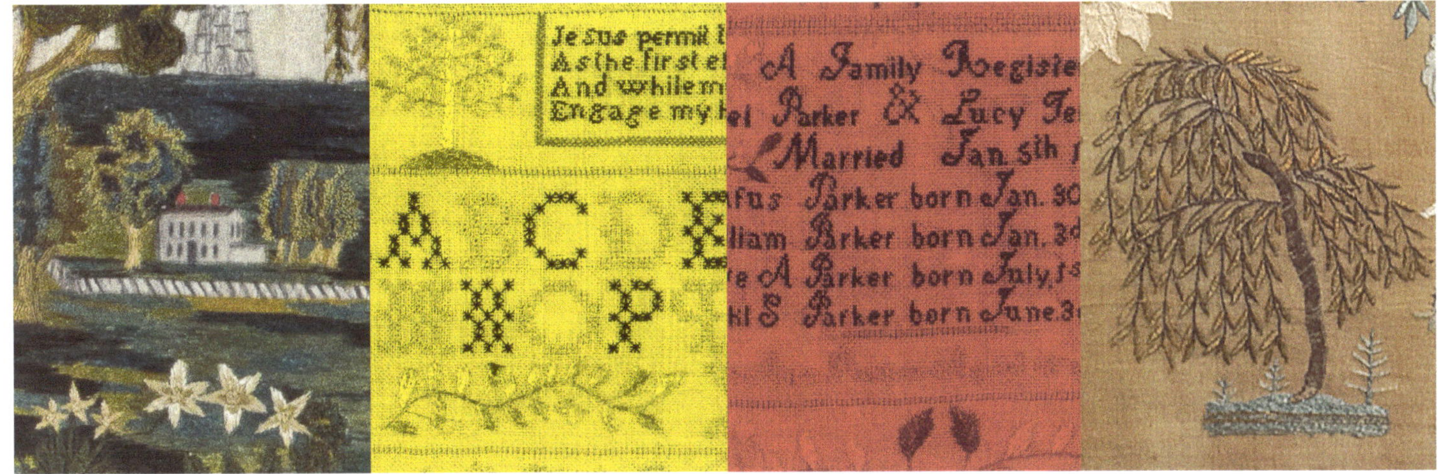

Part Three

How Letters Great and Small Are Wrought:

Individual Creativity and Portland's Influence on Rural Academies

Because styles of Maine needlework often show clear regional differences that may, in the future, help with the identification of other pieces, the works in this section are organized geographically, with those from each town grouped, starting at the southern and western end of Maine and moving in a northerly and easterly direction. Several samplers from one New Hampshire school are included at the end of Part 3.

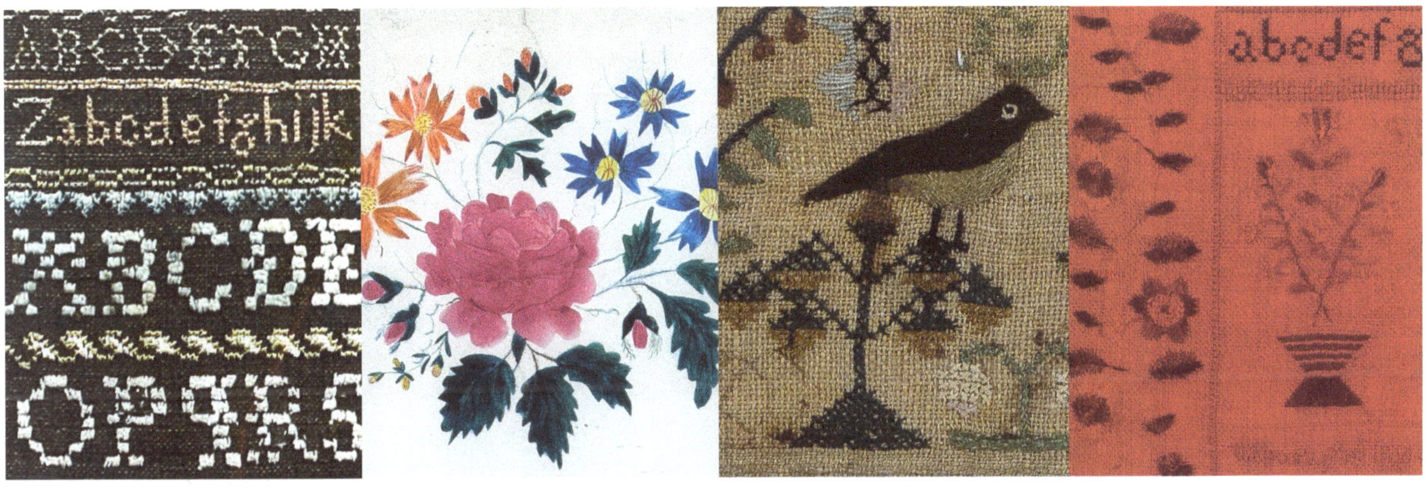

Betsey Fernald (1792–1868)
Marking sampler, 1804
Probably worked in Eliot, Maine, school unknown
Silk thread on linen
Cross, satin, and straight stitches
21 ½ x 14
Collection of the Maine State Museum

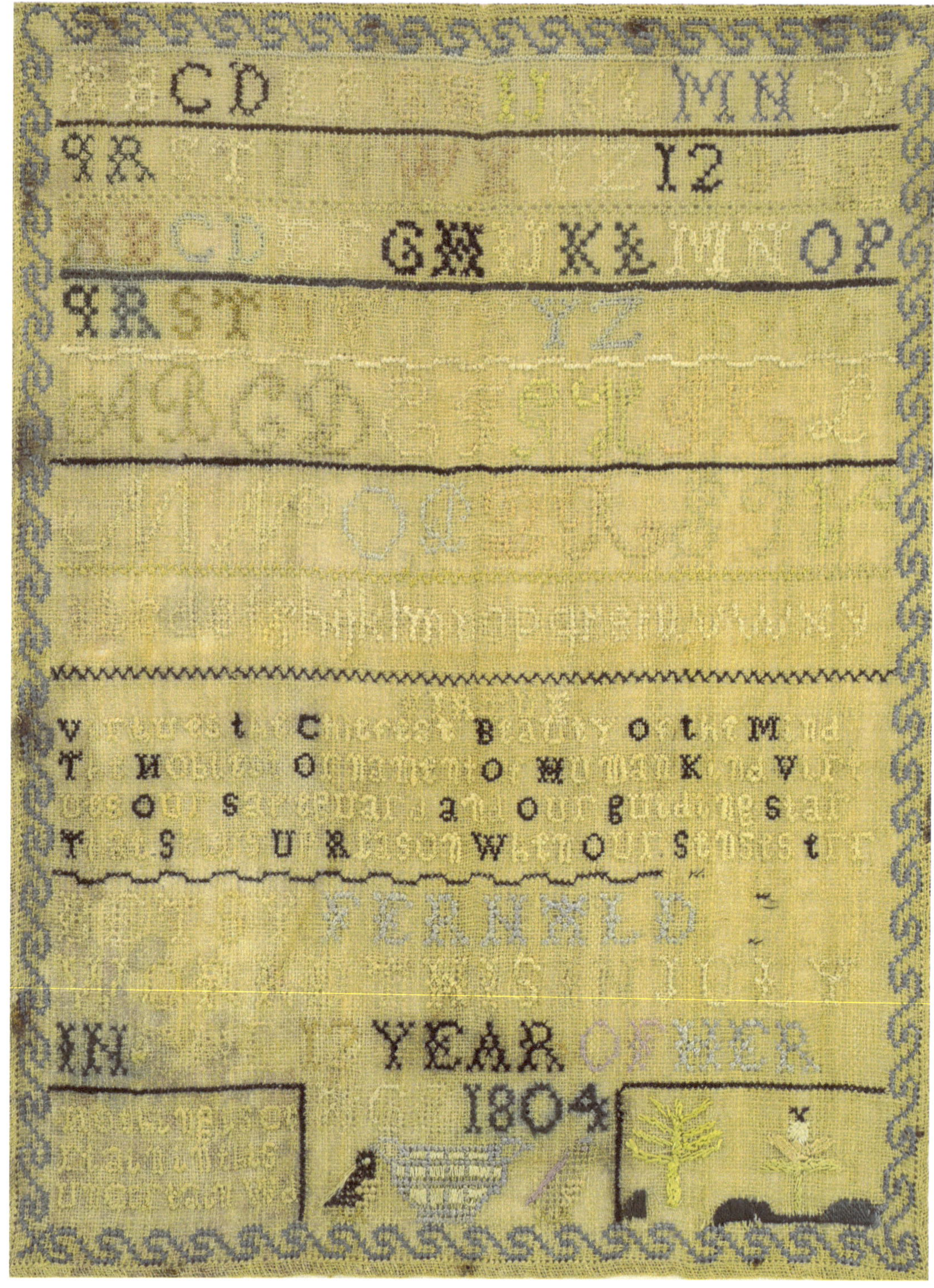

Betsey Fernald was born July 13, 1792, the seventh and youngest child of Captain Mark Fernald and his second wife, Mary Shapleigh. Her father was a blacksmith. After working her sampler in 1804, she went on to marry John Wentworth on November 13, 1819. They were the parents of four children: Mark, born March 11, 1820, a physician and Civil War general; Andrew Pepperell, a ships' carpenter; Mary Elizabeth, born December 10, 1824; and John, born January 2, 1831, a farmer. Betsey's husband, John, died August 15, 1832, leaving her a widow with young children, one of whom, Mary Elizabeth Wentworth, stitched another sampler in the exhibition (p. 58). In later years, Betsey lived with her son, Mark. She died on April 28, 1868 at the age of seventy-six. Betsey's modest work shares common features with others from the southern Maine/coastal New Hampshire region, including birds, an empty basket, and sparse trees at the bottom; it may be a forerunner of the developing style.

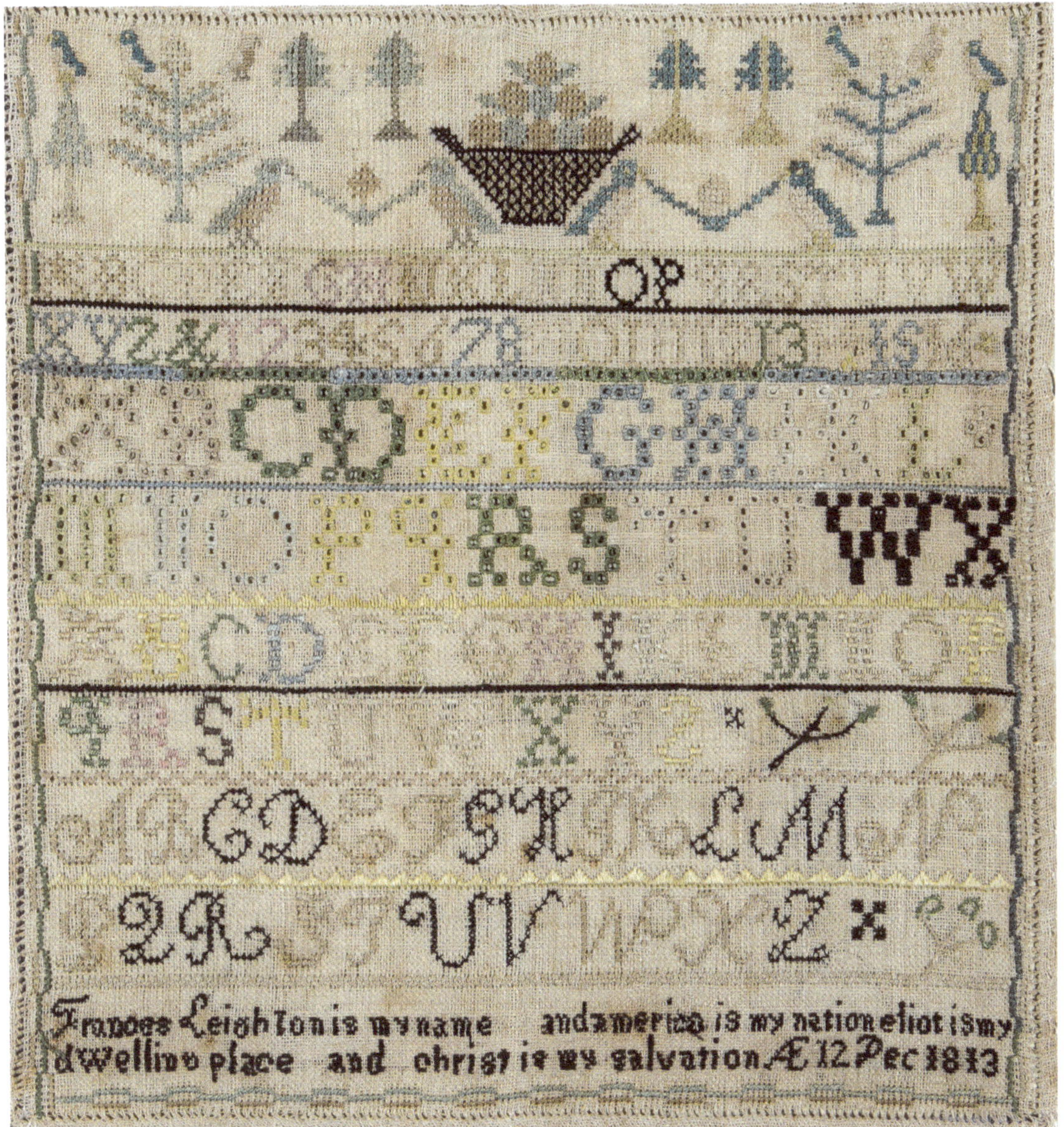

Frances Leighton
(1801–1889)
Marking sampler, 1813
Possibly worked at the school of Betsey Hill, Eliot, Maine
Silk thread on linen
Cross, satin, queen, and straight stitches
24 ½ x 17
Collection of the Brick Store Museum

Frances Leighton was the second of the eight children of Samuel and Frances Usher Parsons Leighton. She was born on December 21, 1801, in Kittery, Maine. Samuel was a state representative in 1809, a justice of the peace for thirty-five years, a judge of the Court of Sessions, and a brigadier general in the state militia. In 1820, the family moved to Alfred, where they operated the Inn at Alfred until Samuel's death in 1848. When she was forty-six years old, on January 31, 1847, Frances married Benjamin Emerson Esq. of Gilmanton, New Hampshire. She was his second wife. After their marriage, they moved to Pittsfield, New Hampshire, where he practiced law until his death in 1878. At various times during their marriage, children of both Frances's brother and a sibling of Benjamin's lived with them, but they had no children of their own. Frances's mother also resided with them for many years. Frances Leighton Emerson died on August 29, 1889. Frances, Benjamin, and Frances's mother are all buried at the Smith Meeting House Burial Ground in Gilmanton.

Frances Leighton's sampler and the sampler by Mary Elizabeth Wentworth (p. 58) have strong stylistic connections to Betsey Fogg's work (p. 56). All three feature some spot decorations that are unique to the southern Maine/coastal New Hampshire region, and they also all have baskets with both fruit and stalks protruding, and mildly elongated birds. Fogg's and Leighton's both have a unique outline of a three-leafed sprig that is not filled in.

Betsey Fogg (1808–1846)
Family register sampler, 1819
Worked at the school of Betsey Hill, Eliot, Maine
Silk thread on linen
Cross, satin, and straight stitches
16 ¾ x 16 ¾
Collection of Burton W. Pearl

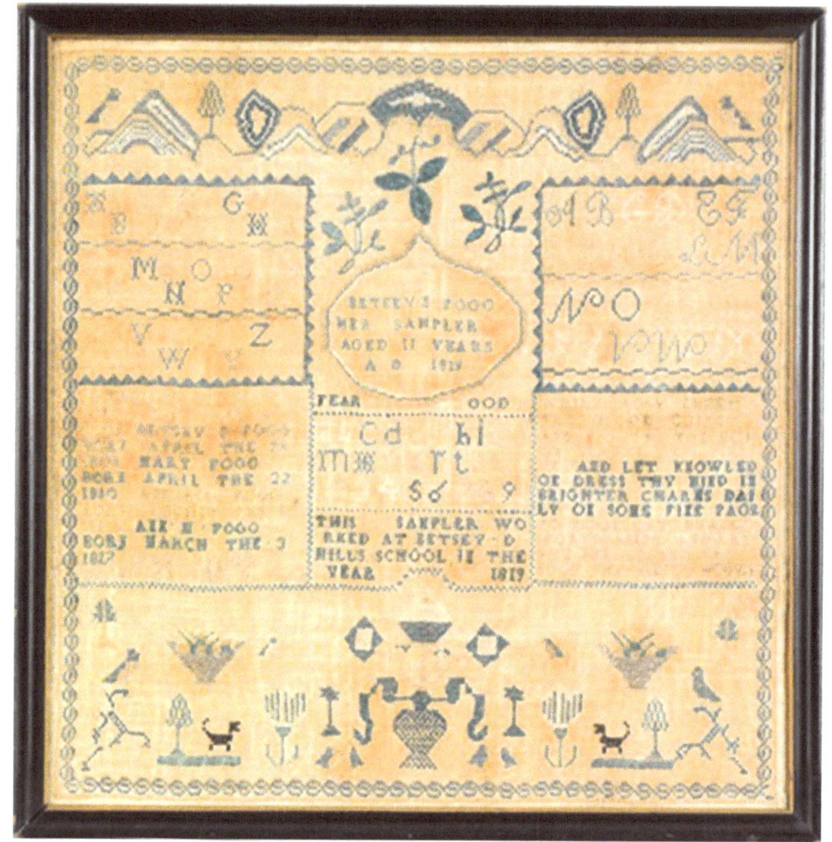

Betsey S. Fogg was the daughter of John and Mary Leighton Staples Fogg. She was born April 26, 1808, the second of nine children, seven of whom were girls. Like two of her sisters, Betsey never married. By 1850, she was living in her mother's household, but Horace Parker, the husband of her younger sister, Abigail, was running the family farm. Betsey and an unwed sister were listed as "domestic." Betsey lived with Horace and Abigail for the rest of her life and died on February 19, 1881, aged seventy-two years, ten months.

On her sampler, Betsey Fogg named Betsey Hill as her teacher. Betsey D. Hill was born in Eliot on August 9, 1790, the only child of Samuel Hill and Rebekah Remick. In 1819, she was teaching in Eliot at her own school. Four other samplers, those by Frances Leighton (p. 55), Mary Elizabeth Wentworth (p. 58), and two nearly identical works by Mary Augusta Shapleigh (p. 57), and Susan Y. Remick (sold by Skinner Auctioneers and Appraisers, Boston, in 2012), have strong stylistic connections to Betsey Fogg's work. Fogg's and Leighton's share a unique outline of a three-leafed sprig. Wentworth's, Fogg's, Shapleigh's and Remick's all share identical trees (remarkably similar to those that appear on samplers made in the 1801 to 1808 Portsmouth, New Hampshire, academy of the Reverend Timothy Alden), and similar and sometimes identical bands between rows of text. On June 16, 1821, Betsey D. Hill married William Fogg, the son of John and Abigail Fogg and uncle of Betsey Fogg. They were the parents of five children. William Fogg held many political offices during his career: he was appointed postmaster by President Monroe and subsequently served during the terms of six following administrations. Betsey Hill died January 24, 1846.

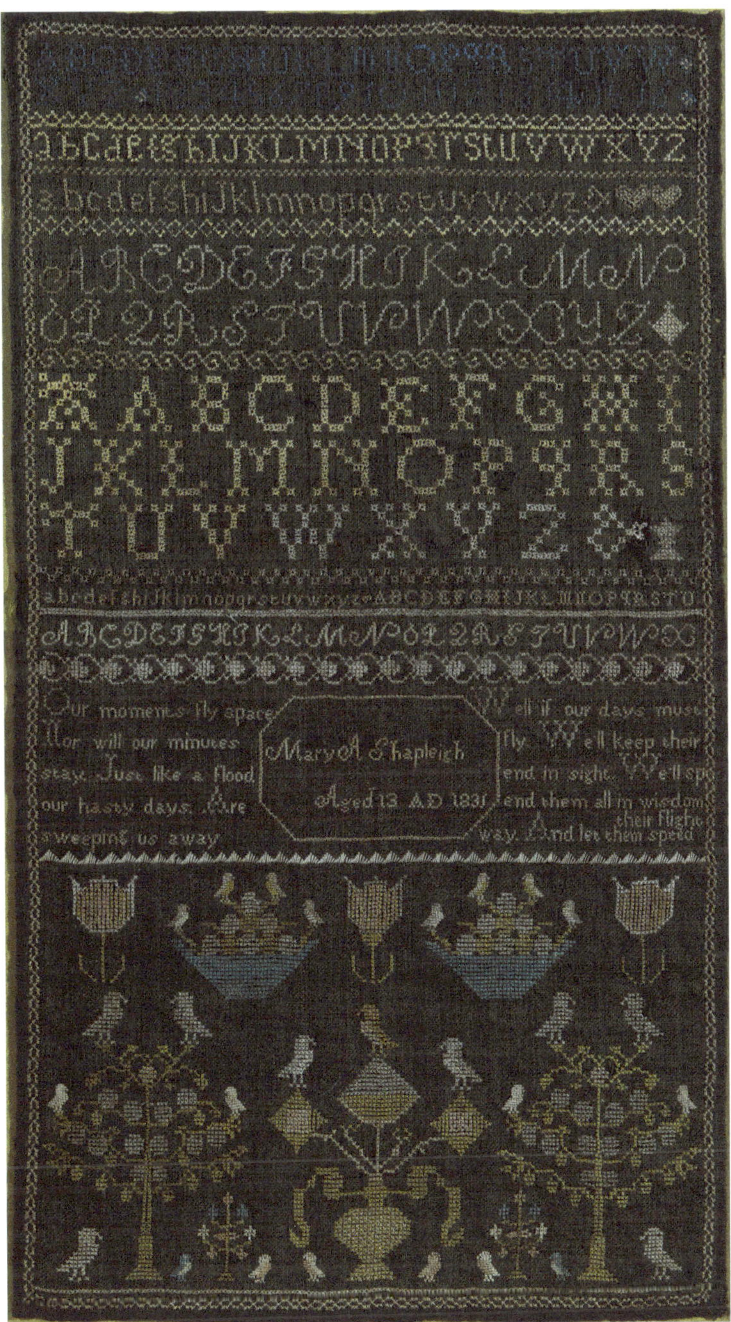

Mary Augusta Shapleigh
(1818–1901)
Marking sampler, 1831
Probably worked at the school of Betsey Hill, Eliot, Maine
Silk thread on linen
Cross over one and two threads, Algerian eye, and satin stitches
21 ¾ x 12 ¼
Collection of the Portsmouth Historical Society

Mary Shapleigh was the seventh of the eight children of Captain Elisha and Martha Fernald Shapleigh of Eliot, Maine. Elisha was a farmer. Mary was born September 25, 1818. Connections between the Shapleigh and Fernald families were complex. Mary's parents were second cousins. Her sister, Elizabeth, married George Washington Fernald, who was also her second cousin. Sampler maker Betsey Fernald was related to Mary both through her Fernald father and her Shapleigh mother. In the small town of Eliot, Mary would almost certainly have known both Betsey Fernald (p. 54) and her daughter, sampler maker Mary Elizabeth Wentworth (p. 58), who may have been taught by Betsey Hill. Susan Y. Remick of Eliot made a sampler identical to Mary's the same year. On May 28, 1839, Mary married Dennis Ferguson and moved to his South Berwick farm. They were the parents of twelve children, including a pair of twins who were named Augusta and Augustus. After spending the last few years of her life living with an unmarried daughter, Mary died May 28, 1901, in South Berwick.

Mary Elizabeth Wentworth
(1824–about 1900)
Marking sampler, 1835
Probably worked at the school of Betsey Hill, Eliot, Maine
Silk thread on linen
Cross, queen, satin, and straight stitches
23 x 23 ½
Collection of the Maine State Museum

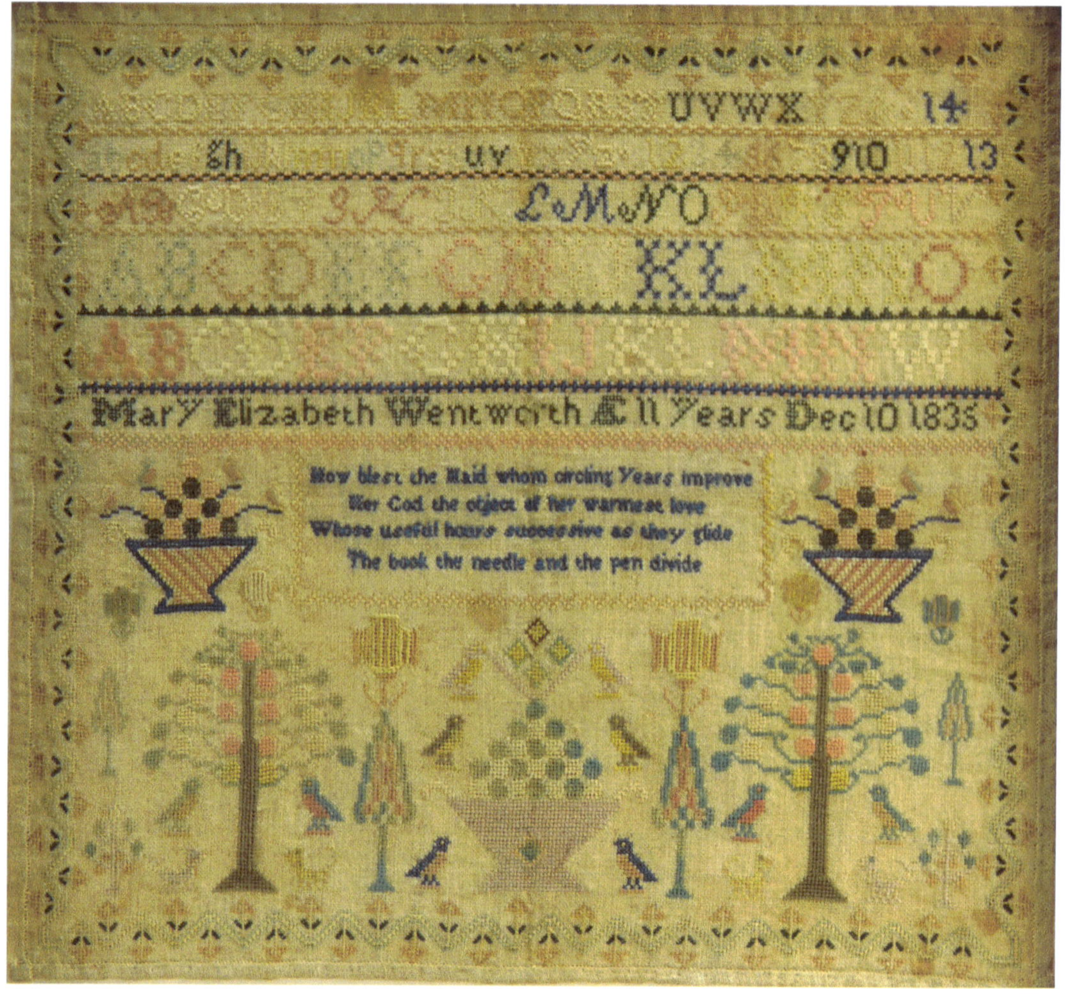

Mary Elizabeth Wentworth was the third child of four and the only daughter of John Wentworth and sampler maker Betsey Fernald (p. 54) of Eliot. She was born December 10, 1824. She was only seven years old when her father died. On December 10, 1835, her eleventh birthday, she completed her needlework piece, proudly stitching her name and the date. She may have been taught by Betsey Hill, who was a distant relative. Betsey Hill (Fogg) was the teacher for Betsey Fogg, and may have continued to teach a few girls even after her marriage. There are very strong stylistic connections between Mary Wentworth's work and those of Mary Shapleigh and Susan Remick. The birds and overflowing baskets with protruding stalks are common features on samplers from southern Maine, but Mary's also features trees that are identical to Shapleigh's and Remick's, and some bands between sections that are identical to those on the sampler of Frances Leighton. According to the 1850 census, Mary was residing in Roxbury, Massachusetts, with no job listed. After that, she probably found work as a teacher. Sometime in the late 1850s, she married Massachusetts Baptist minister Aaron Perkins, who was twenty-four years her senior. Their first child, Harold, was born in Maryland in 1860. Maud Pepperell, their only other child, was born in 1863 in Atchison, Kansas. By 1870, the small family had moved to Red Bank, New Jersey. Even though it was unusual for a married woman of that era to have a career, Mary worked there as a teacher. Sometime shortly after 1870, the family moved to Ossining (Sing Sing), New York, where Aaron continued his ministerial work in the prison and Mary opened her own school, the Cedar Glen Seminary for Young Ladies, that offered "all the substantial and ornamental branches." Aaron died August 31, 1892. Both Mary and her daughter Maud had died by 1900.

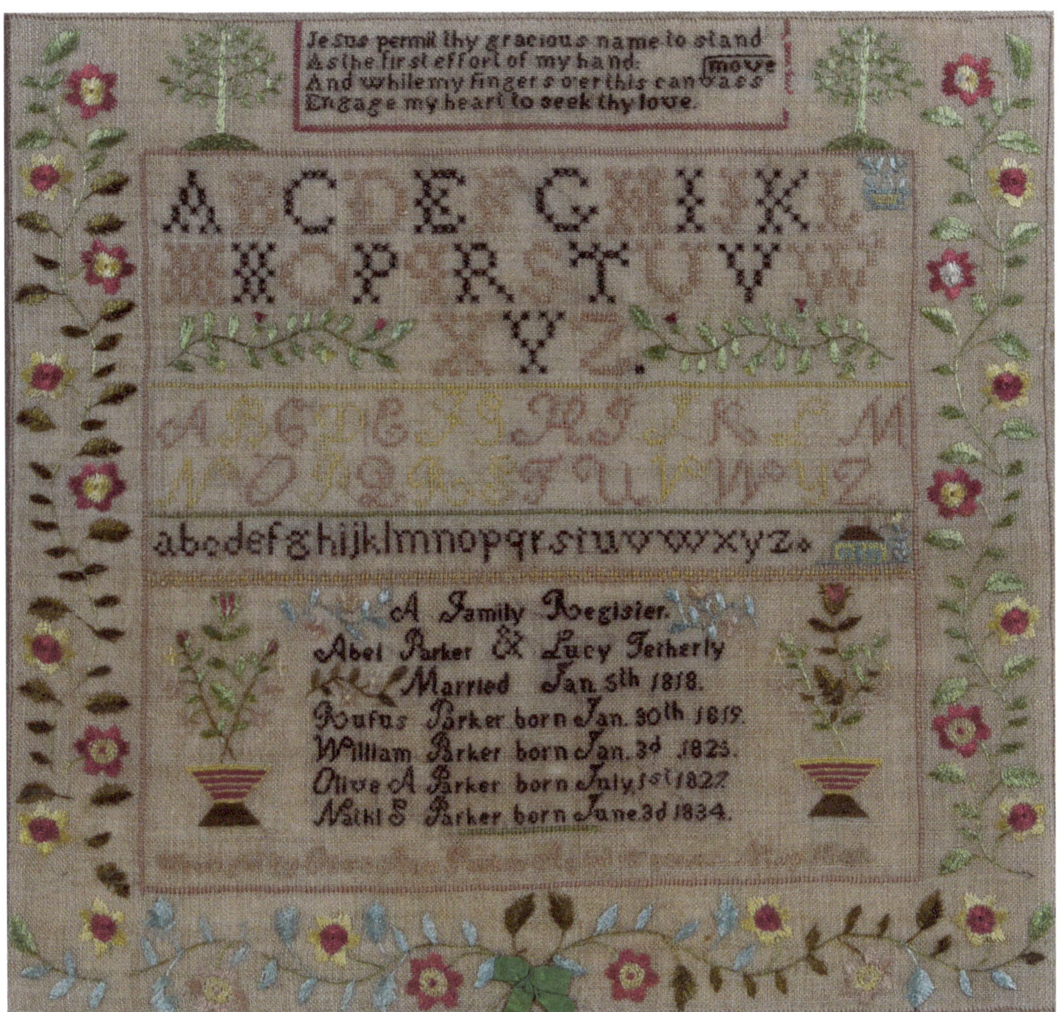

Olive Ann Parker (1827-1904)
Family register sampler, 1840
Probably worked in Eliot, Maine (school unknown)
Silk thread on linen
Cross, satin, outline, and straight stitches
18 ½ x 19 ½
Collection of the Dyer Library and Saco Museum

Olive Ann Parker was born July 1, 1827, the daughter of Eliot farmer Abel and his wife, Lucy Tetherly Parker. This close-knit family stayed together for many more years than was usual. The 1860 U.S. Federal Census shows Abel and Lucy living on their farm with all four of their adult offspring: Rufus, 41, a farmer; William, 35, a farmer; Olive, 32, a "tailoress"; and Nathaniel, 26, also a farmer. Ten years later, Lucy and Abel had died, but Nathaniel and Olive were still living together and William was living right next-door. On December 7, 1893, Olive married her other next-door neighbor, John Garland, a widower and Civil War veteran who was several years younger. Olive died October 27, 1904, and is buried in Eliot. Olive's sampler, with its tidy silk bow, remains quite fresh after about 175 years. It includes baskets, a common southern Maine sampler feature, but otherwise it is not particularly similar to earlier works from the region. Olive must have stitched the decorative elements first, since she ran completely out of room when adding her verse that begins, "Jesus permit thy gracious name to stand . . . ," which is one of the most commonly seen on Maine samplers.

Abigail Donnell (1802–1832)
Marking sampler, 1813
Worked in southern Maine/
coastal New Hampshire
(school unknown)
Silk thread on linen
Cross, Algerian eye,
buttonhole, and
outline stitches
15 ½ x 12
Collection of the Museums
of Old York

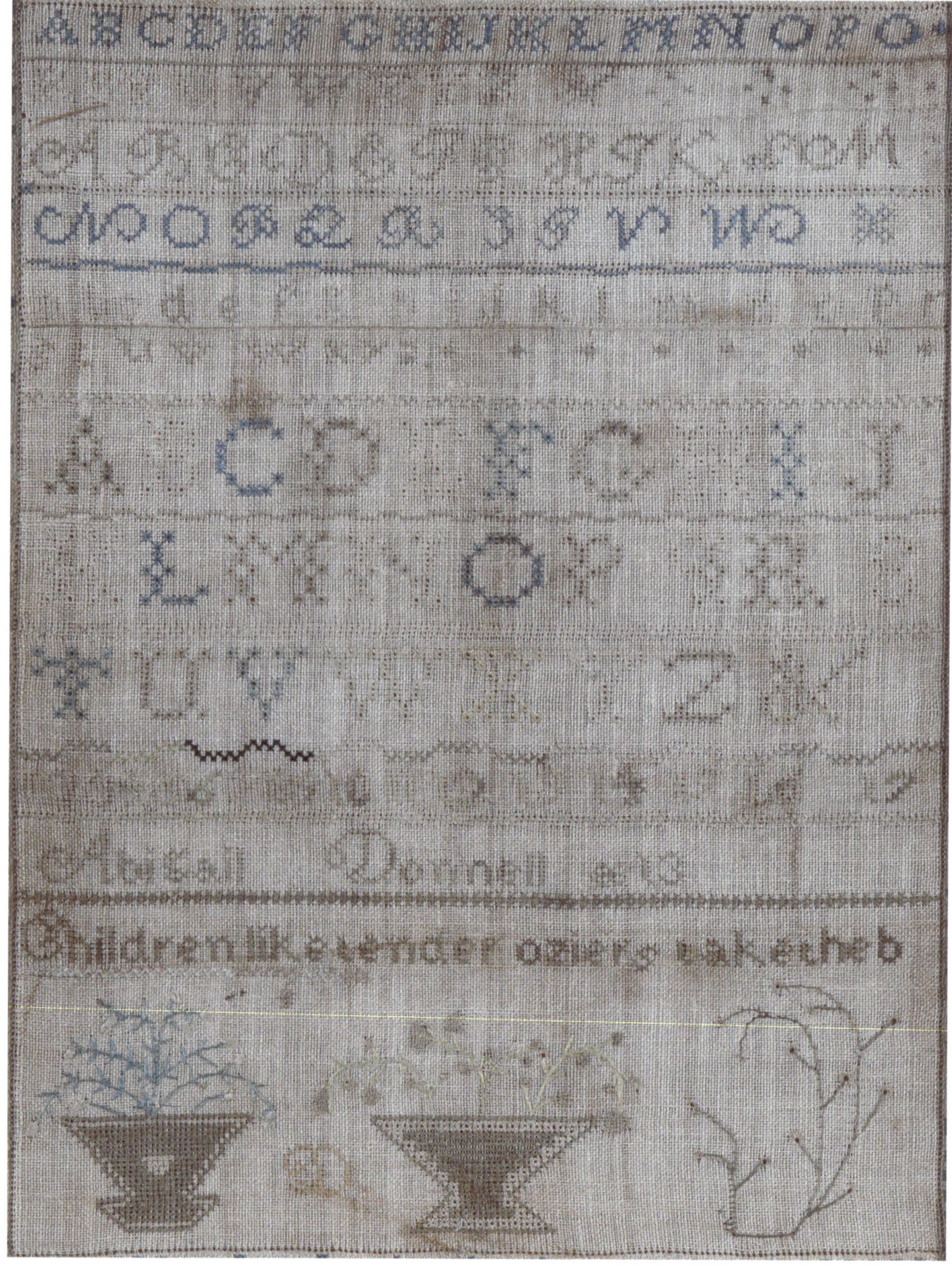

Both **Abigail Donnell** and her daughter, Lydia Ann Brooks (p. 61), have samplers in this exhibition. Abigail, born in 1802, was the daughter of Samuel and Abigail Toppan Donnell of York, Maine. She included part of the first line of a verse that appeared in *A Little Pretty Pocket-book Intended for the Amusement of Little Master Tommy and Pretty Miss Polly with Two Letters From Jack the Giant Killer*, which is considered to be the very first children's book: "Children, like tender osiers, take the bow/ and as they are fashioned always grow/ for what we learn in youth, to that alone/ in age we are by second nature prone." The book was published in 1744 by John Newbery; however, the original source is Decimus Lunius Luvenalis (Juvenal), a Roman poet, making this surely one of the oldest of sampler verses. Abigail became the second wife of Colonel Jeremiah Brooks in 1820. Jeremiah was a devout Methodist minister and successful merchant in York, Maine. They were the parents of seven children. Abigail died in childbirth in 1832.

Lydia Ann Brooks
(1822–1884)
Marking sampler, 1831–2
Worked in southern Maine/
coastal New Hampshire
(school unknown)
Silk thread on linen
Cross and satin stitches
7 ¾ x 17
Collection of the Museums
of Old York

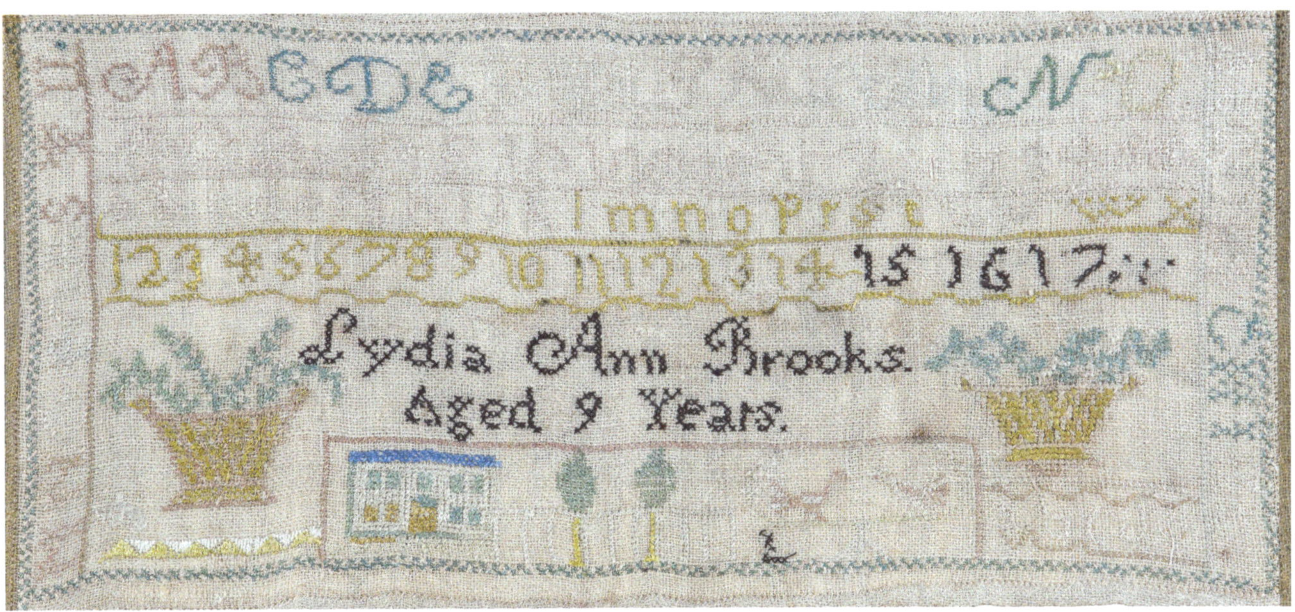

Lydia Brooks was the eldest daughter and second-born of the seven children of Jeremiah Brooks and his second wife, Abigail Ann Donnell, all born in York, Maine. After her mother's death when Lydia was ten, Jeremiah remarried, and his third wife gave birth to an additional six children. The youngest was born in 1846, the same year Lydia's eldest child was born. Lydia married Joseph T. Donnell, a well off cordage maker, and relocated to Bath, Maine. They were the parents of three sons, one of whom died in infancy. Lydia died September 9, 1884. The shape of Lydia's simple marking sampler is more typical of those made much further north and inland in Maine, but it does have a couple of elements that are commonly seen on samplers from southern Maine and coastal New Hampshire: baskets with foliage spilling out and birds.

Narcissa Lyman (1813–1873)
Family register sampler, 1827
Probably worked in southern Maine/coastal New Hampshire (school unknown)
Silk thread on linsey-woolsey
Cross over one and two threads, Algerian eye, and satin stitches
16 ½ x 15 ¼
Collection of the Museums of Old York

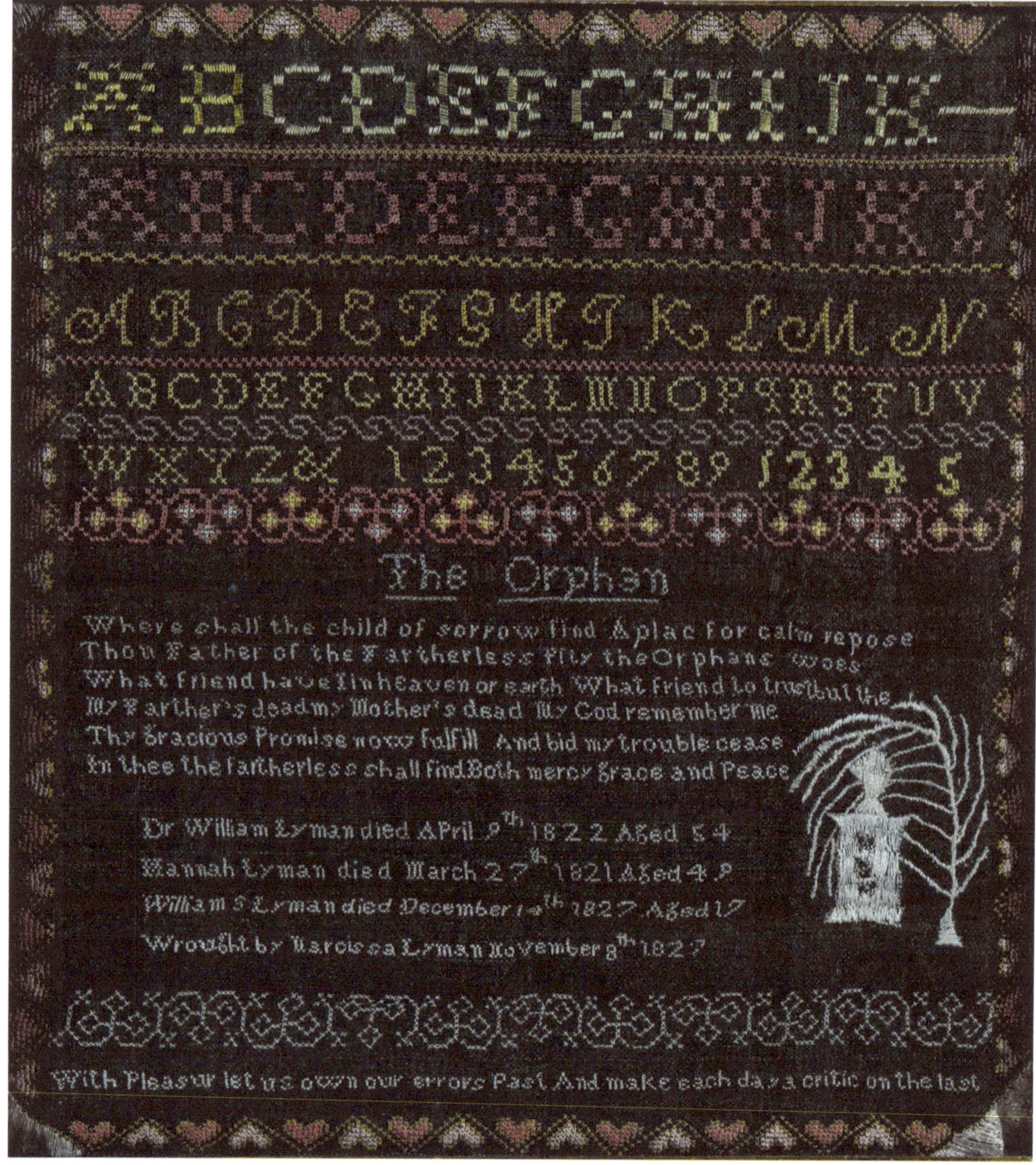

Narcissa Lyman's linsey-woolsey sampler is very typical of the southern Maine/coastal New Hampshire region, both for its ground and the motifs stitched on it. Samplers stitched on a fabric woven of a green or black vertical thread (warp) and horizontal wool thread (weft) were made in some profusion in that area and adjacent Massachusetts. (They were also made, as noted by Glee Krueger in *A Gallery of American Samplers*, 1984, p. 15, in some parts of Connecticut, the Boston area, and two well-known Pennsylvania schools.) The poem that Narcissa, born August 22, 1813, stitched on her sampler had appeared in *The Religious Intelligencer* in 1826 as part of an anonymous spiritually uplifting tale (p. 505). By 1829, it had been set to music. Narcissa had just one brother, William, when they were orphaned by the deaths of their parents, Dr. William and Hannah Sewall Lyman, in 1821 and 1822. Her brother William died just weeks after she stitched the completion date of her work; she carefully added his name. Narcissa's name appears on the list of students for Misses Martin's School for Young Ladies in Portland, but since the linsey-woolsey is so typical of her hometown and not of Portland works, it's more likely that she stitched her sampler either before or after she attended there. In 1832, Narcissa married the Reverend Eber Carpenter, a Connecticut native and graduate of Yale College who was the Congregational minister in York. He was later called to Southbridge, Massachusetts, where they lived for many years, and then to Cambridge, Massachusetts, where they both died, Narcissa in 1873. She and Eber are buried with her family in York.

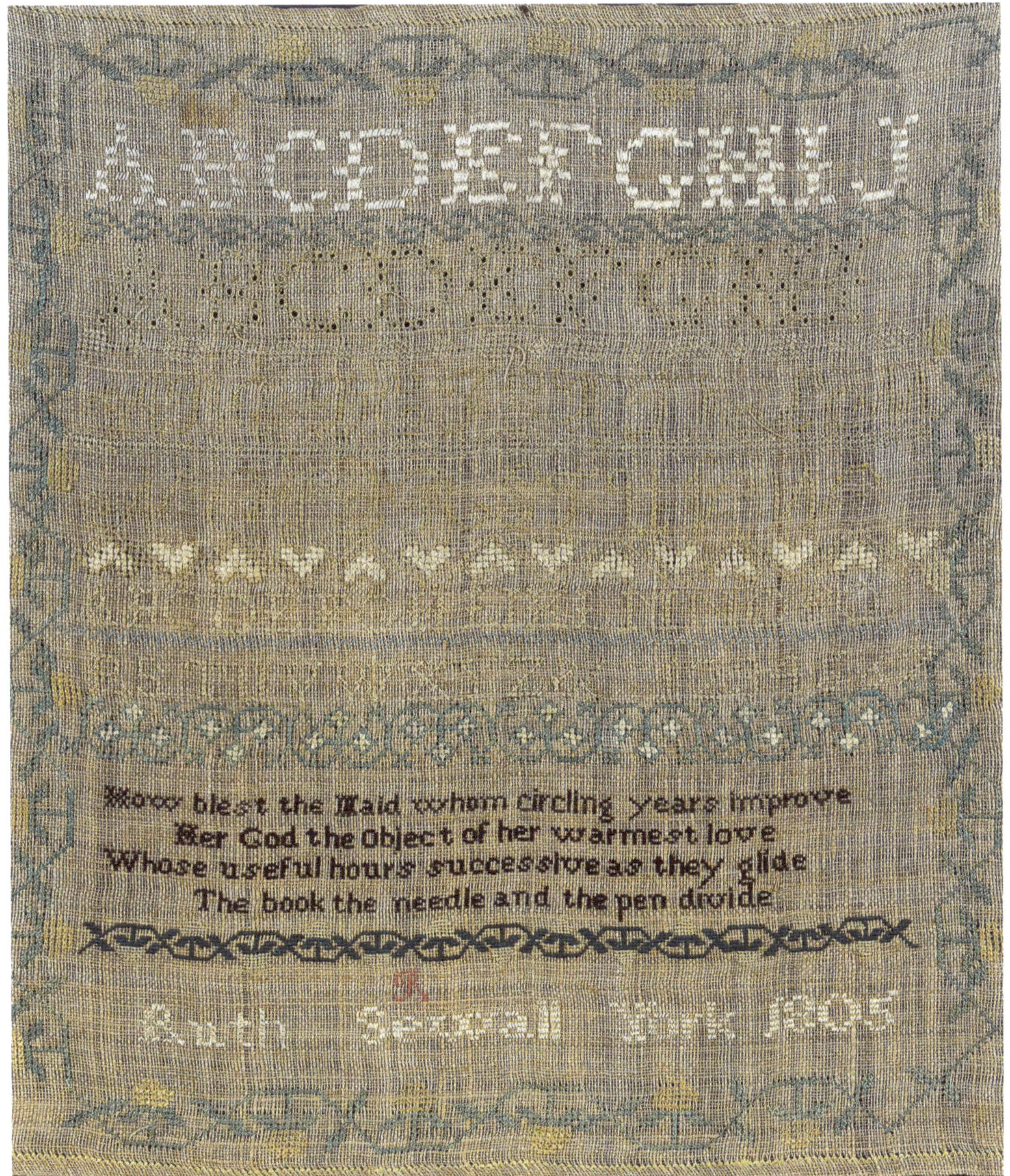

Ruth Sewall (1799–1868)
Marking sampler, 1805
Worked in southern Maine/ coastal New Hampshire (school unknown)
Silk thread on linen
Cross over one and two threads and Algerian eye stitches
17 x 16
Collection of the Museums of Old York

Ruth Sewall completed her sampler at the age of eight, the same year her mother died. She was the youngest of the six daughters of Captain Samuel Sewall and Hannah Moulton. Ruth married Captain James Brown Thornton of Saco, Maine, a merchant, in 1818. At the time of their marriage he was forty-seven and she was just nineteen. They had no children. After he died in 1825, she married Dr. Jeremiah Smith Putnam of York. Together they had two children, a daughter who died as a teen and a son. Ruth died in 1868. Ruth's meandering trefoil and heart bands are typically seen on samplers from the southern Maine, coastal New Hampshire area. Very similar ones appear on the sampler of Narcissa Lyman (p. 62).

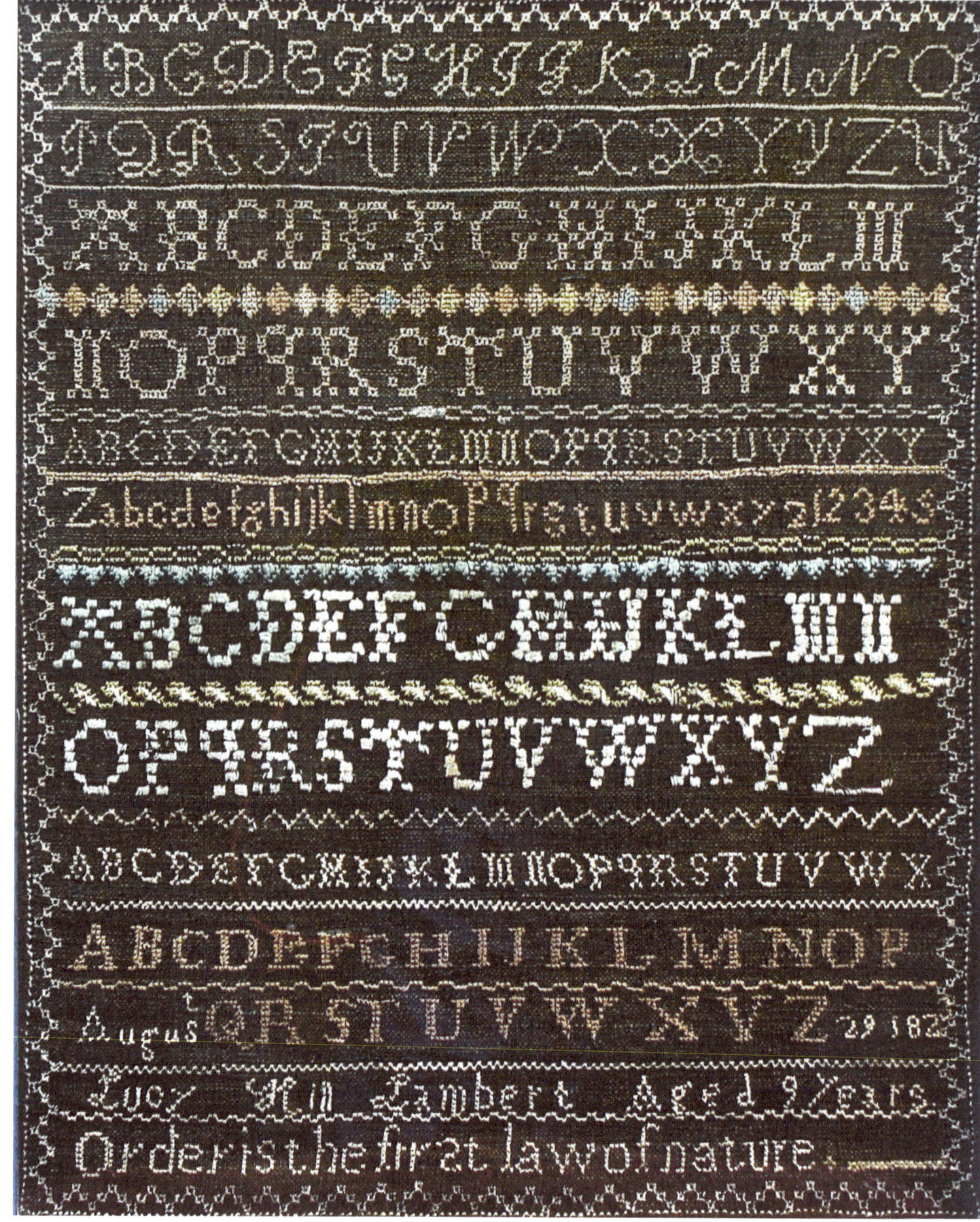

Lucy Hill Lambert
(1812–1902)
Marking sampler, 1821
Worked in southern Maine/
coastal New Hampshire
(school unknown)
Silk thread on linen
Cross, satin, and straight
stitches
23 ½ x 17
Collection of Julie Lindberg

Like the majority of linsey-woolsey samplers, **Lucy Hill Lambert**'s was made within the geographic area that encompasses southern Maine/coastal New Hampshire and northeastern Massachusetts. Lucy Hill Lambert was from Berwick, Maine, born April 23, 1814. She was the daughter of respected South Berwick attorney William Lambert and his second wife, Abigail Ricker. Lucy's only brother grew up to be a minister. She married John Parker Hale of nearby Dover, New Hampshire. They were the parents of two daughters, Elizabeth and Lucy L. In an interesting historic footnote, John Wilkes Booth was engaged to marry Lucy L. at the time that he assassinated Abraham Lincoln, and he was carrying her photo in his pocketbook. John Parker Hale, an ardent abolitionist, served for sixteen years as a United States Senator, was a presidential candidate in 1852 (against Franklin Pierce) and was Minister to Spain from 1865 to 1869. After her husband's death, Lucy made her home in Dover, New Hampshire. She died March 29, 1902, in Washington, New Hampshire.

Sarah "Sally" Wentworth (1805–1822)
Silk mourning embroidery, 1815–22
Worked in southern Maine/coastal New Hampshire (school unknown)
Silk thread and paint on silk
Satin, stem, lazy daisy, chain, long and short, and split stitches
12 ¾ x 15
Collection of the Museums of Old York

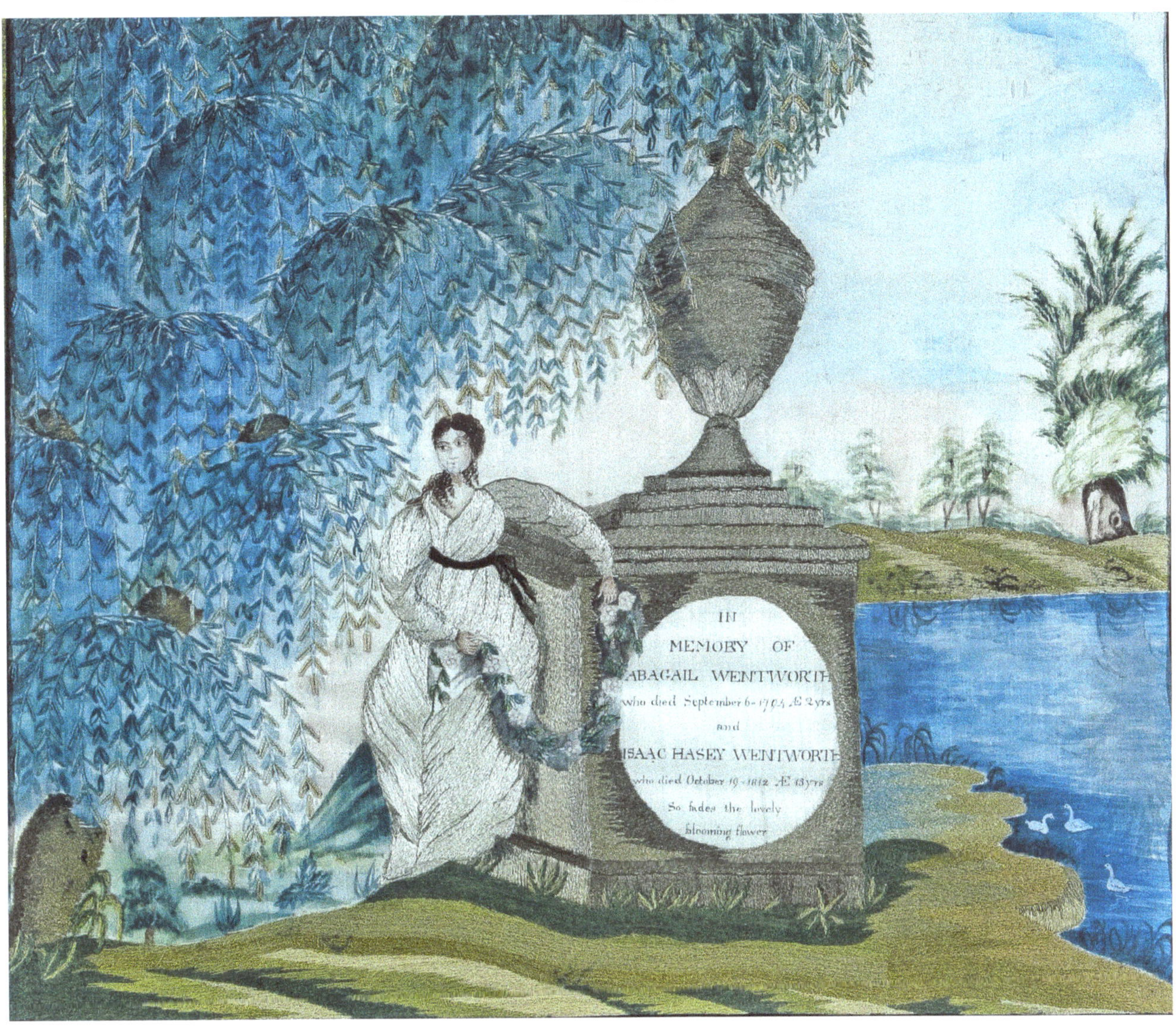

"So fades the lovely blooming flower," **Sally Wentworth** stitched on her silk embroidery in mourning for her two deceased siblings: Abigail who died at age two, long before Sally was born; and Isaac, who died in 1812 at age thirteen, whom she may only have distantly remembered. It is not known where Sally stitched her intricate silk embroidery, but the attractive frame and églomisé mat were made by John Trundy, Gilder, of Penhallow Street in Portsmouth (according to a paper label on the back). Although Sally was from Lebanon, Maine, she may have stitched this work in Portsmouth before having it framed there, or it may have been made in southern Maine and just taken to Portsmouth for framing—not a typical rural trade. Sally was one of the children of Thomas Millet and Rebecca Hasey Wentworth, who married in 1789. She died at age seventeen in 1822; the story that accompanied the needlework when it was donated to the Museums of Old York in 1999 was that she made this piece only shortly before her own death, the fading of yet another "lovely blooming flower."

Hannah Hill (1816–1838)
Family register sampler, 1827
Probably worked in Wells, Maine (school unknown)
Silk thread on linen
Cross, satin, and straight stitches
16 ½ x 17 ¼
Collection of the Wells Public Library

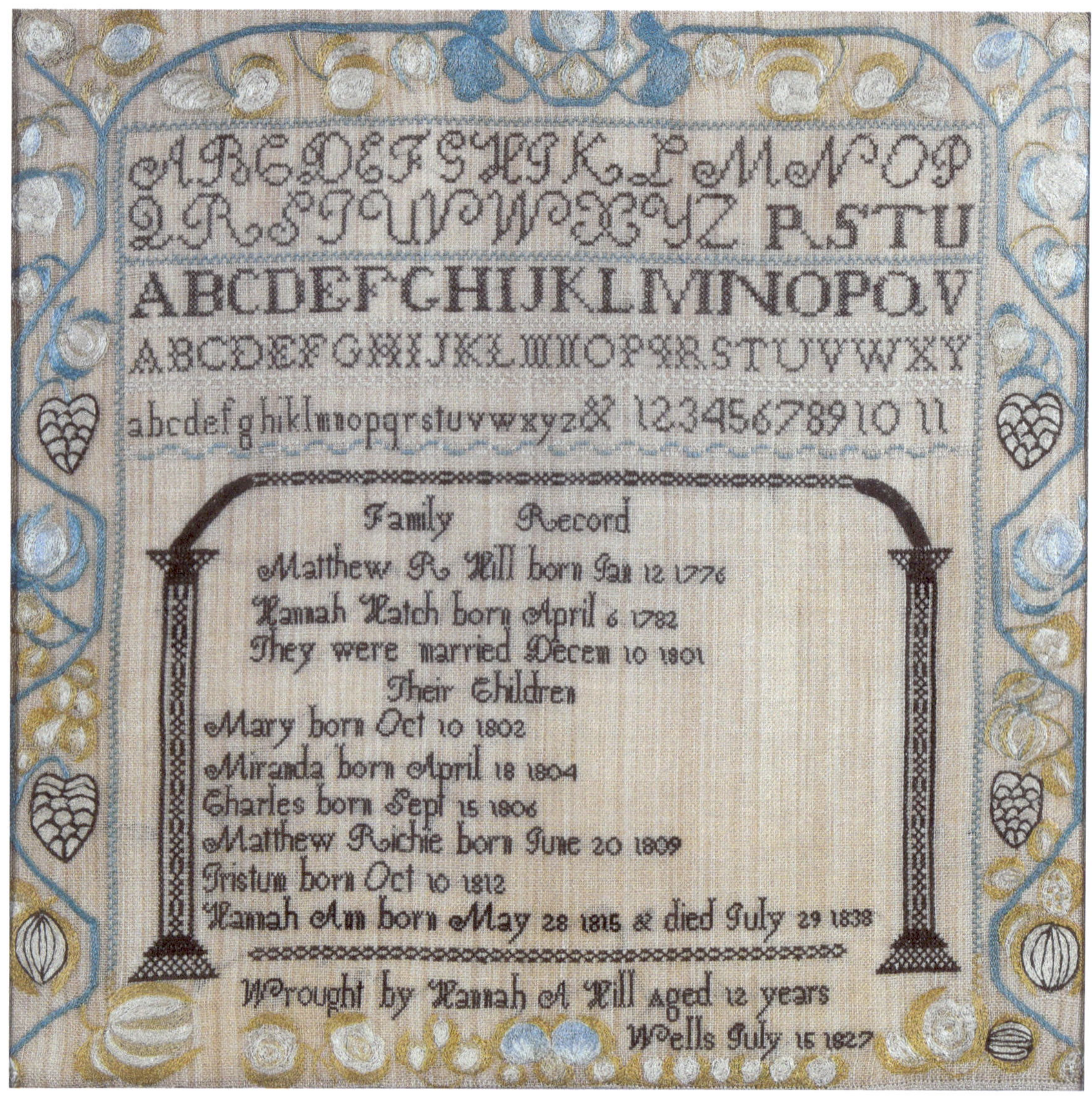

Hannah Hill was named for her mother, Hannah Hatch. On her arch-decorated sampler she lists the marriage of her parents and the births of herself and her five siblings. Later, someone added the date of her death. Matthew Hill, her father, was a farmer, with his land located on what is now U.S. Route 1 just south of the Wells Public Library, which owns this sampler. In the years that followed Hannah's death, her siblings all married and had children. Her brother Charles named his eldest daughter for his deceased sister. She would be one of only two of his five children to survive childhood. Tristram, another brother, also named a daughter after Hannah. Hannah's father died at the age of ninety-six, in 1872, survived by all of his children except Hannah. Nothing is known of where Hannah made her sampler, but it shares a strong stylistic connection with the Wells sampler of Abigail Bragdon.

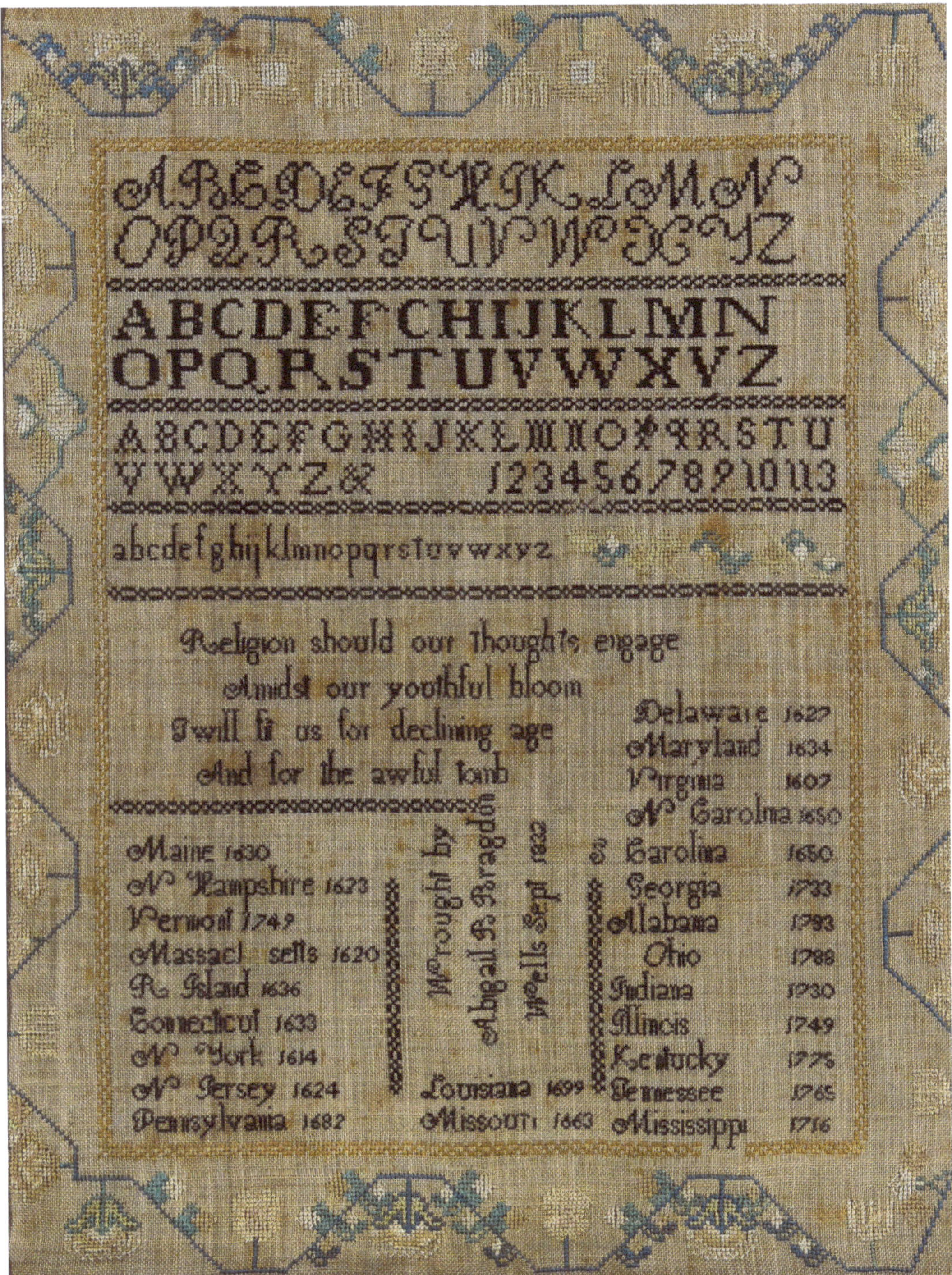

Abigail Bragdon
(1820–1893)
Marking sampler, 1832
Probably worked in Wells, Maine (school unknown)
Silk thread on linen
Cross stitch
20 ¾ x 16 ¾
Collection of Strawbery Banke

Abigail Bragdon stitched her unusual sampler, complete with the dates of settlement of various states, five years later but at the same school as Hannah A. Hill made hers, almost certainly in Wells, Maine. While the overall theme of the two samplers is quite different, there are many common features, including alphabets, the style of dividing bands, and the included information about the girls themselves. Abigail was the daughter of Abner and Nancy Eaton Bragdon. Her father was a carpenter and farmer. He died when Abigail was just five years old. In 1827, Abigail's mother Nancy remarried, to Joshua Winn. Abigail married Benjamin Bonin in 1841 and moved shortly afterward to Badger's Island off of Kittery, where her husband worked as a ships' carpenter. They were the parents of nine children. Abigail was widowed in 1884 and lived on until 1893. She is buried with her husband in Portsmouth, New Hampshire.

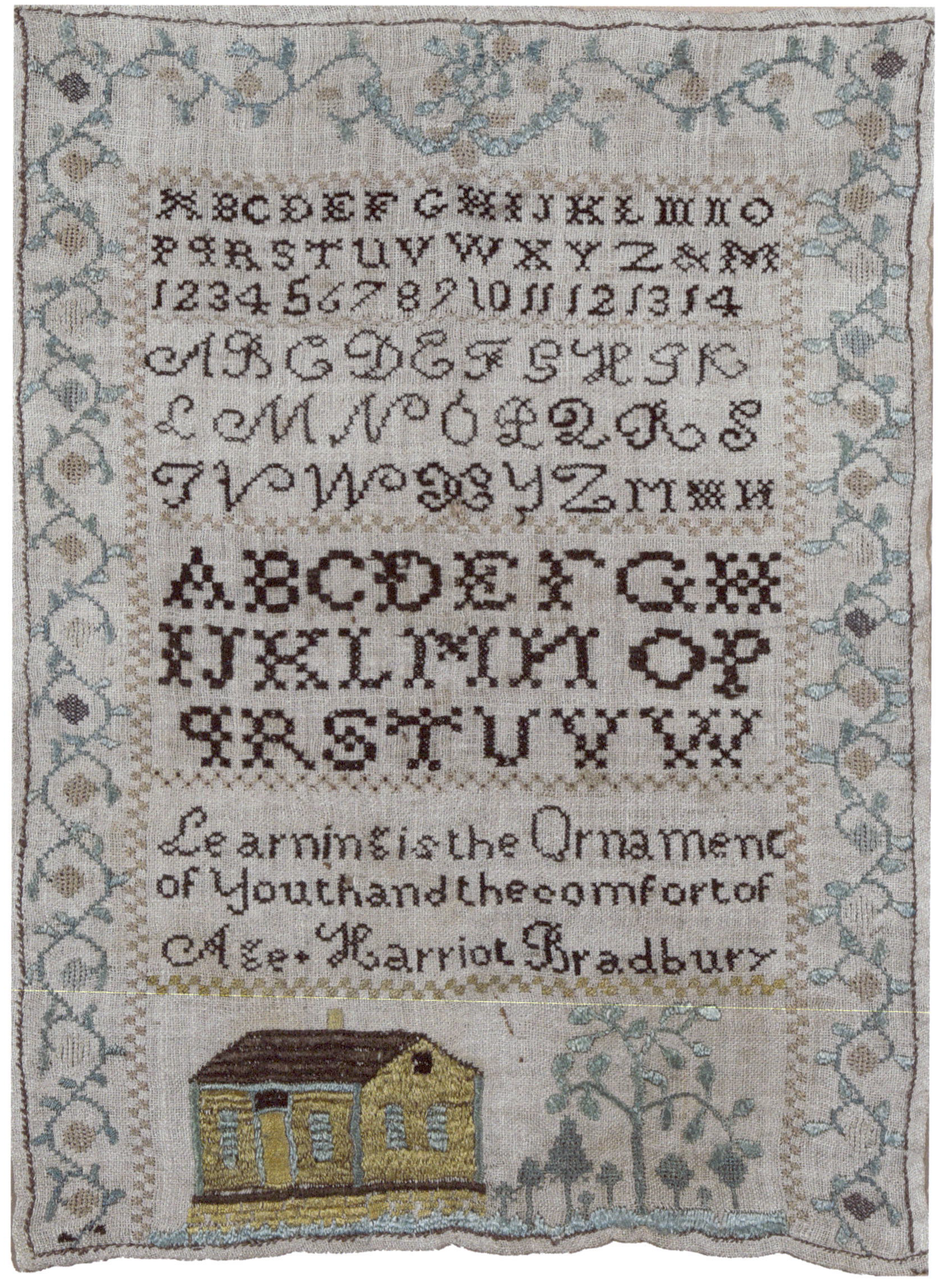

Harriot Bradbury
(1793–1814)
Marking sampler, circa 1805
Probably worked in Kennebunk, Maine (school unknown)
Silk thread on linen
Cross, satin, and queen stitches
22 x 15
Collection of the Brick Store Museum

Harriot Bradbury, the daughter of sea captain Smith Bradbury and Mary Hovey, was born December 26, 1793, and died just twenty-one years later on February 28, 1814. Harriot had three sisters and a brother. Kennebunk cemeteries include the graves of her parents, her sister Caroline, and her nephew Charles, but there seems to be no marker for Harriot. Perhaps she is buried with her parents and her name was never added to their stone.

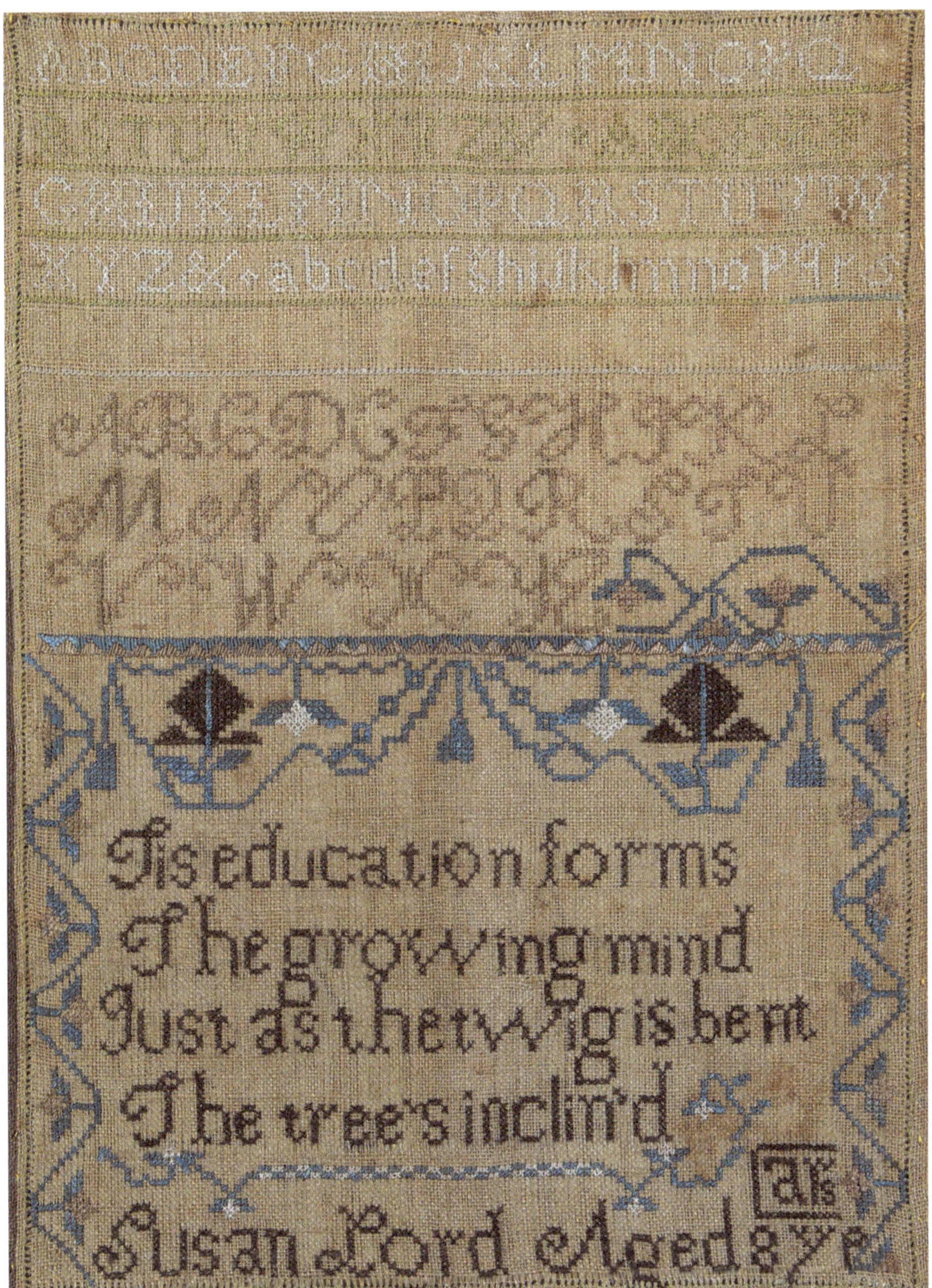

Susan Lord (1812–1890)
Marking sampler, circa 1820
Probably worked in the school of the Misses Sarah and Ann Grant, Kennebunk, Maine
Silk thread on linen
Cross stitch
20 x 14
Collection of the Brick Store Museum

Susan Lord was the eighth of the nine children of Kennebunkport shipbuilder Nathaniel Lord and his wife, Phoebe Walker, who was just sixteen when they married in 1797. Susan was born December 5, 1812, in the house now known as the Captain Lord Mansion; just three years later her father died, leaving her widowed mother to raise the large family of young children. Susan probably stitched her undated work in about 1820, perhaps under the instruction of the Misses Sarah (1782–1850) and Ann (1793–1829) Grant, whose Kennebunk school was open from at least 1813 to 1826. Susan creatively squeezed in her age when she ran out of room. In 1834, she married Peter Clark but was widowed just seven years later. She died November 5, 1890, in New York.

Harriet Stevens (1817–?)
Marking sampler, 1825
Probably worked in the school of the Misses Sarah and Ann Grant, Kennebunk, Maine
Silk thread on linen
Cross, straight, and queen stitches
21 x 17
Collection of Natalie Larson

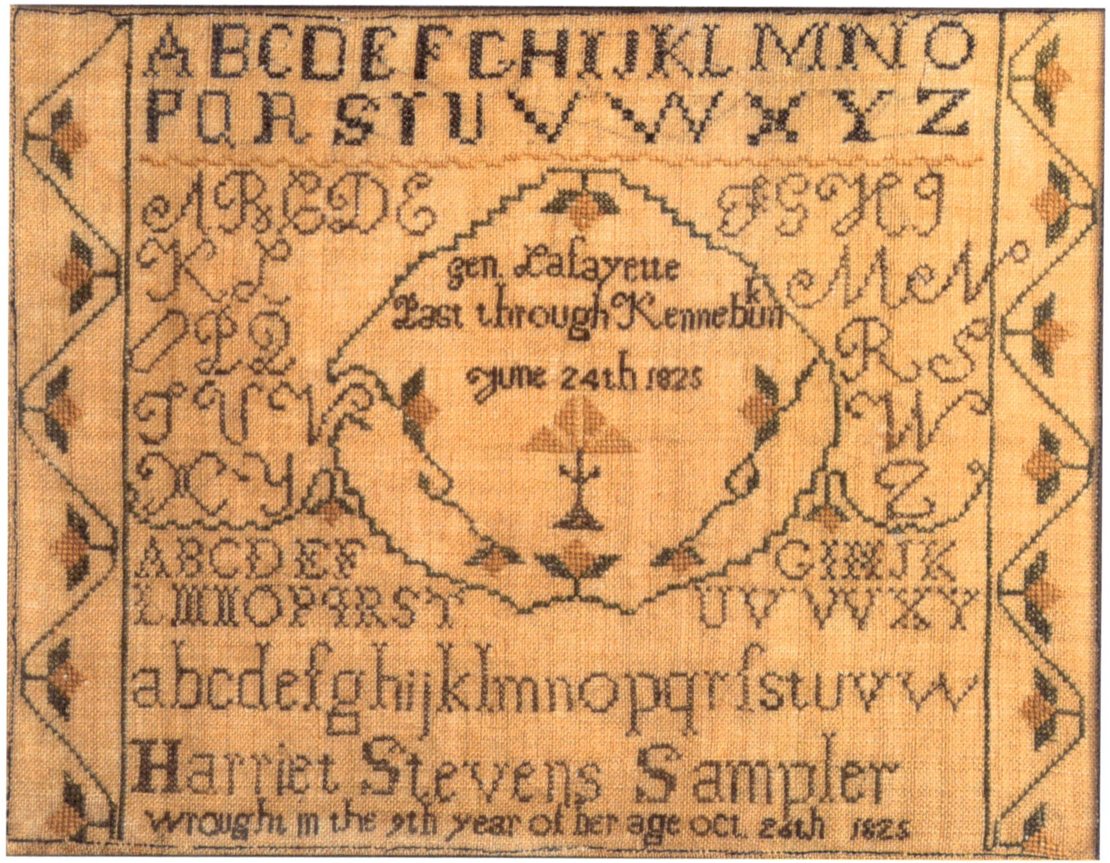

From July 1824 to September 1825, the Marquis de Lafayette, hero of the Revolutionary War, paid an extended visit to America, traveling a vast distance and enjoying great public acclaim. **Harriet Stevens** used her schoolgirl embroidery skills to memorialize the event when on June 24, 1825, "Gen. Lafayette past through Kennebunk." She was born July 18, 1817, in Kennebunk, the eldest daughter of the six children of Phineas and Hannah Fairfield Stevens. Phineas was a silversmith and watchmaker in Kennebunk. The family's patriotism is evident, not only in this sampler, but also in that they named one of their sons George Washington. No further records have been found for Harriet.

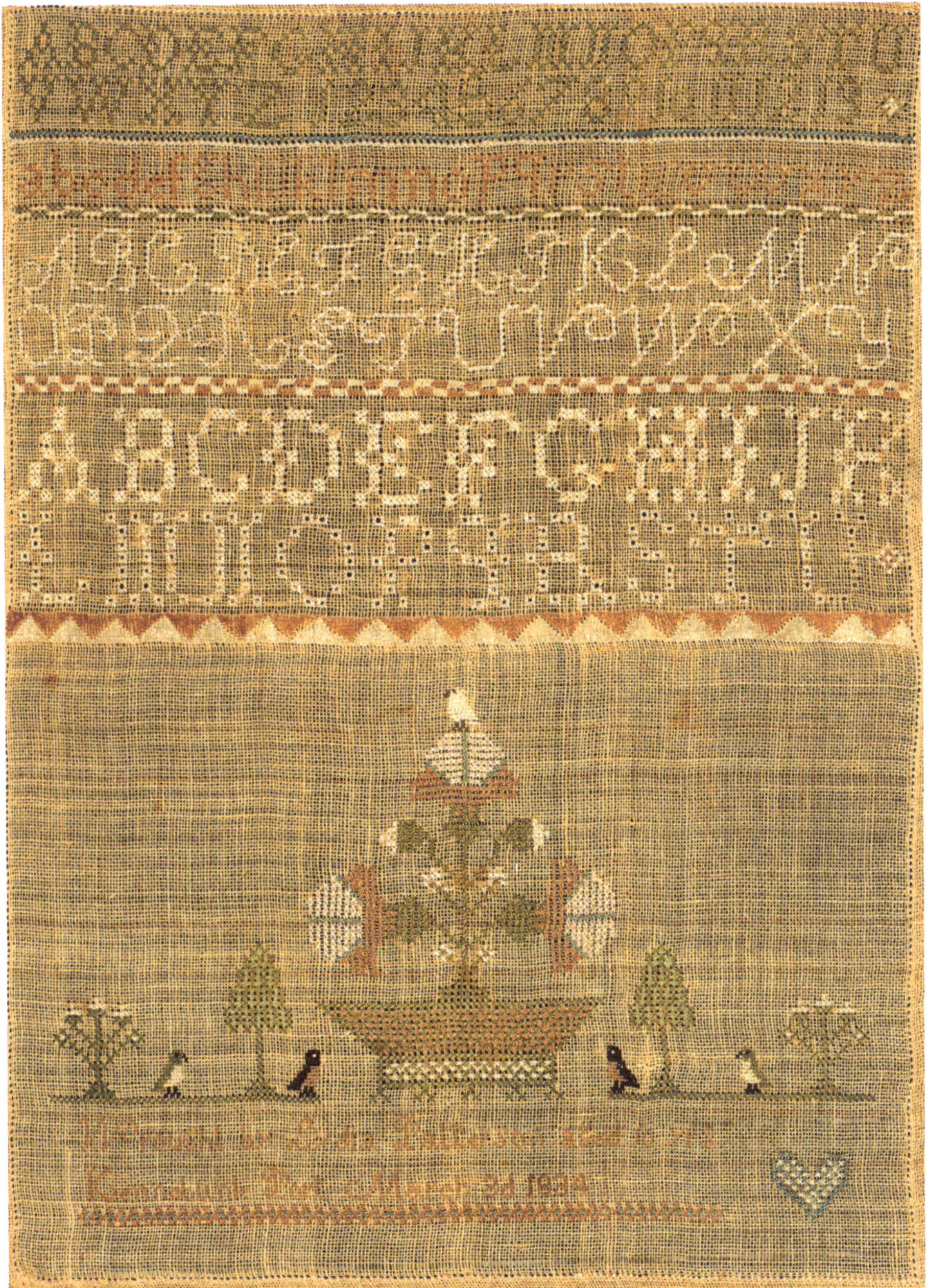

Lydia Patterson (1823–1885)
Marking sampler, 1834
Probably worked in the school of Mary A. Jewett, Kennebunkport, Maine
Silk thread on linen
Cross, satin, straight, and outline stitches
16 x 12
Courtesy of Historic New England. Gift of Mary P. Lord, 1939, 232.

Born in Kennebunk, Maine, on April 26, 1823, **Lydia Patterson** was a daughter of Captain Actor Patterson and his wife, also named Lydia. In 1853, she married Daniel Walker Lord, a wealthy merchant and shipbuilder of Kennebunkport who was about twenty-three years her senior, not long after his first wife, a third Lydia, had died. They had a son and a daughter. In old age, the Lords relocated to Massachusetts and resided with their adult son. Widowed for several years, Lydia died June 4, 1885, and is buried with her family in Kennebunk.

Lydia stitched her sampler in 1834. There were several teachers active in Kennebunk and Kennebunkport in the early part of the nineteenth century, but the only one advertising in the period appropriate for Lydia's sampler was Miss Mary A. Jewett, who ran a "School for Young Ladies" and promised that "No pains will be spared on her part to improve their minds, manners and morals." She charged three dollars a quarter for the subjects "usually taught at Academies" and an additional two dollars for the teaching of French and Latin. She also mentioned, "Her pupils will be instructed in the fashionable exercise called Calisthenics which is highly recommended as a salutary exercise for young Ladies."

Sarah Moody (1786–1865)
Marking sampler, circa 1800
Worked in Saco, Maine
(school unknown)
Silk thread on dark green
linsey-woolsey
Cross and straight stitches
11 ½ x 8 ¼
Collection of Glee Krueger

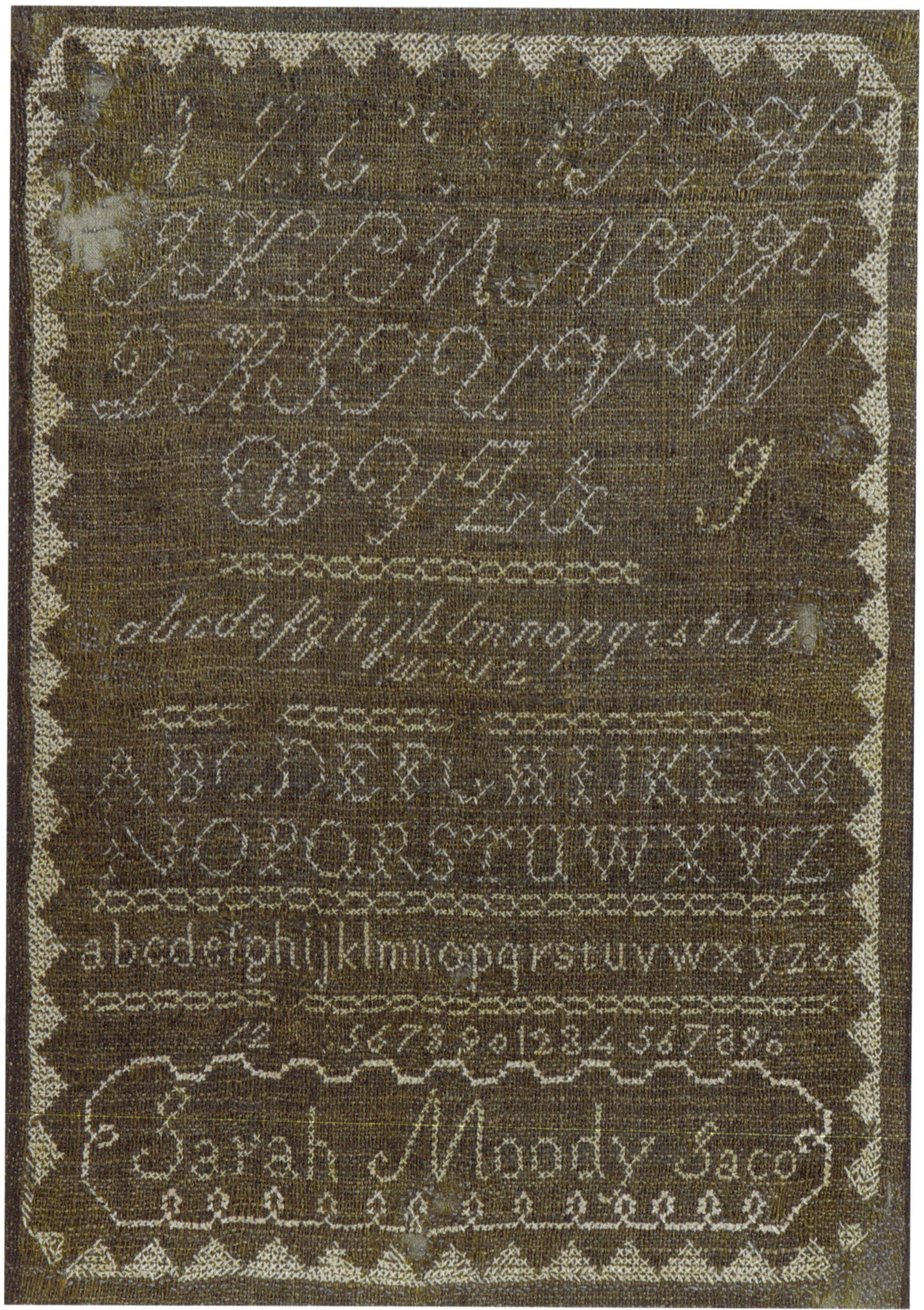

Sarah Moody, the youngest daughter of William and Elizabeth Scamman Moody, was born in Saco December 5, 1786. It is unknown when she worked this very plain marking sampler, but it is typical of the work done by young schoolgirls. Thus, it probably represents the earliest of a remarkably large body of work. Sarah not only completed several pieces herself but also operated a small academy in Saco. Two stylistically related pieces were worked by Elizabeth Kindrick (p. 76) and Martha Waterhouse (p. 75), both students at her school. All of the pieces demonstrate a certain folk-like simplicity that implies a lack of extensive instruction in needle arts. Sarah's father died when she was just three years old. Insufficient family funds may have prevented Sarah from receiving a boarding-school education and may also have influenced her to begin earning money on her own. Sarah was the aunt of another Sarah Moody, who worked a more artful piece that names the Cony Female Academy in Augusta (p. 115). The teacher, Sarah, who made this sampler, married John Means of Augusta in 1811 and relocated there. He was the brother of sampler maker Hannah Means (p. 114). The mother of six children, Sarah died in Augusta July 12, 1865.

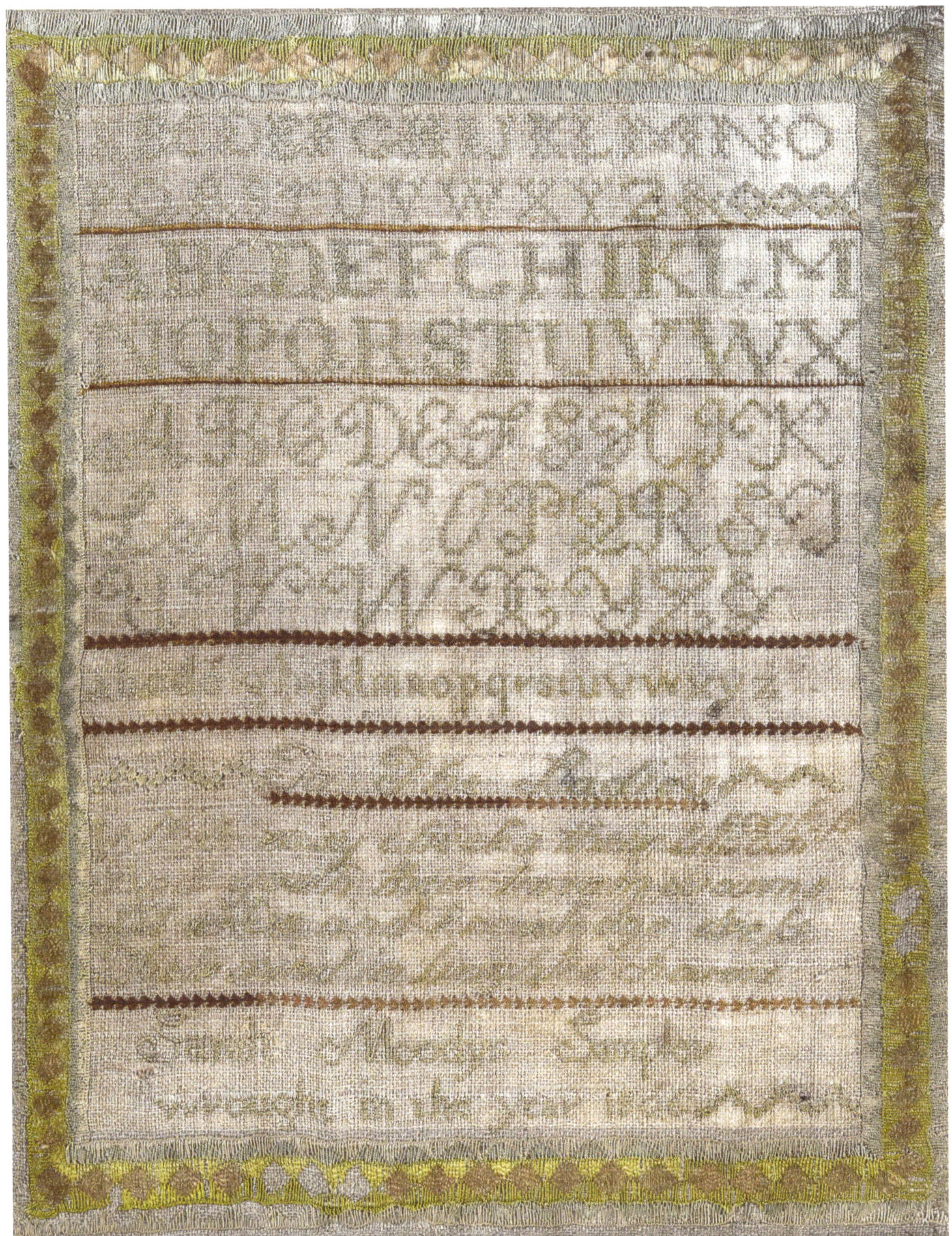

Sarah Moody (1786–1865)
Marking sampler, 1806
Worked in Saco, Maine, possibly in the school of Sarah Moody
Silk thread on linen
Cross, satin, queen, and straight stitches
17 x 14
Collection of the Dyer Library and Saco Museum

Sarah Moody employed the verse "To the Ladies," on her own marking sampler, sadly faded, and used it again when designing the sampler Elizabeth Pike Kindrick (p. 76) stitched a few years later in her school.

Sarah Moody (1786–1865)
Family register sampler, 1812
Worked at the school of Sarah Moody, Saco, Maine
Silk thread on dark green linsey-woolsey
Cross and straight stitches
16 ½ x 14 ¼
Collection of the Dyer Library and Saco Museum

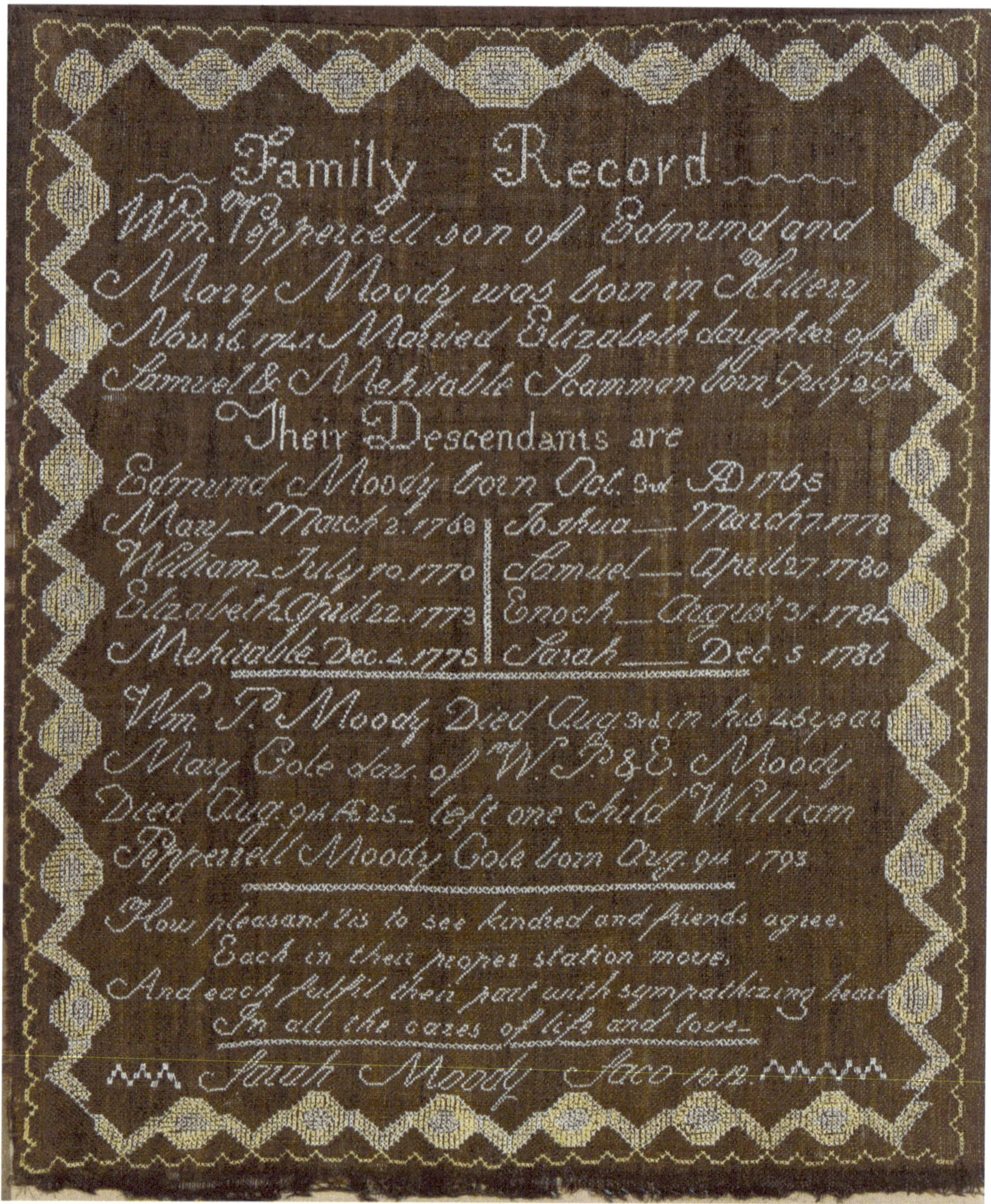

Sarah Moody worked this very plain but large family register sampler at the age of twenty-six, making her the oldest sampler maker in the exhibition. The sloping alphabets and other text, the use of simple geometric borders, and the very large size make Moody-related works easy to identify. She may have stitched it to use as an example for her students.

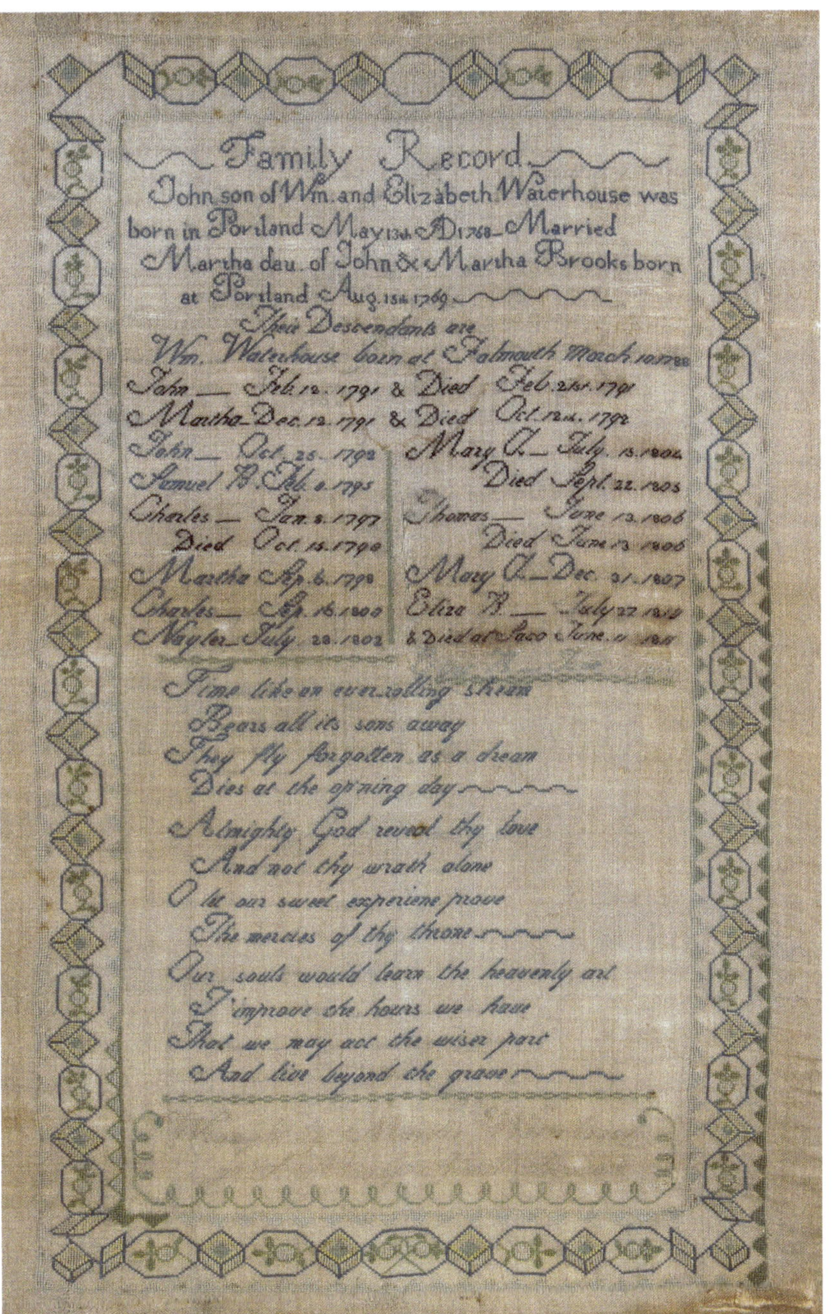

Martha Waterhouse (1798–?)
Family register sampler, 1812
Worked at the school of Sarah Moody, Saco, Maine
Silk thread on linen
Cross, straight, and satin stitches
32 x 23
Collection of the Dyer Library and Saco Museum

Martha Waterhouse stitched her grandly-sized genealogical sampler in the school of Sarah Moody of Saco. We only know of Sarah's fairly short-lived school because she is named as the instructor on this sampler. The contrast is sharp between the designs of Sarah and ones being created contemporaneously just a short distance away in Portland. Sarah clearly was not, like Mary Rea (who also began her teaching career in a small town), looking to sophisticated city schools to influence her work.

Martha was one of the large Waterhouse family from the Stroudwater village, near Portland. They later relocated to Saco for a period of time. There, Martha married James Coffin of Deerfield, New Hampshire. Whether he had a connection to the James Coffin family of Saco is unknown. After their marriage, there is no further conclusive record of Martha or James.

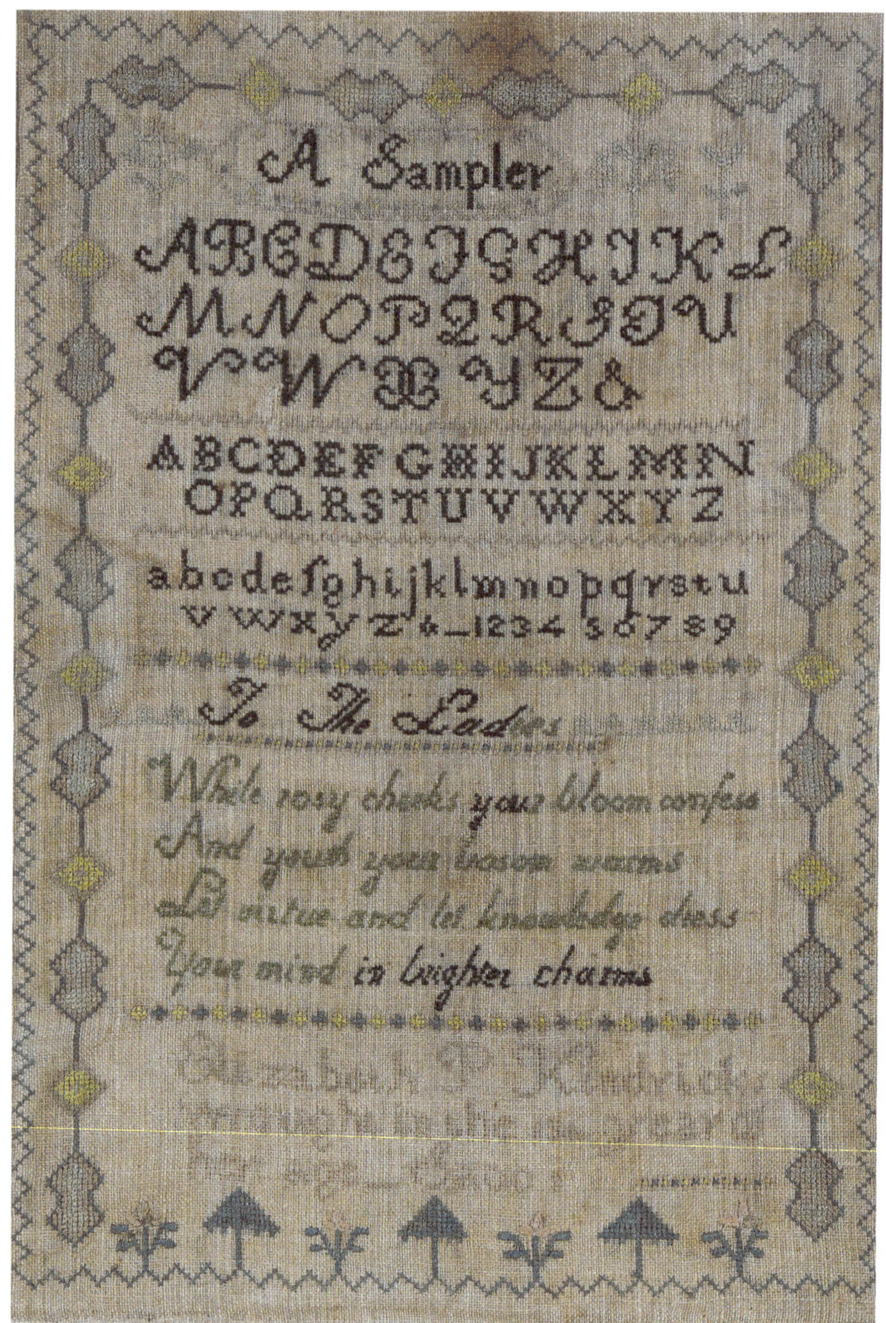

Elizabeth Kindrick
(1800–1862)
Marking sampler, 1812
Worked at the school of Sarah Moody, Saco, Maine
Silk thread on linen
Cross, straight, and satin stitches
28 x 17
Collection of Linda Danielson

Elizabeth Kindrick was the second child of Noah and Abigail Pike Kindrick of Saco, born September 19, 1800. Seven more children would follow, including two sons named Humphrey Pike, the first of whom died only a month after he was born. Elizabeth married John Adams, a Saco shoemaker, and they were the parents of ten children. Their oldest child, George, died at the age of twenty-one after being struck by lightning. The following year, when their last child was born, they named her Georgiana in honor of the brother she would never know. Tragically, she lived only to the age of twenty, dying four years after her mother passed away on May 17, 1862. A Saco school is named after Elizabeth's niece, Clementine Kendrick Burns, a daughter of her brother, Humphrey. Elizabeth is buried with her husband and several of her children in Saco's Laurel Hill Cemetery. She stitched her sampler under the instruction of Sarah Moody of Saco, and it bears a close resemblance to several other samplers associated with Moody's school.

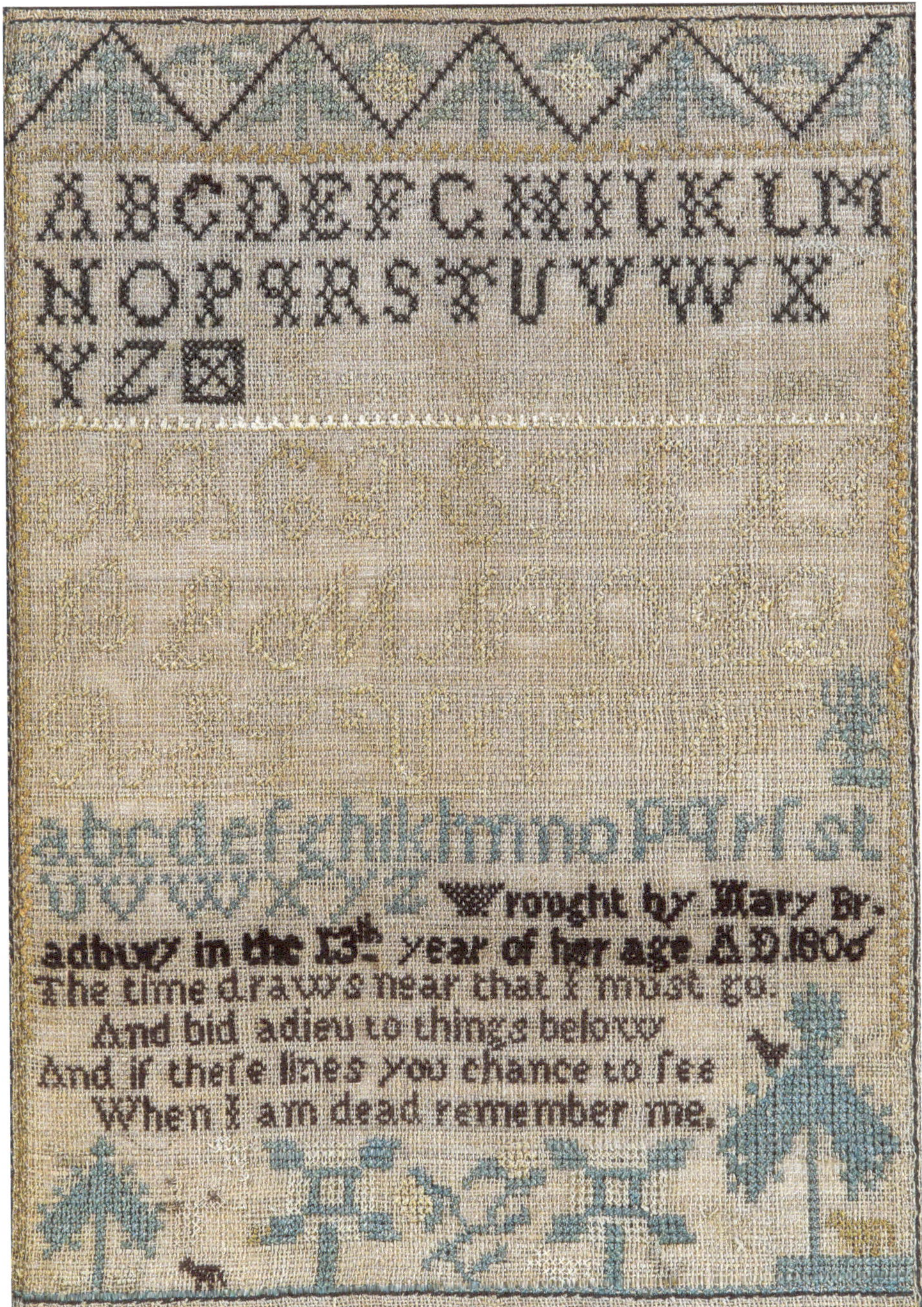

Mary Bradbury (1792–1867)
Marking sampler, 1806
Probably worked in Biddeford, Maine (school unknown)
Silk thread on linen
Cross, satin, and queen stitches
13 x 10 ½
Collection of the Dyer Library and Saco Museum

Mary Bradbury's simple, naive marking sampler offers a contrast to the many more elaborate works that were being done by young ladies of her age (thirteen) in the Federal era. She may have worked this sampler at home under the guidance of an older female relative, or perhaps it was made in a one-room schoolhouse in the Biddeford area. It is not likely to have been completed at one of the many fancier Maine female academies that were already in existence by 1806. While the motifs she worked across the bottom of the sampler are certainly unique in appearance, there is little to link this work to a particular region or teacher. However, Mary Bradbury almost certainly was a Maine girl, quite likely the eldest child of Nehemiah Bradbury and Betsey Cole of Biddeford, Maine, born August 24, 1792, about six months before her parents posted their intentions of marriage. Mary married Moses Bradbury, a farmer, and gave birth to at least four children between 1817 and 1831. She died October 10, 1867, in Biddeford.

Sally Chase
(1793–after 1880)
Marking sampler, 1800
Probably worked in Saco, Maine (school unknown)
Silk thread on linen
Cross, satin, straight, queen, and outline stitches
18 x 17
Courtesy of Historic New England. Bequest of Frances S. Marrett, 1959, 743.

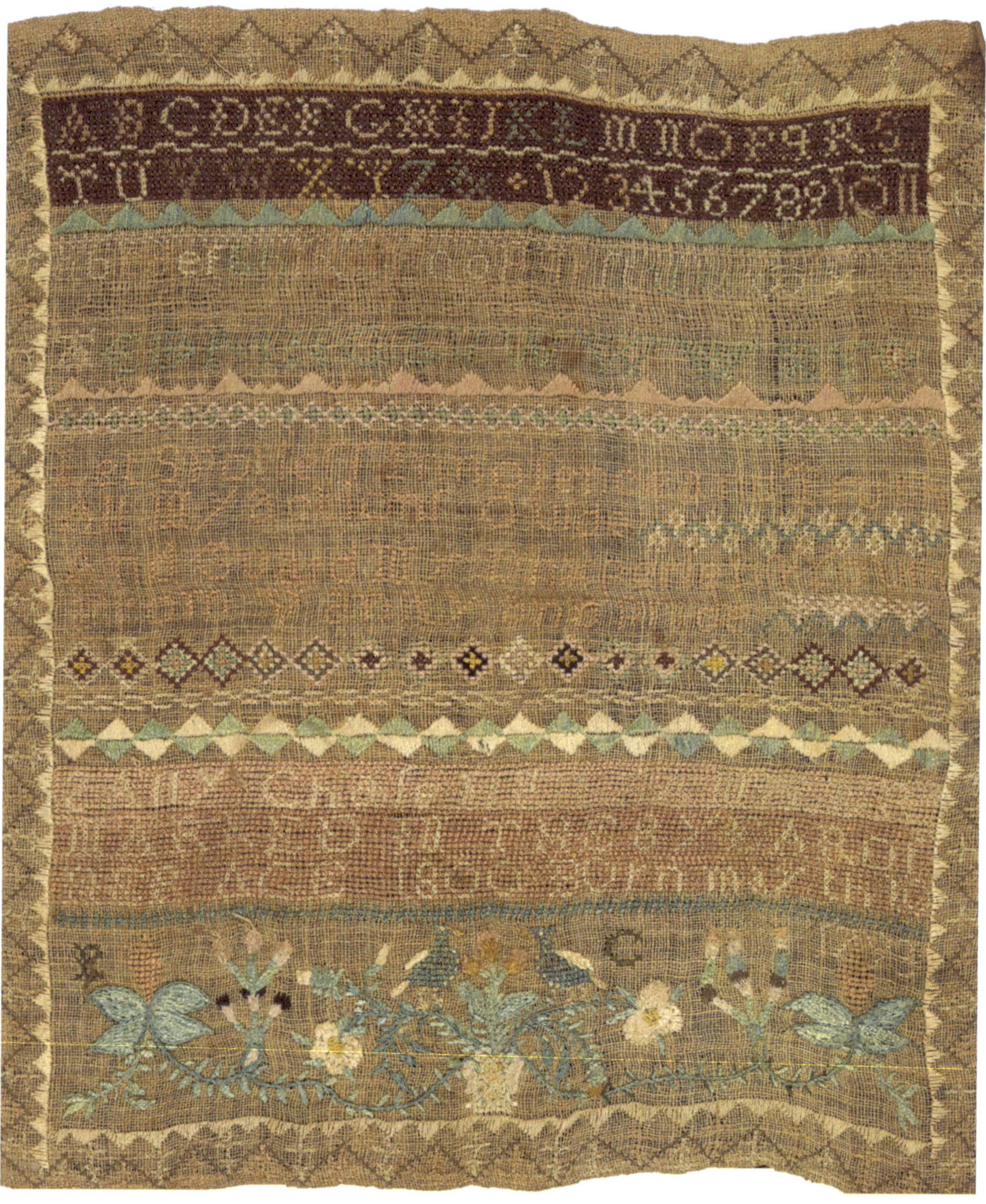

Sally Chase's unusual marking sampler perfectly captures her youthful, eight-year-old exuberance with its charming basket, birds, leaves and vines, and very remarkable flowers, truly a one-of-a-kind work. It was described in *American Samplers* in 1921, and eventually found its way to the collection of Historic New England. Sally was born May 10, 1793, the second eldest of the seven children Daniel and Elizabeth Chase of Saco. She married the Reverend James Weston of Bath in 1816. They seem to have resettled in Lebanon and eventually moved to Standish. They were the parents of at least seven children, one of whom served in the Civil War. By 1870, Sally was a widow. Through 1880, when she was eighty-seven years old, the U.S. Census lists her as head of a household that also included her unmarried daughter Sarah and son John. The date of her death is unknown.

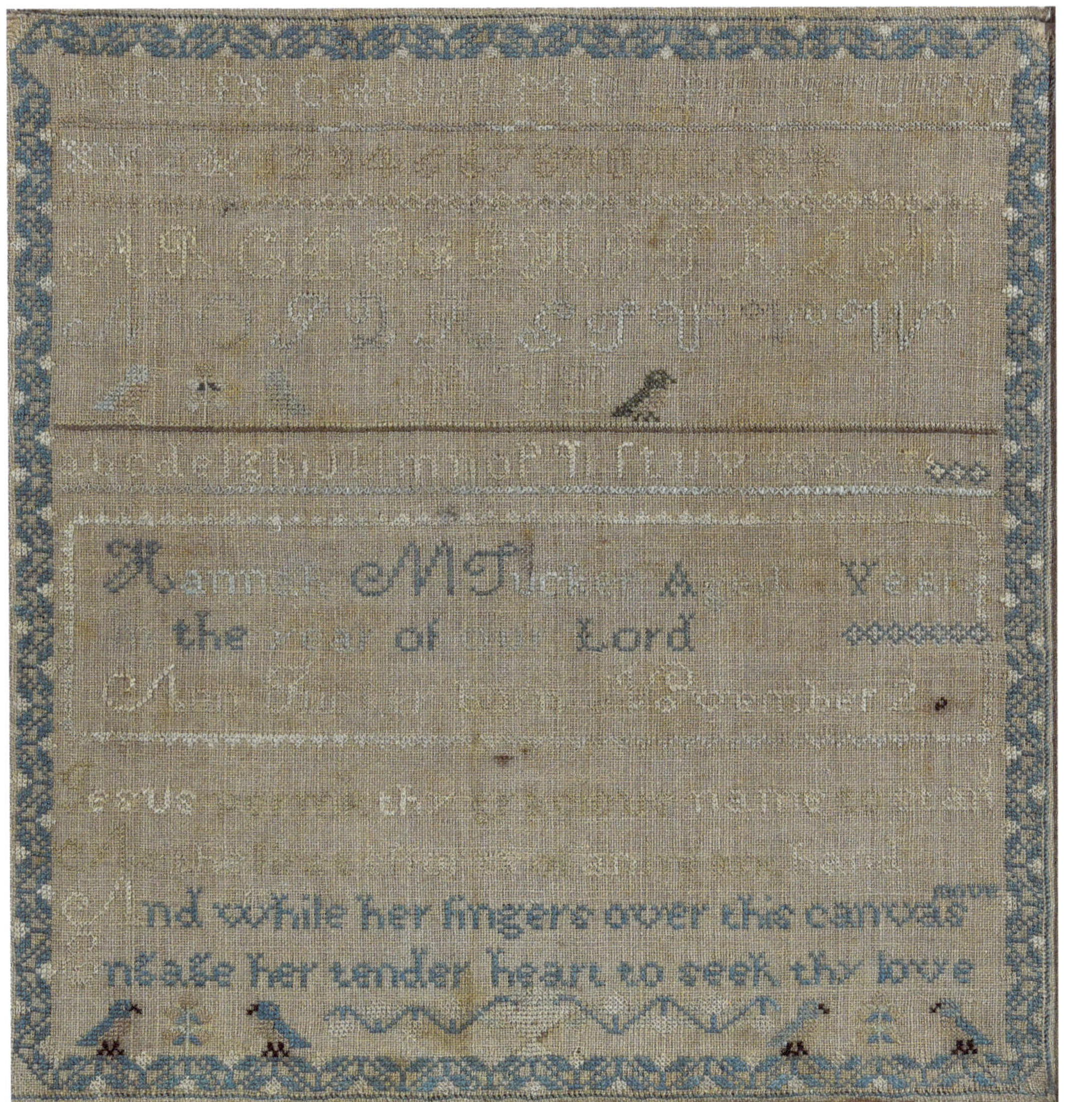

Hannah M. Tucker
(1816–1886)
Marking sampler, circa 1826
Probably worked in Saco, Maine (school unknown)
Silk thread on linen
Cross over one and two threads
16 ¼ x 16 ¼
Collection of the Dyer Library and Saco Museum

Hannah Marcia Tucker, known as Marcia in adulthood, was one of the nine children of Jonathan Tucker and Hannah Scamman of Saco, Maine. On May 1, 1835, she married Daniel Cleaves of Biddeford. Daniel was president of the Saco Bank at the age of twenty-one, a highly successful merchant, and co-owner of several ships. By 1860, his personal estate was valued at a remarkably large $30,000, with an additional $16,000 of real estate. They were the parents of seven children, but sadly, four of them died in infancy. Hannah died in May 1886 and was buried near her parents in Saco's Laurel Hill Cemetery.

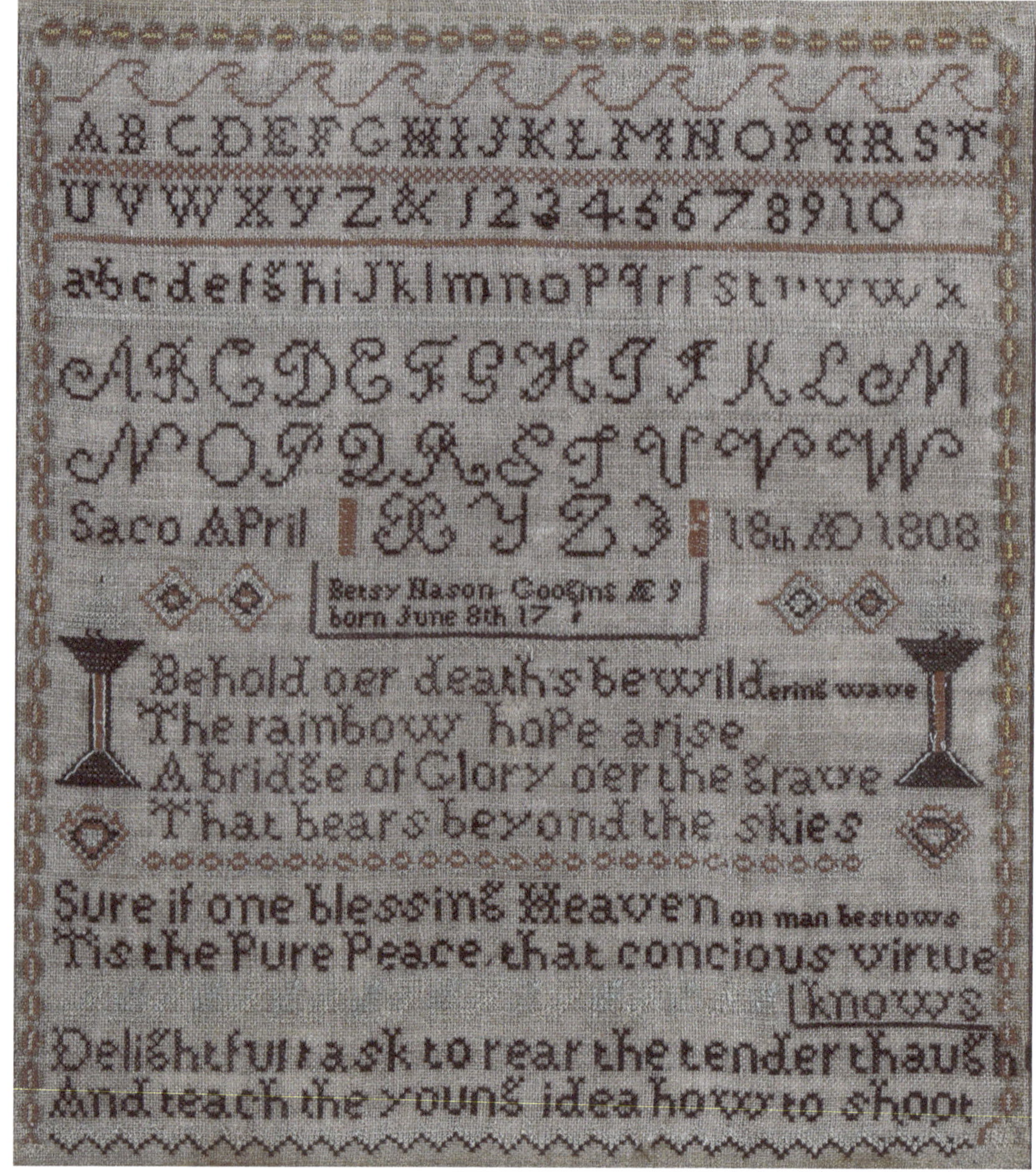

Betsy Nason Googins
(1799–1884)
Marking sampler, 1808
Probably worked in Saco,
Maine (school unknown)
Silk thread on linen
Cross, satin, queen, and
straight stitches
17 x 15 ½
Collection of the Dyer Library
and Saco Museum

Betsy Googins (Elizabeth in later life) was born June 8, 1799, the daughter of Daniel and Olive Junkins Googins of Saco. Olive was the sister of sampler maker Lucy Junkins (p. 21). Betsy was not yet four when her father died. Her mother remarried, to Stephen Fairfield. In 1824, Betsy married Captain Moses Merrill of Wells and they became the parents of seven children. By 1846, they were living in Bangor, where Merrill operated a fur clothing store and served as harbor master. By 1865, Moses had died. Betsy continued to reside in Bangor until she passed away on June 6, 1884. Sometime after she stitched her sampler, when she became more conscious of the passing of the years, Betsy picked out the year in which she was born, not at all unusual. What is a bit more amusing is that she left the century—17. Since she was born in its very last year—1799—any age viewers of the sampler might now assign to her would be no younger than her actual one. The border and a band on Betsy's sampler matches in form and color a band used by Ann Matilda Nye on her sampler (p. 83), also stitched in Saco, not many years later. Betsy crafted unusual spool-like decorations on which she perched birds. The motif of birds on tall objects also appears on the sampler of Dorothy Lancaster (p. 22), who worked her piece a few years earlier in neighboring Scarborough. Betsy also included the common rural Maine motif of concentric triangles.

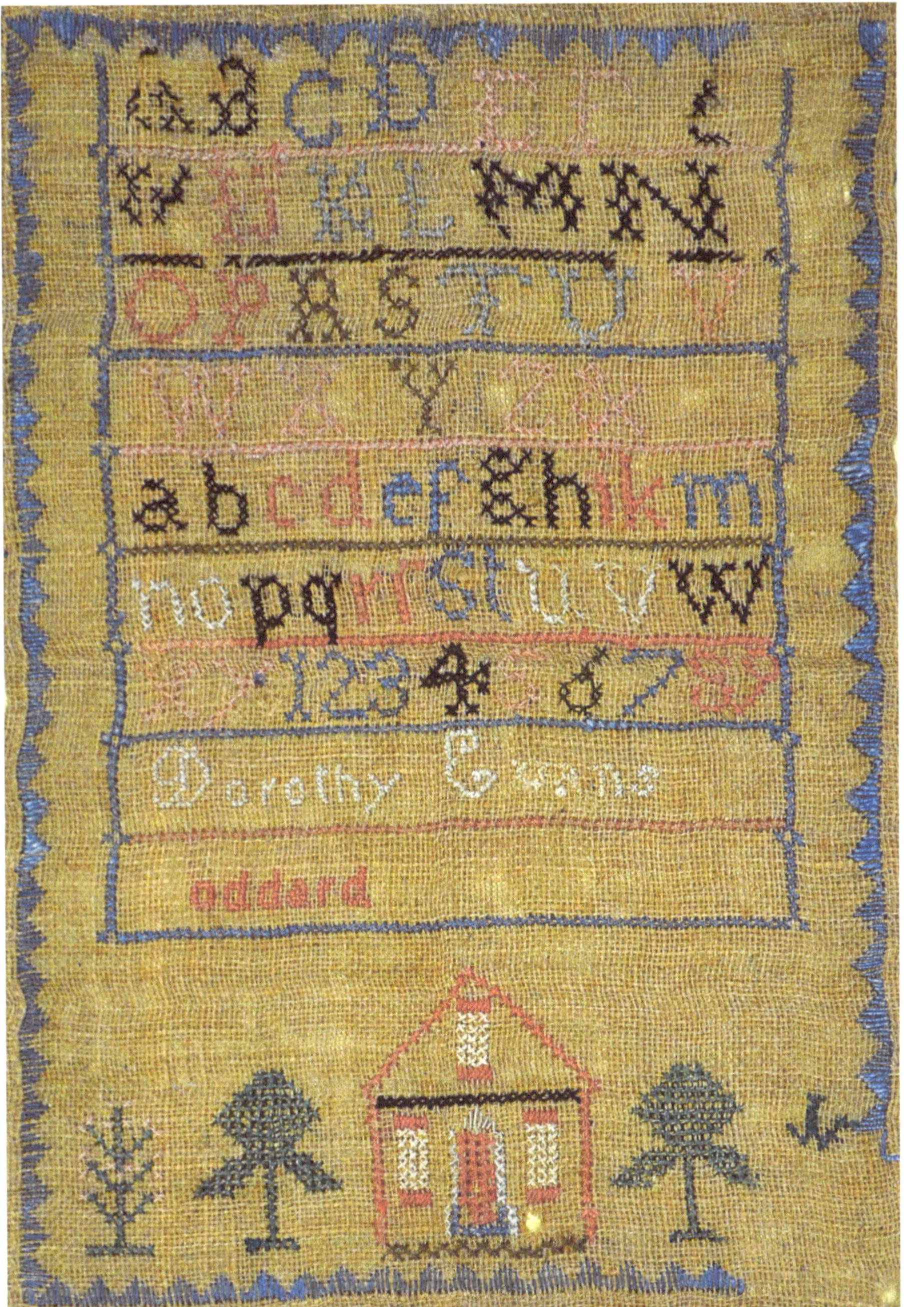

Dorothy Evans Stoddard
(unknown)
Marking sampler, circa 1820
Possibly made in Saco, Maine
(school unknown)
Silk thread on linen
Cross, satin, and
straight stitches
11 x 8
Collection of the Dyer Library
and Saco Museum

Nothing is known of **Dorothy Evans Stoddard**. The tree on the bottom of her sampler resembles one worked by Mary Bradbury (p. 77), perhaps coincidentally. Since she never completed her sampler, it was most likely never displayed, leaving the colors as vivid as the day she selected them, a reminder that schoolgirl embroidery of the Federal era was nearly always vividly polychromatic when created. The muted colors that seem so attractive in the twenty-first century do little justice the exuberance of the stitchers' color choices.

Sarah Cutts Thornton
(1801–1891)
Marking sampler, circa 1810
Probably worked in Saco,
Maine (school unknown)
Silk thread on linen
Cross, satin, and
straight stitches
8 ½ x 12 ½
Collection of the Dyer Library
and Saco Museum

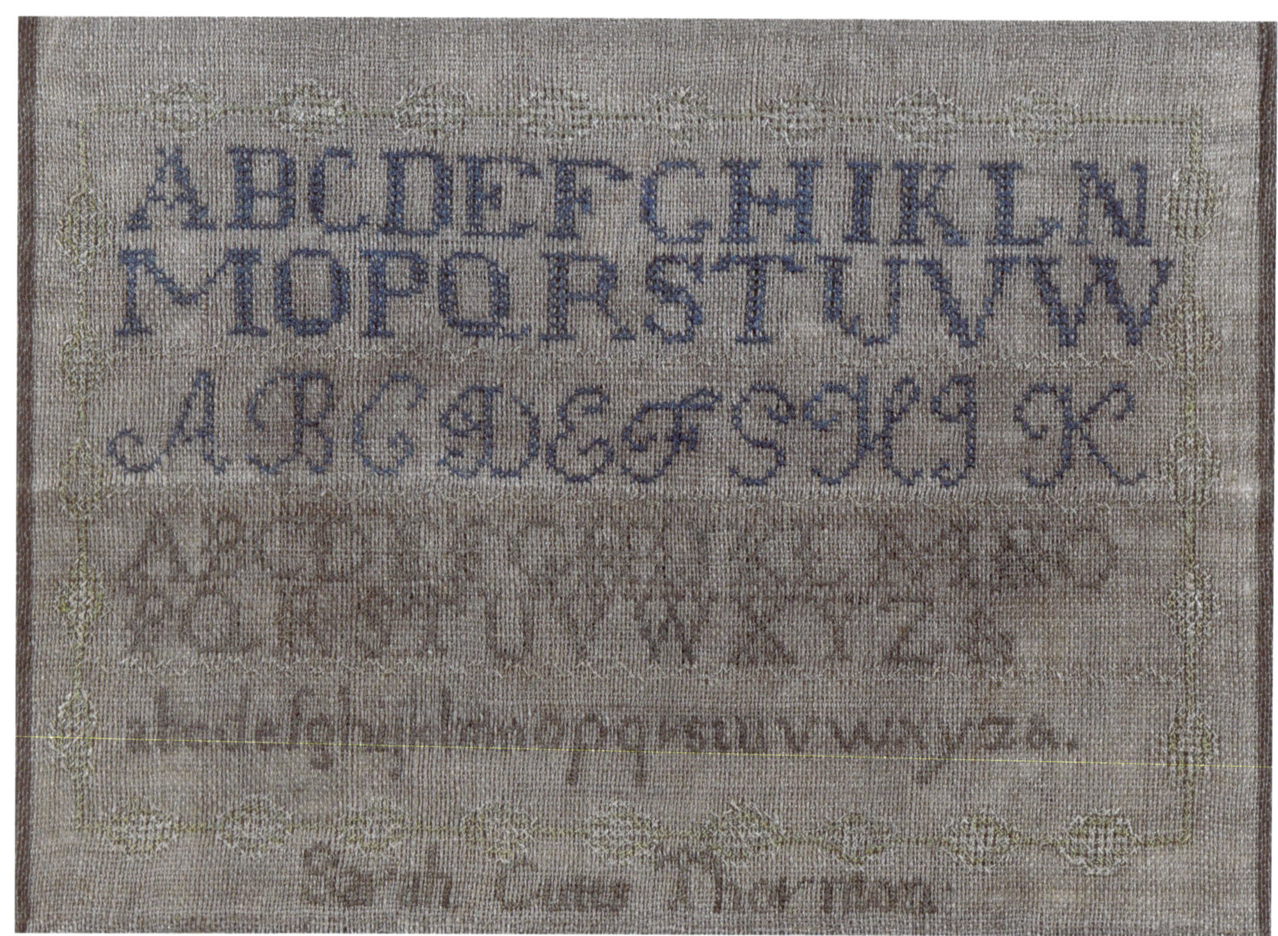

Sarah Cutts Thornton, like sampler maker Ann Matilda Nye (pp. 83–84) a granddaughter of wealthy Saco merchants Colonel Thomas and Elizabeth Cutts, was one of the twelve children of Sarah Cutts and Thomas Gilbert Thornton. Sarah stitched a small and very simple marking sampler. The most distinctive feature is the first alphabet, the block style of which is associated with Quaker-made samplers. She was born March 19, 1801. She grew up in Saco, and on November 27, 1823, she married Moses Emory, an attorney who was practicing law in Wiscasset at the time. The couple later moved back to Saco where their five children were born. Sarah died January 15, 1892.

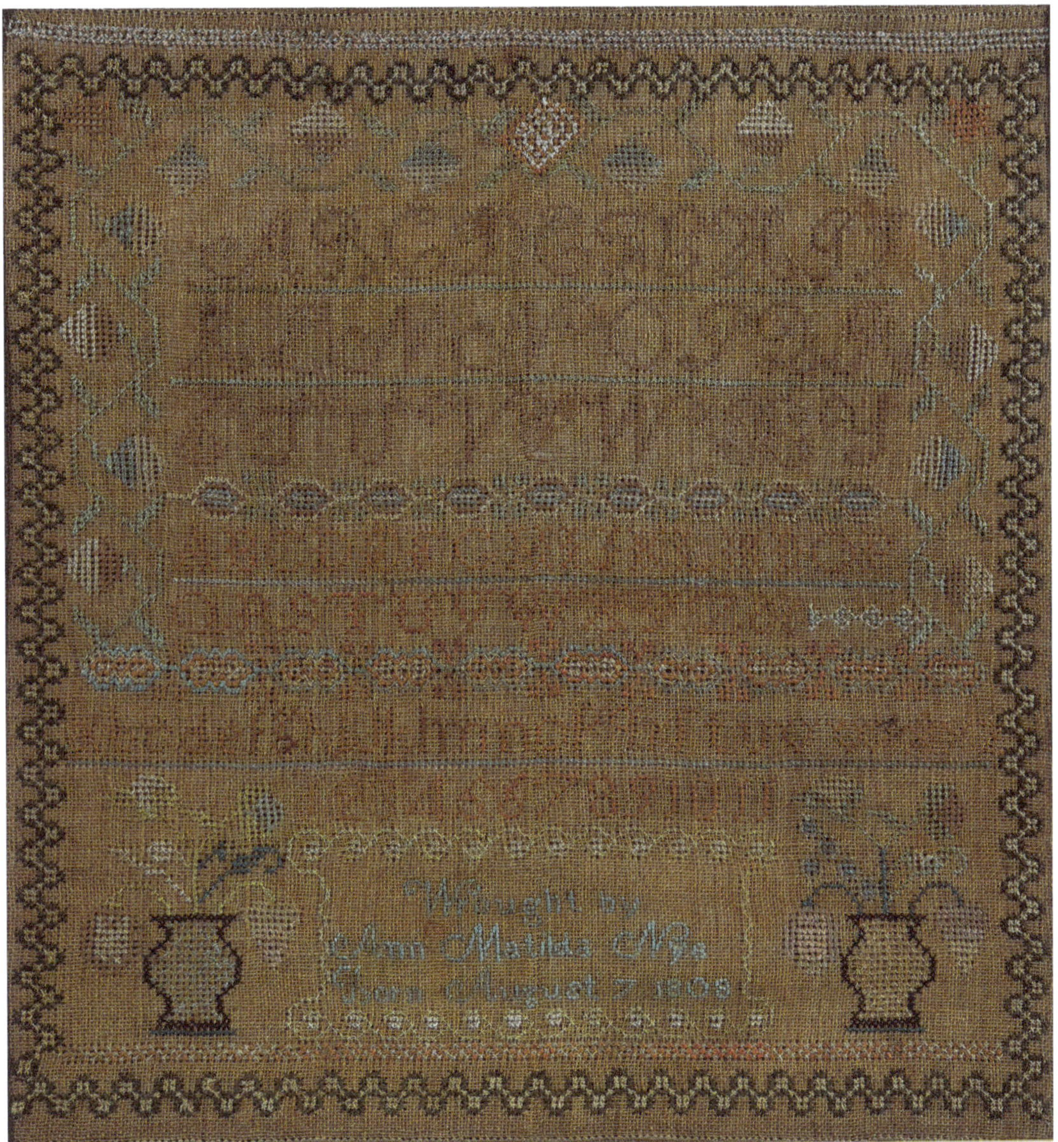

Ann Matilda Nye (1808–1891)
Marking sampler, circa 1822
Worked in Saco, Maine (school unknown)
Silk thread on linen
Cross stitch over one and two threads
14 ¼ x 14 ¼
Collection of the Dyer Library and Saco Museum

Ann Matilda Nye was born August 7, 1808. She was the third child of Eunice Cutts (p. 16) and Samuel Nye. Eunice Cutts had been born and raised in Saco, the daughter of well-to-do parents Colonel Thomas and Elizabeth Cutts, who are the subjects of two very large portraits by John Brewster Jr. in the Saco Museum collection. Ann's father was a physician. Her parents were married in 1803 in Boston. After the War of 1812, they moved to Saco into a large home constructed for them by Thomas Cutts. The house initially stood on the corners of Main, North, and Elm Streets but was later moved to 17 Clark Street, where it still stands, now a multifamily home. Of Ann's nine siblings, three died in childhood. Five of the seven remaining children grew to adulthood but never married. In 1860, Ann was living with one of her unmarried brothers, a sister who was a widow, and another sister, Eunice. Eunice and Ann remained unwed and lived together in gradually worsening poverty for the rest of their lives, dying in 1889 and 1891 in the family home.

Ann's sampler is worked entirely in cross stitch with two unusual borders and an additional border on top that may have been added to accommodate a frame. Nothing is known of her schooling. Saco's Thornton Academy was accepting female students at about the right time for this sampler to have been stitched there, but never employed a preceptress, so almost certainly did not teach decorative needle arts.

Ann Matilda Nye (1808–1891)
Silk mourning embroideries,
circa 1821
Probably worked in Saco, Maine (school unknown)
Silk thread on silk
Satin, outline, and straight stitches
Top: 15 ½ x 17
Bottom: 17 ¾ x 15
Collection of the Dyer Library and Saco Museum

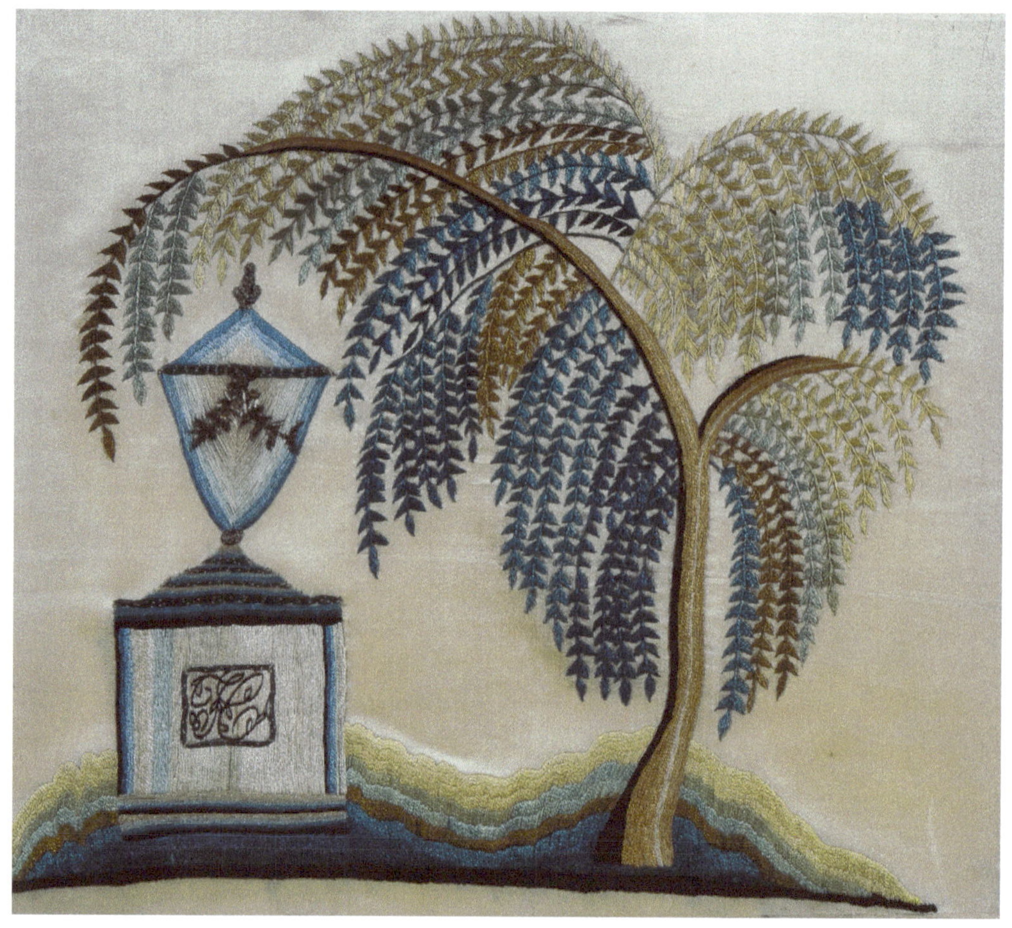

Having already worked an attractive sampler, **Ann Matilda Nye** then went on to stitch two similar but not identical mourning embroideries in honor of her Cutts grandparents, Thomas and Elizabeth, whose initials appear on the urns. Stitching silk on silk was a more exacting skill than embroidering on a linen ground. The design of these two pieces is simple compared to the elaborate mourning embroideries emerging from Portland and other metropolitan areas during the Federal era, making it more likely that they were stitched in a less sophisticated location, perhaps in Saco, where Ann grew up. The Nye family seems to never have been wealthy, and throughout the nineteenth century their financial situation steadily worsened, perhaps making an out-of-town education unavailable for the nine Nye children.

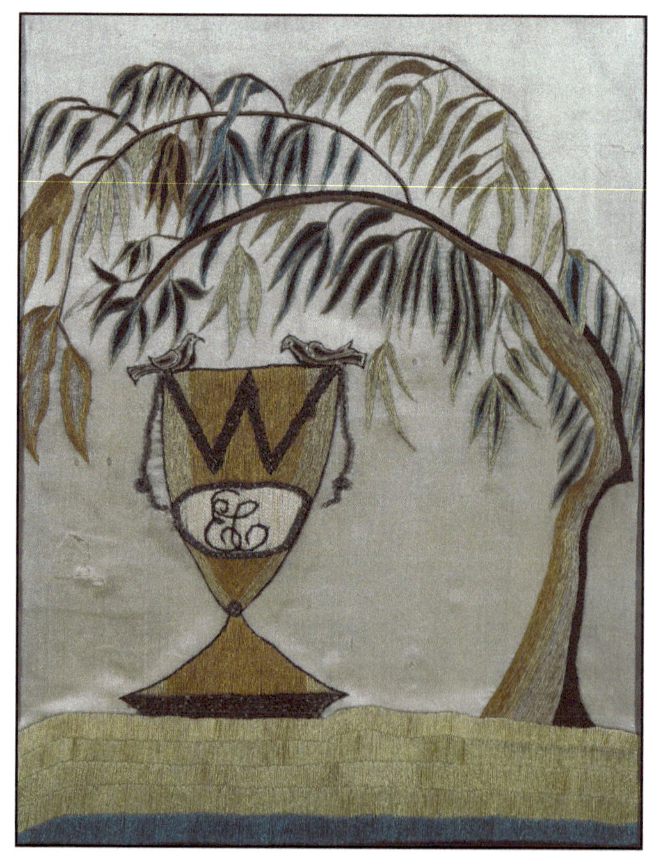

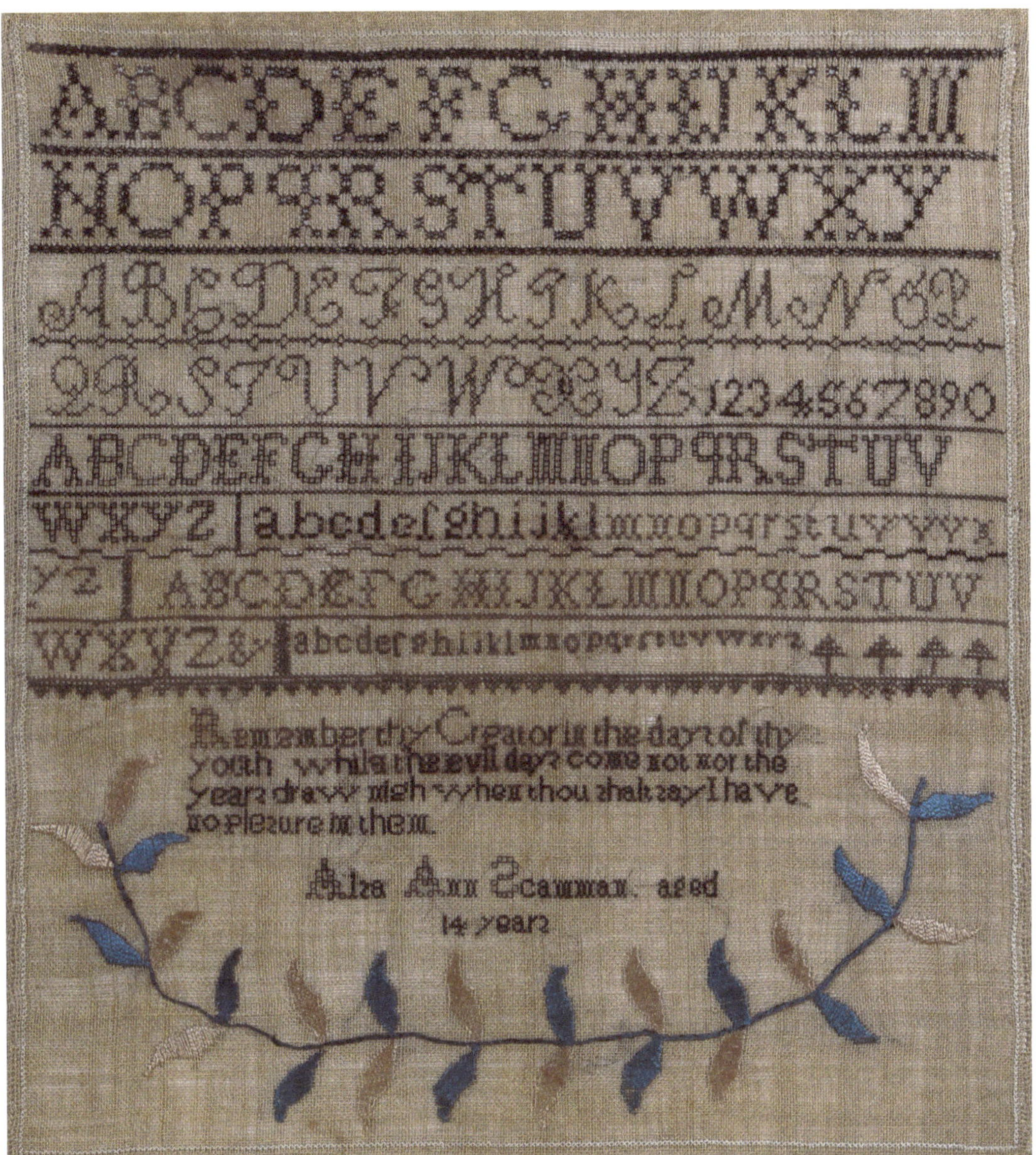

Alsa Ann Scamman
(1821–1837)
Marking sampler, circa 1835
Probably worked in Saco, Maine (school unknown)
Silk thread on linen
Cross, satin, and straight stitches
18 x 16 ¾
Collection of the Dyer Library and Saco Museum

Alsa Ann Scamman was the daughter of Aaron Scamman, born December 15, 1775, and his second wife, Alsa Whitney Dennett, who was also the second wife and widow of Nicholas Dennett Jr. Aaron and his first wife, Jane Dearing, were the parents of five children by the time of Jane's death in 1819. After her 1820 marriage to Aaron Scamman, Alsa (sometimes spelled Elcy) gave birth to just one more child (in addition to the three children she bore during her first marriage), Alsa Ann Scamman, born August 26, 1821. Alsa worked her marking sampler with its leafy decoration at the bottom in 1835, when she was fourteen. Sadly, the vital records of Saco note the death of Elcy Ann Scamman, aged sixteen, on October 15, 1837. One elder brother and one elder sister of Alsa married first cousin siblings but had no children of their own; none of the other Scamman children seem to have survived childhood.

Maker unknown
Silk embroidery,
circa 1800–1830
Possibly worked in Saco,
Maine (school unknown)
Silk thread on silk
Satin stitch
14 ¾ x 12 ¾
Collection of the Dyer Library
and Saco Museum

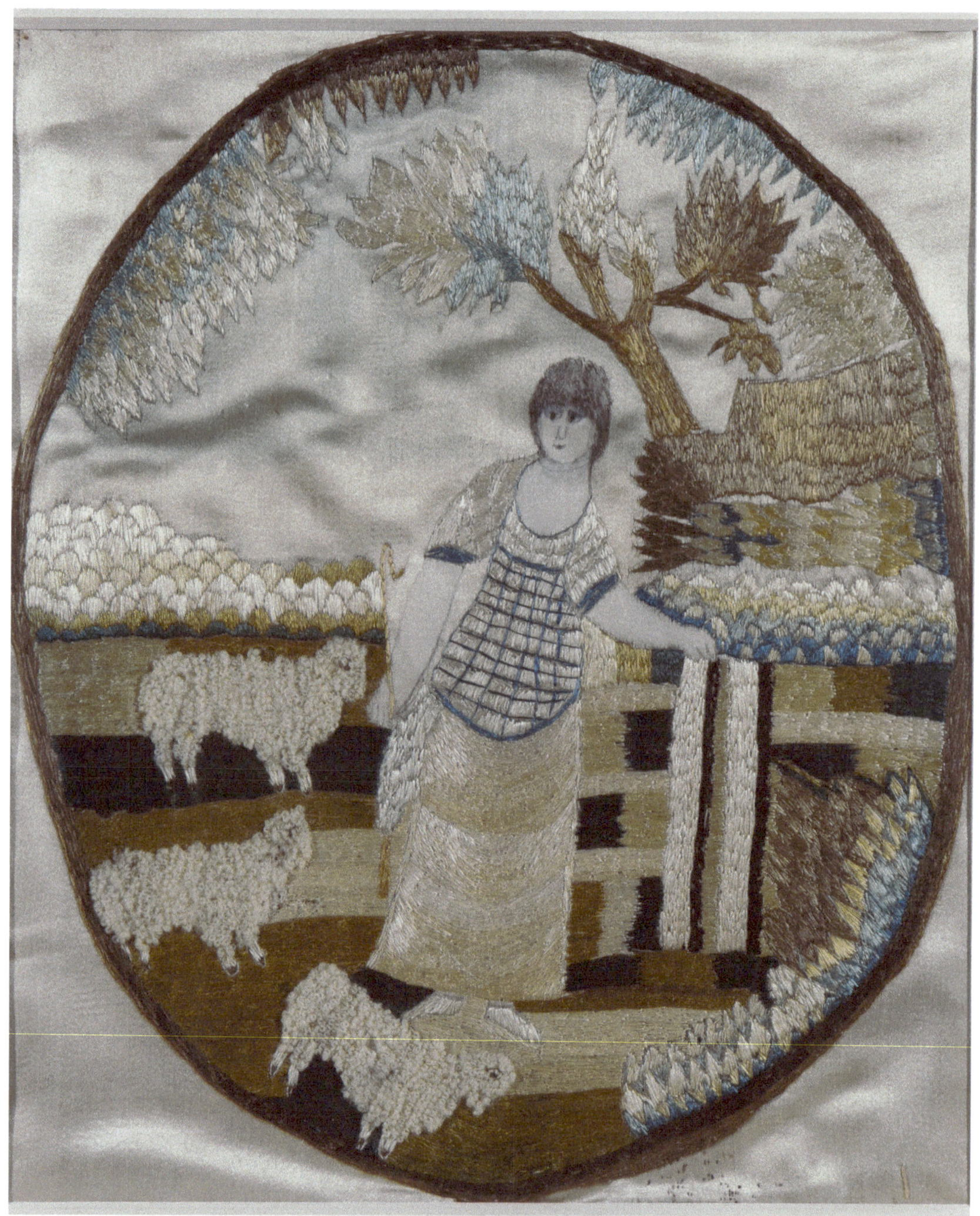

The naïve nature of this thick-armed shepherdess, accompanied by her lopsided sheep, makes it very likely the work of a small town school, drawn by an inexperienced teacher. At larger academies, teachers frequently resorted to tracing or copying prints of the era; the resulting needlework has a sophistication of design and level of artistry that belie the age of most of the embroiderers. This shepherdess appears to have been drawn by an unskilled hand, but is nonetheless charmingly unique.

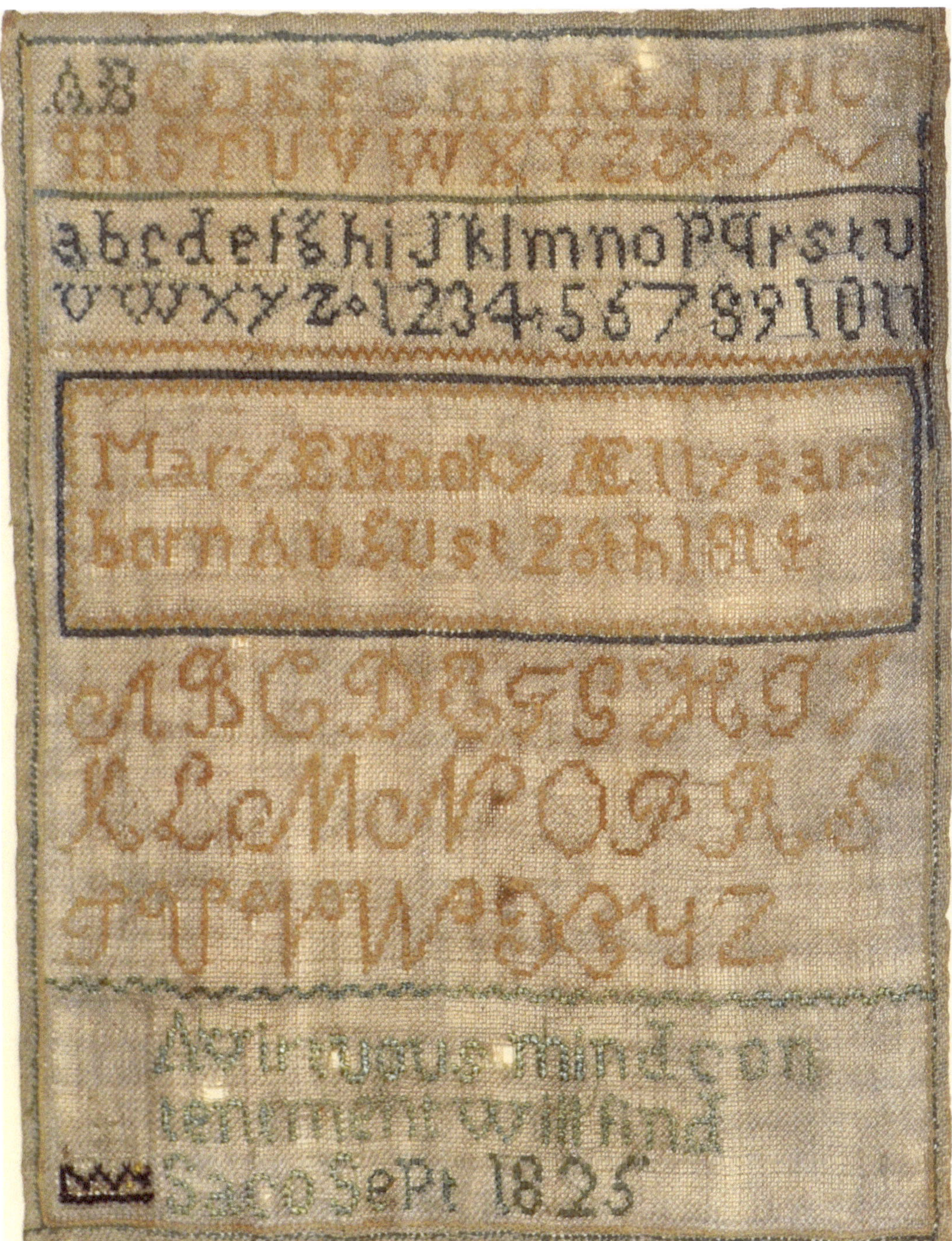

Mary E. Hooky (1814–1895)
Marking sampler, 1825
Probably worked in Saco, Maine (school unknown)
Silk thread on linen
Cross and straight stitches
11 x 12 ¾
Collection of the Dyer Library and Saco Museum

Mary Edgecomb Hooky was one of the two children, both daughters, of Saco native Patience McArthur and John Hooky, who was born in England. Sometime between 1825, when Mary stitched her sampler in Saco, and 1830, the family relocated to York, Maine. The next time records appear for them is in 1850, when Patience and John were residing in the home of their daughter Mary and her husband, John Ricker, in Brownfield, Maine. John Hooky was not working, but John Ricker was a shoemaker with a modestly valued home. John and Mary Ricker had three children. Mary died December 6, 1895, in Des Moines, Iowa. Since the 1890 census is not available, it's hard to know if she had moved there or was perhaps visiting at the time of her death.

Abigail Leavitt (1801–?)
Family register sampler, 1818
Possibly stitched in Scarborough, Maine (unknown school)
Silk thread on linen
Cross, satin, straight, and lazy daisy stitches
26 x 21
Collection of Burton W. Pearl

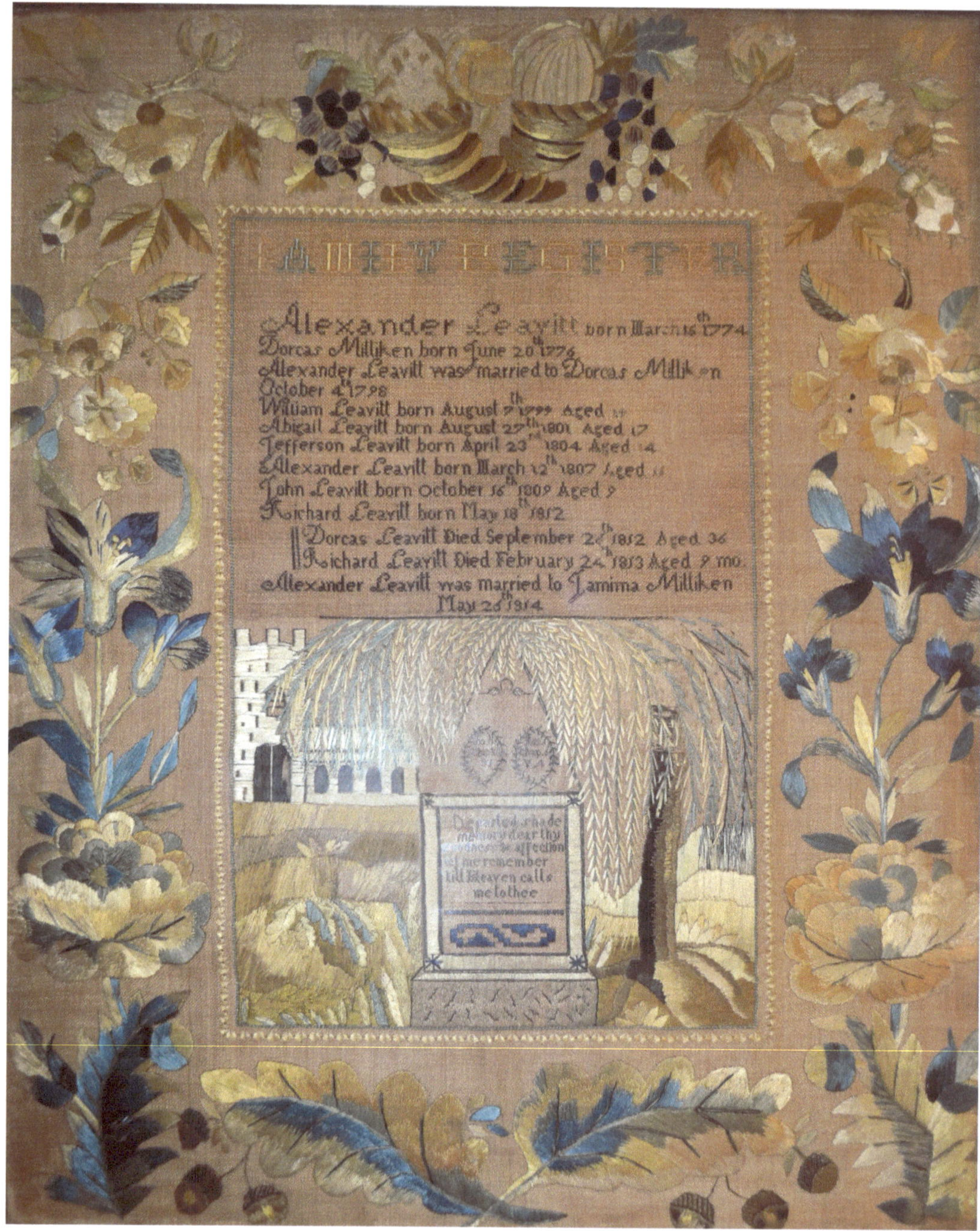

In 1818, when she was seventeen years old, **Abigail Leavitt** carefully recorded the births of her parents, her brothers, and herself. It must have pained her to stitch the date of death of her mother, followed five months later by that of her baby brother. Just a few months later, her father remarried; very often the time between the death of a beloved spouse and remarriage was brief in that era. It may have been some comfort to the Leavitt children that their new mother was their aunt, the younger sister of their mother. Alexander Leavitt appeared on the 1800 census in Scarborough, and he may be the Alexander Levitt recorded on the census for Frankfort, Maine, in 1810 and 1820, since there is no further mention of Alexander, his wives or children on any Scarborough records. Abigail's highly sophisticated genealogical sampler must have been stitched under the watchful eye of a talented teacher.

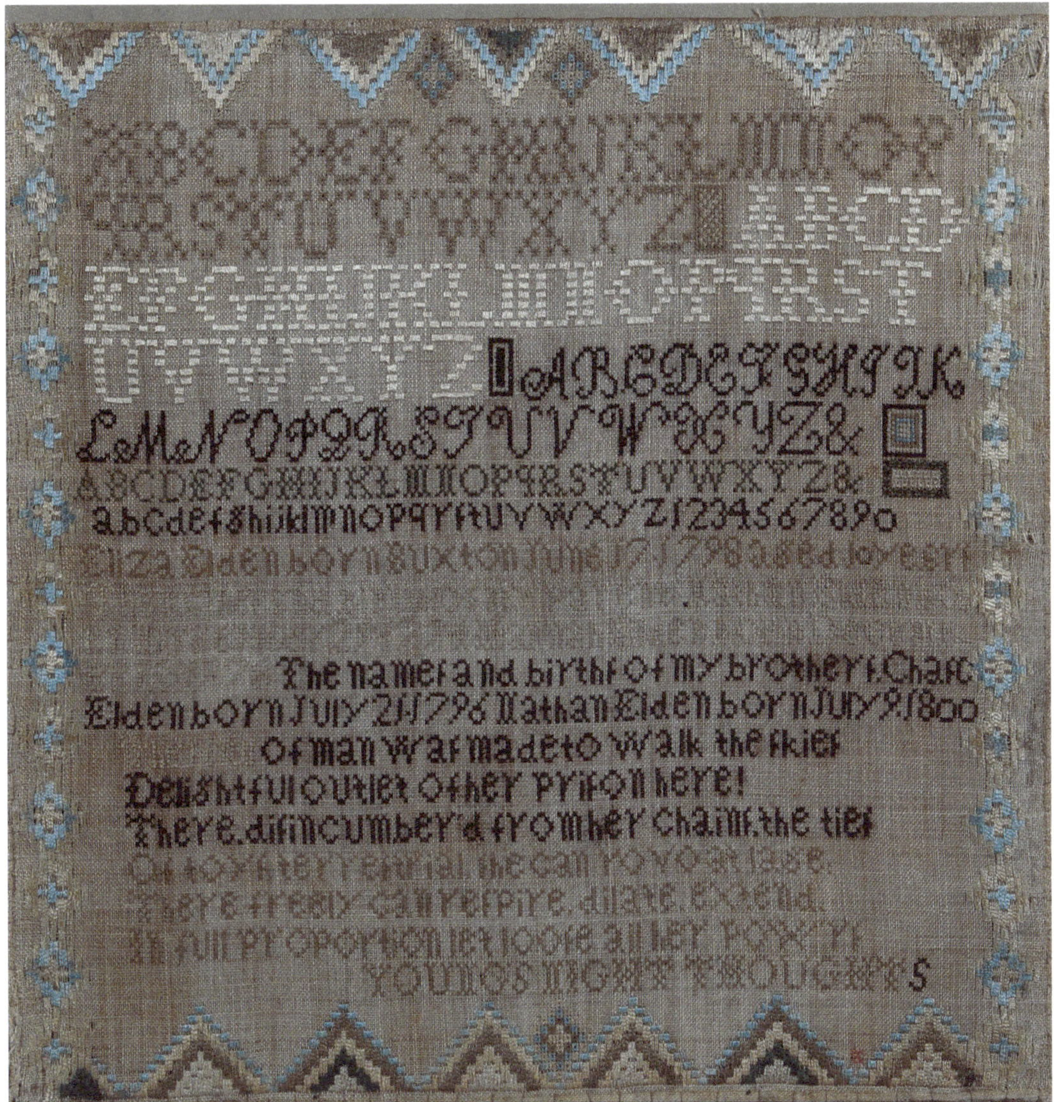

Eliza Elden (1798–1816)
Family register sampler, 1808
Probably worked in Buxton, Maine or possibly at the Misses Martin's School for Young Ladies, Portland
Silk thread on linen
Cross, satin, and Algerian eye stitches
17 ½ x 17 ½
Collection of Dr. and Mrs. Peter Larrabee

Eliza Elden was born in Buxton, Maine, on June 17, 1798, the only daughter of Hannah and Nathan Elden Jr. Her great-grandfather was known as one of the founders of the town. She was related to Gibeon Elden Bradbury (1833–1904), an artist of some fame in the region. Eliza's brother Chace died in 1811 at the age of fifteen, and Eliza herself died March 29, 1816, at the age of seventeen, not very long after she completed her sampler. She is buried in Emery Cemetery in Buxton Center. Like most complex schoolgirl needlework of that era, Eliza's sampler was almost certainly worked in a school setting, most likely in a female academy. The border is rather distinctive, and with any luck another similar one may turn up. But the interesting question that Eliza's sampler raises is that her name appears on the list of students of Misses Martin's School for Young Ladies. Did she work the sampler there? It's unlikely, since no others like it have been discovered, especially when taking into consideration the large number of students who were taught there.

Nancy Favour (1815–1882)
Family register sampler, circa 1815
Probably worked in Limerick, Maine (school unknown)
Silk thread on linsey-woolsey
Cross stitch
26 x 18
Collection of the Baxter House Museum

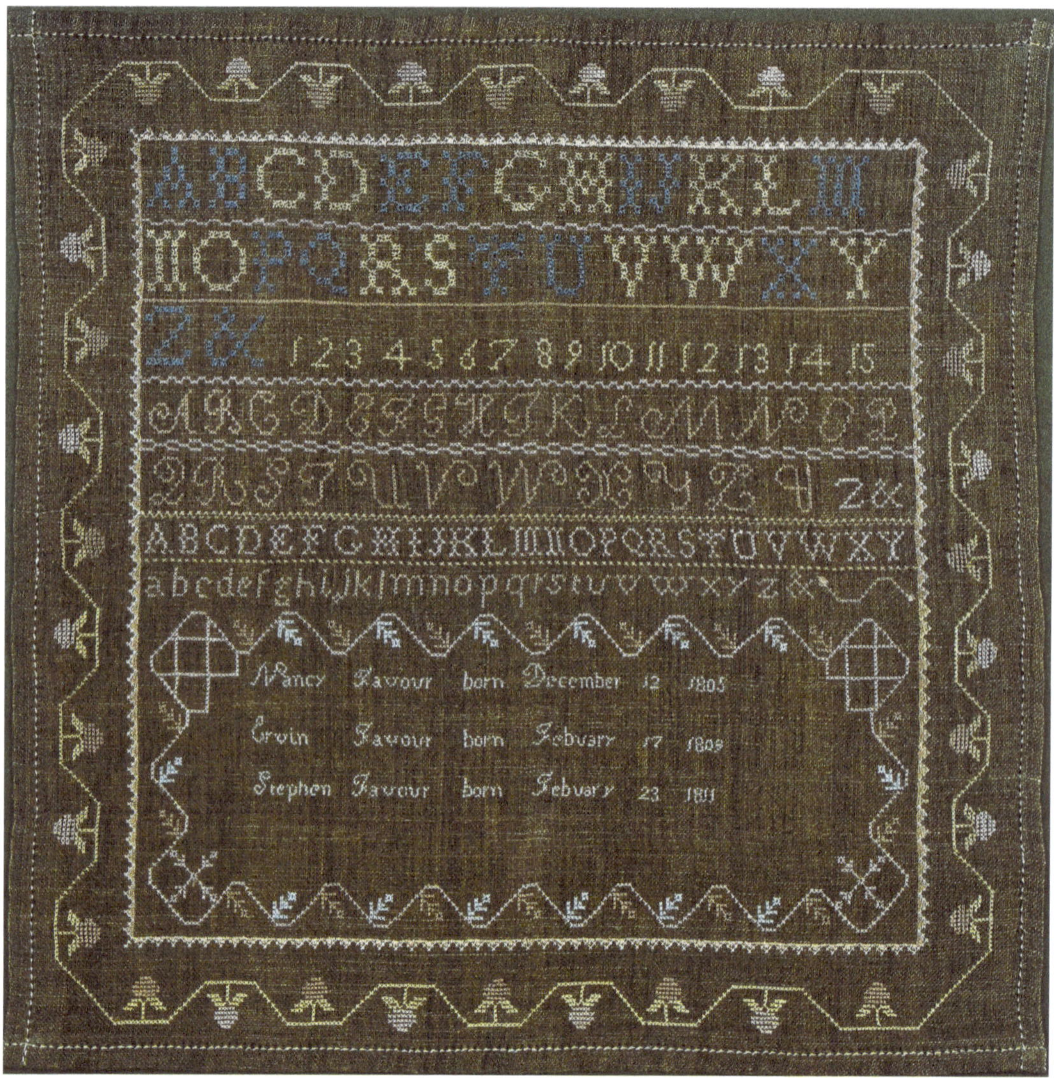

Nancy Favour's linsey-woolsey sampler is large and not as decorative as many of the linsey-woolseys that originated further south in Maine and in coastal New Hampshire. Her strawberry border is neat and attractive. The fern-like elements that surround her minimal genealogical information appear on a few other known Maine samplers, often used as space fillers at the ends of lines of alphabets. Nancy provided information about the births of her two brothers and herself. They were the children of Stephen Hook Favour of Saco and Susan L., probably born in Limerick, Maine. Nancy married Ivory Day, and they were the parents of three daughters. He died in 1866. Nancy lived on until 1882 and was buried in the Day family plot in Limerick.

Rebekah Peabody (1798–1886)
Marking sampler, 1810
Possibly worked at the Bridgton Academy, Bridgton, Maine, or the Fryeburg Academy, Fryeburg, Maine
Silk thread on linen
Cross, satin, and straight stitches
24 x 16
Collection of Julie Lindberg

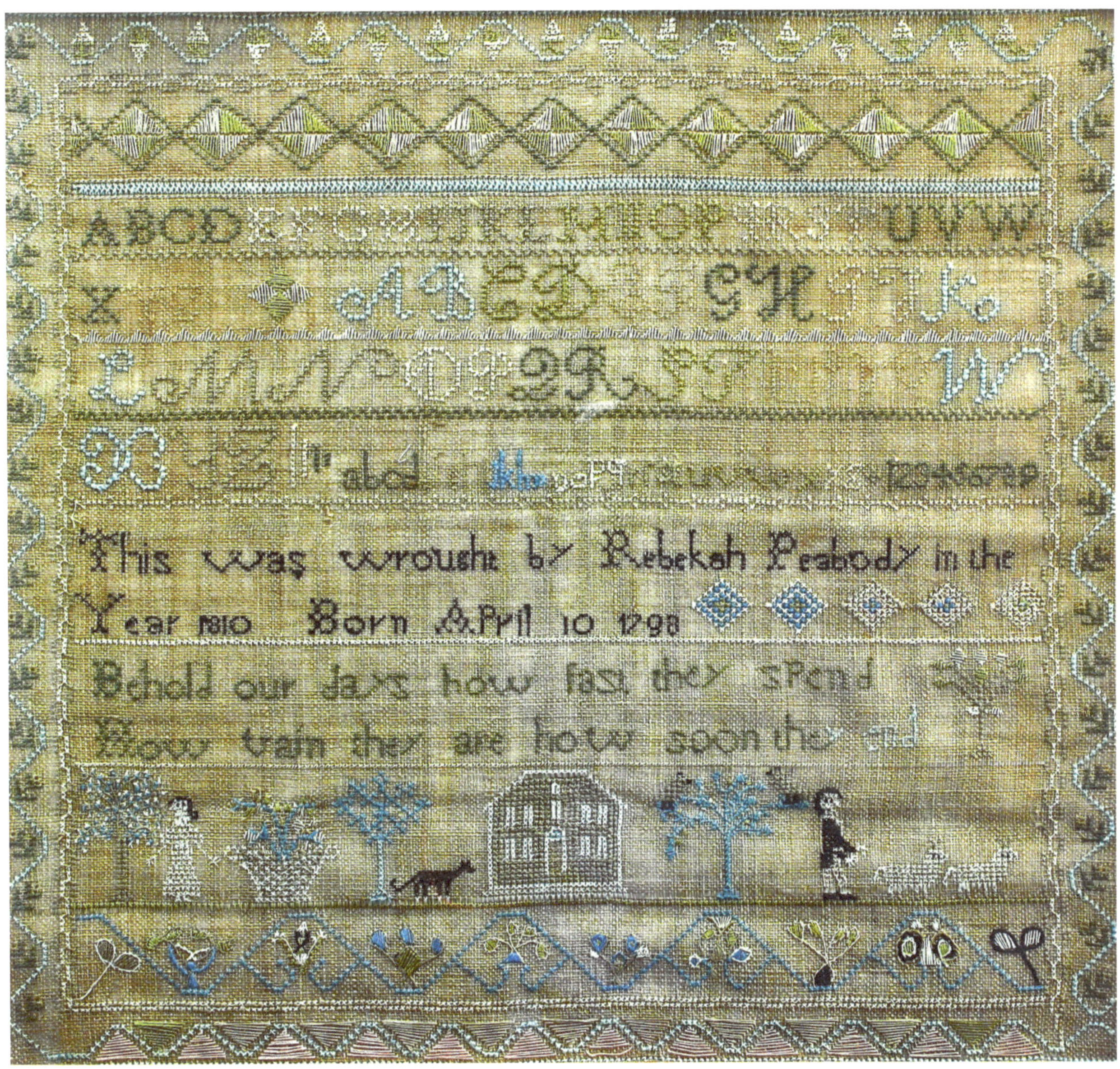

Rebekah Peabody was born April 10, 1798, one of the eleven children of John and Asenath Stevens Peabody of Bridgton, Maine. All three of the Peabody sisters who survived infancy stitched samplers (see also p. 92). Two are included in this exhibition; the whereabouts of the third is unknown. On May 17, 1820, Rebekah married Nathaniel Martin. They were the parents of ten children born between October 1820 and 1844. Rebekah died August 25, 1886. The Peabody samplers share several Maine characteristics, including the use of concentric diamonds as space holders to fill rows. Two academies in the immediate area were educating both boys and girls, raising the intriguing possibility that the Peabody sisters may have stitched their works at either the Fryeburg Academy or the Bridgton Academy. To date there are no other works attributed to either school.

Huldah Peabody (1800–1819)
Marking sampler, 1810
Possibly worked at the Bridgton Academy, Bridgton, Maine, or the Fryeburg Academy, Fryeburg, Maine
Silk thread on linen
Cross, satin, and straight stitches
24 x 16
Collection of Julie Lindberg

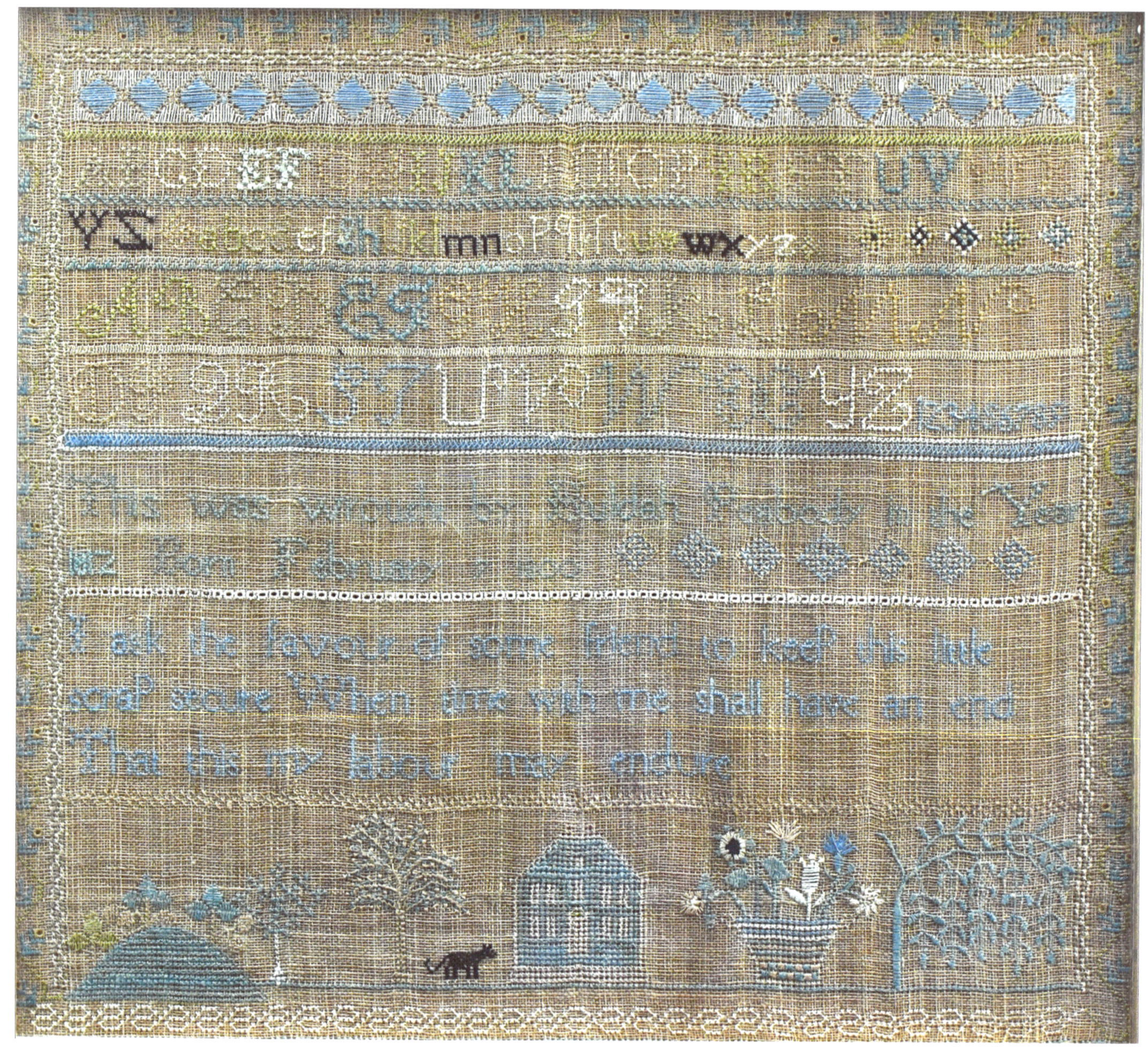

Huldah Peabody was the next child born after Rebekah, daughters of John Peabody and his wife, Asenath Stevens of Bridgton, Maine. Unfortunately, Huldah died at just nineteen on August 15, 1819. She is buried in South Bridgton Cemetery, alongside many members of her family. Years after her death, her brother Israel named his second daughter after her.

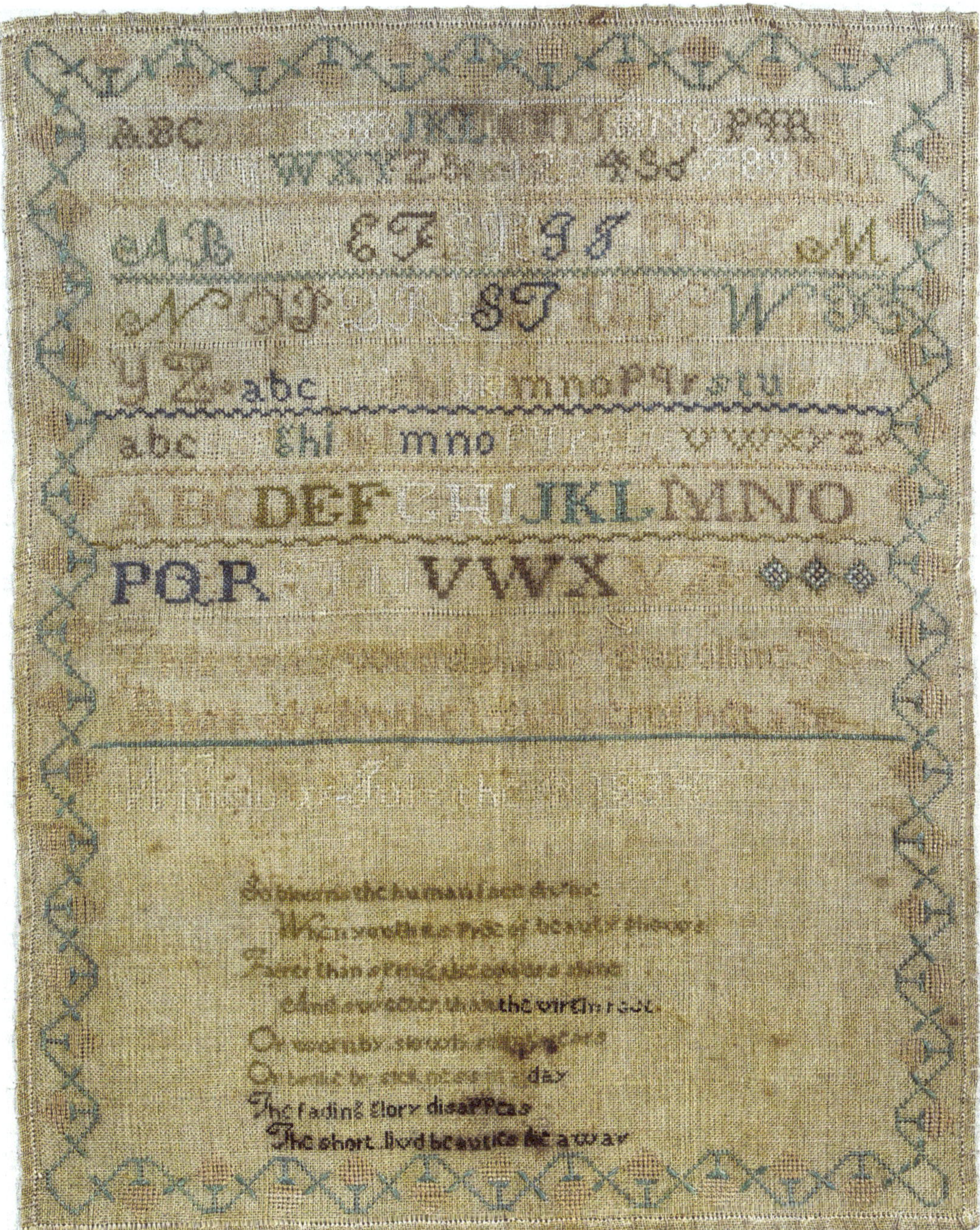

Caroline Blackwell
(1820–1842)
Family register sampler, 1834
Probably worked in Winslow, Maine (school unknown)
Silk thread on linen
Cross stitch
20 ¾ x 16 ¾
Collection of Donna Moir

Caroline Redington Blackwell was the eldest child of Alvin, born in Sandwich, Massachusetts, and his wife, Abigail Hudson Blackwell, who was born in Clinton, Maine. Most of the Blackwell children were born in Winslow, Maine, where Alvin farmed. Caroline married Heman B. Horn, possibly of New York City, on October 14, 1841, and died only months later on May 22, 1842. Abigail Jane Caroline Blackwell, Caroline's younger sister, was born shortly after Caroline died and was named both for Caroline and another sister, Abigail Jane, who died as an infant in 1828; she, too, had a short life, dying before her tenth birthday. In fact, only one of the unlucky Blackwell offspring survived long enough to have children of his own.

Sybil Parker, born on April 7, 1772, in Winslow, Maine, married William Pattee on April 4, 1795. She was widowed only months later when William died on December 4, 1795. She was said to have operated a school in Winslow for many years, and she might have been Caroline's teacher. Sybil died in Winslow on May 16, 1861.

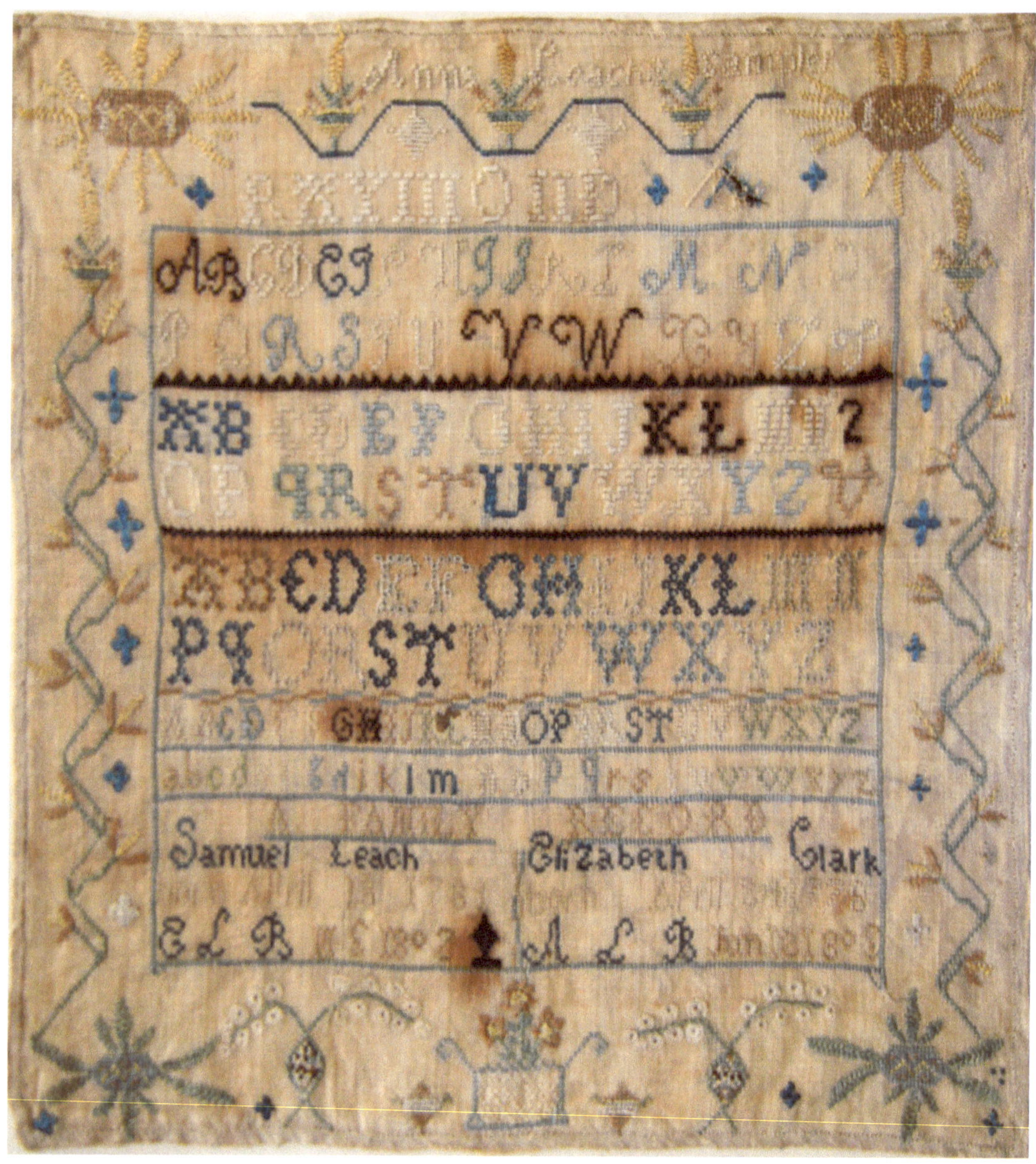

Anne Leach (1805–1870)
Family register sampler, 1818
Probably worked in Raymond, Maine (school unknown)
Silk thread on linen
Cross, satin, straight, and queen stitches and French knots
16 ¼ x 15 ¾
Collection of Mrs. Nancy Mairs

Anne Leach was the third of the eight children of Samuel and Elizabeth Clark Leach of Raymond, Maine. Two of the five girls may have died very young. The family relocated to Naples, Maine, in the 1830s. On July 1, 1832 Anne married Levi P. Holden, a farmer, in Otisfield, Maine. They later settled in Casco, where Anne's younger sister Peggy had also moved. They were the parents of a son and a daughter. Anne, known as Anna in adulthood, died of consumption in December 1870 in Casco. Her sampler demonstrates a charming youthful exuberance, but less success with planning the spacing of all the information she wanted to squeeze in.

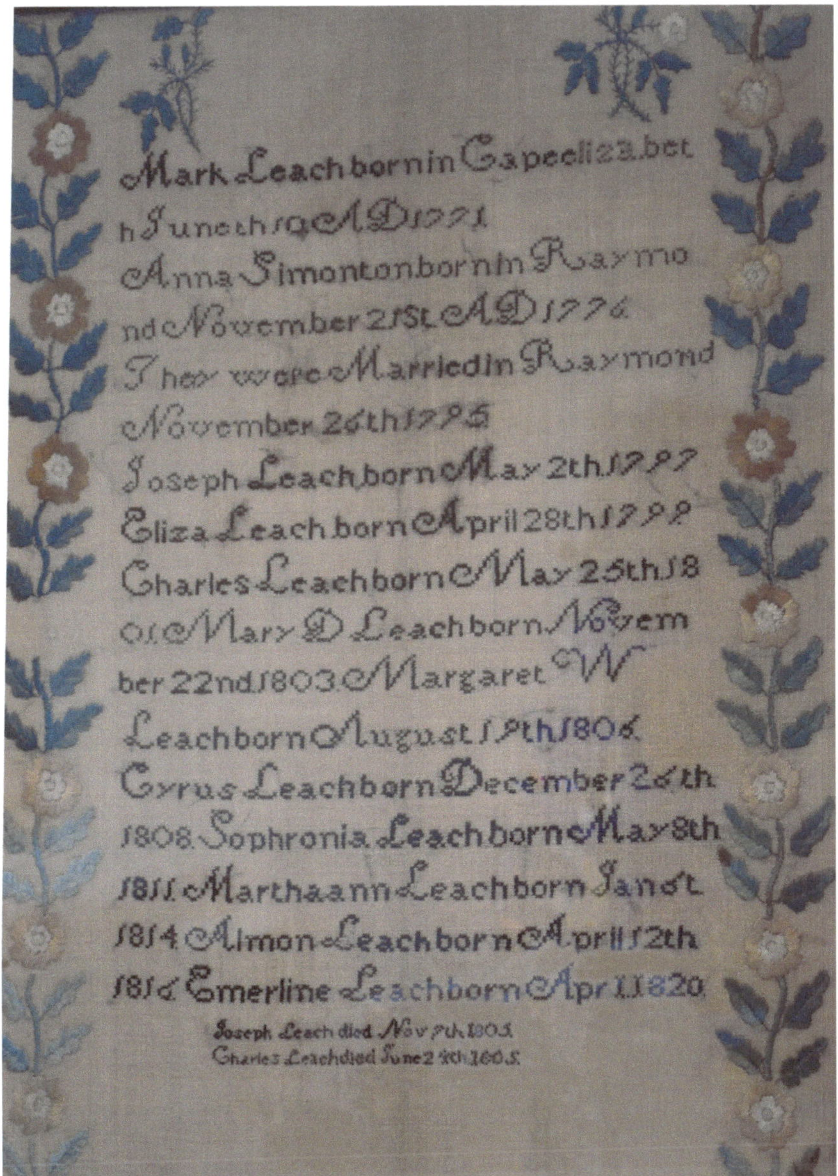

Possibly Sophronia or Martha Ann Leach (1811–?, 1814–1826)
Family register sampler, circa 1822
Probably worked in Raymond, Maine (school unknown)
Silk thread on linen
Cross and satin stitches
23 x 17
Collection of Burton W. Pearl

It's impossible to know who stitched the genealogical sampler of the Mark Leach family, or even when it was completed. It includes the dates of birth of the children through 1820, all seemingly stitched by the same person. Given the rather casual handling of the information, splitting the dates and names between the lines instead of planning in advance in order to make them fit one to a line, it seems likely that it was made by a rather young child, making the most probable candidates **Sophronia or Martha Ann Leach**. Martha Ann died at age twelve in 1826. Elizabeth married John Cook. They were the parents of two young children when she died in 1827. Two years later, he married her younger sister Margaret, and they had a further seven children. Mary died in 1829 at the age of twenty-five. If Emerline had stitched the sampler, she probably wouldn't have done the work until closer to 1830, since she wasn't born until 1820, and then perhaps would have included the deaths of Martha Ann and Mary. There seem to be no further records for Emerline or Sophronia. Raymond, Maine, is located not far from Windham. A Meayberry genealogical sampler made by a child of Edward Meayberry and Mary Johnson of Windham (sold at Freeman's Auction on November 16, 2007, in Philadelphia) features a similar border of casually rendered flowers up each side, with the genealogical information stitched a bit awkwardly in very large letters. These two samplers, both probably stitched in the 1820s, undated and without maker's name, and the also casually designed Anne Leach sampler (p. 94), made by a cousin from Raymond, may be related.

Mary Hawks (1798–1828)
Marking sampler, 1811
Worked in Windham, Maine, possibly under the instruction of Mary Rea
Silk thread on linen,
Cross, straight, and queen stitches
23 x 17
Collection the of Portland Museum of Art, Museum purchase, 1972, 194

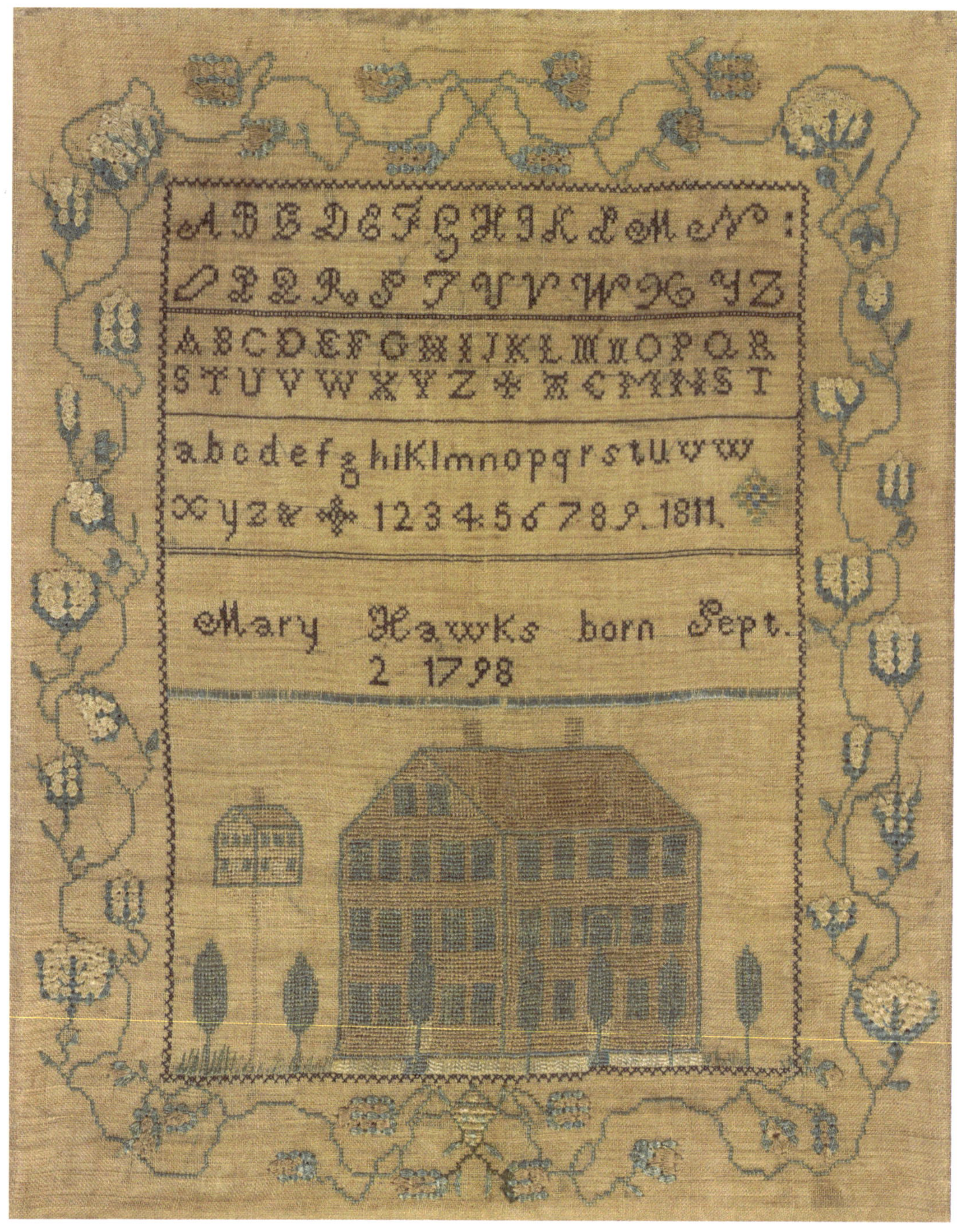

Mary Hawks was the third of the seven children of Amos and Lydia Winslow Hawks Jr. of Windham, Maine. She was a cousin of the Hawks girl who stitched another sampler in this exhibition (p. 97), but while that one was made about 1820, Mary stitched hers at a younger age, in 1811. Mary's sampler includes a meandering queen-stitch border, neatly worked alphabets, and a very large building. While the border relates to known Portland pieces, it is less accomplished than some others of the same period.

Portland teacher Mary Rea was born in Windham in 1787 and is known to have resided there until at least 1822. The other Hawks sampler shows strong evidence of the influence of Portland needlework, and yet was possibly also made in Windham. In 1811, Mary Rea was twenty-three; her mother had been a widow since 1796 and was the mother of six children, at least three of whom were younger than her industrious daughter. It's quite probable that Rea was already gainfully employed by this time, teaching young females of Windham in an effort to help support her family, and may have been the instructor for this Hawks work. Mary Hawks died December 19, 1828, in Windham.

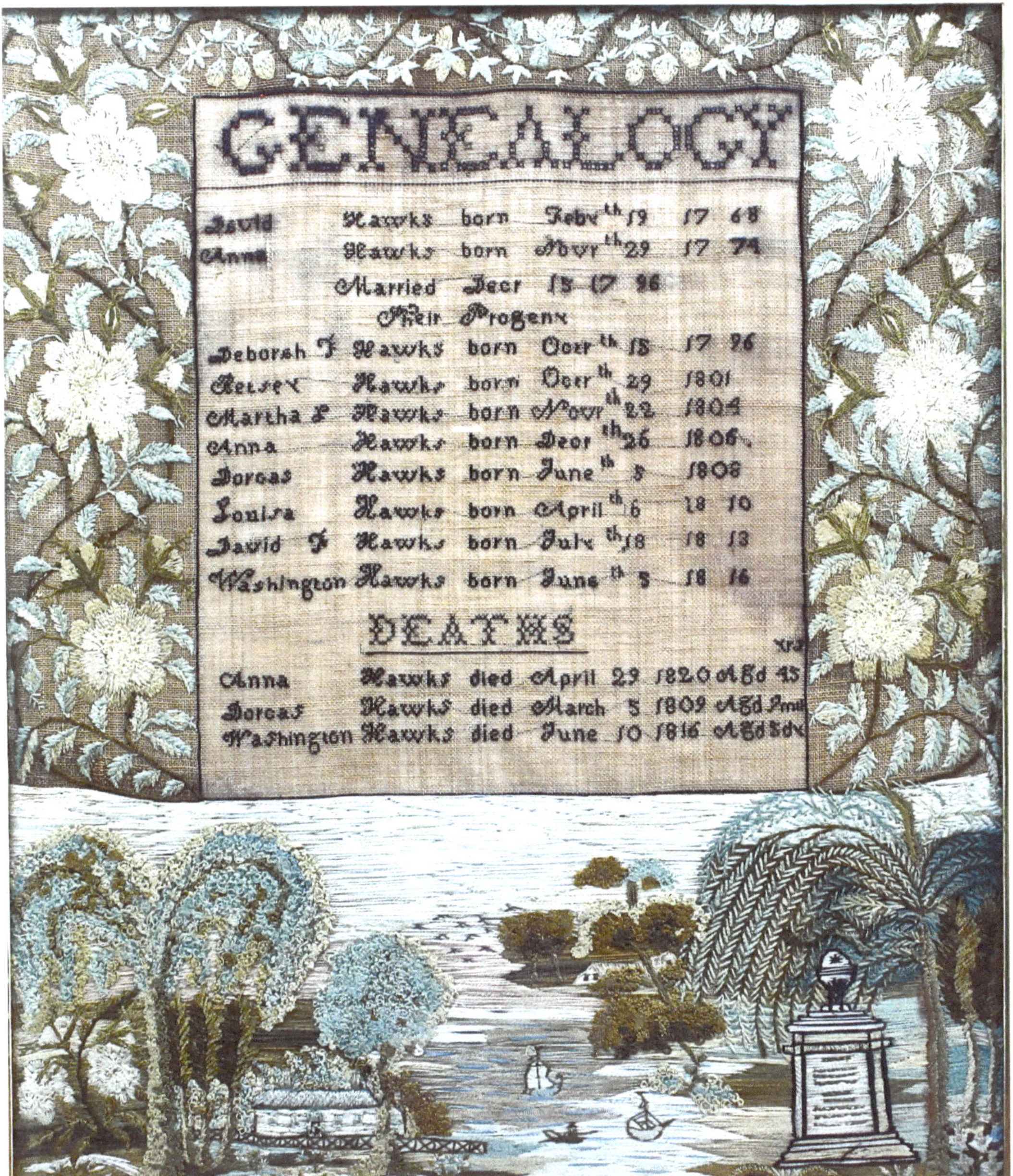

Probably Martha, Anna or Louisa Hawks (1804–?, 1806–?, 1810–?)
Family register sampler, circa 1820
Worked in Windham, Maine, or Portland, Maine, under the instruction of Mary Rea
Silk thread on linen
Cross, satin, and outline stitches
28 ½ x 17
Collection of Julie Lindberg

This attractive rose-bordered sampler with its satin-stitched landscape was created by one of the daughters of Anna and David Hawks of Windham, Maine, who were first cousins. They were the parents of six daughters, five of whom survived to adulthood, and just two sons, of which only one survived. The sampler was stitched no earlier than 1820, making it probable that it was made by one of the younger girls, **Martha, Anna or Louisa Hawks** being the most likely candidates. This Hawks embroidery seems to bear a strong connection to the sampler of Janet Carruthers, with a similar landscape and border, which is believed to have been worked at the recently opened Portland school of Mary Rea in 1824.

Mary Rea was the daughter of Dr. Caleb Rea Jr. and Sarah White. Dr. Rea died when she was just nine years old. Her next-youngest brother, Dr. Albus Rea, opened a medical practice in Portland in about 1822, and shortly after Mary joined him and opened a school there. This Hawks sampler may date from *before* she began teaching in Portland. Given that she was about thirty-five when she moved there, it would not be surprising that she would have been employed in teaching prior to that time. Since the Hawks sampler includes many of the features of Portland work, it may demonstrate the way in which that style had begun to permeate the region and influence some teachers in outlying towns. All of the surviving Hawks daughters married and lived into their middle or later years. Mary Rea operated a school in Portland until at least 1846 and died in 1849.

Narcissa Stone (1801–1877)
Marking sampler, 1810
Probably worked at the school of Catherine Palmer Putnam, Brunswick, Maine
Silk thread on linen
Cross, queen, straight, and satin stitches
24 x 18
Collection of the Portland Museum of Art, Museum purchase, 1973, 9

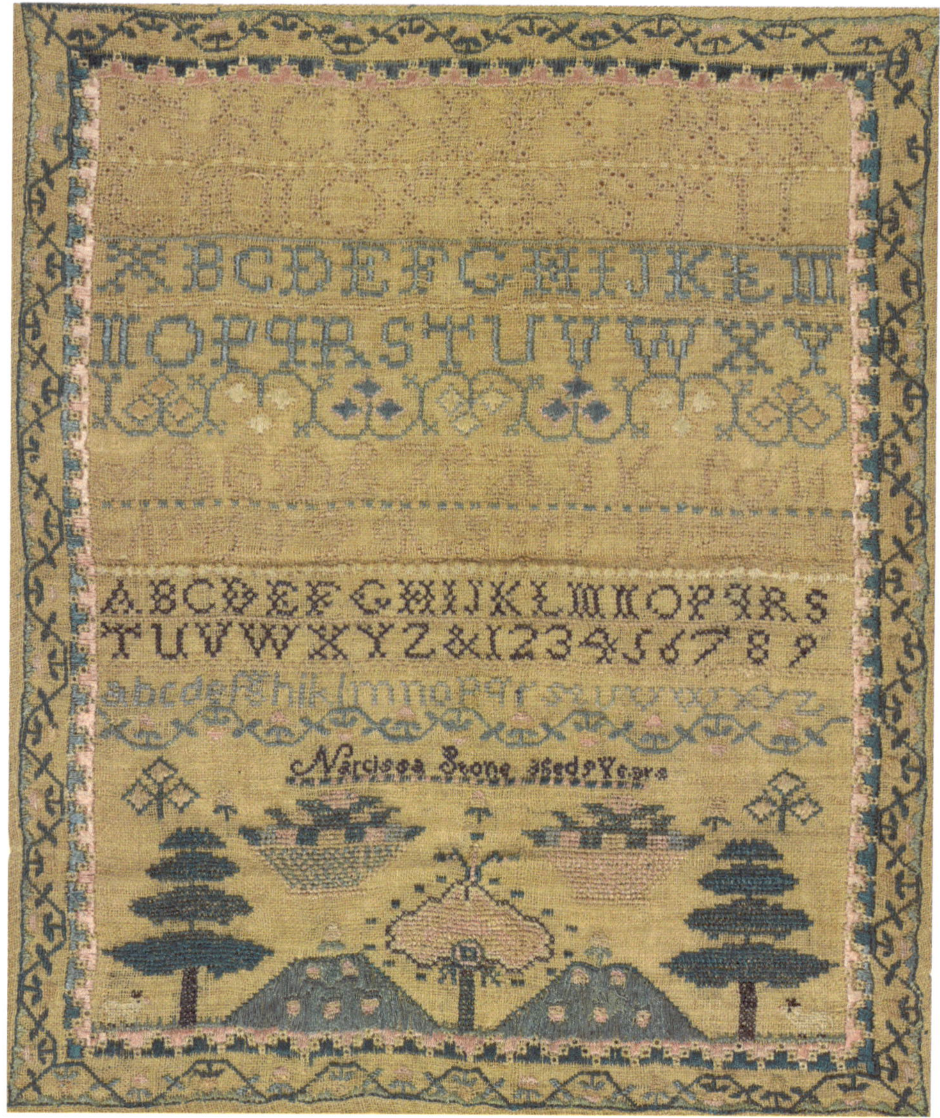

Narcissa Stone was the second-born of the ten children of Captain Daniel Stone and Nancy Hinkley of Harpswell, Maine. Of their seven daughters, she was the only one to live well into adulthood. The samplers of the Stone daughters are all quite similar, no doubt stitched under the eye of the same teacher. This was very likely in the school of Catherine Palmer Putnam, which she ran in Brunswick from 1808 to 1829. Narcissa was an assistant there for many years. When she was four, her father, formerly a sea captain but by then a prominent Brunswick merchant, built the house where she spent the rest of her life, now known as the Captain Daniel Stone Inn. Orphaned by the deaths of her father in 1825 and mother in 1828, Narcissa became responsible for her younger siblings and, trained in business by her father, became actively involved in real estate and part ownership and management of a factory, the Brunswick Company. She died in 1877 after suffering a stroke, with only one sibling, Daniel, outliving her.

According to George Palmer Putnam, the publishing magnate who was Catherine Putnam's grandson, Catherine and Narcissa met as students at Mrs. Rowson's school in Boston and remained fast friends throughout their lives. Since Narcissa was just six when Catherine married Henry Putnam in 1807, this is surely apocryphal. Catherine's husband was an invalid for most of the years of their marriage; she had to find a way to raise money to support their five children. It was supposedly Narcissa that informed Catherine that Brunswick was in need of a school and made arrangements for her to rent the academy's first location from her father. Again, this is unlikely, since Narcissa was only seven when the school opened. After the school burned in 1829, Catherine relocated to New York City and continued to teach, perhaps into the 1840s. She died in 1869.

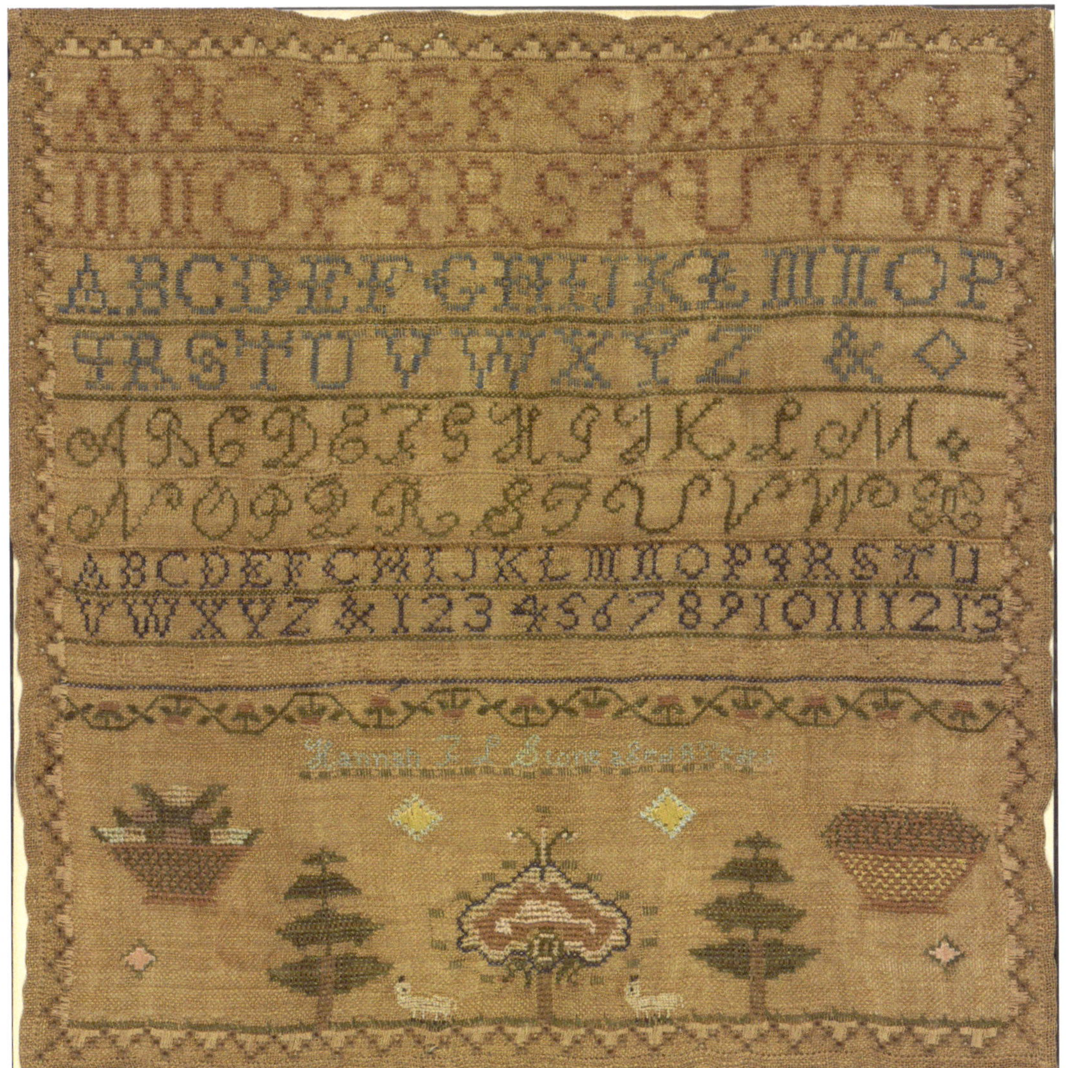

Hannah Stone (1817–1840)
Marking sampler, 1825
Probably worked at the school of Catherine Hunt Putnam, Brunswick, Maine
Silk thread on linen
Cross, queen, straight, and satin stitches
18 ½ x 18
Collection of the Portland Museum of Art, Museum purchase, 1973, 7

Hannah Stone was the seventh of the ten mostly unfortunate children of Captain Daniel Stone and Nancy Hinkley. By the time Hannah was born in Brunswick, her elder sister Narcissa was actively involved in teaching at the school of Catherine Palmer Putnam, where Hannah no doubt made this sampler. Hannah was still quite young when the deaths of her parents made her an orphan, and was largely raised by Narcissa. Hannah died at the age of twenty-three, the same year as her younger sister, Eliza.

Two other Stone daughters, Lydia and Rebecca, also worked samplers, both owned by the Portland Museum of Art. Because of the notable similarity to the works of their sisters, they are not included here. Lydia, born in 1807, was the fourth child of well-to-do Captain Daniel Stone and Nancy Hinkley. Like five of her six sisters, she did not live long enough to marry, dying at the age of just nineteen in 1826. Rebecca was born in 1815, a year after the eldest of the Stone children (their first Rebecca) died at age fourteen. As was the custom of the time, the name was used again. This Rebecca was only slightly more long-lived than the sister she was named for. Rebecca died in 1834, at the age of nineteen. She is buried with her parents and siblings in Brunswick. The series of deaths in the Stone family, occurring during the young adult years, may indicate that they were afflicted with tuberculosis, at the time a very common cause of deaths, especially in that age group. It frequently afflicted whole families, killing one member at a time, rather than creating a cluster of deaths in quick succession.

Mary D. Stone (1809–1828)
Marking sampler, circa 1819
Probably worked at the school of Catherine Palmer Putnam, Brunswick, Maine
Silk thread on linen
Cross, queen, straight, and satin stitches
24 x 18
Collection of the Portland Museum of Art, Museum purchase, 1973, 5

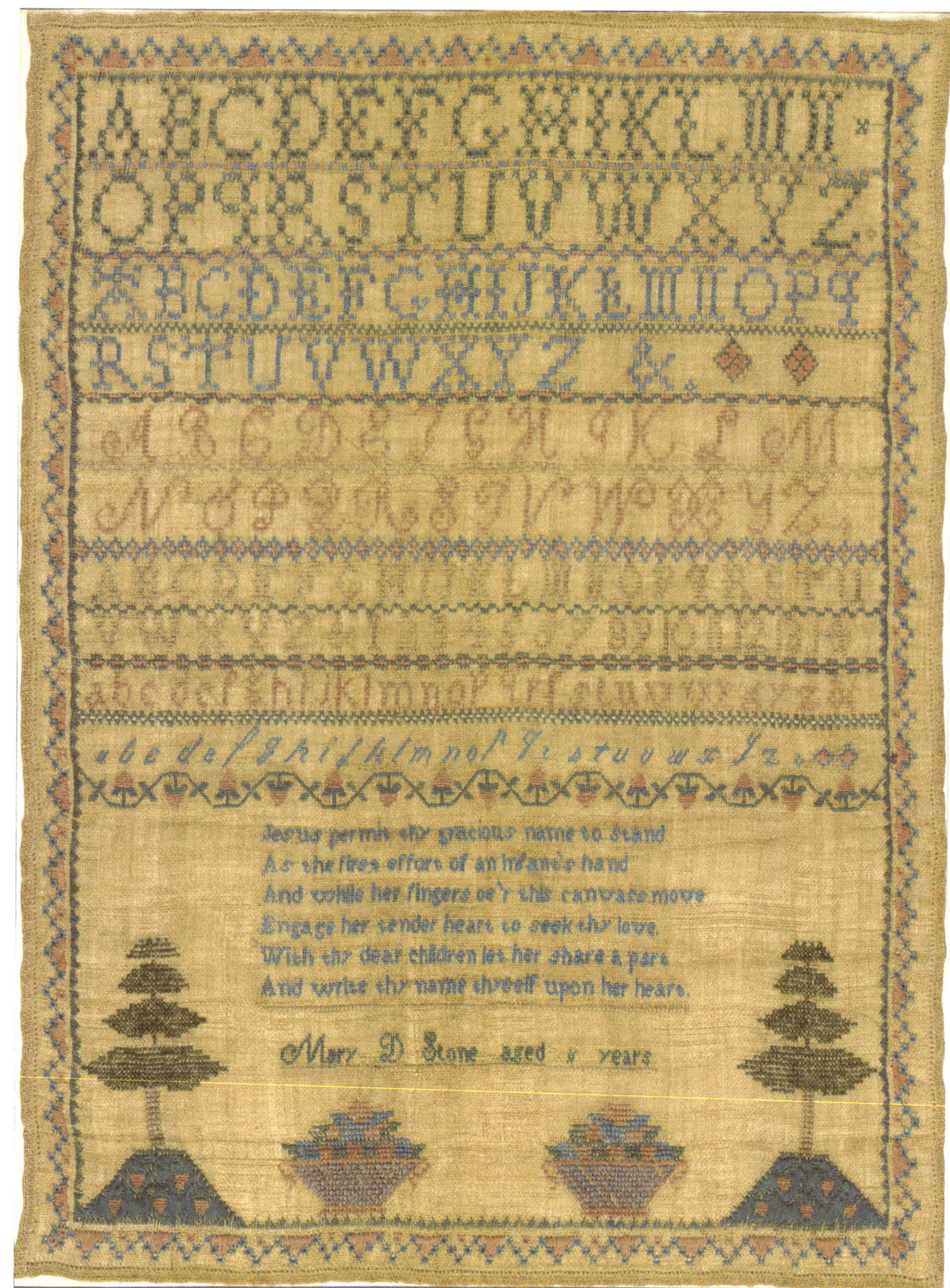

Mary Stone was born in 1809, the fifth of the ten children of wealthy merchant Daniel Stone and his wife, Nancy Hinkley. Like her sisters Lydia and Rebecca, she died at the age of nineteen. Only one of the ten children of the Stone family had children of his own. The youngest child, Daniel, lived to the age of sixty-six and was the father of just one daughter. Like her sisters, Mary likely stitched her sampler under the attentive supervision of her older sister Narcissa and Mrs. Catherine Palmer Putnam.

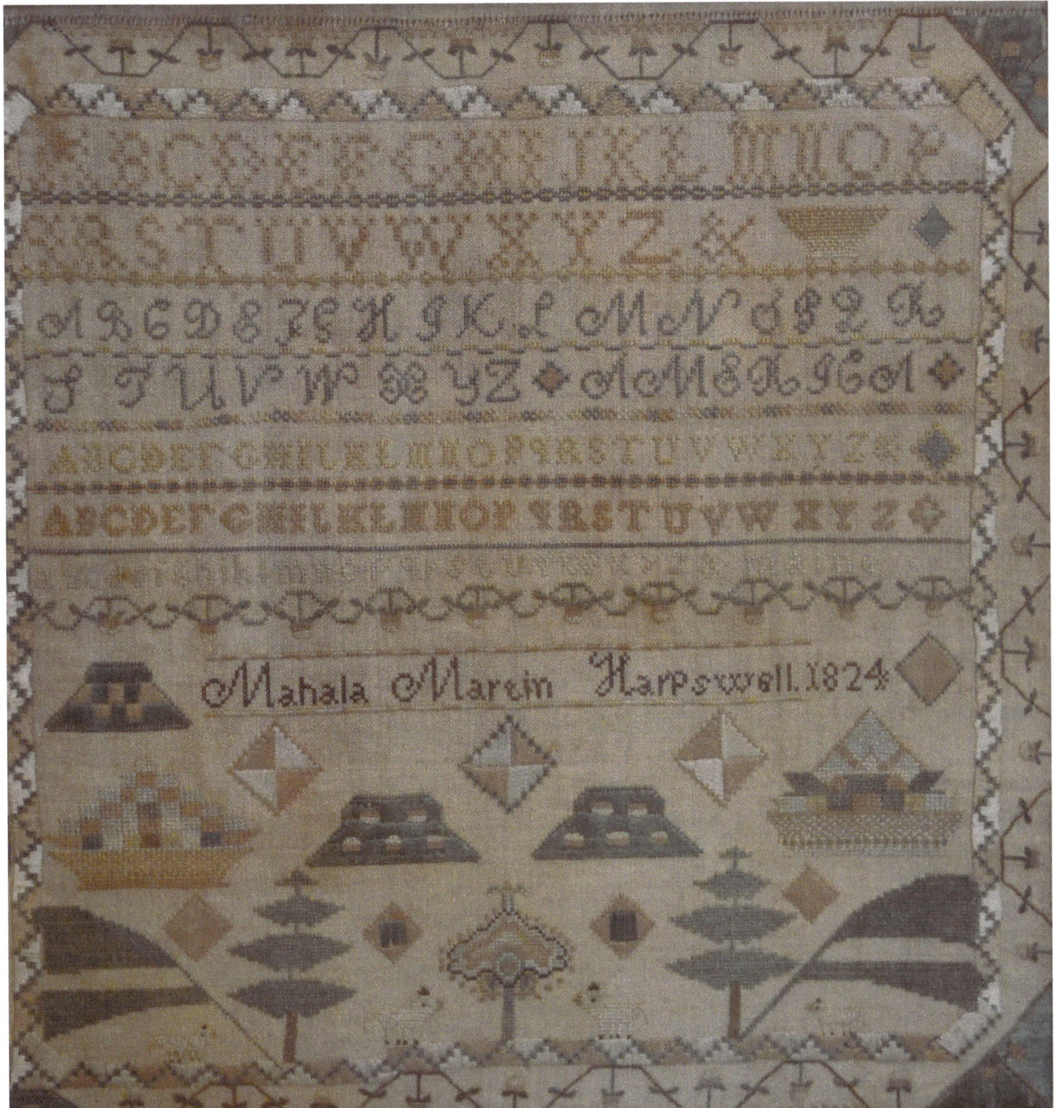

Mahala Martin (1814–?)
Marking sampler, 1824
Possibly worked at the school of Catherine Palmer Putnam, Brunswick, Maine
Silk thread on linen
Cross, satin, straight, and queen stitches
16 ¾ x 17 ¼
Collection of Burton W. Pearl

Mahala Martin's sampler was once part of the Theodore Kapnek collection so a photograph of it is included in Glee Krueger's *A Gallery of American Samplers* (p. 63). (For quite some time it had been believed that Mahala's last name was Marein, making it difficult to research her background.) Mahala was the daughter of Captain Clement and his wife, Abigail Durgin Martin of Harpswell, Maine. Mahala married Captain Robert Giveen of nearby Brunswick in 1838. Their only child, a son, was born in 1841. Mahala died December 5, 1852, in Brunswick. Her lively sampler features tiered pine trees and a carnation-like object that is more typical of samplers made closer to the southern Maine/New Hampshire border. No Harpswell teachers are known, but the twin towns of Topsham and Brunswick are close by. Mahala's remarkably quirky work at first glance seems to have nothing in common with the Stone sisters' samplers. A closer examination reveals that her carnation, trees, and strawberry divider are all nearly identical to Narcissa's (p. 98), making Mahala a likely student of Mrs. Putnam's school in Brunswick. Another possibility is that she was a student of Miss Eliza Chapman, who ran a rival Brunswick school from 1823 to 1829, and could have been copying elements of Putnam's designs, but adding her own unusual flavor. Eliza was the daughter of Abner and Lydia Thorndike Chapman and was born August 31, 1799, in Beverly, Massachusetts.

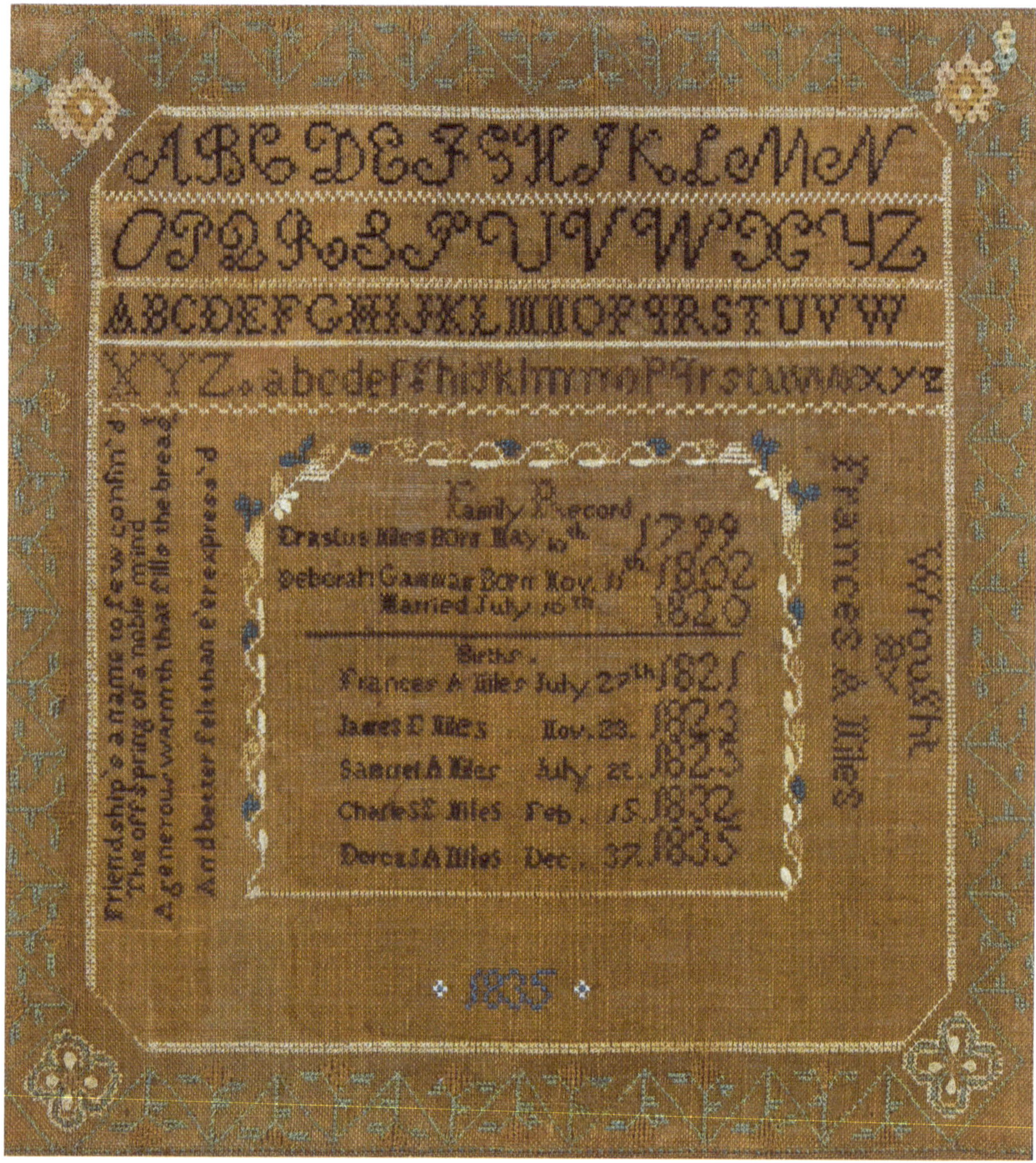

Frances A. Niles (1821–1860)
Family register sampler, 1835
Probably worked at the school of Elizabeth Fields, Topsham, Maine
Silk thread on linen
Cross, queen, and satin stitches
17 ½ x 16 ½
Collection of the Pejepscot Historical Society

Frances Niles was born July 27, 1821, in Topsham, Maine, the eldest daughter and second of the seven children of Erastus and Deborah Gammon Niles. Erastus had served as a musician in the War of 1812 and then became an inn operator. In 1844, Frances married Aaron Adams of Brunswick. They relocated to Harpswell, where he became a very financially successful landlord. He died in 1860, leaving Frances with three still-young sons. In 1874, she remarried, to Abijah Dean, a Malden, Massachusetts, butcher. According to the 1880 census, Frances was living with Abijah, along with two of her married children, their spouses, and a total of five young grandchildren. Frances died in 1914 and is buried with her first husband in Brunswick.

Mrs. Elizabeth Fields, widow of English barrister Robert Fields, who practiced law in Boston for a period of time, relocated to a rented mansion in Topsham in 1831 and opened a boarding and day school that apparently offered a solid academic education as well as instruction in "Sewing of various kinds, embroidery and fancy, in all its branches; also lace mending and fine darning, plain and fancy knitting." (*History of Brunswick, Topsham, and Harpswell* by George Augustus Wheeler, 1878, p. 491). Both the school and Mrs. Fields were well-respected; it closed a year after she resigned its management in 1843. Perhaps the very attractive, well-balanced design of Frances's sampler could be attributed to her.

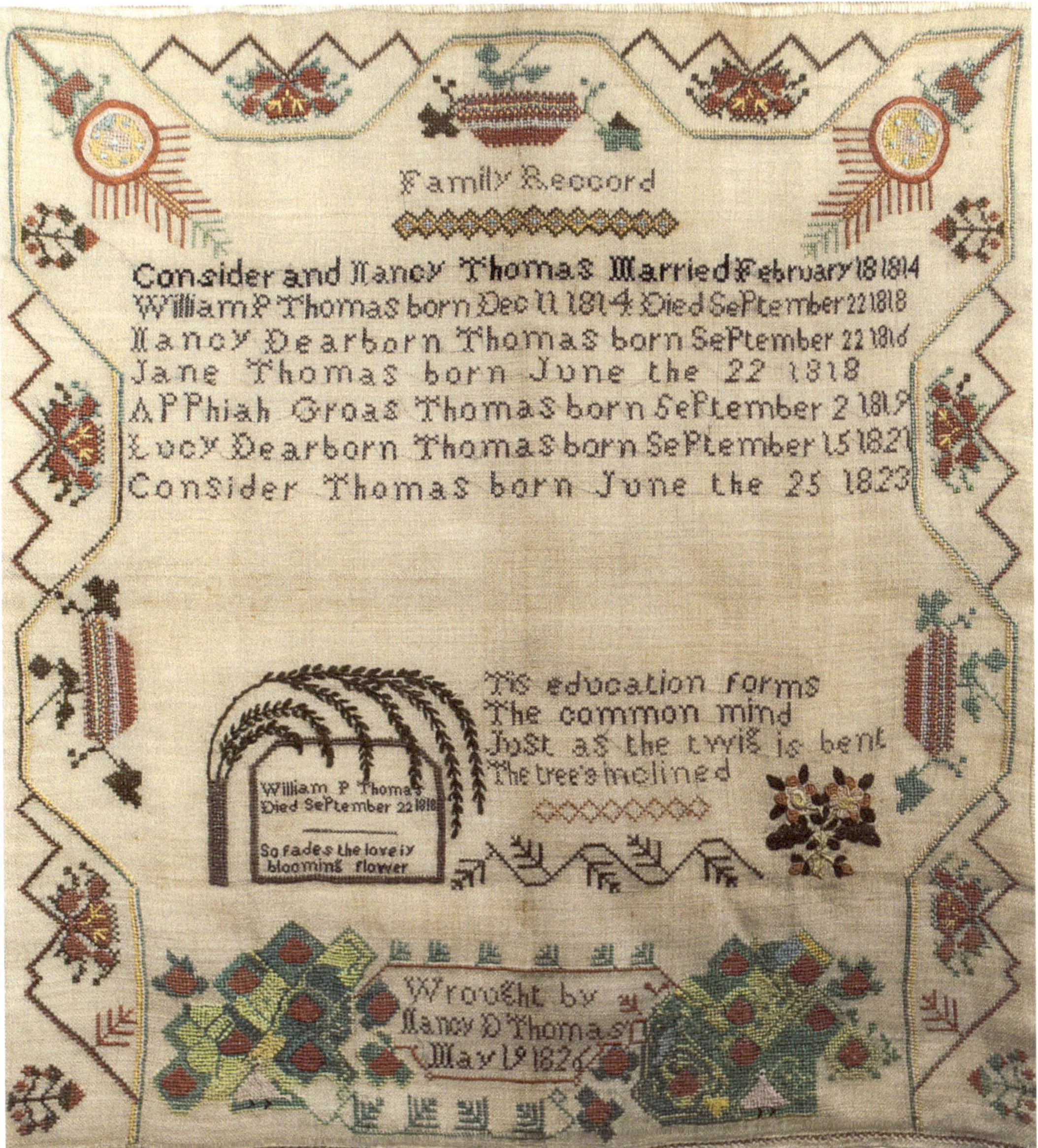

Nancy Dearborn Thomas
(1816–?)
Family register sampler, 1826
Probably worked in Brunswick
or Bath, Maine
(school unknown)
Silk thread on linen
Cross, satin, lazy daisy, and
straight stitches
Collection of the Maine
Historical Society

Nancy Dearborn Thomas was probably born in Brunswick, but the family later relocated to nearby Bath, Maine. Nancy's father was a merchant; her brother Consider became a mariner. Nancy does not appear in known records after the date of her sampler. The same year she completed her sampler, another sister, Sarah, was born, and a couple of years later her brother George was born. Since they were never added to Nancy's work in the ample space still available, perhaps she died very shortly after its completion date. Her father died in Bath in 1855 and is buried with her mother, who died in 1838. In 1870, her sister Sarah, a milliner, was living in Illinois with her twenty-year-old son, Freddie Radcliffe. According to the 1880 census, Sarah, Freddie, and brother Consider were all living with sister Apphia and her husband, George Clark, in San Francisco. Nancy's sampler is highly unusual; it appears to have nothing in common with other works from the Brunswick/Bath area.

Eliza Ann Silsby (1806–1837)
Marking sampler, 1817
Possibly worked at the Bath Female Academy, Bath, Maine
Silk thread on linen
Cross over one and cross over two threads, satin, and outline stitches
17 x 17
Collection of Burton W. Pearl

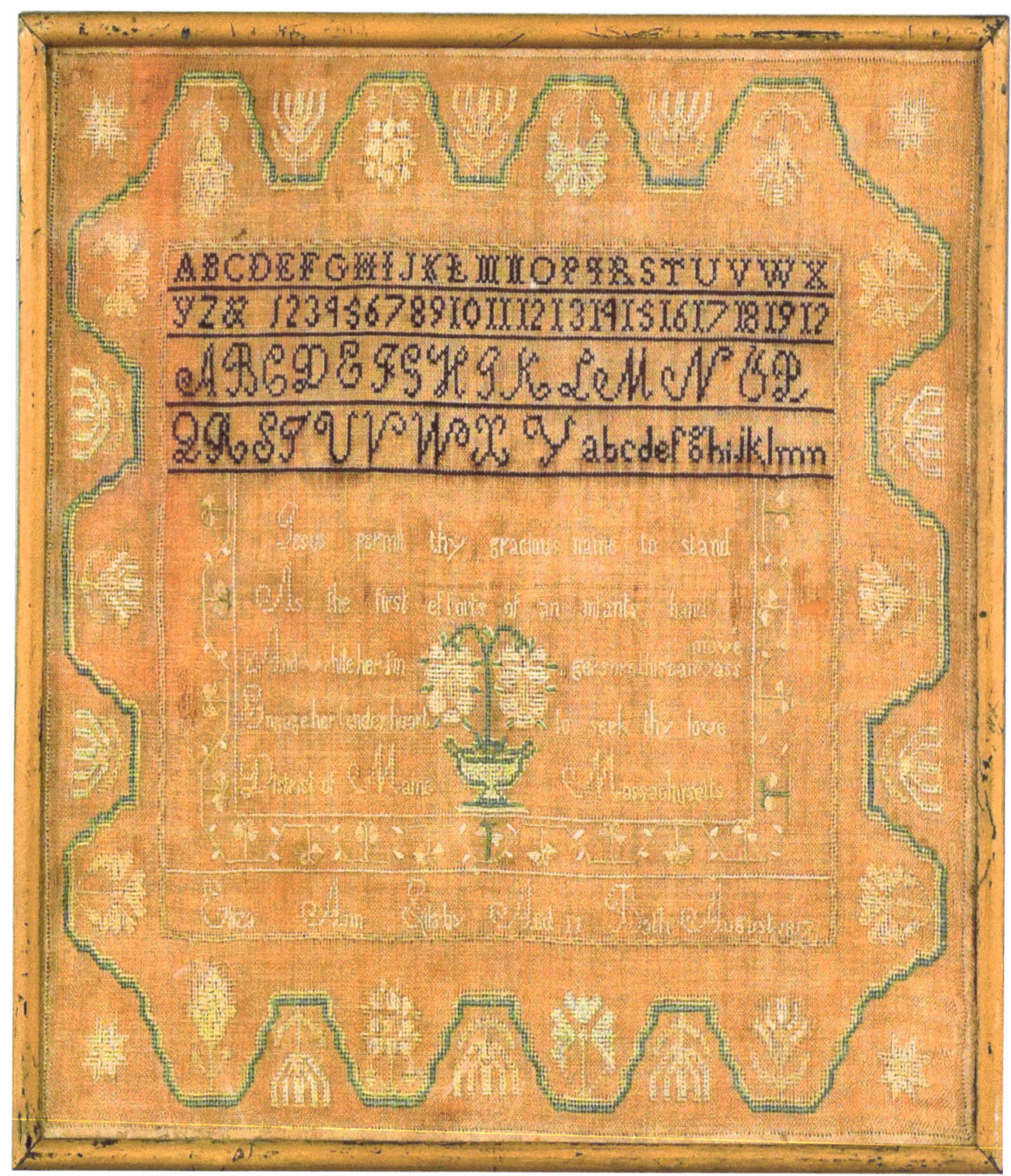

Eliza Ann Silsby quite correctly noted that she made her sampler in the District of Maine, Massachusetts, since statehood for Maine was still three years away in 1817. She was the daughter of Bliss and Bethiah Silsby of Bath, born February 14, 1806. She married James Couillard of Bath on April 10, 1828. They were the parents of a daughter and two sons. She died there on July 2, 1837. All three of Eliza's children grew to adulthood, her daughter living until 1914.

The Bath Female Academy advertised in 1808 that it was intended "for the instruction of females in useful and elegant accomplishments," and that the preceptresses were Harriet Low and Miss Peck. The Bath Female Academy received a substantial grant of land from the state of Massachusetts which it then sold to finance its early operations. In 1810, Lucy Hildreth stitched a family register sampler in Bath that sold at Cyr Auction in 2003. The samplers of Lucy and Eliza have a few common features, especially the uppercase cursive alphabet, and may both have been made at the academy.

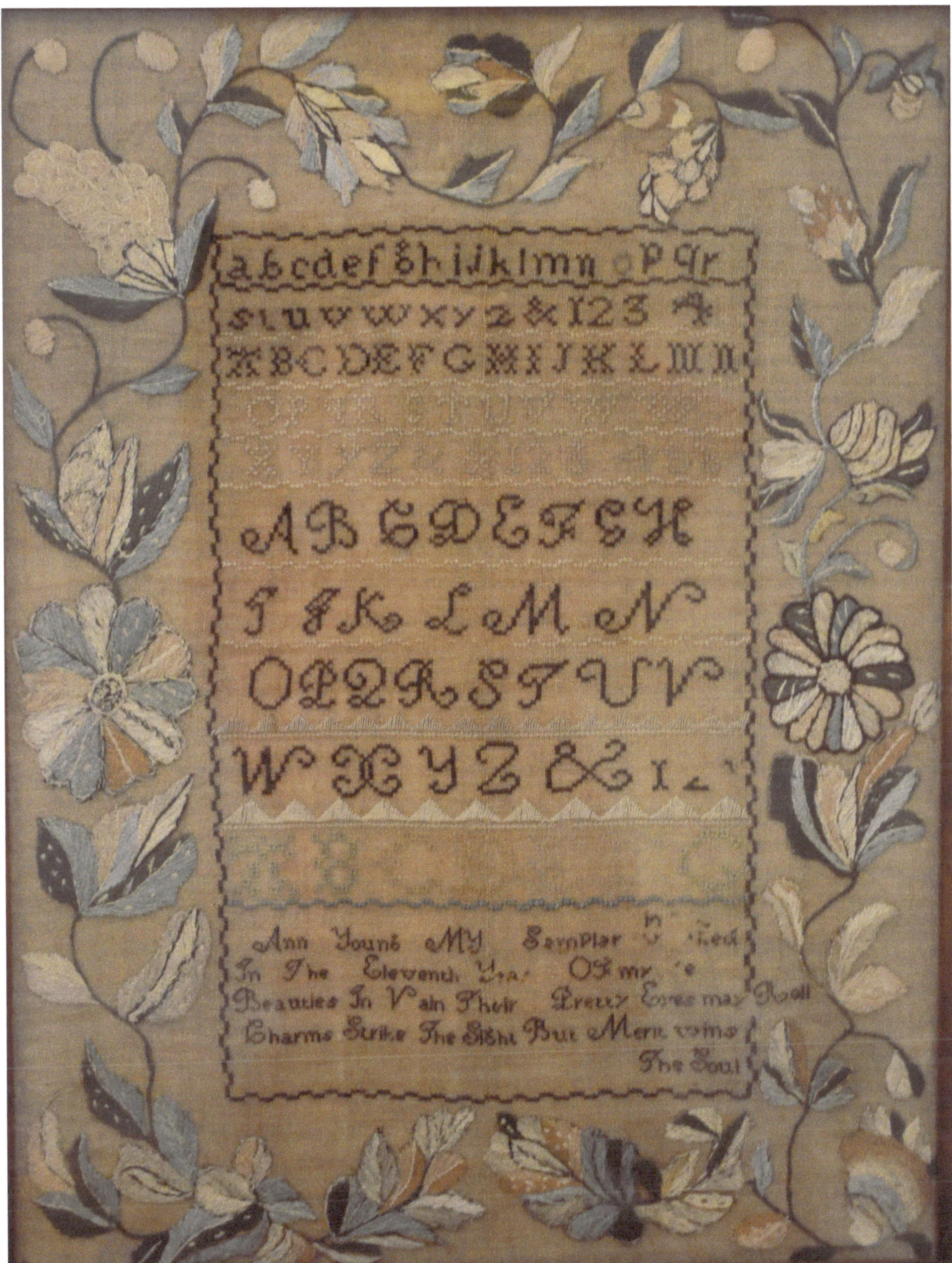

Ann Young (dates unknown)
Marking sampler, circa 1830
Possibly worked in Waldoboro or Hebron, Maine
(school unknown)
Silk thread on linen
Cross, satin, straight, and outline stitches
21 ½ x 16 ½
Collection of Burton W. Pearl

Ann Young, unfortunately, elected to tell us almost nothing about herself, making it hard to conclusively link this very attractive sampler to a particular girl. She might have been the Ann Young, daughter of George and Ann Young, who was born in 1798 in Waldoboro and died there in 1815, or possibly the Ann Young who married Parker Soper, a shoemaker, in Hebron, Maine, in 1822 and was the mother of at least four children. Her sampler shows a high level of sophistication, both in its design and stitchery. A complex border like hers, rendered in satin stitch rather than the more formulaic cross stitch, required a much higher degree of skill. The resemblance between her border and that of Abigail Leavitt (p. 88) may be a random coincidence—or it may indicate that the girls were taught by the same artistic preceptress.

Lucy Ann Trask (1823–1884)
Marking sampler, 1833
Probably worked in Wiscasset, Maine (school unknown)
Silk thread on linen
Cross, satin, Algerian eye, running, and stem stitches
17 x 17
Collection of Burton W. Pearl

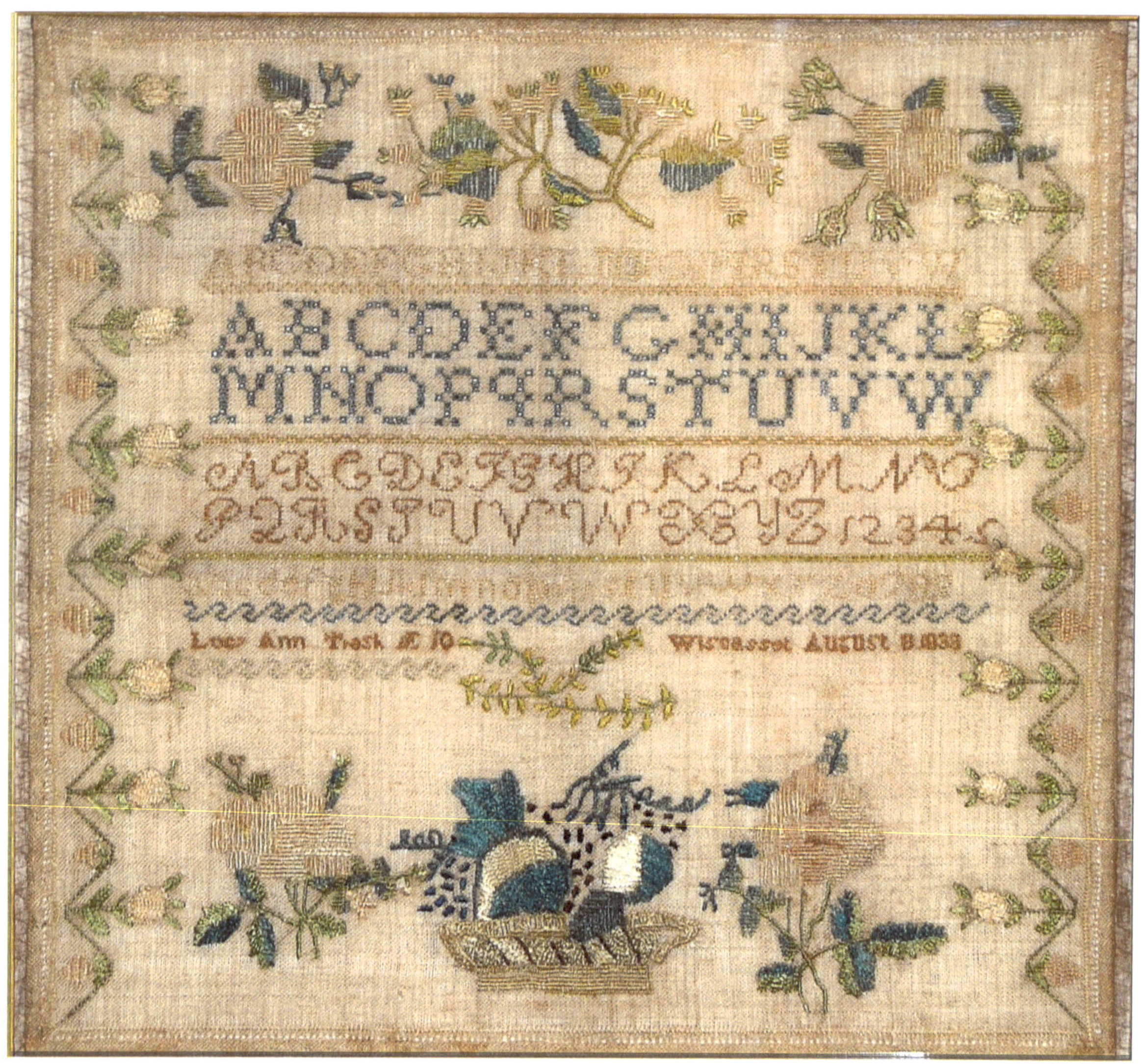

Lucy Ann Trask was the daughter of John and Hannah Nael Trask, who were married in Wiscasset in 1819. In 1842, Lucy married sea captain George W. Chapman, who had been born in Saco, Maine, in 1814. They were the parents of a daughter and a son. George died of paralysis in Hyde Park, Massachusetts, in 1868. According to the 1870 U.S. Census, Lucy was living in the home of her son, George W. Trask, a bookkeeper in Hyde Park. She died of "apoplexy" there on June 11, 1884. Lucy's sampler includes some of the same alphabets as Almira Prescott's 1825 Wiscasset sampler, which is in the collection of the Maine State Museum but not included in this exhibition. They also share similar dividing bands, and Lucy's includes a pair of leafy sprigs that closely resemble a single sprig on Almira's work. The tall stalked flowers in Lucy's border are reminiscent of those on Nancy Chamberlain's 1819 sampler, worked in nearby Bristol, Maine (p. 111).

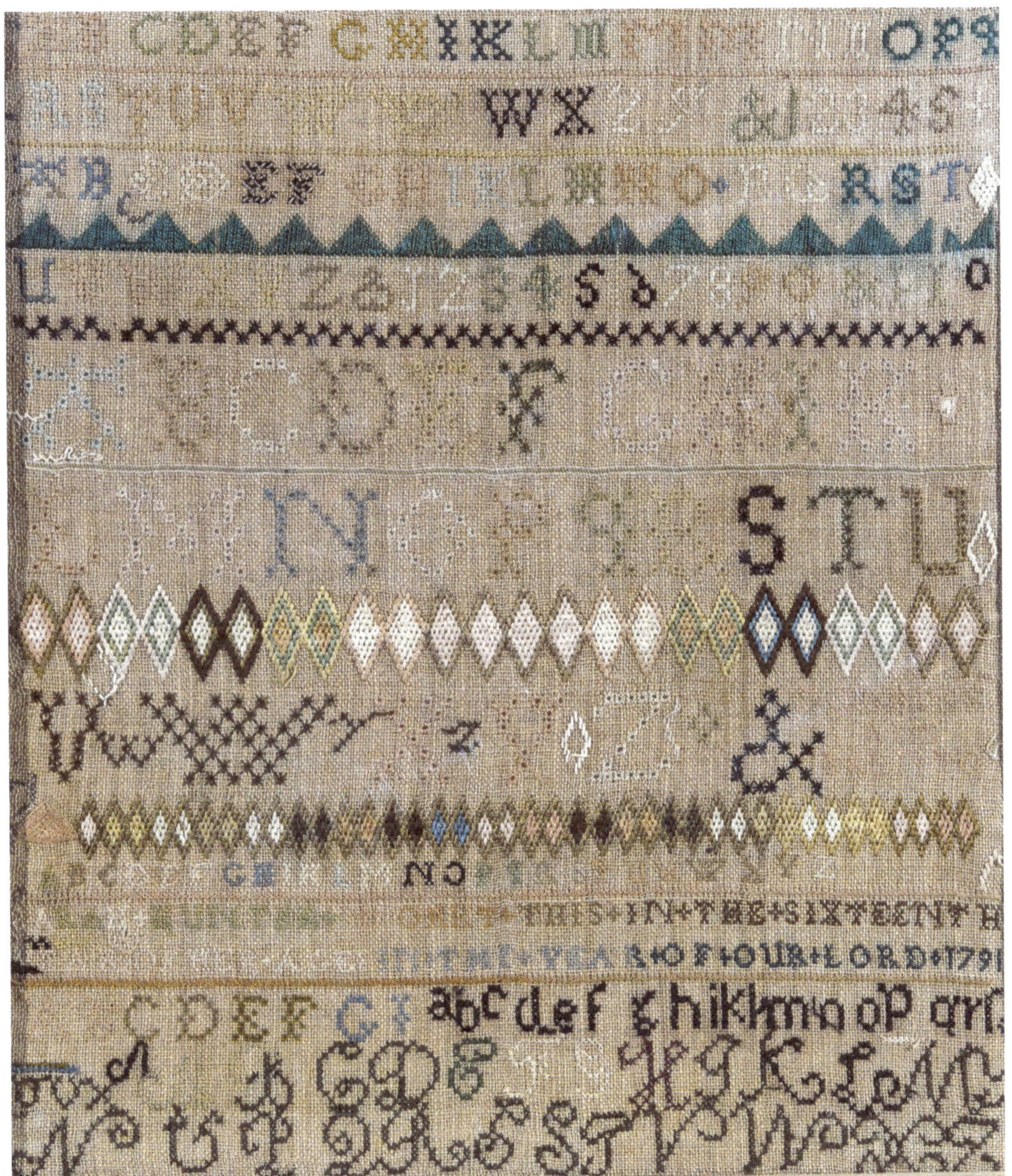

Sarah Hunter (1775–1837)
Marking sampler, 1791
Worked at the school of Mrs. Brunto (Mary Bruntin/Brunton), Bristol, Maine
Silk thread on linen
Cross, satin, and Algerian eye stitches
16 ½ x 14 ½
Collection of the Lincoln County Historical Society

Sarah Hunter's sampler is important for several reasons. The first of these is that it is currently the earliest identified Maine sampler that exhibits the iconic concentric diamond motif that appears so frequently on rural Maine works. Secondly, it names her teacher, in thread that is so faded it is difficult to read: "Taught by Mrs. Brunto." Could this be the Mary Bruntin, aged sixty to seventy, who appeared on the 1830 Bristol census as a head of household, living with another woman between the ages of sixty and seventy? No other records have been identified for Mary, but Brunton (the more typical spelling) is a very unusual name in New England. Sarah's sampler also exhibits an oversized sawtooth border that is another common feature on Maine samplers.

Sarah was born October 17, 1775, in Bristol, the daughter of Henry and Sarah Wyer Hunter. She married William Chamberlain, and they were the parents of ten children, including Sarah Ann and Nancy (pp. 108–112), both sampler makers whose works are included in this exhibition. Sarah Hunter died May 1, 1837.

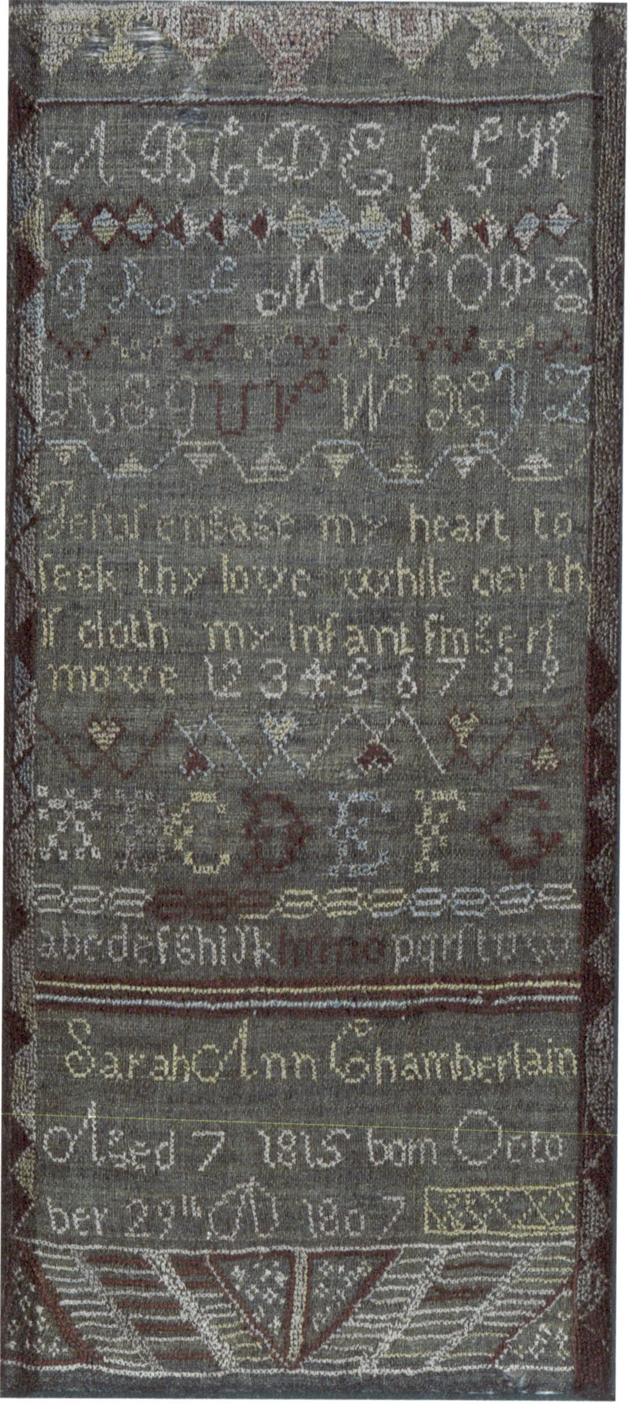

Sarah Ann Chamberlain
(1807-after 1880)
Marking sampler, 1815
Worked in Bristol, Maine, possibly at the school of Mrs. Brunto (Mary Bruntin/Brunton)
Silk thread on linsey-woolsey
Cross and Algerian eye stitches
18 x 8 ¼
Collection of the Lincoln County Historical Society

Sarah Ann Chamberlain, daughter of sampler maker Sarah Hunter (p. 107), stitched three samplers, all owned by the Lincoln County Historical Society (see also pp. 109 and 110). Her bright linsey-woolsey work—made very far downeast for this type of ground—was stitched when she was just seven. It demonstrates a youthful enthusiasm, but lacks the competence she would be able to demonstrate even just a year later.

Sarah Ann was born October 29, 1807, in Bristol. She became the second wife of Alexander Fossett, a veteran of the War of 1812, who had one young son by his first wife. They were the parents of two more children, a son and a daughter, before Alexander died in 1850. Sarah never remarried. In 1880, she was the head of a household that included her son, her married but perhaps widowed daughter, and that daughter's son. No record has been found for her death.

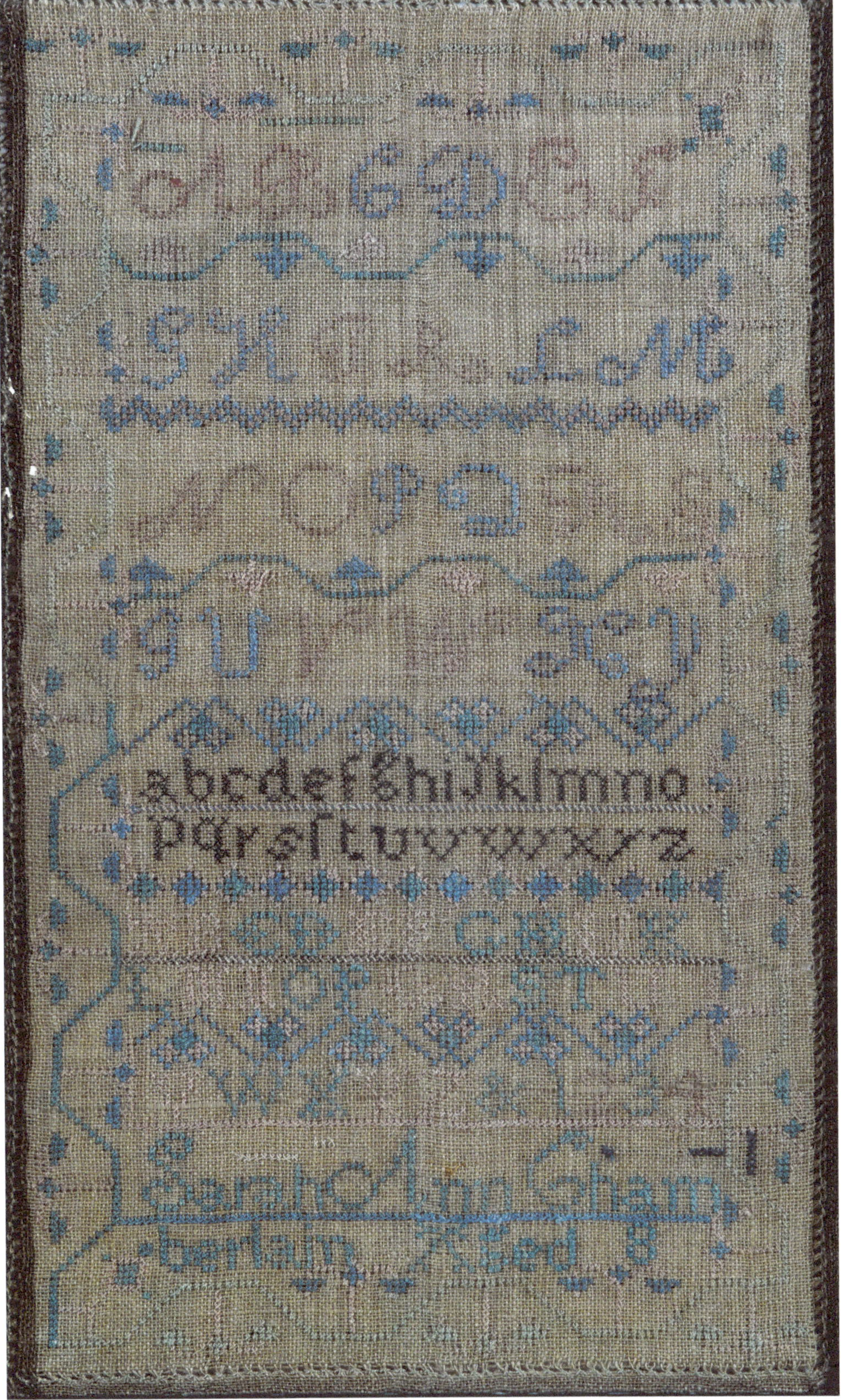

Sarah Ann Chamberlain (1807-after 1880)
Marking sampler, 1815
Worked in Bristol, Maine, possibly at the school of Mrs. Brunto (Mary Bruntin/Brunton)
Silk thread on linen
Cross and hem stitches
16 x 10
Collection of the Lincoln County Historical Society

Sarah Ann Chamberlain's second sampler effort dates from when she was eight. Her meandering fruited border is quite distinctive, but her heart band echoes a similar one on her earlier work.

Sarah Ann Chamberlain (1807–after 1880)
Marking sampler, 1815
Worked in Bristol, Maine, possibly at the school of
Mrs. Brunto (Mary Bruntin/Brunton)
Silk thread on linen
Cross, Algerian eye, satin, padded satin,
stem, and chain stitches
15 ¼ x 17 ½
Collection of the Lincoln County Historical Society

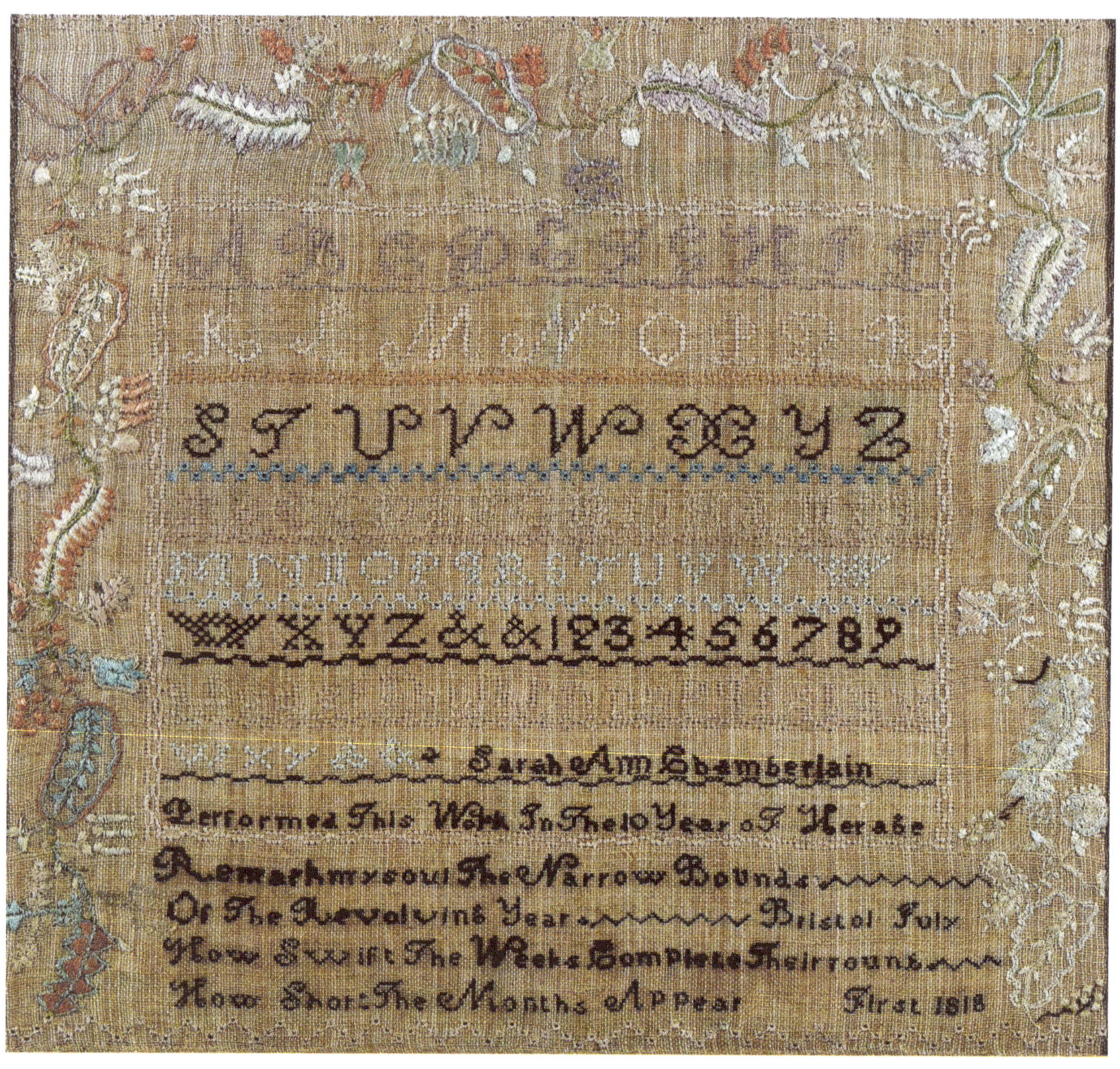

With this work, at the young age of ten, **Sarah Ann Chamberlain** demonstrated a full mastery of complex needlework. The attractive design of this lovely effort is very similar to a glorious sampler that her sister Nancy worked in 1822 in Bristol (p. 112). The teacher for these works in unknown, but she was clearly also a very talented person. Could it have been the same instructor who taught Sarah's mother?

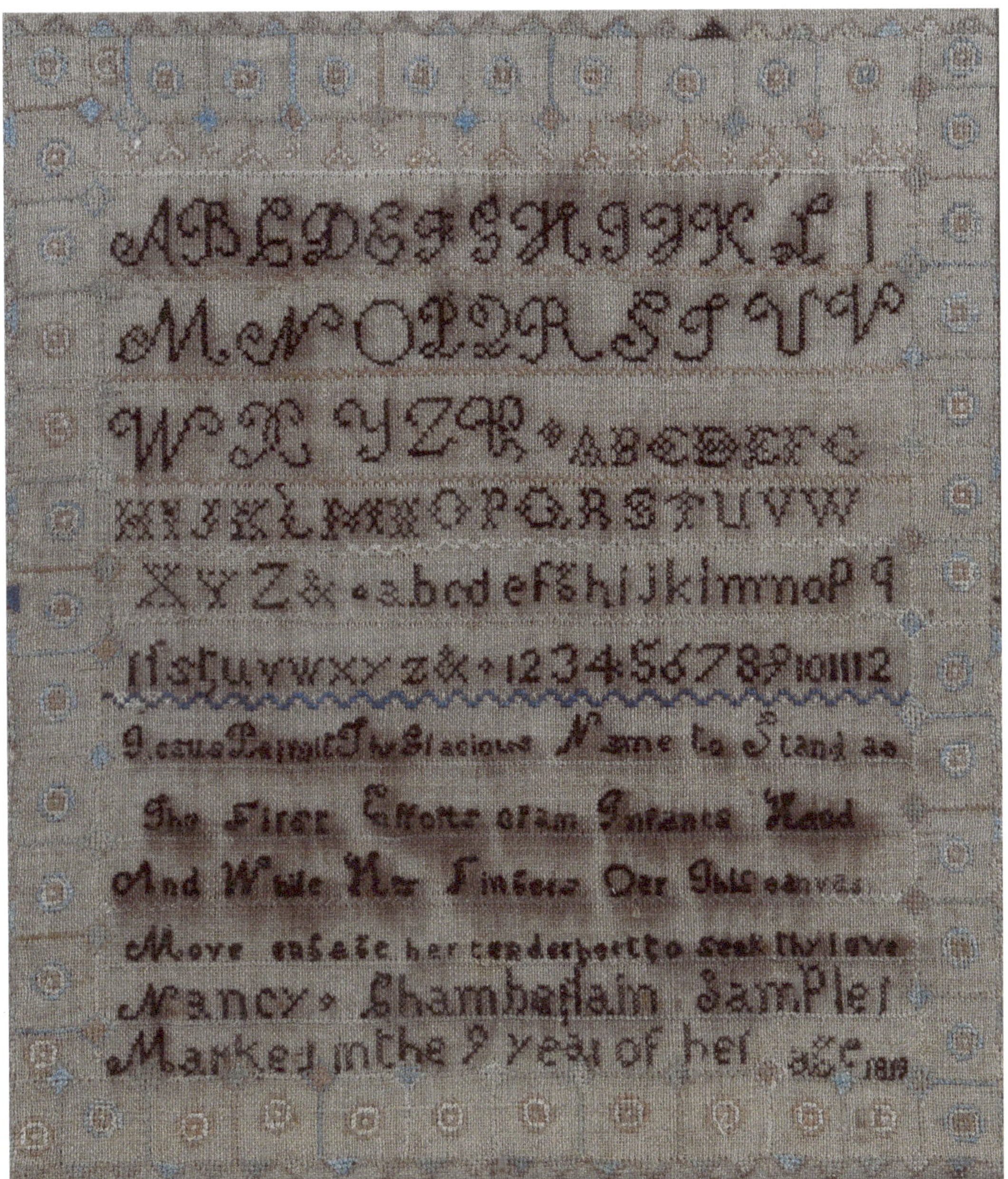

Nancy Chamberlain
(1811–1858)
Marking sampler, 1819
Worked in Bristol, Maine,
possibly at the school
of Mrs. Brunto
(Mary Bruntin/Brunton)
Silk thread on linen
Cross stitch
17 x 15 ½
Collection of the Lincoln
County Historical Society

Nancy Chamberlain was two years younger than her sister, Sarah, but no less talented. When she worked this attractive piece she was just nine years old. It features an unusual border. Nancy never married. On the 1850 census, she was residing with her elderly father and three unmarried adult siblings. She died March 3, 1858, and is buried in the Chamberlain family cemetery in Round Pond, Maine.

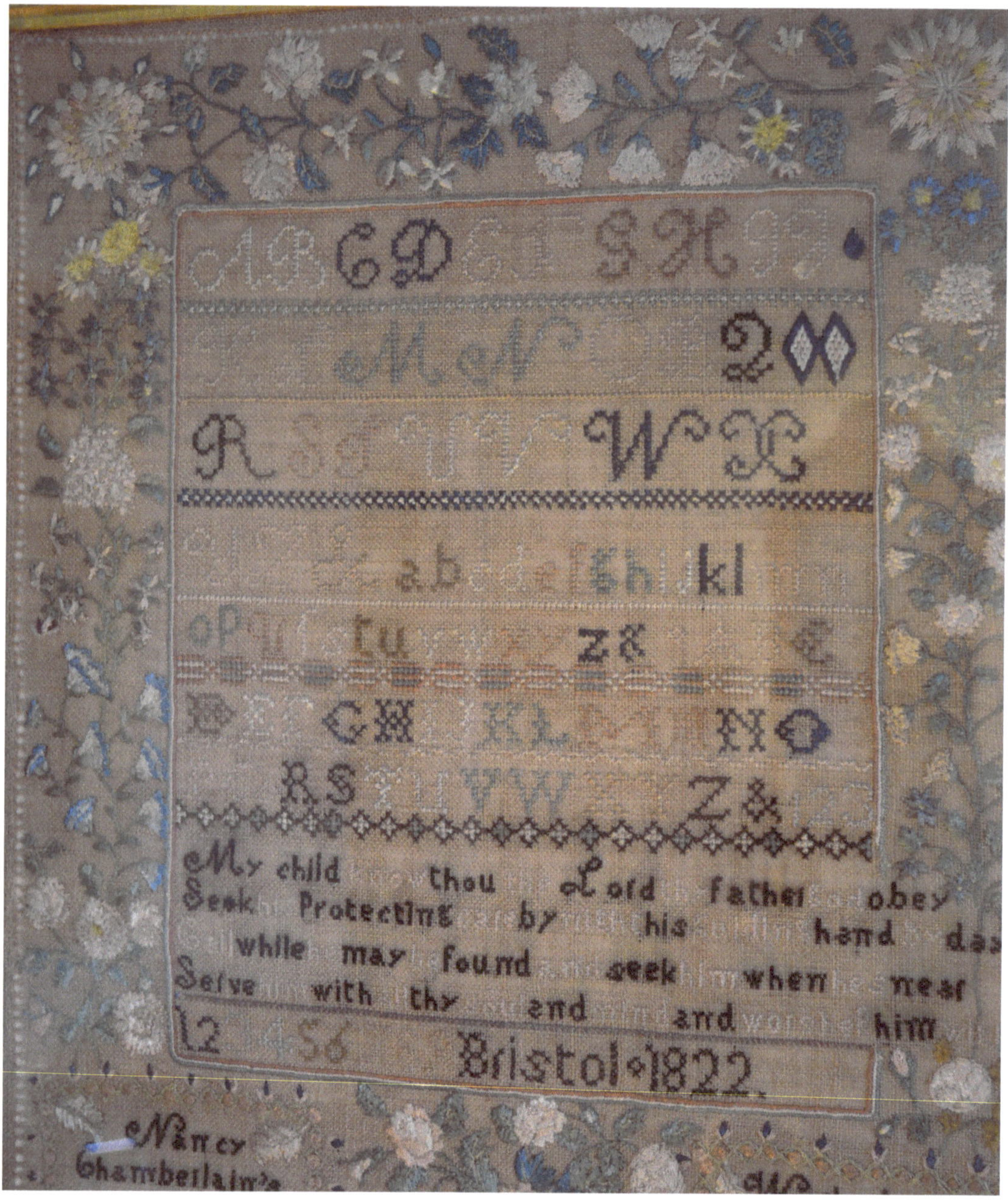

Nancy Chamberlain
(1811–1858)
Marking sampler, 1822
Worked in Bristol, Maine,
possibly at the school
of Mrs. Brunto
(Mary Bruntin/Brunton)
Silk thread on linen
Cross over one and two
threads, split, stem, and
satin stitches
19 x 16
Collection of Burton W. Pearl

Like her older sister, **Nancy Chamberlain** made more than one sampler. In this work, she demonstrated, that like Sarah, she had now fully mastered complex stitchery.

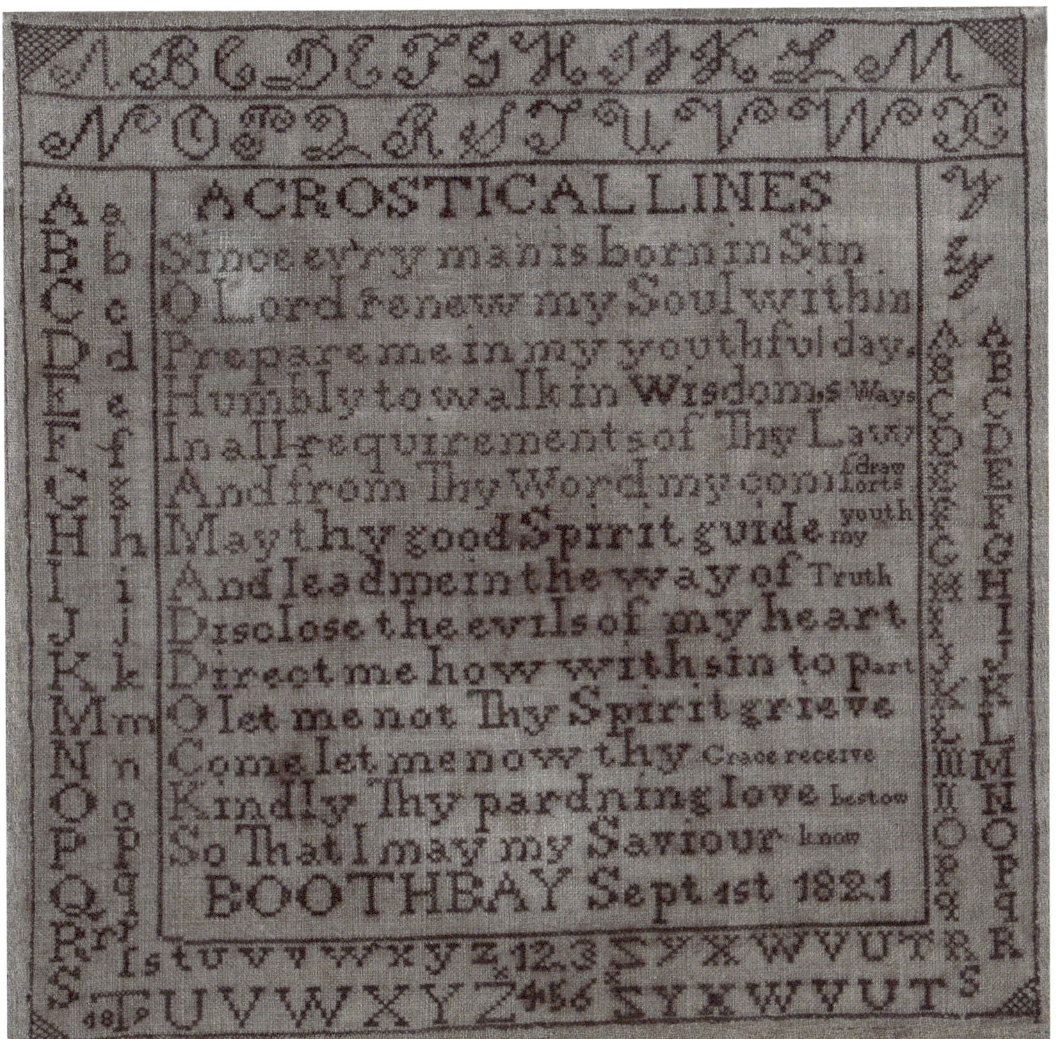

Sophia Maddocks
(1807–1881)
Acrostic marking sampler,
1821
Worked in Boothbay, Maine
(school unknown)
Silk thread on linen
Cross and straight stitches
23 ½ x17
Collection of the Boothbay
Historical Society

Sophia Maddocks's father was born in Kennebunkport but moved to Cape Newagen Island as a young man, where he married Rhuhama Pierce in 1804. Sophia was their eldest daughter, born April 16, 1807, the second of their thirteen children. Sophia's father was a successful fisherman. Cape Newagen later became Townsend, Maine, and then Southport. Her acrostic sampler is very unusual and clever. No others have been found. In 1830, Sophia married Freeman Grover, a fisherman and astute businessman who had moved to Cape Newagen as a young man. In 1837, they relocated to Flagstaff, Arizona but returned to Maine in 1844. They were the parents of eleven children (just three of them girls), of whom four died young. Sophia died September 26, 1881.

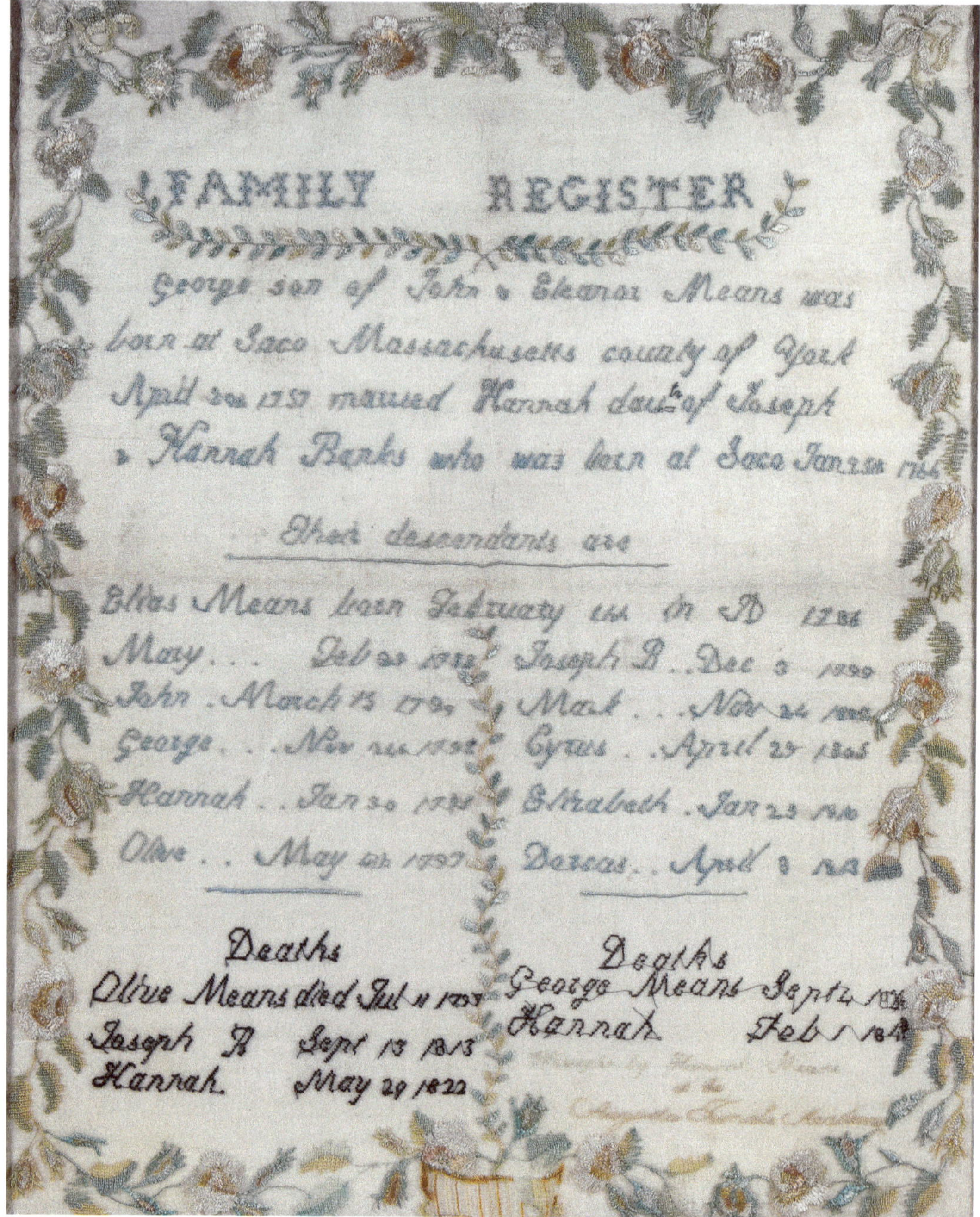

Hannah Means (1795–1822)
Family register sampler, 1815
Worked at the Cony Female Academy, Augusta, Maine
Silk thread on tiffany
Cross, satin, outline, and straight stitches
Frame attributed to Cumston & Buckminster, Saco
24 ½ x 17
Collection of the Dyer Library and Saco Museum

Hannah Means was one of the eleven children of George and Hannah Banks Means. She was born January 30, 1795. George Means was a farmer. Hannah attended the Cony Female Academy in Augusta, the city where her older brother John, a baker, had recently relocated shortly before he married. Around the same time, John married sampler maker Sarah Moody of Saco (pp. 72–74). Hannah's sampler, with its delicate leafy borders, is very typical of those that were worked at the Cony school. Not so typical is the fact that it was done on a very thin, gauzy material called tiffany, which required excellent needle skills. Hannah probably returned to Saco after her period of schooling in Augusta. She may be the female between the ages of sixteen and twenty-six who appeared on the 1820 census, living with George and Hannah. She died May 29, 1822. Her brother John named his daughter, born in 1824, after Hannah. Sometime after her death, another person added several death dates, including hers, to the sampler.

The frame for Hannah's sampler was made by the Saco furniture making company of Cumston and Buckminster. David Buckminster was married to Hannah's first cousin, Eleanor Means.

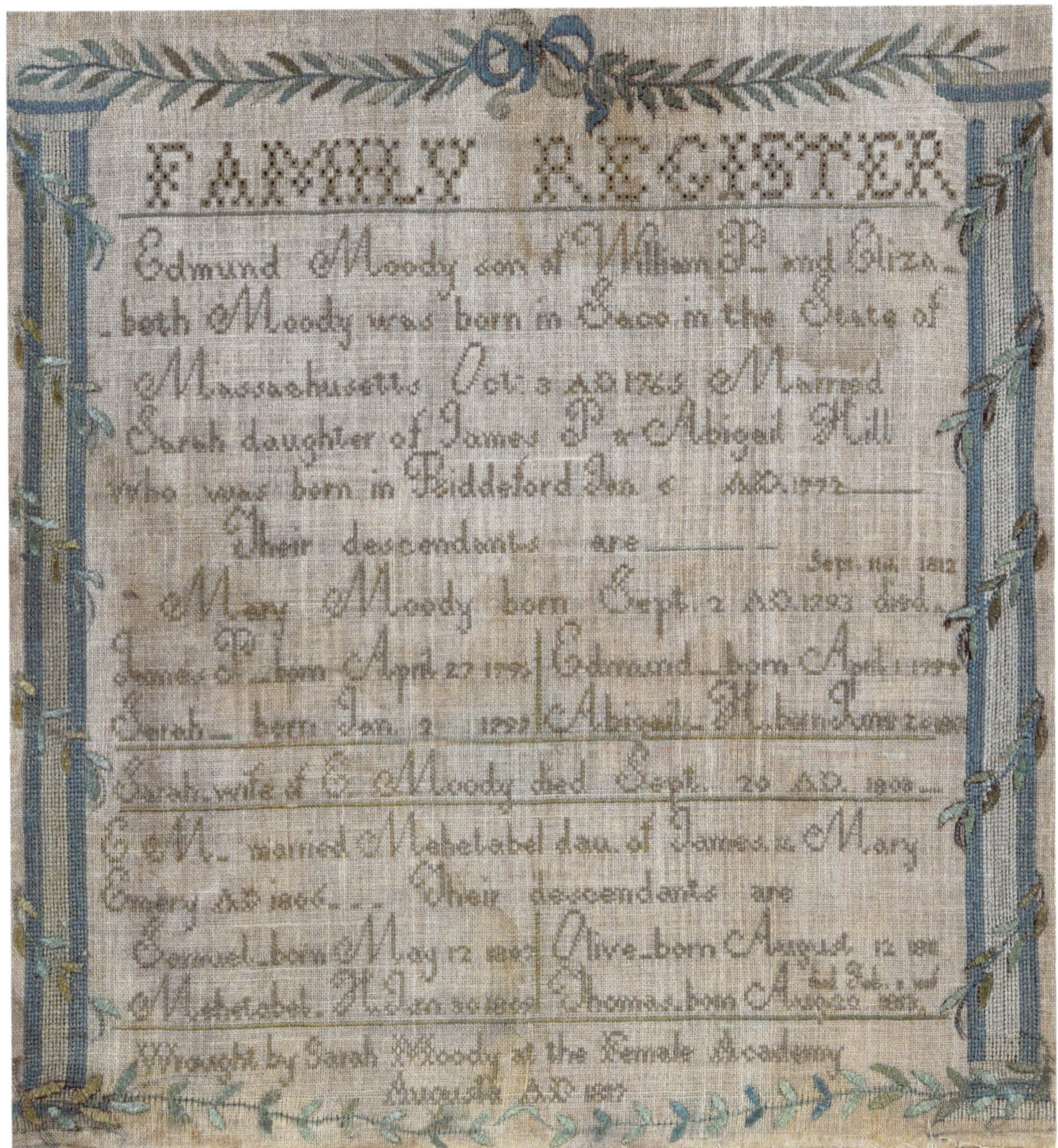

Sarah Moody (1797–1849)
Family register sampler, 1817
Worked at the Cony Female Academy, Augusta, Maine
Silk thread on linen
Cross, satin, outline, and straight stitches
25 x 17
Collection of John and Elizabeth DeSimone

Sarah Moody was the niece of the Sarah Moody who operated a school in Saco in 1812 (pp. 72–74). The younger Sarah Moody made her family register sampler at the Cony Female Academy in Augusta, and it shares stylistic elements with many of the samplers made there, including the fact that it names the school. Most of the works from that academy feature finely worked leafy vines and genealogical information.

Sarah Moody was the daughter of Edmund Moody and Sarah Hill; she was born January 2, 1797. While it may seem slightly strange that she traveled all the way to Augusta to attend the Cony Female Academy when Portland female academies existed in profusion much closer to home, Sarah had a strong family connection in the capital city. Her aunt, the woman for whom she was probably named, had moved there after marrying John Means a few years earlier. After her period of schooling, Sarah moved back to Saco. She never married; she died of consumption on June 13, 1849.

The Cony Female Academy had been founded in 1815 by the Honorable Daniel Cony, who was the father of at least four grown daughters (one of whom appears on the list of students of Misses Martin's School for Young Ladies in Portland). He wanted to find a way to provide young women with a quality education closer to home than Portland. For more on the Cony Female Academy, see pp. 9–10.

Dulcena Dunbar (1794–1880)
Family register sampler, 1816
Worked at the Cony Female Academy, Augusta, Maine
Silk thread on linen
Cross, satin, outline, and straight stitches
25 x 18 ½
Collection of the Maine Historical Society

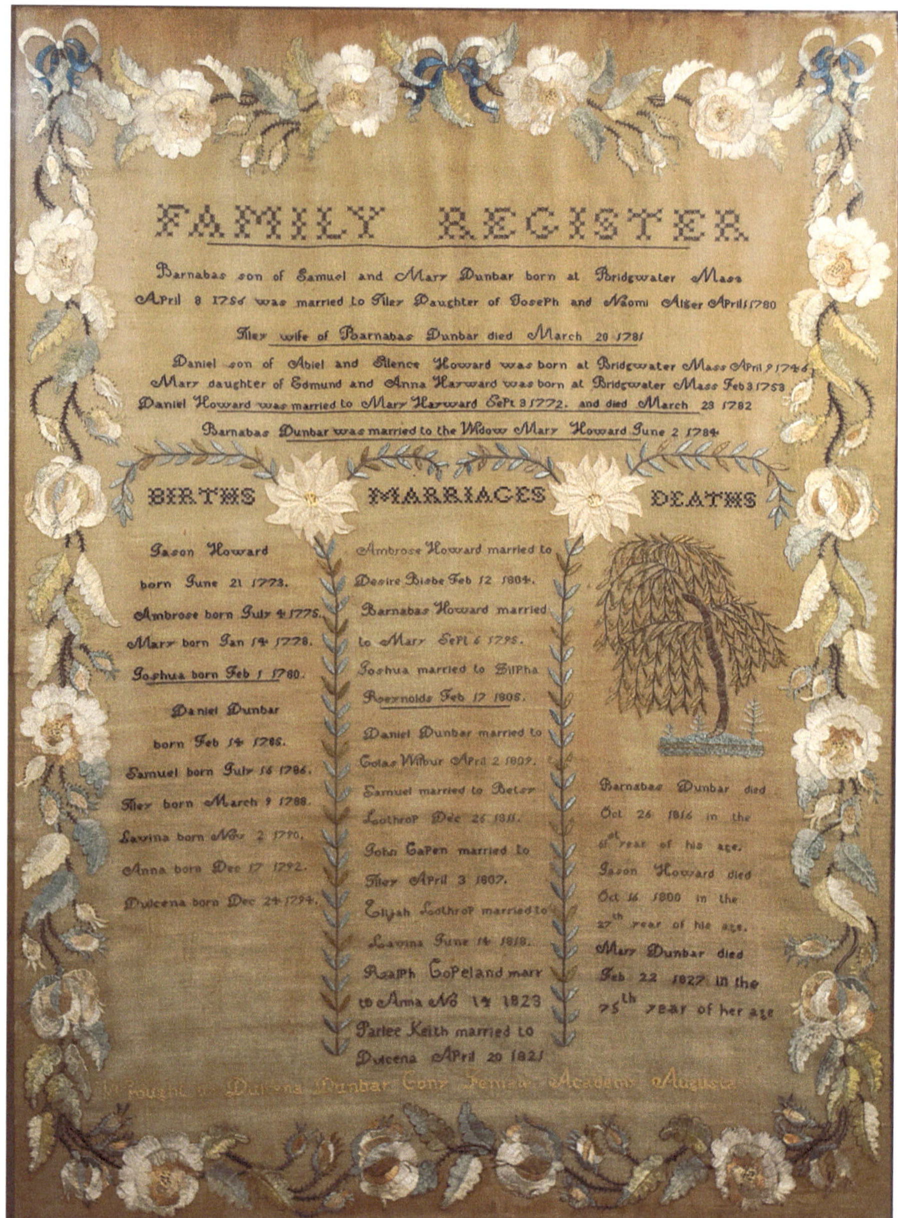

When looking at **Dulcena Dunbar**'s Cony Female Academy genealogical sampler, the first question that comes to mind is how this Massachusetts girl ended up making a sampler in central Maine. Dulcena's father Barnabus, of Bridgewater, Massachusetts, first married Silence Alger, who died only a year after their marriage, perhaps in childbirth with their first baby. Barnabus then married Mary Hayward Howard, who not only became the mother of the rest of the Dunbar children, all born in Bridgewater, but was the widow of Daniel Howard and the mother of just one child from that marriage, Ambrose Howard. In 1815, Ambrose was living in Winslow, Maine, very close to Augusta, when his first child was born. It seems likely that Dulcena, already a mature twenty-one years old, traveled to Maine to help out with her step-brother's new baby. Regardless, she attended the Cony Academy, no doubt quite a lot older than many of the students. In a time of sometimes sporadic educational opportunities for young women, the Cony Academy, with its strong academic base, must have seemed like an experience that was too good to pass by. Dulcena ultimately returned to Bridgewater, where she married Captain Perley Keith, a farmer, in 1821. They were the parents of three children. Dulcena died December 9, 1880, in East Bridgewater, Massachusetts, at the age of almost eighty-six. Dulcena's work, with its well-developed rose border and neatly stitched, small leafy vine dividing the sections, is very typical of Cony work. The preceptress at the time she made it was Miss Hannah B. Aldrich, also a Massachusetts native.

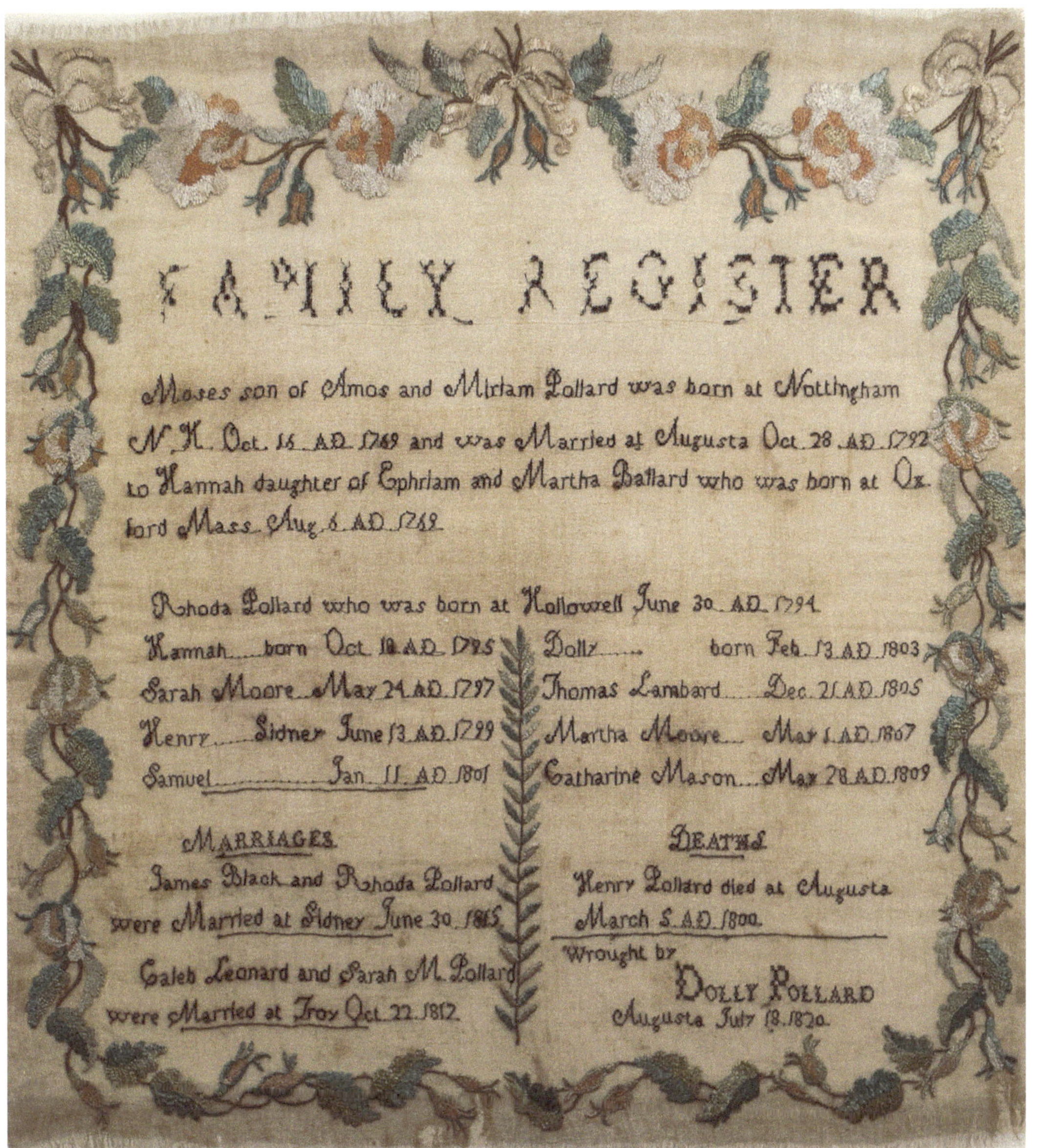

Dolly Pollard (1803–1888)
Family register sampler, 1820
Worked at the Cony Female Academy, Augusta, Maine
Silk thread on linen
Cross, satin, outline, and straight stitches
27 x 17 ½
Collection of the Maine Historical Society

Dolly Pollard, the maker of this sampler, was a granddaughter of Martha Ballard, the remarkable woman described in historian Laurel Thatcher Ulrich's *A Midwife's Tale*. Ephraim and Martha Ballard migrated from Oxford, Massachusetts, to a rural, nearly unsettled region of Hallowell, Maine, in October of 1777. With them were their five surviving children, including Hannah and Dorothy, "Dolly," who was six. They left behind the graves of three of their young children (including their first Dorothy), who had perished within ten days of each other during a severe epidemic of diphtheria in 1769, just weeks before daughter Hannah was born. Once established in Maine, Martha took up the calling that she had begun in Massachusetts: she delivered babies and kept track of her work in her diary, over the course of decades. For this reason, we have small snippets of information about Hannah, the mother of the maker of this sampler that was completed at the Cony Academy in 1820. The rough-and-ready way of life that characterized the Maine of Hannah's childhood differed immensely from the snapshot of sophistication that the Cony Academy would offer her daughter. Since Dolly completed her sampler in July of 1820, her preceptress might either have been Miss Aldrich, or perhaps Miss Bancroft, who replaced her at Cony sometime that year. Dolly's sampler is very similar to that of Dulcena Dunbar (p. 116) who stitched hers several years earlier. Dolly married Jonas Farrar, a farmer about seven years her junior, in 1836. They were the parents of a son and a daughter. By 1860, Jonas had died. Dolly lived on, eventually in the home of her unmarried daughter who worked as a seamstress, until she died in Augusta on February 1, 1888.

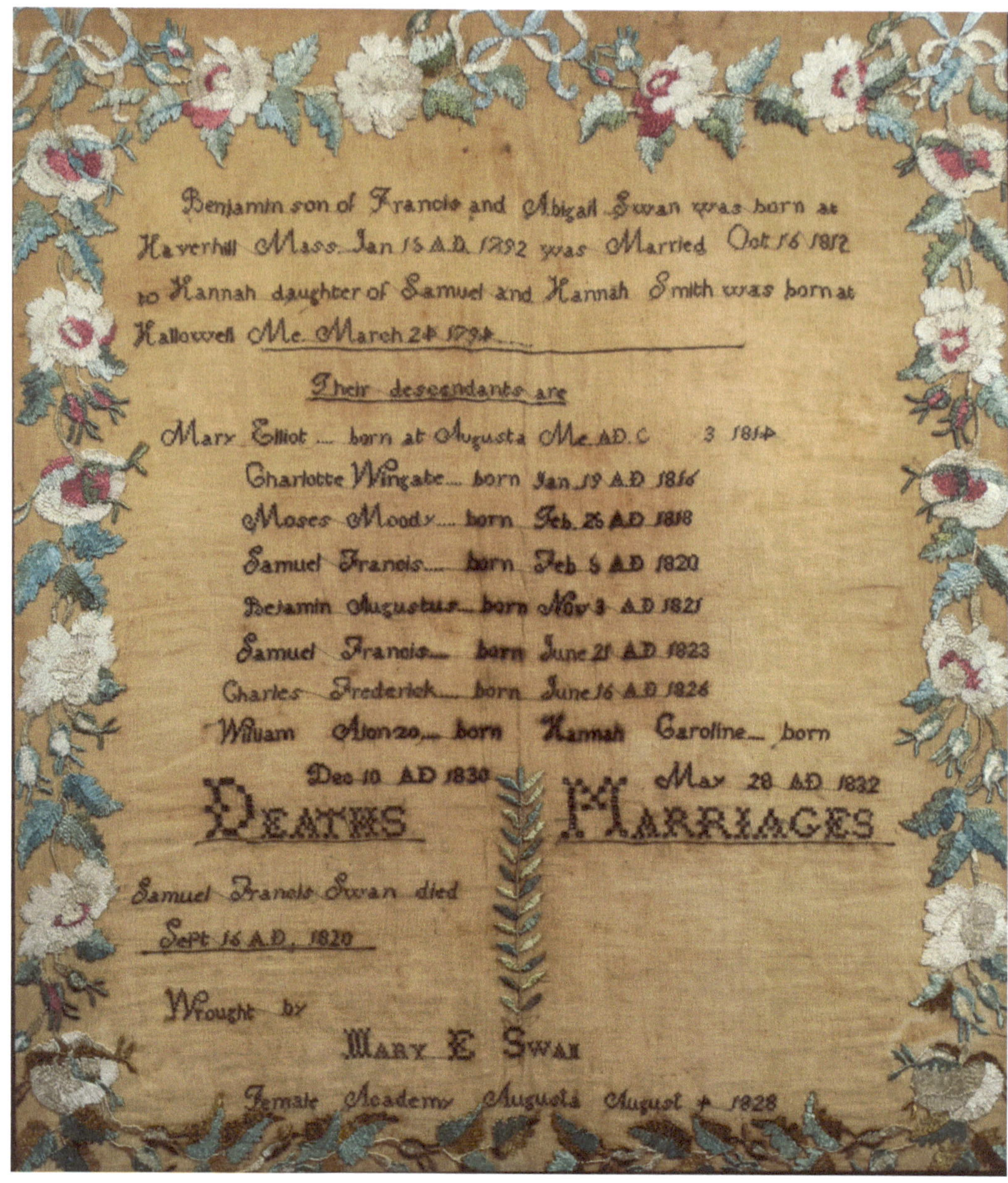

Mary E. Swan (1814–1896)
Family register sampler, 1828
Worked at the Cony Female Academy, Augusta, Maine
Silk thread on linen
Cross, satin, and outline stitches
26 ½ x 17
Collection of the Maine Historical Society

Mary Eliot Swan was the eldest of the nine children of Benjamin, a jeweler, and Hannah Smith Swan of Hallowell, Maine. Two of her siblings were born after Mary completed her sampler at the Cony Female Academy, and she had to squeeze their names in, altering the format a bit to accomplish that. The delicate, leafy vine that separates the "Deaths" section of her work from the "Marriages" is a common feature on Cony embroideries, although it is used in a variety of ways. Most Cony works also include an attractive floral border. Mary Swan married a very successful door and sash maker, Josiah P. Wyman, and lived in Augusta. They were the parents of seven children (including a set of twins born when Mary was forty-two years old). Four survived childhood. Mary outlived her husband, dying on April 29, 1896 in Augusta.

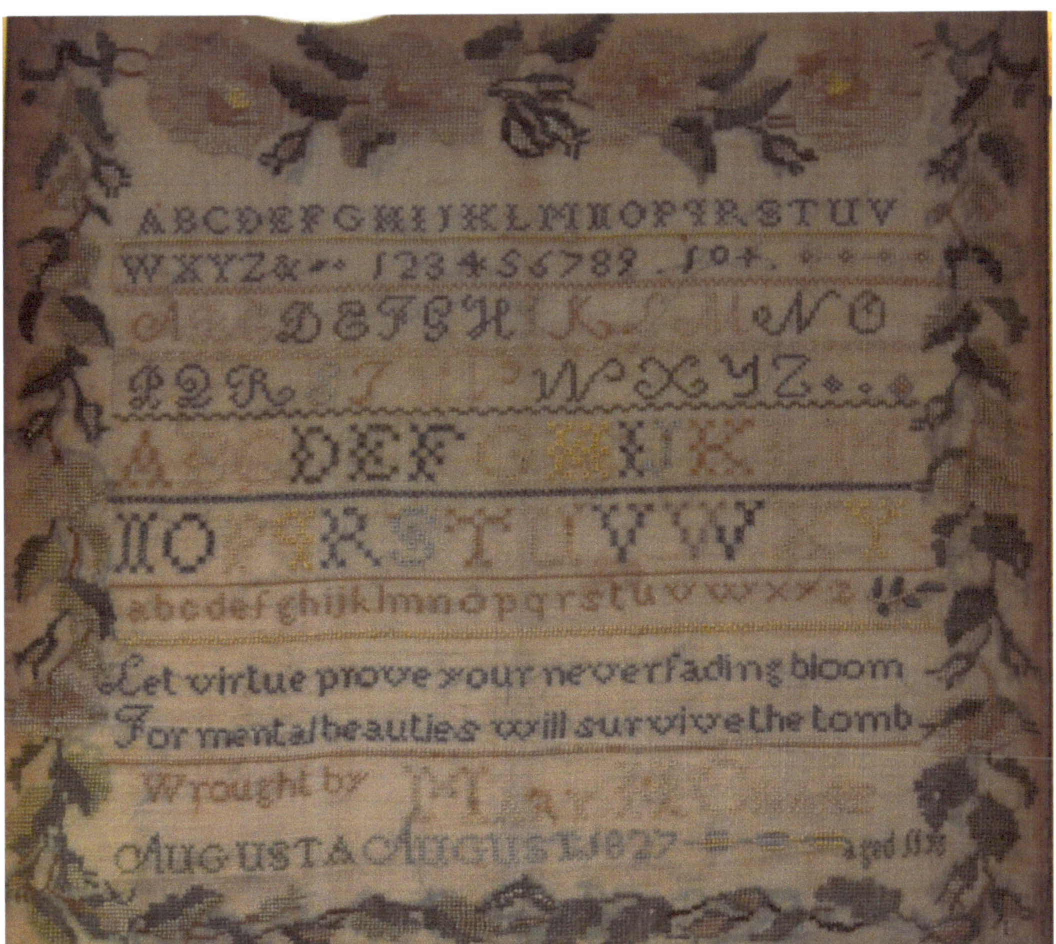

Mary M. Chase
(about 1816–1832?)
Marking sampler, 1827
Worked in Augusta, Maine
(school unknown)
Silk thread on linen
Cross and Algerian
eye stitches
16 ½ x 16 ½
Collection of Burton W. Pearl

Unlike many other Augusta samplers of the 1820s, **Mary Chase**'s cannot readily be attributed to the Cony Female Academy, having none of the typical features of that iconic group. Mary's sampler, however, is sophisticated in design and meticulously worked. She provided us with very little information to track her down. Her birth is not recorded in Augusta vital records, if she is even from that town. She may have been a daughter of Benjamin Chase, who was the only Chase noted on the U.S. Federal Census in Augusta in 1820 and 1830, and who had a daughter of the right approximate age to be Mary. If that is correct, then she very likely died in Augusta at the young age of sixteen on July 26, 1832.

Lucy Ann Babcock
(1820–circa 1849)
Marking sampler, 1831
Possibly worked in Augusta, Maine (school unknown)
Silk thread on linen
Cross, outline, and straight stitches
23 x 16
Collection of the Maine State Museum

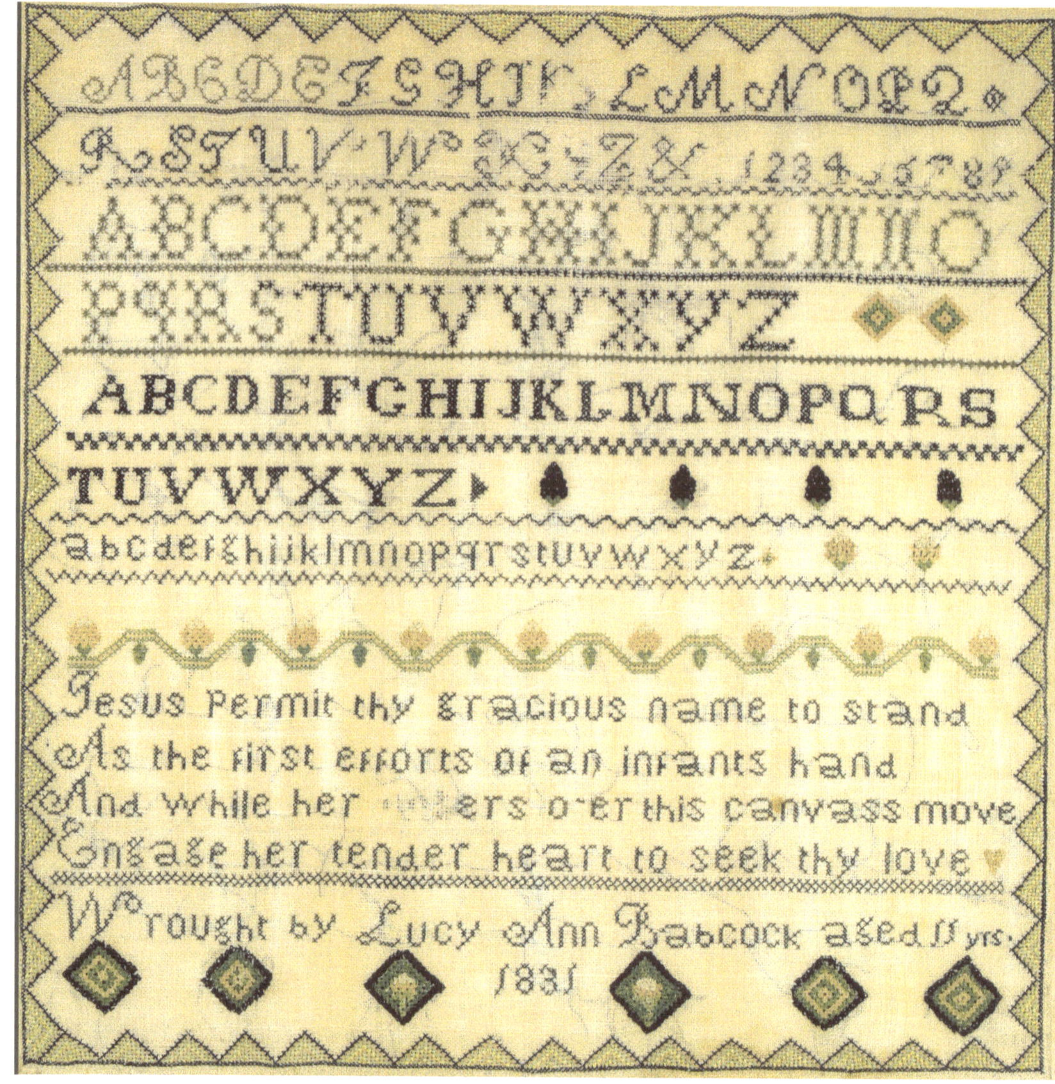

Lucy Ann Babcock's story is a rather convoluted and uncertain tale. She was probably the daughter of Abel Babcock and his wife, Lucy Stone, and was born in Augusta in 1820. On November 28, 1839, Lucy Ann married William T. Pierce who was, at the time, teaching school in Windsor, Maine. When her descendants donated the sampler to the Maine State Museum, they included a considerable amount of family history. It was believed that Lucy died in Maine, perhaps shortly after the birth of her second daughter, and that her husband then placed their two young children with a local family who raised them. Sometime afterward, he purportedly relocated to Lowell, Massachusetts, where he remarried in 1851. But, in fact, Lowell death records reveal that Ferdinand Pierce, the one-year-old son of Lucy A. and William T. Pierce, who was born in Lowell, died there on September 5, 1849, so Lucy must have accompanied William on the move to Massachusetts. Later census records seem to indicate that there might have been three surviving daughters: Albina, Havilla, and Aurelia. Where and when Lucy died is unknown, but it must have been around 1849 to 1850. Lucy's sampler includes concentric diamonds, a common rural Maine motif, used sometimes as space holders at the ends of alphabets, or as in hers, eye-catching decorative elements.

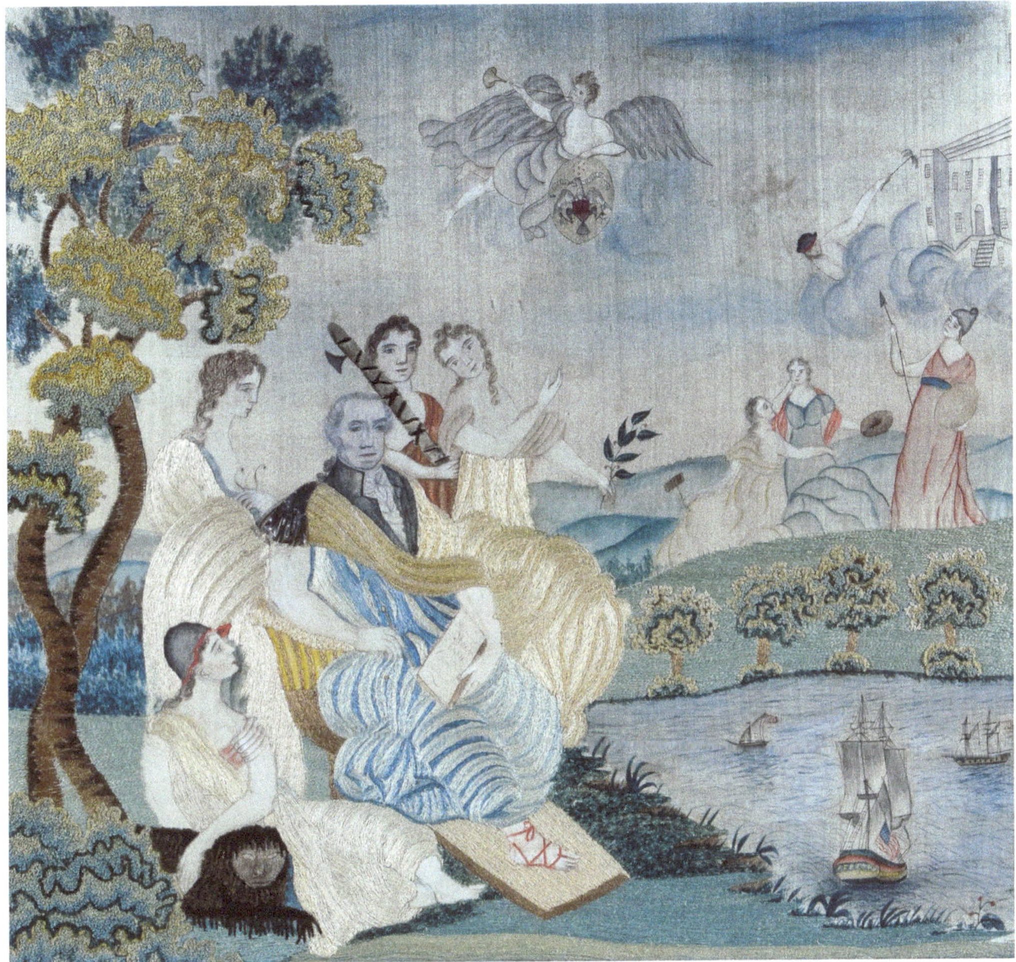

Mary Guild (1794–1872)
Silk embroidery, 1810–14
Worked at the school of Rhoda Remington, Hallowell, Maine
Silk and metallic threads, pencil, pen and ink on silk over linen
Satin, outline, and straight stitches
23 x 23
Collection of Mr. and Mrs. Dan Scheid

Mary Guild was born April 17, 1794, in Hallowell, Maine, the only child of Benjamin Guild and Zilpha Hardy. On October 16, 1814, she married David Page. They were the parents of eight children and lived in a home on Lincoln Street in Hallowell that still stands. She died on April 5, 1872, in Hallowell. Her lavish embroidery, worked in colored silks, metallic threads, pencil, paint, and ink on a painted plain-weave silk ground, is a copy of an engraving entitled "Washington Giving the Laws to America," circa 1800. Mary Guild completed this silk embroidery at the school of Mrs. Rhoda Remington in Hallowell.

Betty Ring first documented Mrs. Remington's academy in Providence, Rhode Island, where for several years her school was the primary competition for the much better-known Mary Balch's school. Mrs. Remington initially advertised her Providence school in 1807, but just the year before, she had advertised in Boston for a school she operated in Dedham, Massachusetts. She first advertised her school in Hallowell on May 29, 1810, and she continued to advertise until June 1815.

Rhoda Bullen was born January 30, 1774, the eldest child of Elizabeth Legg and Samuel Bullen. On February 21, 1796, she married William Remington, a merchant from New York. She gave birth to at least two daughters, Charlotte in 1801 and Caroline in 1803, both of whom died in the 1860s. William Remington disappeared from records after 1803. In his absence, Rhoda needed to support her children, which was most likely the motivating factor behind opening a school in Dedham. The opportunities may have appeared better in the much larger city of Providence, prompting her move there. The next move, to distant Hallowell, seems less obvious, although there were several Bullens on the Hallowell census for 1810; they may have been relatives. On December 23, 1815, Rhoda married Lieutenant Jedediah Lakeman of Boston in Charlestown, Massachusetts. Several books list Lieutenant Jedediah Lakeman in Captain S. G. Ladd's company, Major Chandler's Battalion of Artillery, raised in Hallowell and serving in 1814. Rhoda and Jedediah had no children. Rhoda died July 17, 1838, in Charlestown, Massachusetts.

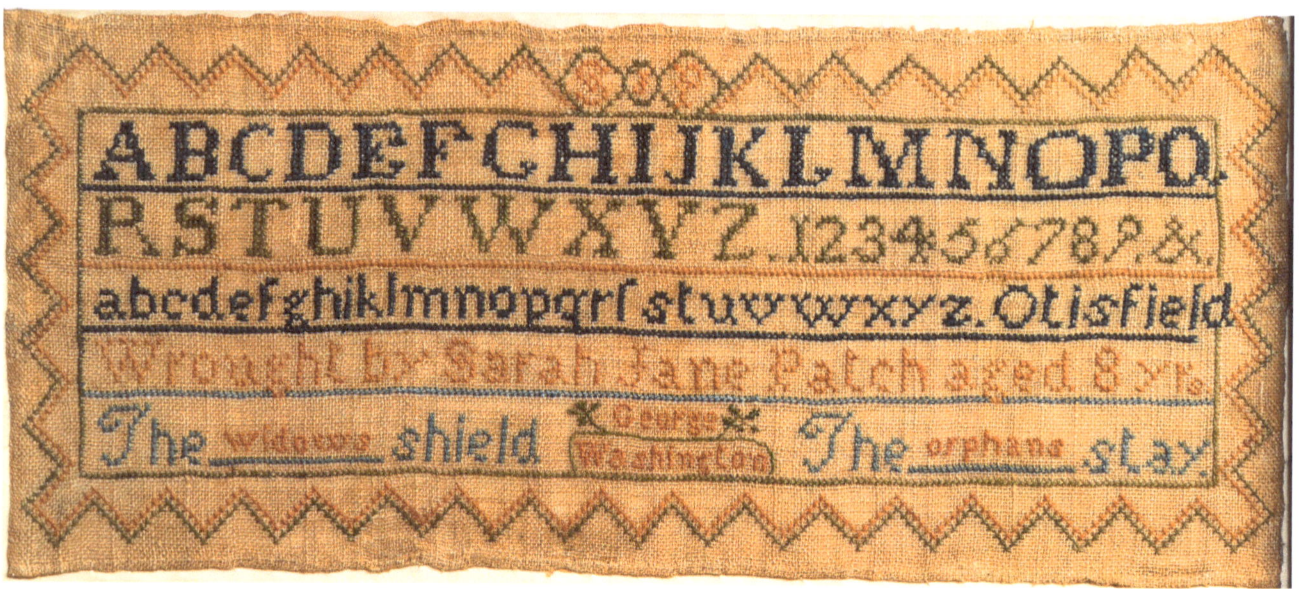

Sarah Jane Patch
(1819–1847)
Marking sampler, 1827
Probably worked in Otisfield, Maine (school unknown)
Silk thread on linen
Cross over one and two threads, satin, and outline stitches
7 x 17 ½
Collection of Natalie Larson

The sampler **Sarah Jane Patch** stitched in about 1827 is of a shape that is very typical for Maine's lakes region. The long, rectangular shape doesn't represent the work of a particular school, but rather a regional choice. Sarah Jane used her sampler to memorialize George Washington. Shortly after his death in December, 1799, there was an outpouring of memorial poetry, artwork, decorative wares, and needlework in his honor. However, Sarah Jane made her sampler many years later, so the choice to honor him may instead have been inspired by the recent fifty-year anniversary of the new nation in 1826. The sampler features an uppercase alphabet style that is often associated with Quakers, although most of the early settlers of rural Otisfield were Congregationalists. Sarah Jane's father, Tarbell Patch, a farmer, was the son of one of the first settlers of Otisfield; he married Elisa Shed. Sarah had a brother and two sisters, one of whom, like Sarah, died just as she reached adulthood. Sarah was born December 20, 1819, and died August 7, 1847. She, her sisters, and her parents are all buried under the same substantial marble monument in Otisfield.

Julia Ann Patch (1807–1848)
Family register sampler, circa 1824
Probably worked in Otisfield, Maine
(school unknown)
Silk thread on linen
Cross, satin, Algerian eye,
and split stitches
17 ½ x 17 ½
Collection of the Otisfield
Historical Society

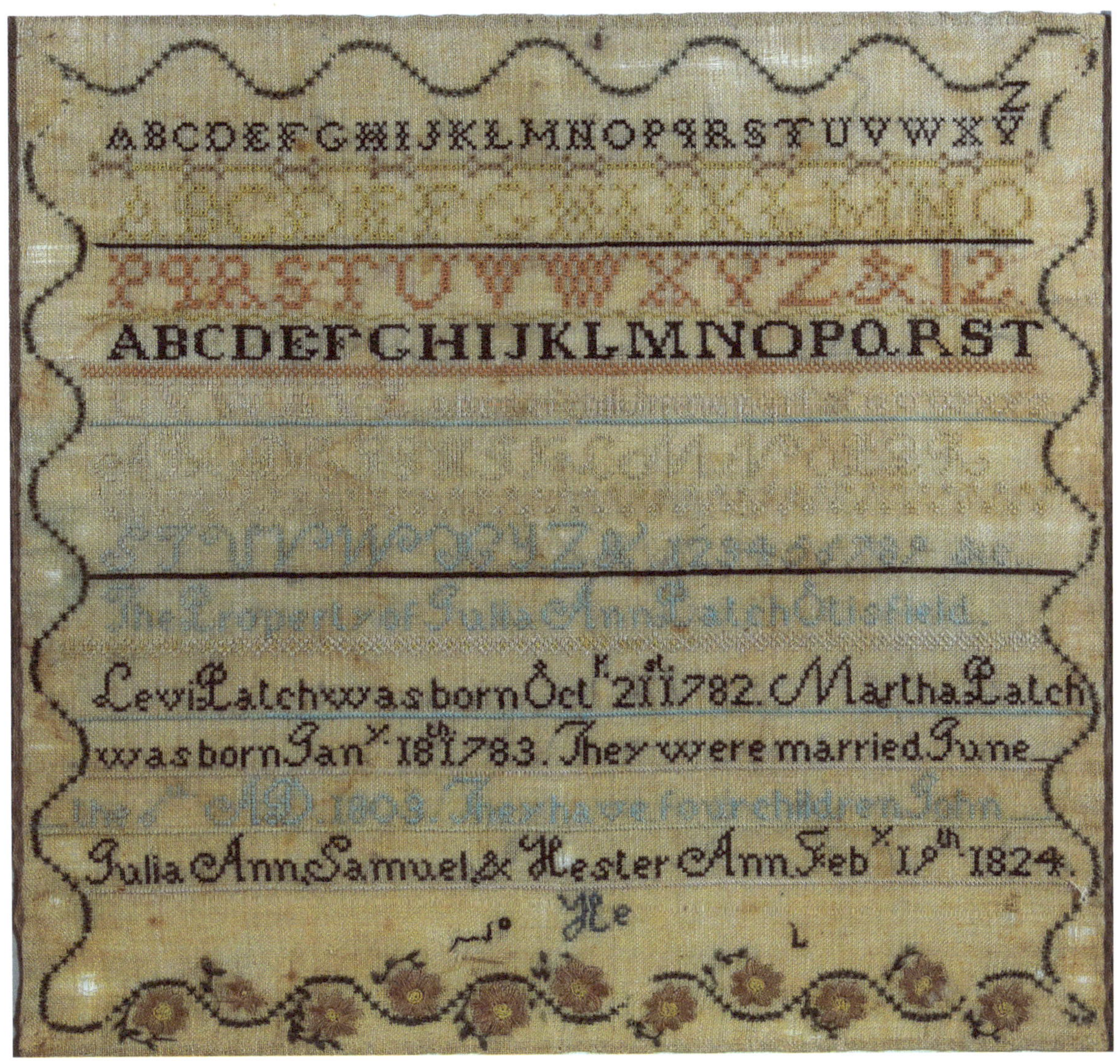

Julia Ann Patch, born on April 28, 1807, was one of the four children of Captain Levi Patch and Martha Barnes of Otisfield. Levi was the brother of Tarbell Patch, making Julie Ann the first cousin of Sarah Jane Patch (p. 122). Levi's father, Benjamin, was one of the two original settlers of Otisfield. Levi inherited the family farm and, in about 1810, erected a handsome two-story home there to replace the log cabin his father had built. That house still stands, one of the largest constructed in town during the Federal era. There are some similarities between Julia Ann's work and that of her cousin, including the use of a Quaker-style uppercase alphabet and the blue and orange color palate. Julia Ann's meandering border with its Algerian eye vine is very unusual. Also distinctive is the way she included her name on her work: "The property of Julia Ann Patch." Julia Ann's siblings, John, Samuel, and Hester Ann all lived to adulthood and married. Julia Ann never married, and she died on June 12, 1848. She is buried in Otisfield near her parents.

Rosetta Stoddard
(1822–1920)
Marking sampler, 1832
Worked at the school of Edee
Pease, Chesterville, Maine
Silk thread on linen
Cross, queen, and straight stitches
14 ½ x 23
Collection of Glee Krueger

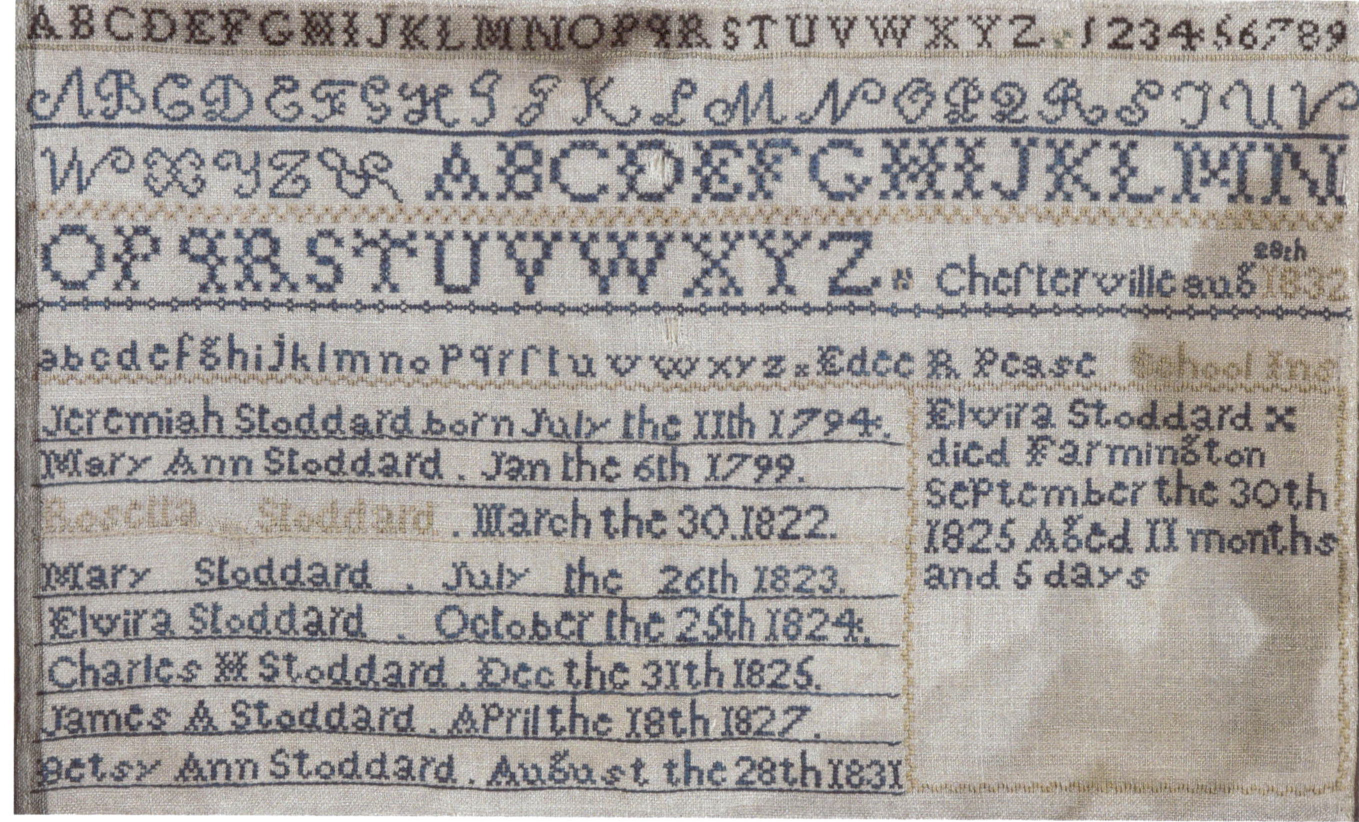

Rosetta Stoddard cooperatively provided a great deal of information on her sampler, and then lived long enough to personally pass all that family lore on to succeeding generations. Not only that, but she also named her teacher, providing insight into the career of an otherwise anonymous young woman. Rosetta's father was a minister; the family moved frequently throughout the early 1800s to fulfill the needs of his work. Rosetta was living in Maine at the time she worked her sampler, in Chesterville, under the instruction of Edee Pease. Rosetta was one of the six children of the Reverend Jeremiah Stoddard and his wife, Mary Ann Smith Stoddard. She married Charles B. Rose of Livermore, Maine, becoming Rosetta Rose. They were the parents of two sons. Eventually, the couple moved with two of Rosetta's siblings to Illinois and then Kansas. She died at the age of ninety-eight in New Cambria, Kansas, in her sons' home that she had, until 1915, also shared with her long-lived sister, Betsey (later "Lizzie").

Edith Richardson (Edee) Pease, Rosetta's teacher, was the youngest daughter of Abisha and Mary Abigail Raymond Pease, born in Wilton, Maine, on March 4, 1804. She married Benjamin Barry in 1832 and divorced him in March 1869. Later she appeared on the 1880 U.S. Federal Census in Scituate, Rhode Island, where she described herself as a widow and was "keeping house." She died in Fall River, Massachusetts, on March 25, 1891, but was buried in Hope, Rhode Island.

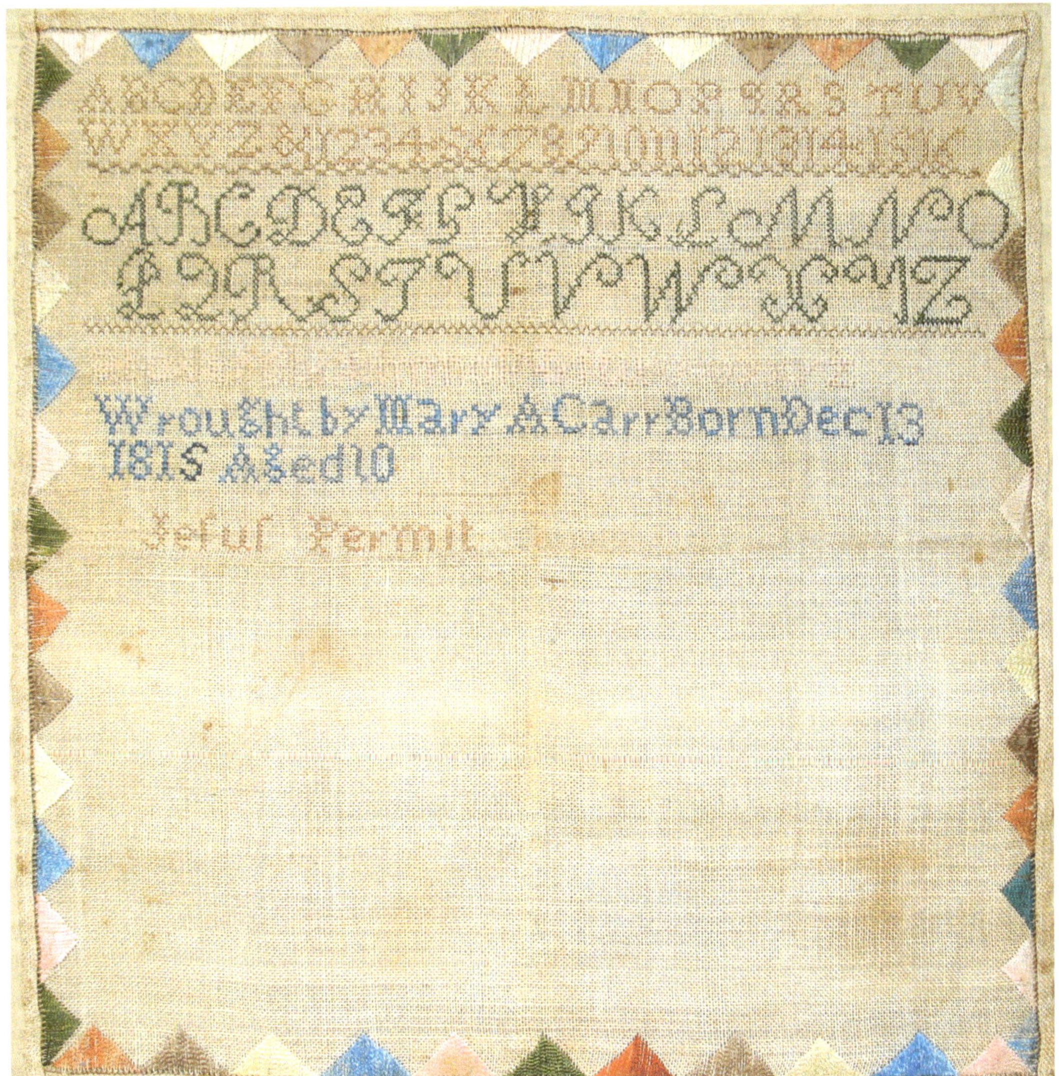

Mary Carr (1815–1826)
Marking sampler, 1825
Worked in Winthrop, Maine
(school unknown)
Silk thread on linen
Cross and satin stitches
16 ½ x 17
Collection of Lynne Anderson

Mary Carr was the oldest of the seven children of Daniel and Polly Joy Carr. Daniel was born in Newburyport, Massachusetts, but moved to Winthrop, Maine, in about 1811. He fought in the War of 1812, where he was wounded and lost an arm. When Mary died at age eleven on November 23, 1826, she became the third child they had lost. In all, of their seven children, only two lived past young adulthood. Although she never finished, Mary planned to stitch the most common of all verses seen on Maine samplers: "Jesus permit thy gracious Name to stand/As the first efforts of an infant's hand/And while her fingers on the canvas move/Engage her tender hear to see thy love./With thy dear children let her have a part./And write thy name thy self upon her heart." After her early death, Mary's sampler seems to have been folded up and put away, leaving it as pristine as the day she laid it down.

Lydia Holt (1805–?)
Marking sampler, 1815
Worked in Bethel, Maine
(school unknown)
Silk thread on linen
Cross, satin, and
outline stitches
17 ¼ x 18 ¼
Collection of the Bethel
Historical Society

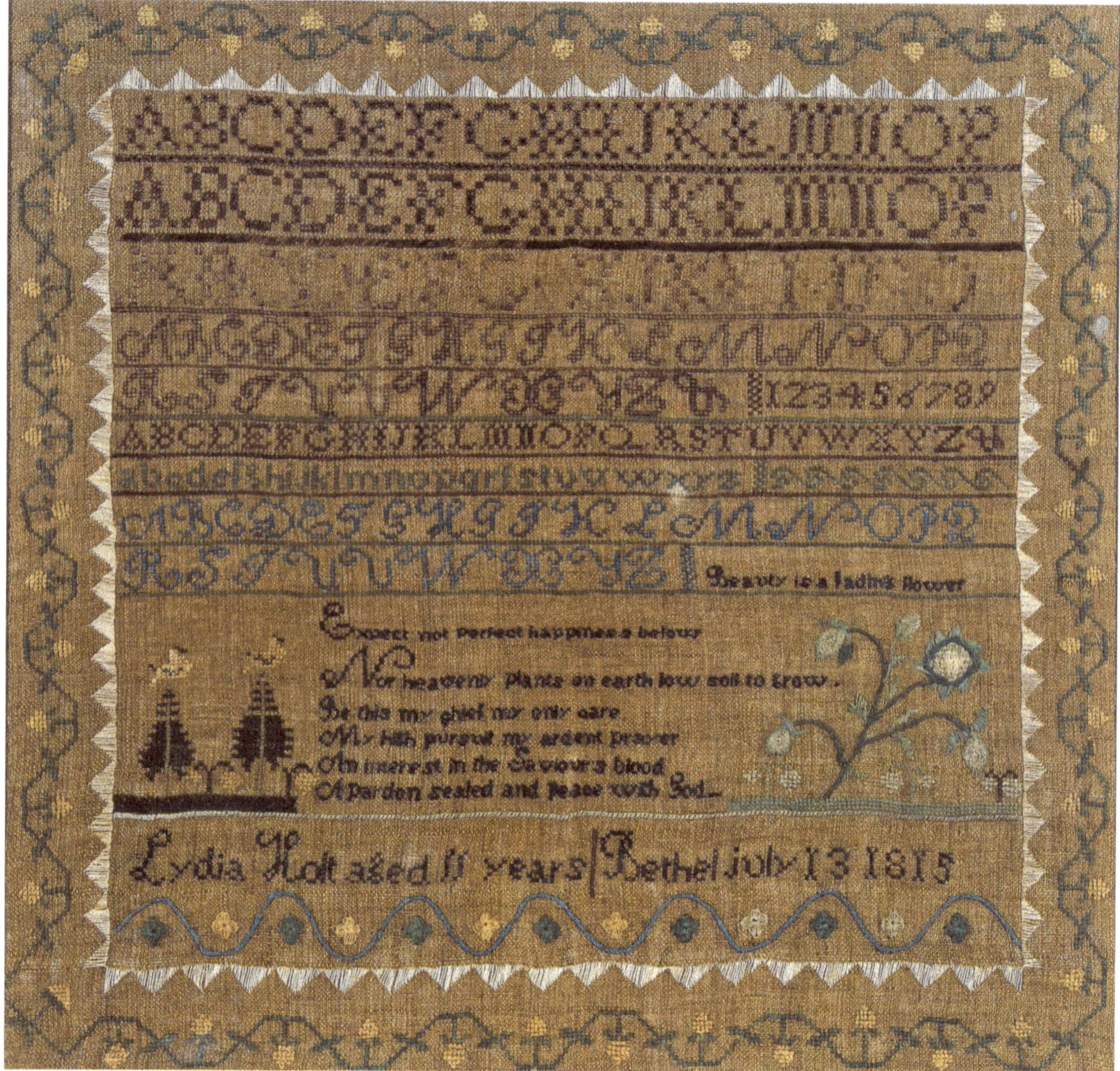

Lydia Holt's sampler has a couple of elements in common with the later Bethel work of Sarah Abbot (p. 127). They both have unusual pine trees with oversized birds perched in the treetops, and they each feature a large plant with drooping flowers. The droopy plant also appears on the nearly anonymous sampler of S. B. (p. 128), also from Bethel. Lydia may have stitched her sampler at one of the district schools that were already well established by 1815, or at a small private academy. Born November 17, 1805, she was the ninth and youngest child of John Holt, who had moved to Bethel from Tewksbury, Massachusetts, and his wife, Lydia Russell Holt. Lydia married Humphrey Bean, a well-to-do farmer, and they were the parents of at least five children, one of whom, Hiram, they resided with for many years as they grew old. Lydia died in 1891 in Bethel. Although separated from Lydia's work by fifteen years, the sampler of Olive Wheeler, stitched in 1830 and sold at Cyr Auction in 2003, is strikingly similar and includes an identical strawberry border and a very similar configuration of alphabets, including the unusual repetition of the largest upper case one.

Sarah Abbot (1806–1874)
Marking sampler, 1823
Worked in Bethel, Maine
(school unknown)
Silk thread on linen
Cross and satin stitches
18 ½ x 16
Collection of the Bethel
Historical Society

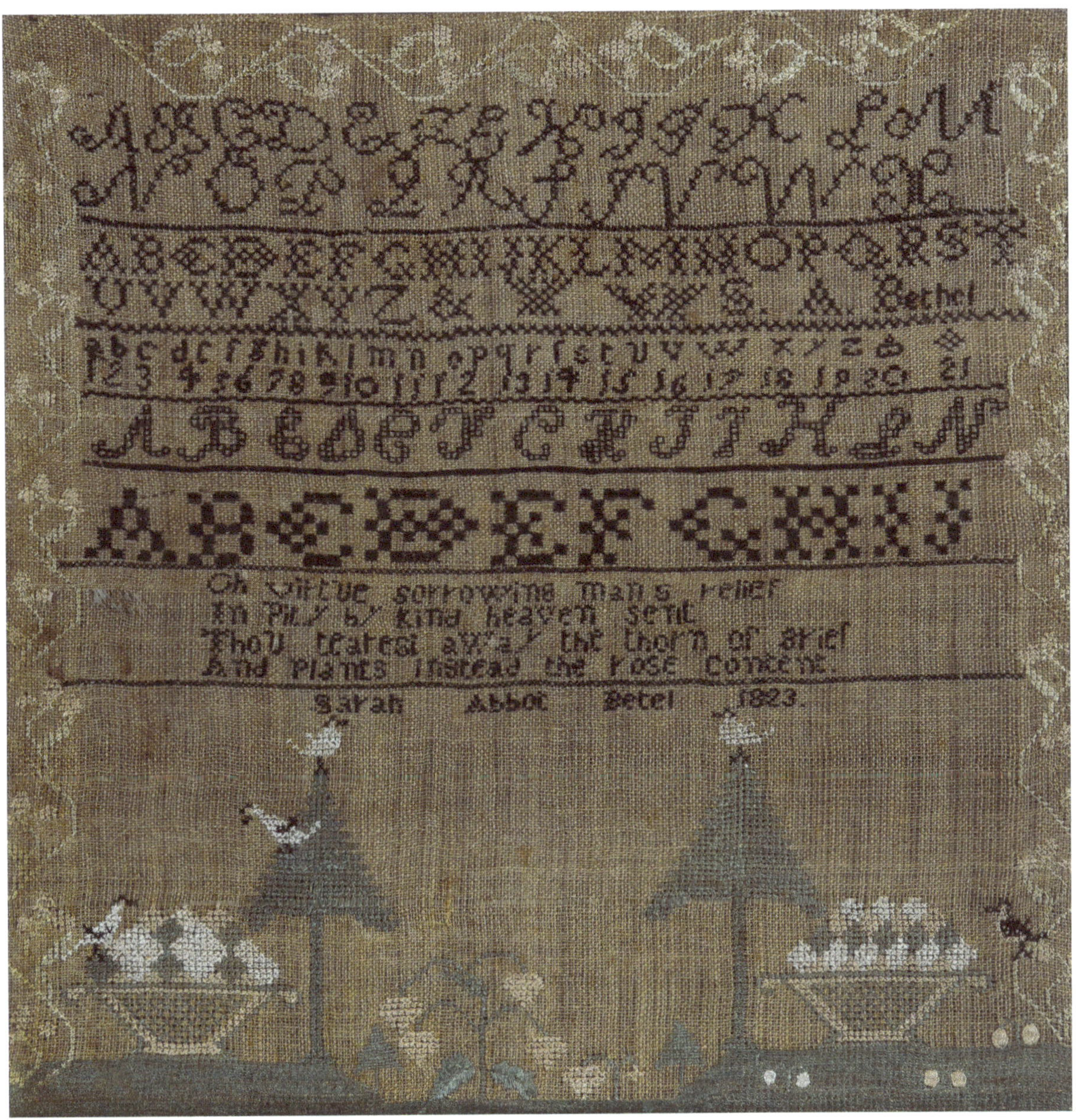

Sarah Abbot, the daughter of Aaron and Sarah Abbot, was born March 12, 1806, in Concord, New Hampshire, where both her parents were from. By 1812, they had relocated to Bethel, Maine. Around 1834, Sarah married Timothy Capen, a Bethel farmer several years her senior. They were the parents of three boys and one girl. In later years, Sarah and Timothy shared their home with a married son, his wife, and children, with a second married son living right next door. Timothy died in 1872 and Sarah on April 14, 1874. Her naive sampler shares several design elements with other Bethel works.

S. B. (dates unknown)
Marking sampler, 1826
Worked in Bethel, Maine
(school unknown)
Silk thread on linen
Cross over one and two
threads, and satin stitches
8 ½ x 13 ½
Collection of Burton W. Pearl

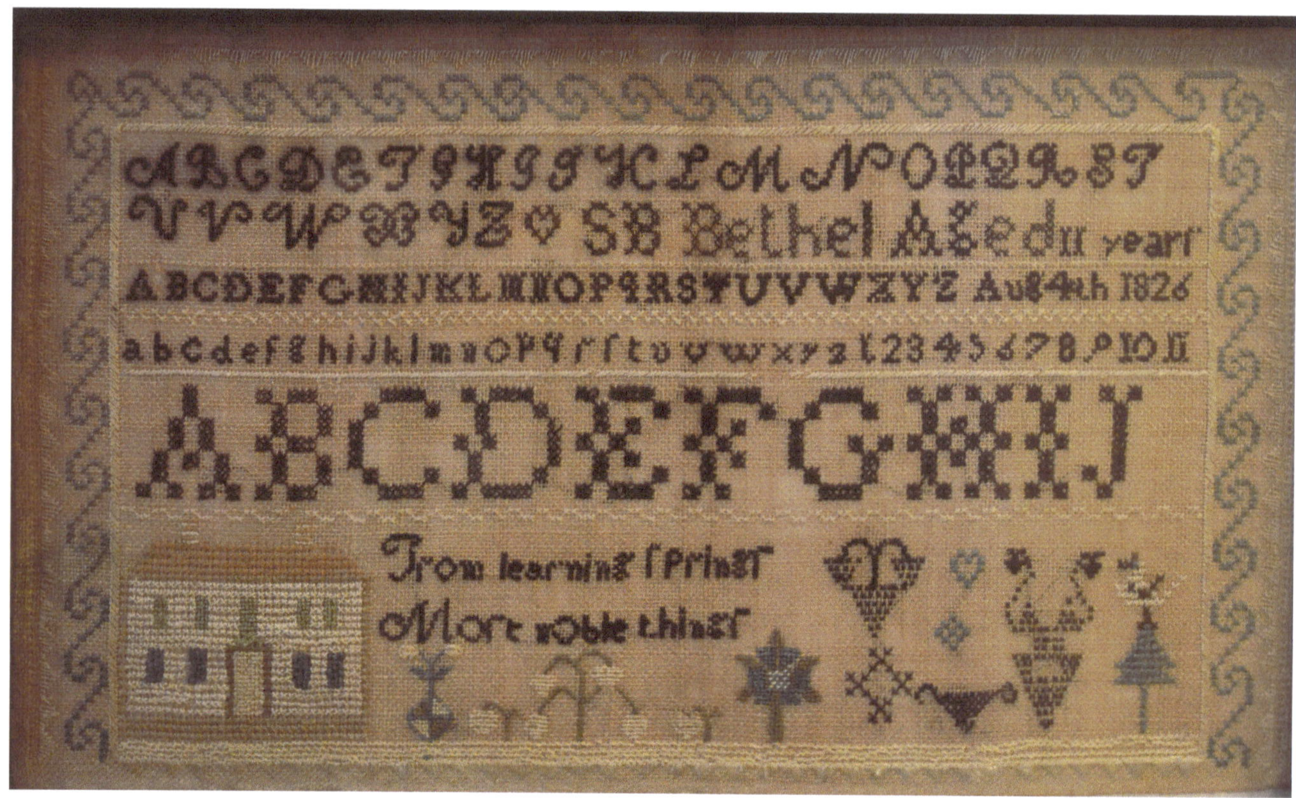

Although **S. B.** didn't provide much information about herself, her sampler strongly relates to others stitched in Bethel, Maine, in the Federal era and beyond. It is notable that such a large body of work that extends over a long period of time can be connected to this small town. She may have been **Sarah Stickney Barker**, born September 9, 1814, the daughter of Samuel Barker and his second wife, Abigail Blanchard, the fourteenth of Samuel's fifteen children. She is the only girl whose birth is noted on Bethel's vital records that has the right age and initials to match S. B. Sarah married Thomas Beach. They were the parents of two daughters. By 1850, Sarah had become a widow. In 1870, she was listed as the "Mother of the House" for a large orphans' school in Boston, the Children's Friend Society, where her unwed younger daughter, Ellen, was also employed as a teacher. She later lived with her older daughter, who was also widowed at a young age. No record was found for Sarah's death.

Lucy R. Eames (1827–1849)
Marking sampler, 1841
Worked in Bethel, Maine
(school unknown)
Silk thread on linen
Cross stitch
14 x 13
Collection of the Bethel
Historical Society

Lucy Russell Eames was the daughter of Luther Eames, a farmer, and his wife, Abigail Pierce Russell; she was born February 19, 1827. Lucy had both a younger and an older brother. When she stitched her simple, unfinished sampler in 1831, Bethel did not yet have a public academy to provide its children with a high school-level education, but was being served by fourteen schoolhouses spread across the rural, hilly town. The strawberry border on Lucy's sampler is very similar to the one stitched by Lydia Holt on her 1815 work (p. 126). Lucy died January 23, 1849. Her parents would outlive both their only daughter and also their eldest son.

Melissa Russell (1833–1907)
Family register sampler, 1841
Worked in Bethel, Maine
(school unknown)
Silk thread on linen
Cross, satin, and outline stitches
15 ½ x 16 ¼
Collection of the Bethel
Historical Society

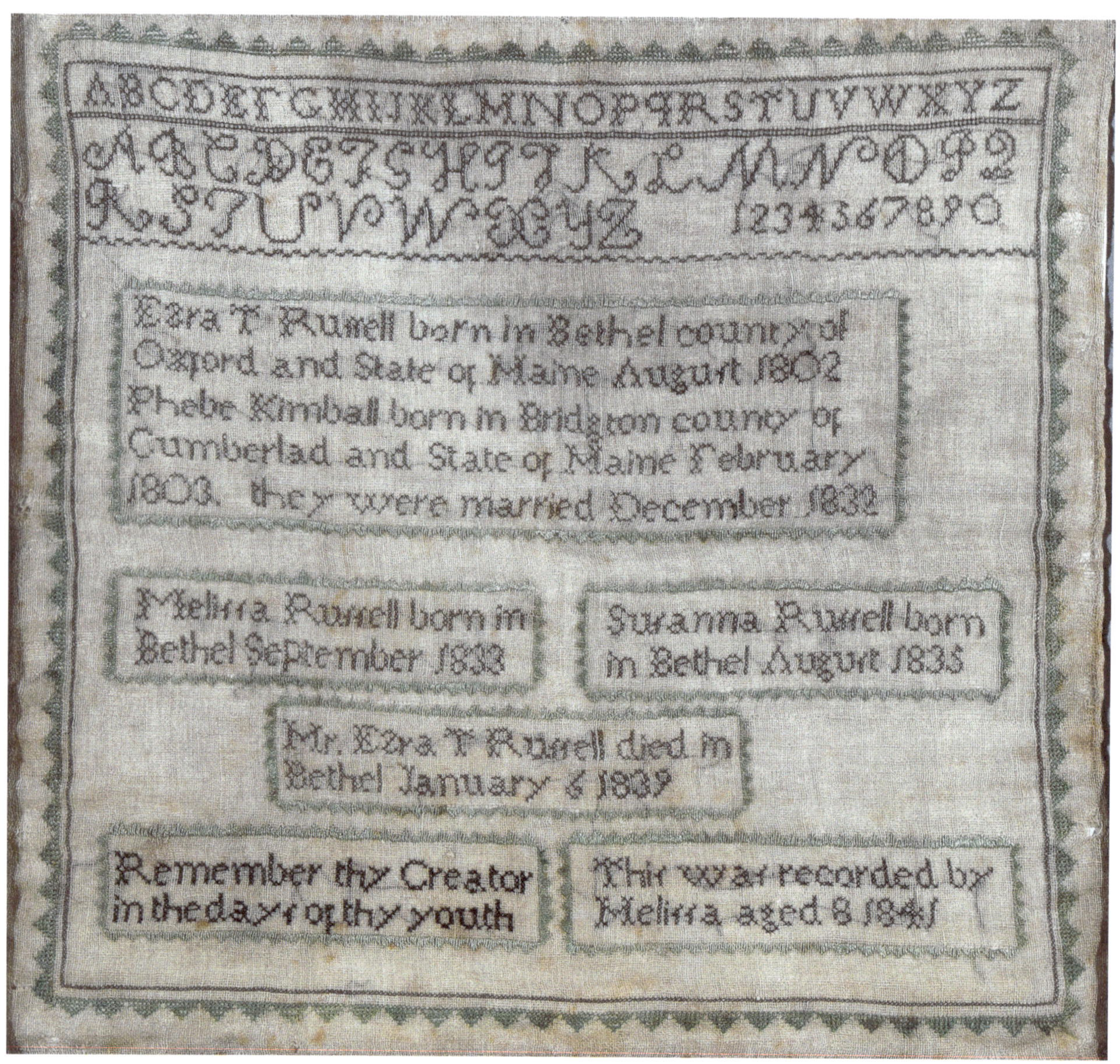

Melissa Russell's mother, Phebe, was widowed at an early age when her husband, Ezra Twitchell Russell, died in 1839, leaving her with two very young girls to raise. Melissa may have stitched her sampler at one of Bethel's many district schools. By 1860, Phebe had remarried, to Winslow Heywood, a Bethel trader. Phebe's daughter Susannah, a milliner, lived with the couple. A few doors down, Melissa was living with her husband of seven years, Charles Mason (a very successful merchant), and their three young daughters. By 1871, there were an additional three children, two sons and a daughter. In 1900, the couple was living with two of their unmarried daughters. Charles died in 1903 and Melissa on April 2, 1907, in Bethel. Melissa's sampler has a sawtooth border like the Bethel works of Cyrene Ayer and Lydia Holt (pp. 131, 126), but lacks the typical Bethel spot motifs of the others.

Cyrene Straw Ayer
(1834–1910)
Marking sampler, 1842
Worked in Bethel, Maine
(school unknown)
Silk thread on linen
Cross stitch
13 x 15 ¼
Collection of the Bethel Historical Society

Cyrene Ayer is listed in the 1891 *History of Bethel* (page 288) as one of the graduates of Gould's Academy "who have become distinguished in some one of the learned professions or in other pursuits." Since many of this group of samplers pre-date the founding of Gould's Academy, that is not the source. She was the daughter of Cyrene Ayer Straw and James Ayer (whose parents were from Saco, Maine). She was born December 11, 1834, so her sampler dates from about 1842, relatively late for a traditional marking sampler. Her sampler includes a pair of motifs that appear on other Bethel samplers in the exhibition, a distinctive basket (Sarah Abbot, p. 127) and a leafy tree (Lucy R. Eames, p. 129). The cursive R in her second alphabet is also similar to those on the samplers by Melissa Russell (p. 130) and Lucy Eames: they all have a very long, angular front leg.

Cyrene married Daniel Twitchell, who was in trade. They were the parents of two daughters: Mary, who died as an infant in 1857, and Ada, born in 1858. Daniel died of diphtheria in 1863. Cyrene later married Orange Littlehale. In 1878, widowed again, she filed a suit in Superior Court, alleging that Littlehale was insane when he assigned to his father instead of to her his benefits from the Odd Fellows Mutual Relief Association. It's uncertain whether or not she won her case, but it is telling that after she died on September 12, 1910, she was buried not with Littlehale, but with her first husband and infant daughter.

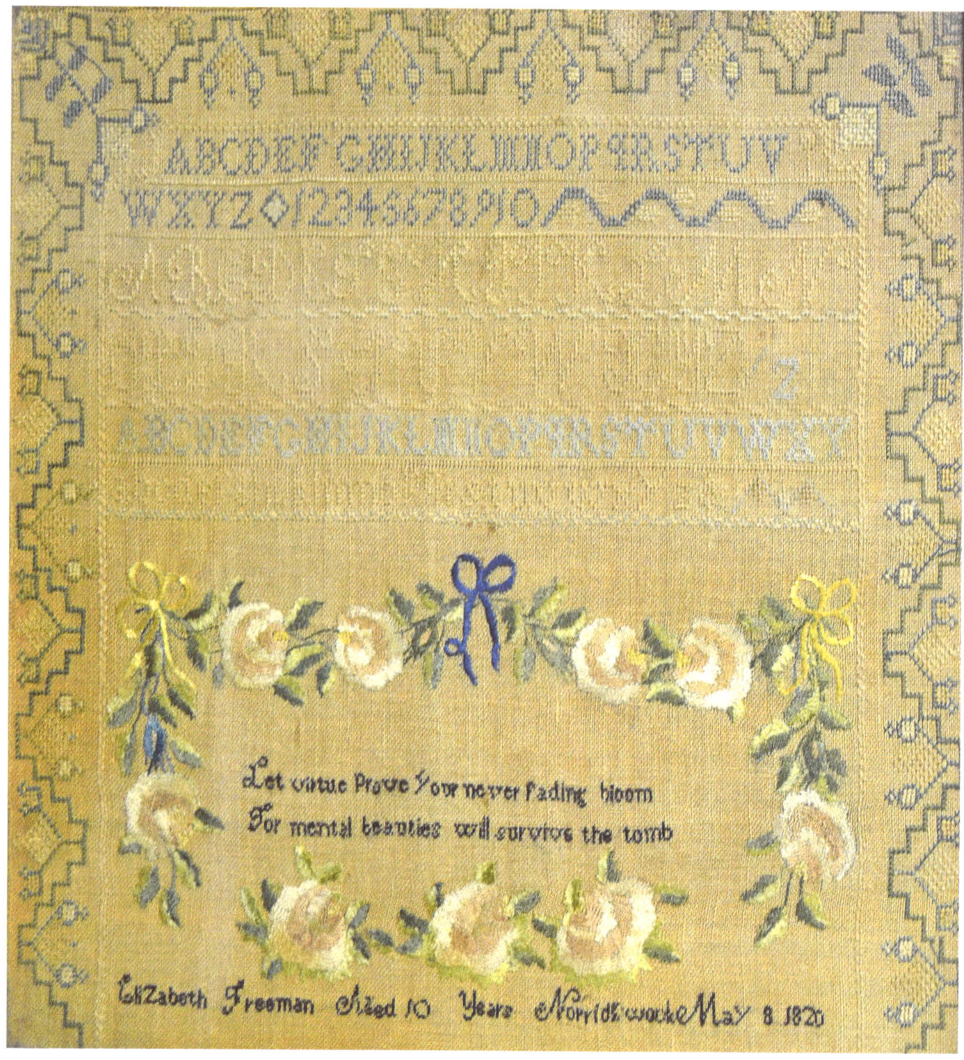

Elizabeth Freeman
(1810–1847)
Marking sampler, 1820
Probably made in the school of Catherine Swan Lyman, Norridgewock, Maine
Silk thread on linen
Cross, satin, straight, outline stitches
25 x 18
Collection of Historic New England

Born in Norridgewock, Maine, on May 17, 1810, **Elizabeth Freeman** was the eldest of the seven children of Abraham Williams and his first wife, Nancy Fairfield. In 1831, she married Captain William Handy Jr. of Sandwich, Massachusetts, (the town where her father was born), one of a family of mariners and shipbuilders. They were the parents of seven children. Their daughter Paulina, named after Elizabeth's younger sister, died at the age of just two. Two of their sons died at sea in young adulthood. Elizabeth herself died September 5, 1847, while on a visit to western Massachusetts. She is buried with her husband and some of her children in Sandwich.

Elizabeth almost certainly made her sampler under the instruction of Catharine Swan Lyman, who was the daughter of Caleb Lyman and Catharine Swan of Northbridge, Massachusetts, and was born March 19, 1797. She came to Norridgewock around 1820 and opened a school there that she operated for several years. She may have moved to that area because her uncle, William, had relocated there more than ten years before. On August 16, 1829, she married the Reverend Thomas Adams; he had been married previously to her first cousin, who had died three years earlier. They moved to Vassalboro, where she continued to teach for several more years. As the wife of a minister, she had to move frequently, as far as Ohio, but by about 1860 the Adamses had returned to Maine. For the last several years of her life, Catharine was confined to the Augusta Lunatic Asylum, suffering from a mental illness that she was said to have inherited from her grandfather. She was the mother of two sons. She authored at least eight religiously oriented books. She died in the asylum November 28, 1870. A sampler by Susan Crosby (in the collection of the Maine State Museum) was also made under her instruction, as was a sampler by Hadassah Thompson (p. 133), in a private collection, both stitched in Norridgewock. An 1833 sampler by Lydia Cartland of Vassalboro, in a private collection, can be attributed to Swan, as well.

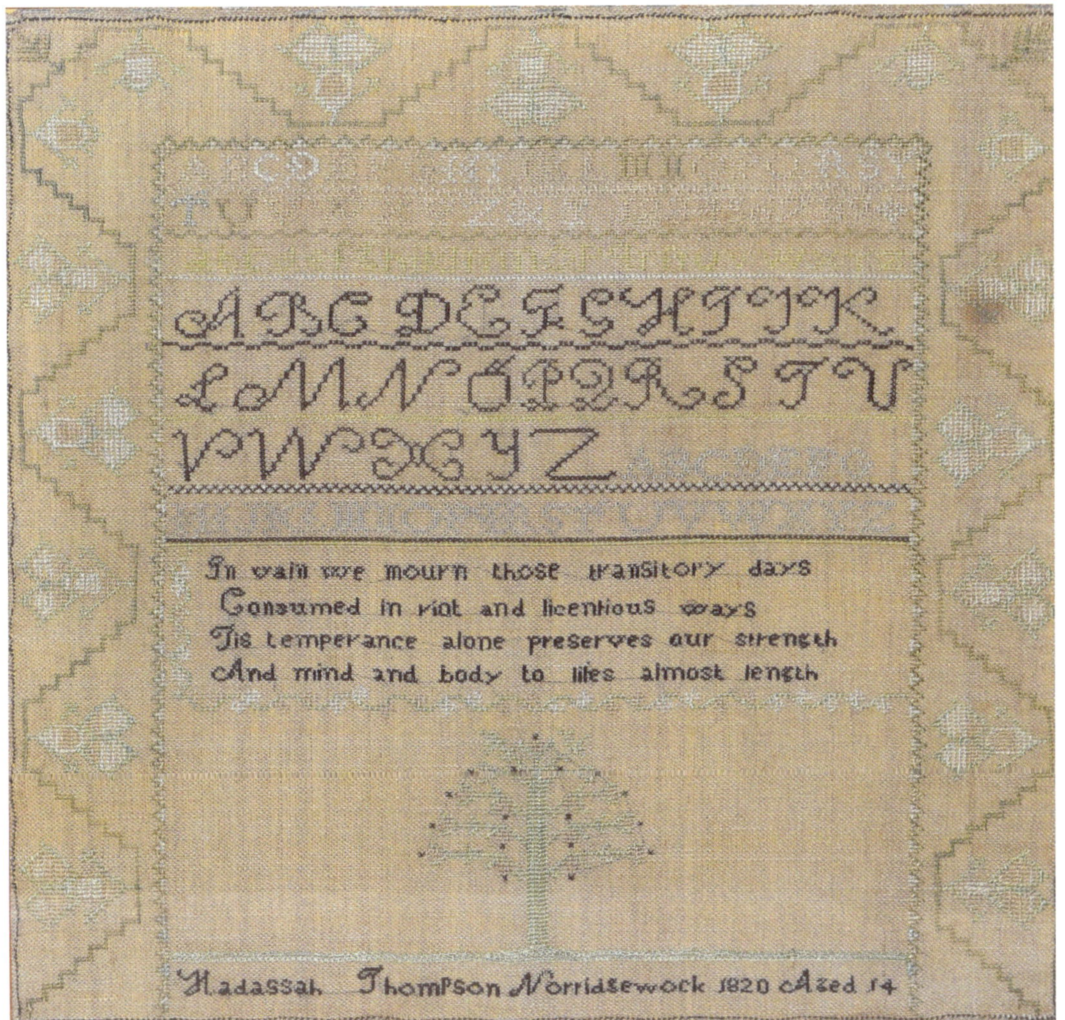

Hadassah Thompson
(1806–1832)
Marking sampler, 1820
Probably made in the school of Catherine Swan Lyman, Norridgewock, Maine
Silk thread on linen
Cross, satin, straight, and outline stitches
16 ¾ x 17 ¼
Collection of the Hinkle family

Hadassah Thompson was the eldest of the five children of Dr. Asaph Thompson, who was born in Halifax, Massachusetts, and his wife, Mary "Polly" Wood of Norridgewock. At a time when per capita alcohol consumption was approaching an all time high and alcoholism was disrupting many families, Hadassah stitched an unusual sampler verse praising the importance of temperance. Her verse had appeared in the *Columbian Calendar or New York and Vermont Almanack* of 1817. Hadassah married James M. Wilder, a chair maker, from nearby Temple, Maine. After their marriage, they moved to North Anson. Hadassah gave birth to a son, Francis, in 1831, then died in 1832.

Anonymous
Plain sewn shirt,
circa 1810–1840
Worked at an unknown school
Woven cotton sewn with
cotton thread
Hand sewn, straight, running
stitches, French seams
8 x 7
Collection of Leslie Rounds

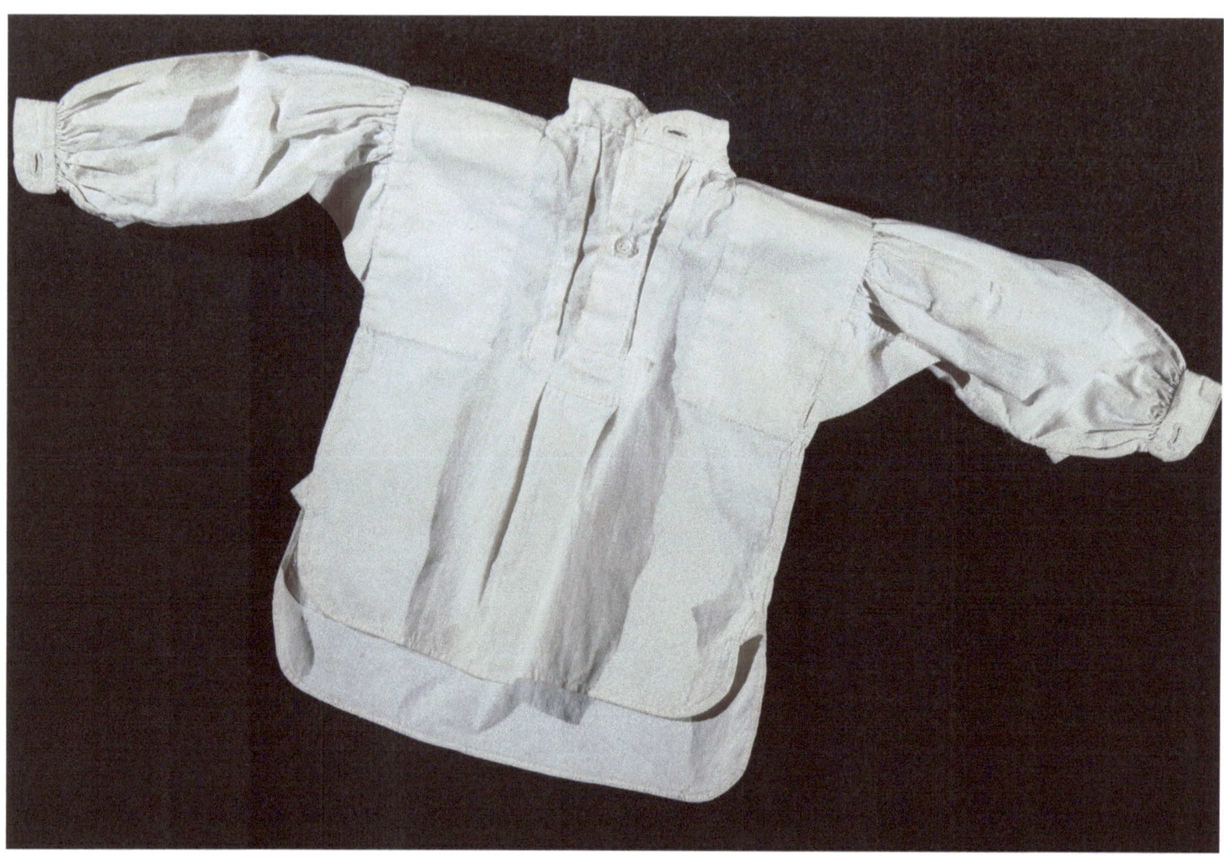

Girls of the Federal era grew up in a world in which all textiles were still stitched by hand. The first truly functional sewing machine would not be invented until 1846. While the wealthy often paid others to sew their clothing, many of the sampler makers would continue to need good sewing skills for most of their lives. Nancy Stone of Brunswick wrote to Eliza Mayo, apparently inquiring about the Mayo's curriculum. Eliza replied, "The first piece of work with which our ladies all commence is a shirt, as that embraces all the variety of plain work so essential for a lady to be perfected in before she takes up ornamental needlework" (Portland Museum of Art collection). Not all schools advertised that plain sewing was offered. This tiny shirt is an example of a plain-sewing exercise and includes the underarm and side seam gussets that men's shirts of the era usually featured. Some schools would, no doubt, teach these skills on a full-sized garment. Shirts like this one are unusual.

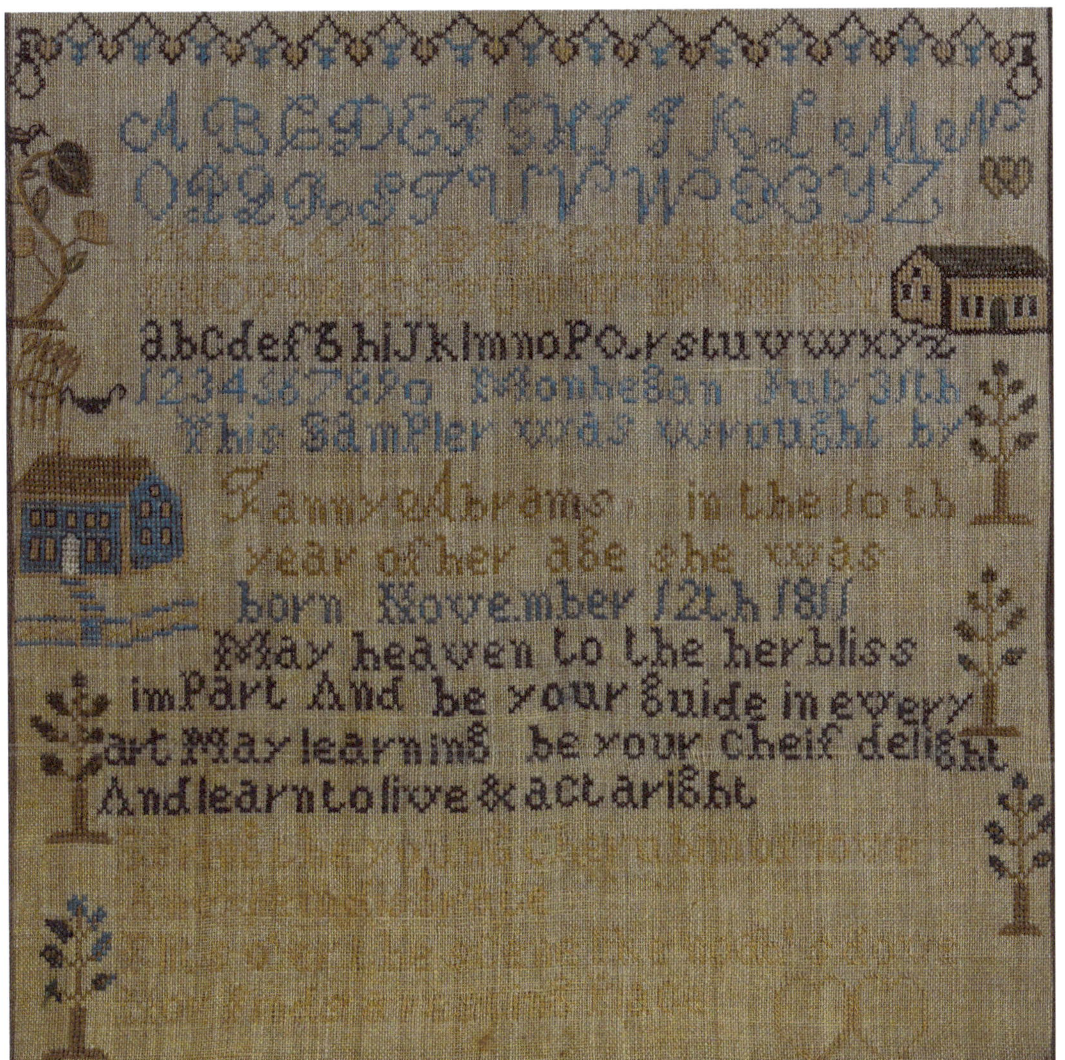

Fanny Abrams (1811–1890)
Marking sampler, 1821
Worked on Monhegan Island
(school unknown)
Silk thread on linen
Cross, satin, and
queen stitches
26 x 18
Collection of Ocean Park
Community

Fanny Abrams recorded on her sampler that she was born November 12, 1811, and that she stitched her needlework on Monhegan Island. She was the daughter of John Abrams (sometimes spelled Abrahams), who appeared on the 1810 census in Monhegan, a rocky mile-long island twelve miles off the coast of Maine. He resided on Monhegan for many years and married Phebe Starling, a member of a longtime Monhegan family. They relocated to Kittery sometime around 1820, reportedly having moved their house there by boat, and were recorded on the federal census in Kittery in 1830. Fanny—Frances—married Jacob Cilley of Atkinson, Maine, in 1837. She gave birth to a daughter, Mary, in 1838, possibly her only child. In 1850, Jacob died. By 1870, she was married to John Clark, a farmer in Corinth, Maine. She died in 1890 and is buried alone in Corinth. A small plaque that is exhibited with Fanny's sampler says, "She was a woman, intelligent, far above average, and gave liberally to the Free Baptist Church and the Woman's Missionary Society."

Almira Flye (1821–1896)
Family register sampler,
circa 1837–1846
Worked in the school of
Phebe T. Flye, Sedgwick, Maine
Silk thread on linen
Cross, satin, and
outline stitches
26 ¼ x 17 ½
Collection of Burton W. Pearl

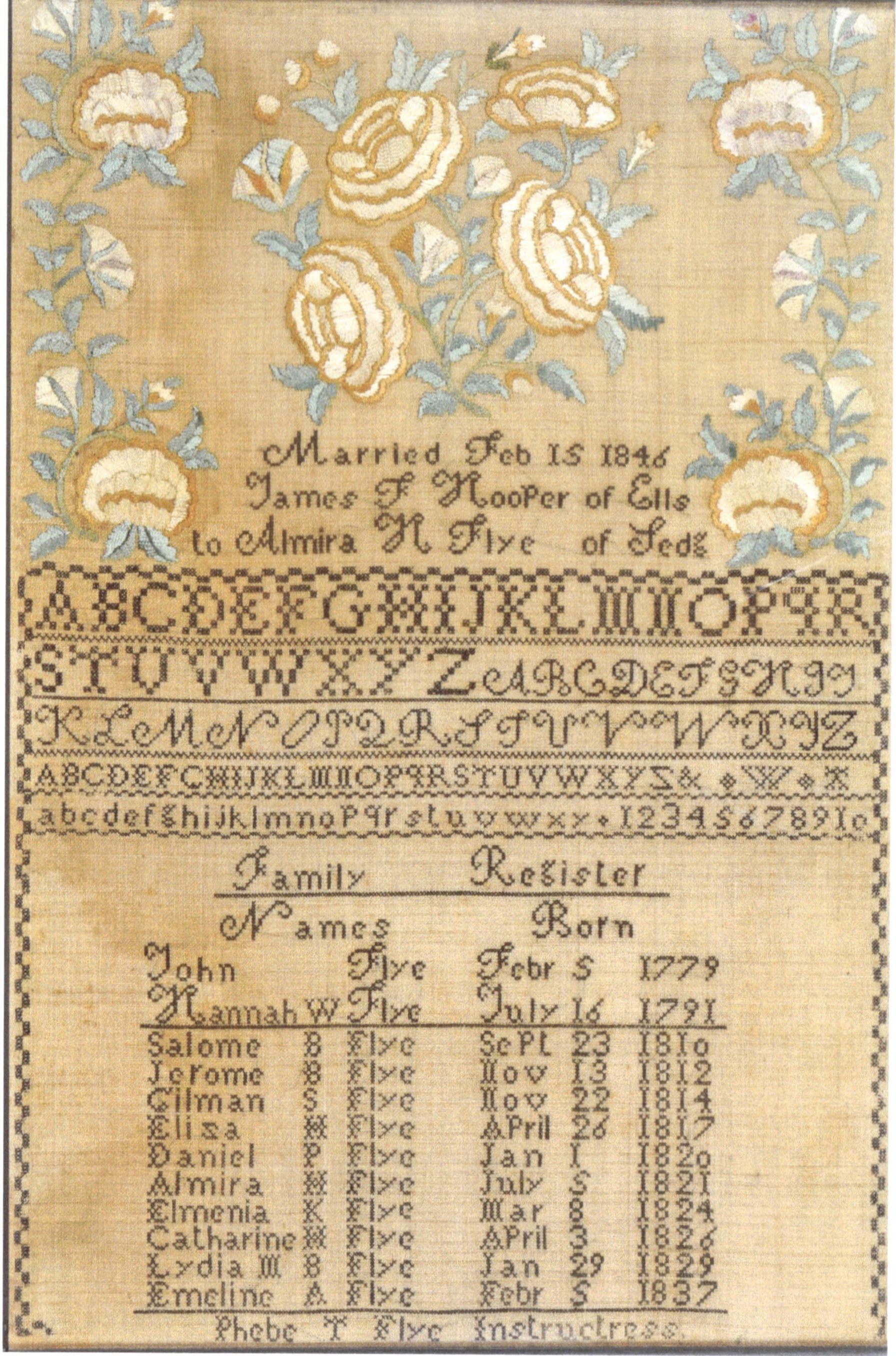

Almira Flye did something quite unusual when she stitched her large, attractive family register sampler in Sedgwick, Maine, near Blue Hill. She recorded her own marriage in the location that was often reserved, on related works, for noting the marriage of parents. She also provided the name of her instructor, Phebe T. Flye, who was her aunt. A nearly identical sampler, stitched by Louisa Heath in 1836, named Mount Desert, Maine, as the location where it was made. It was illustrated in Gloria Seaman Allen's *Family Record* (p. 68). Louisa included the name S. B. Flye after one of her alphabets, presumably naming her teacher. This might refer to Almira's oldest sister, Salome B. Flye. Louisa Heath's father and Almira Flye's mother were brother and sister. Almira married James Hooper, who later became the postmaster of West Ellsworth, Maine. Almira operated a millinery shop in town. They were the parents of four sons and a daughter. James was listed as both a farmer and manufacturer of lumber, in addition to his postmaster duties. Almira died February 15, 1896, in Ellsworth of a disease of the spine.

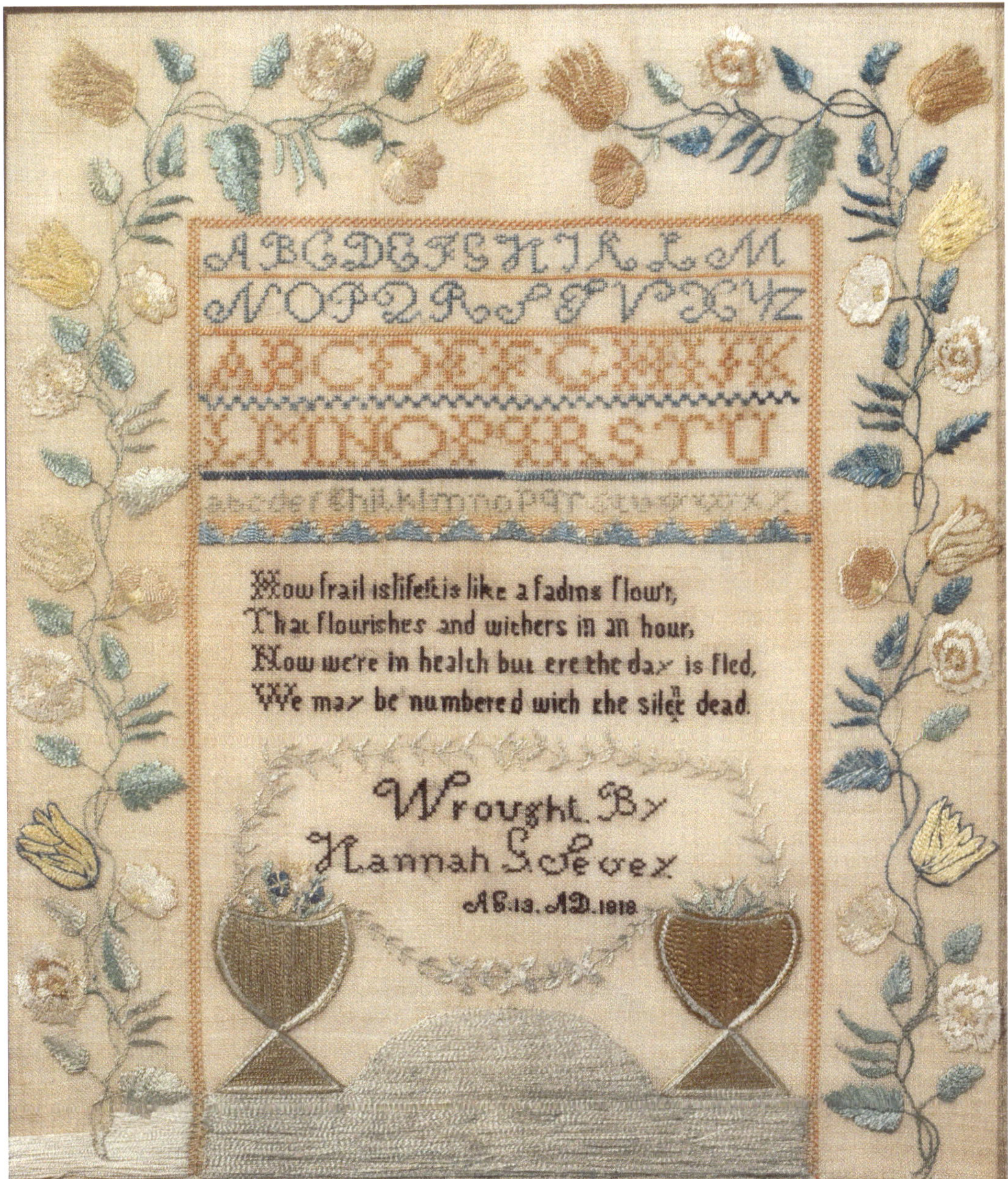

Hannah G. Sevey
(1805–1876)
Marking sampler, 1818
Worked in Machias, Maine
(school unknown)
Silk thread on linen
Cross, satin, stem, lazy daisy, and Algerian eye stitches
20 ½ x 17 ½
Collection of Amy Finkel
(M. Finkel & Daughter)

Hannah Gooch Sevey was born in Machias, Maine, on March 16, 1805, the second of the nine children of John Sevey and his wife, Esther Chase. Hannah was named for her paternal grandmother, Hannah Gooch Sevey. She never married. Her younger brother, James, lived with her from at least 1850 to 1870, but she was always listed as the head of the household, and her modest wealth increased over the years. She died in Machias in 1876. Hannah's instructor is unknown but was clearly a talented designer and teacher. Although the paired urns at the bottom of the sampler are simple, the delicate stitchery that surrounds them and the elaborate floral border combine to create a visually satisfying work.

Sarah A. Cheney (1835-?)
Family register sampler, 1846
Worked in Eastport, Maine
(school unknown)
Silk on Penelope weave linen
Cross and straight stitches
24 x 20 ½
Collection of Dan and
Marty Campanelli

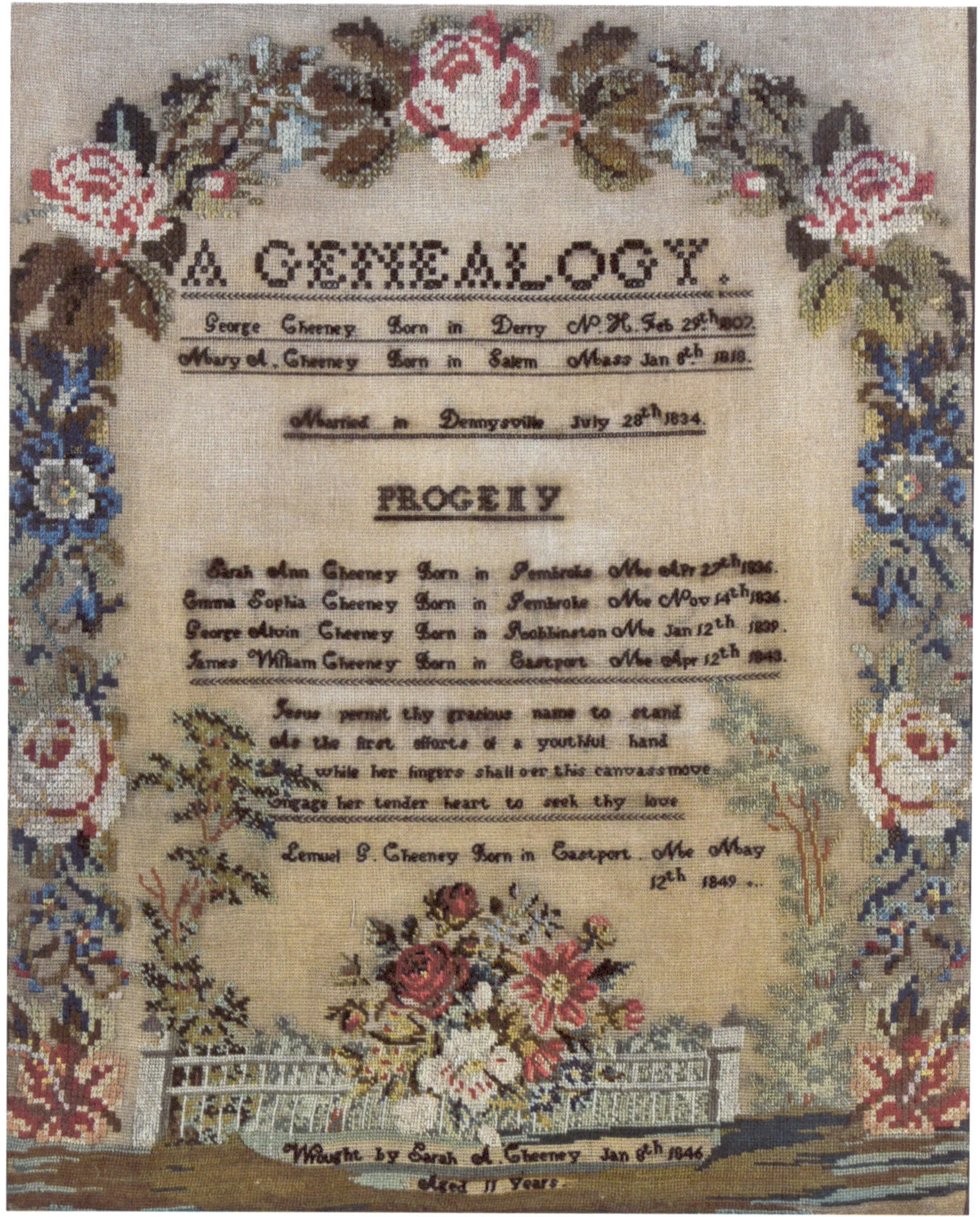

Sarah Cheney's sampler is the "newest" of all the samplers in the exhibition, and shows many signs of the new styles of needlework that were emerging at the time. However, it also continues to demonstrate stylistic elements that clearly tie it to the earlier works in the exhibition, with its lavish rose border and family register format that appears to be a near-copy of many Portland samplers. Sarah worked her sampler on much more forgiving Penelope weave canvas, with a combination of traditional cross stitch and the now trendy needlepoint stitch, otherwise known as tent stitch. She was mimicking the Berlin work that was quickly becoming the needle arts rage of the era—leading to the numerous "God Bless This Home" pieces worked on either Penelope weave or punched paper that now decorate flea market stalls in profusion. Sarah Ann Cheney was the eldest of the five children of George Cheney and his wife, Mary. They were wed in Dennysville, Maine, which is in Washington County, "downeast," or near the coastal border with Canada. On the 1850 census, George was listed as a "trader" and the family was residing in Eastport. On July 20, 1858, Sarah married George Kilborn in Boston, Massachusetts. He had been born in Newburyport and was thirty-seven; the bride was just twenty-three. He was a store clerk and later bookkeeper. The Kilborns seem to have lived in Boston for the rest of their lives. Their only son, George Jr., was born there in 1860.

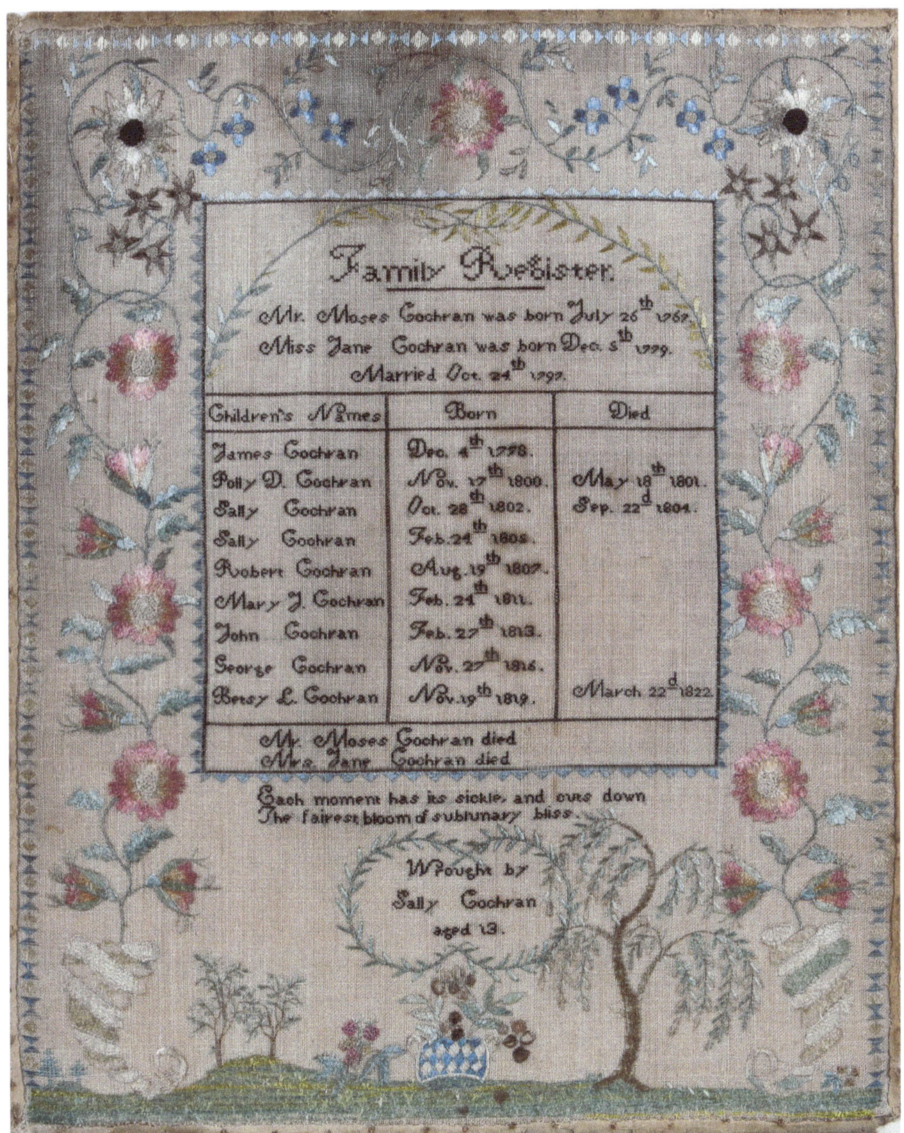

Sally Cochran (1805–1833)
Family register sampler, 1818
Worked at the Pinkerton Academy, Londonderry, New Hampshire
Silk thread on linen
Cross, satin, and straight stitches
23 x 18
Collection of the Dyer Library and Saco Museum

Sally Cochran's lovely sampler is one of a group that has now been connected to the Pinkerton Academy in Londonderry, New Hampshire, as is Eliza Hills's similar work (p. 140). Some of the group of Pinkerton samplers, which date from 1818 to about 1825, have elements that strongly link them to samplers made in Lynn, Massachusetts, a few years earlier, many of which are in the collection of the Lynn Historical Society. Mary Knight was the preceptress in the year Sally made her sampler. It's unknown if she was the source for the design, but she did have familial connections to the northeastern Massachusetts area.

Some of the stories that accompany the samplers in this exhibition are sad—girls that died young, or women who lost most of their children to early deaths, or suffered early widowhood and poverty afterward—but Sally's is almost certainly one of the most unfortunate. Sally Cochran was the daughter of cousins Moses and Jenny Cochran. After growing up in Londonderry, she moved with her parents to Pembroke, New Hampshire, sometime between 1818 to 1820. There she must have had more contact with her first cousin, Chauncey Cochran. They were wed on November 26, 1828. She moved into the Pembroke farmhouse of his mother, where Chauncey ran the family farm, since his father had already died. They hired a teen-aged boy, Abraham Prescott, to help out with farm chores. On June 23, 1833, Sally, by then the mother of two toddlers, went out to pick strawberries in the field behind the house with eighteen-year-old Abraham. For some unknown reason—perhaps in a fit of passion—he murdered her there. He was eventually executed for his brutal crime. Chauncey relocated to Corinth, Maine, and later remarried and raised a large family, one of whom eventually settled in Saco, bringing Sally's sampler with him. Sally's two children both died in young adulthood.

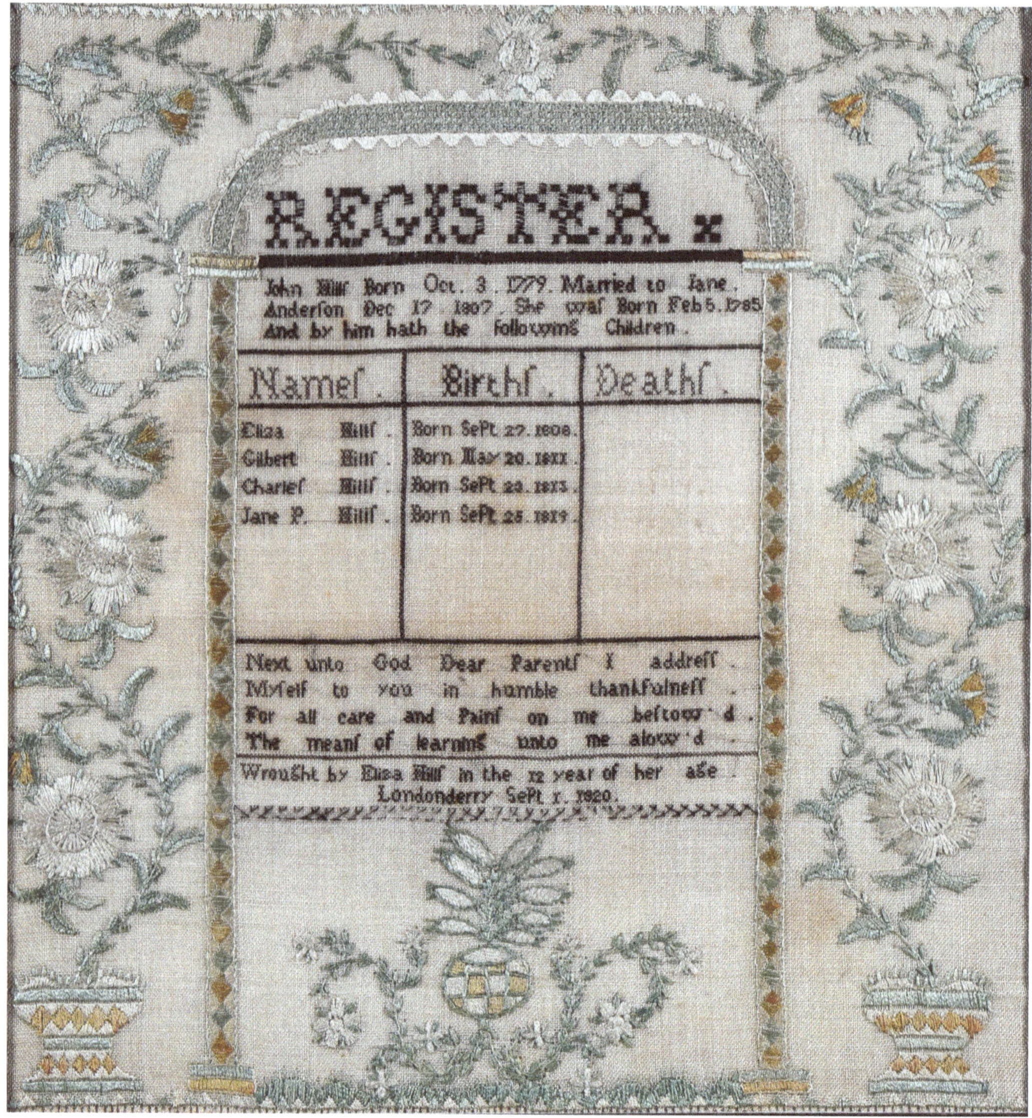

Eliza Hills (1808–1863)
Family register sampler, 1820
Worked at the Pinkerton Academy, Londonderry, New Hampshire
Silk thread on linen
Cross, satin, and straight stitches
21 ½ x 17
Collection of Dan and Marty Campanelli

Eliza Hills, like Sally Cochran, stitched her genealogical sampler at the Pinkerton Academy in Londonderry, New Hampshire. Other related pieces that are very similar and most likely made at the same school are those by Jane Davidson, 1821 (being sold by Dawn Lewis of Needleworkantiques.com, which includes period documents that firmly link it to the Pinkerton Academy); Margaret Anderson, 1818 (being sold by Stephen and Carol Huber); Nancy Anderson, 1824–25 (the New Hampshire Historical Society); Dolly Abbot, 1817 (p. 141); and Anna D. Campbell. (The undated Campbell sampler, which appeared in *A Gallery of American Samplers* by Glee Krueger, was stitched by a Windham, New Hampshire, girl.) Preceptresses of the academy were Sarah Fitz in 1816, Mary Knight in 1817–18, and Mary Adams in 1819. In 1821, the Pinkerton Academy stopped accepting females, but the closely related Adams Female Academy opened in Derry, New Hampshire, and the young women attended there. In 1824, Mary Lyon and Zilpha Grant took over as preceptresses and steered the school more toward academics, a change that the trustees did not warmly welcome.

The samplers of Sally, Eliza, and Dolly, while not made in Maine, are included in the exhibition because the Cochran sampler is one of the treasures of the Saco Museum collection, and this new body of work connected to the Pinkerton Academy is worthy of being brought to the attention of collectors and scholars. Eliza was the eldest of the four children of John Hills and Jane Anderson, born on September 27, 1808. Eliza married Benjamin Franklin Wilson, a shoemaker. They were the parents of four children. She died April 5, 1863 in Windham, New Hampshire.

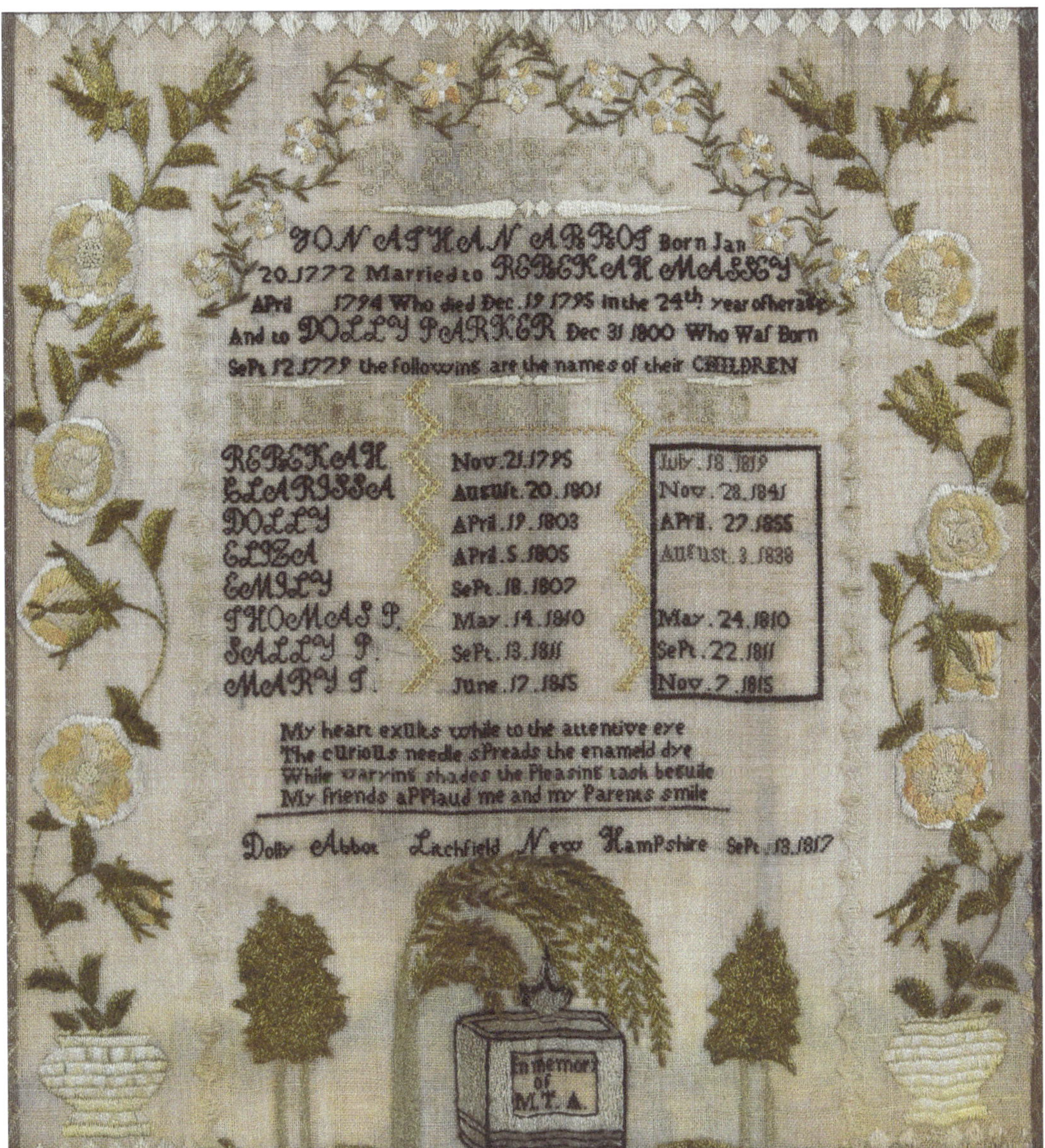

Dolly Abbot (1803–1855)
Family register sampler, 1817
Worked at the Pinkerton Academy, Londonderry, New Hampshire
Silk thread on linen
Cross, satin stitches
17 ½ x 16 ½
Collection of Dan and Marty Campanelli

Dolly Abbot was the third-born of the eight children of Jonathan Abbot and his second wife, Dolly Parker. They named their first-born daughter after his first wife, Rebekah. Dolly noted the initials of her recently deceased youngest sister on the satin-stitched memorial at the bottom of her sampler. Only her sister Emily outlived Dolly; nearly the whole group of seven sisters and their sole brother died young. Although Dolly named her hometown of Litchfield on her work, it was very likely stitched at the Pinkerton Academy in Londonderry. Dolly died, unmarried, in Claremont, New Hampshire in 1855.

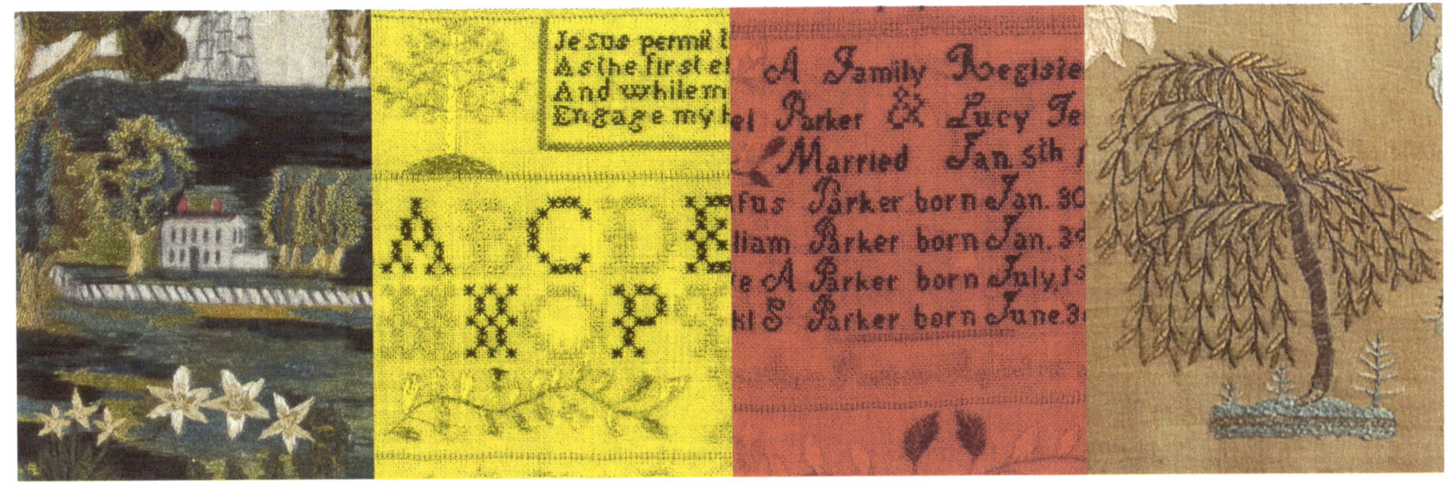

Part Four

The Various Texture of the Twining Thread:
Where Did All That Creativity Lead?

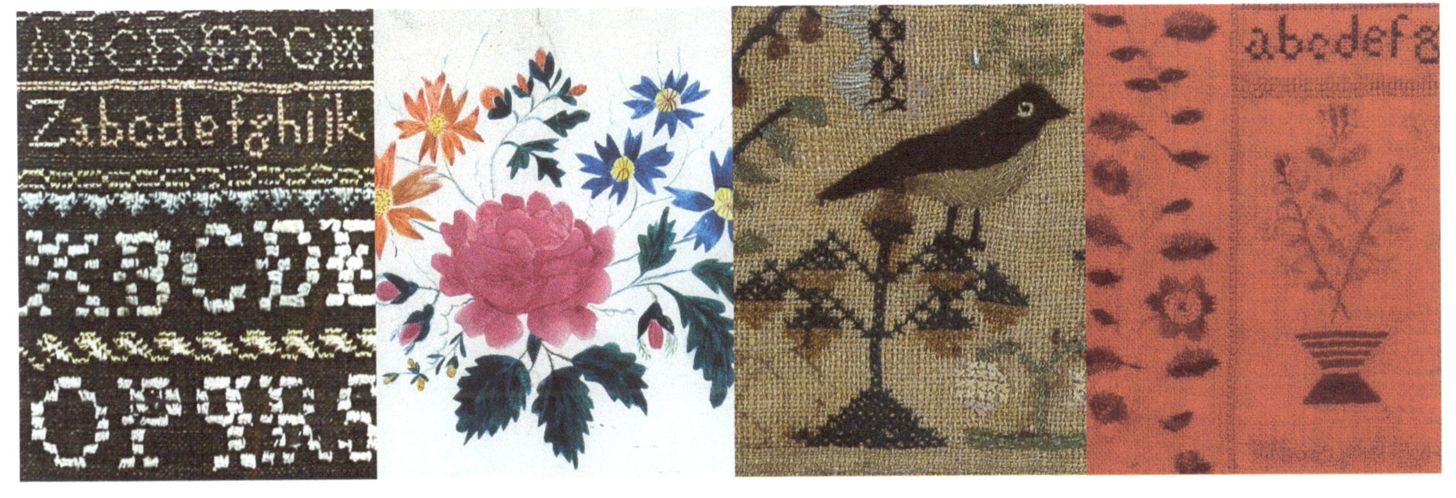

Clockwise, from top left: Berlin work strawberries, wool on perforated paper, 1860

Infant dress with Van Dyke decoration, hand stitched cotton, circa 1835

Lady's reticule, hand stitched cotton, embroidered decoration, 1800–1850

Berlin work motto, wool on perforated paper, 1860–1890

Berlin work parrot, wool on perforated paper, circa 1860–1890

Lace pelerine, needle lace and embroidery, 1830-1850

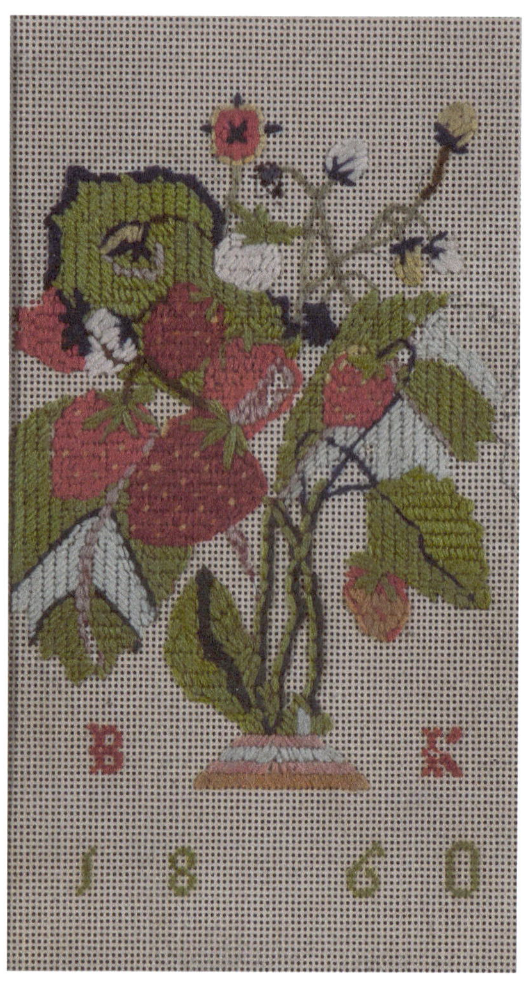

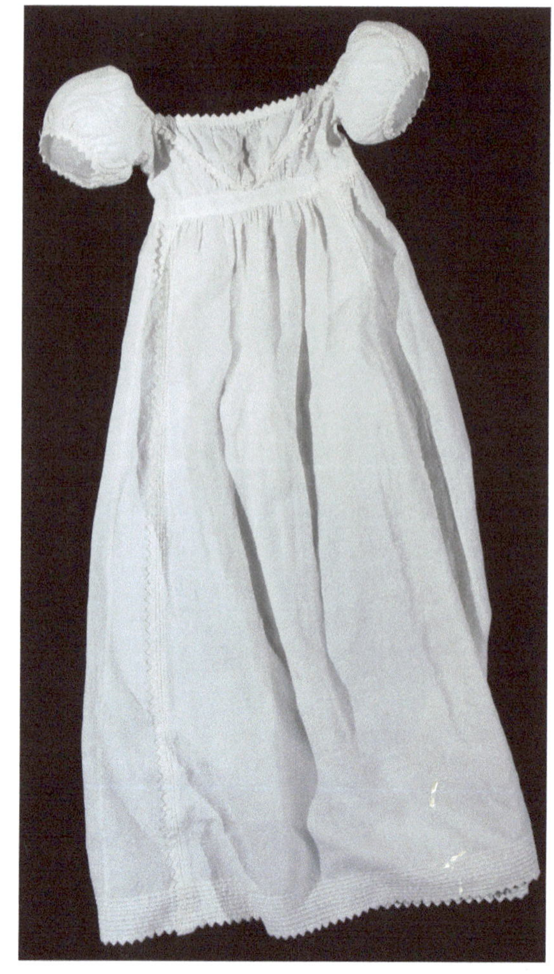

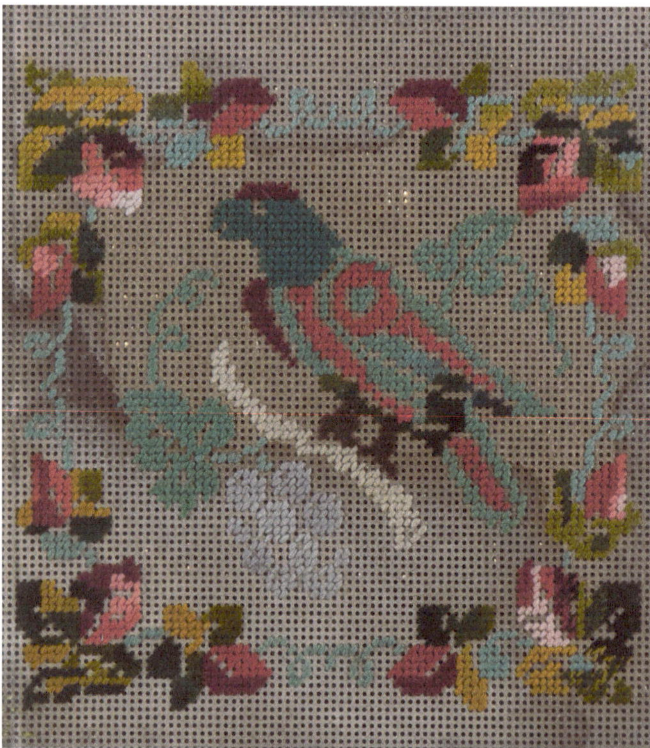

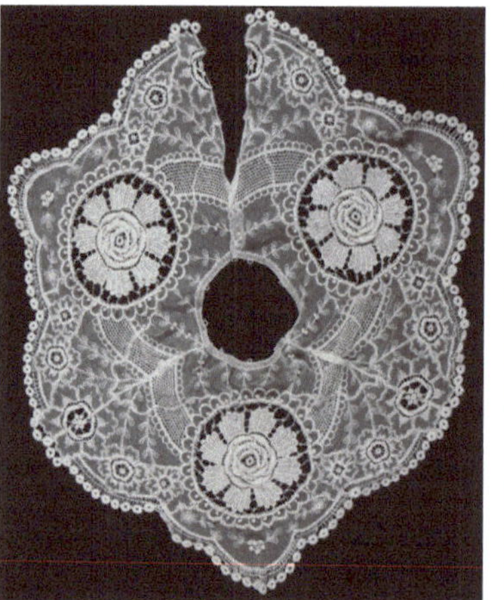

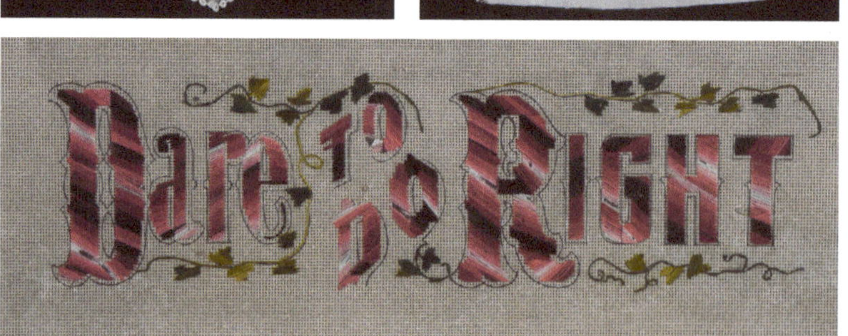

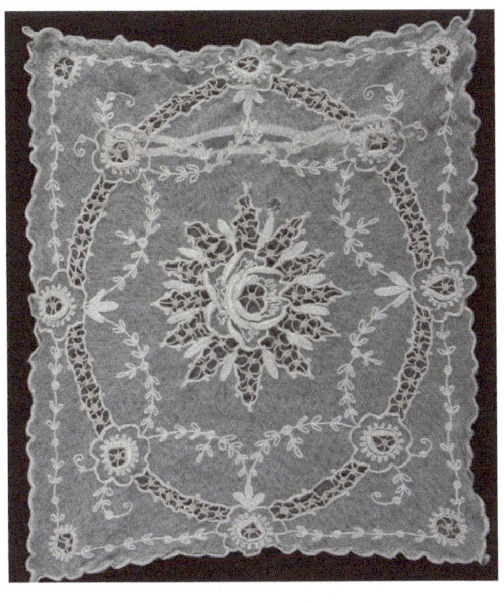

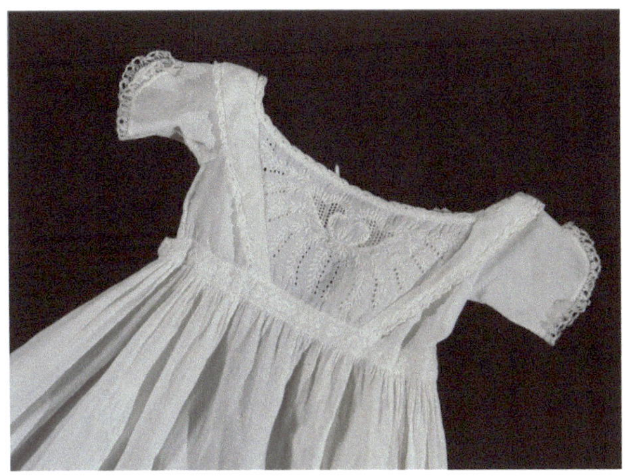

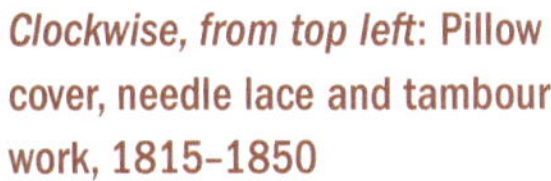

Clockwise, from top left: Pillow cover, needle lace and tambour work, 1815–1850

Infant dress bodice, hand stitched cotton, cut work and embroidery, 1840–1860

Lady's day cap, hand stitched cotton, applique and net lace, 1830–1850

Infant socks and mittens, knitted wool, 1875-1930

Infant petticoat, hand stitched cotton flannel, cut work and embroidery, 1850–1875

Lace collar, Irish crochet, circa 1850–1860

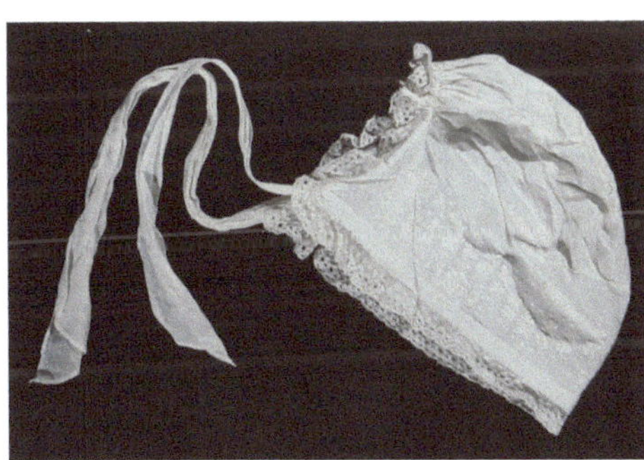

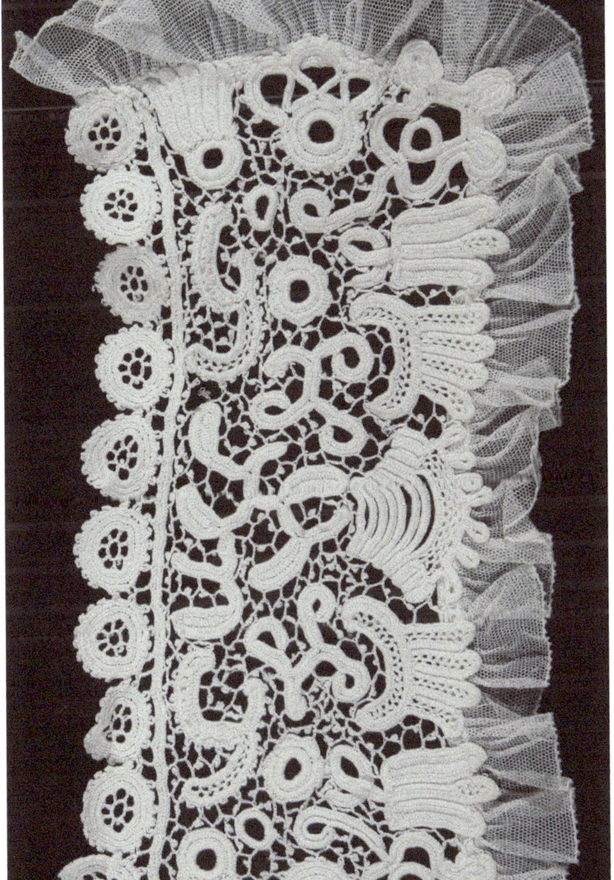

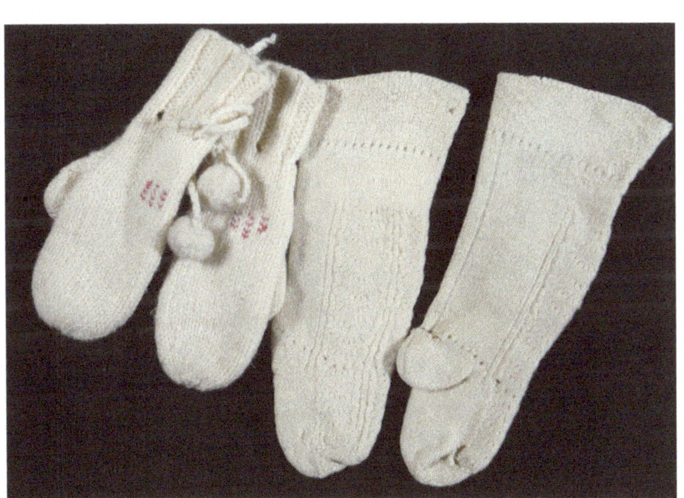

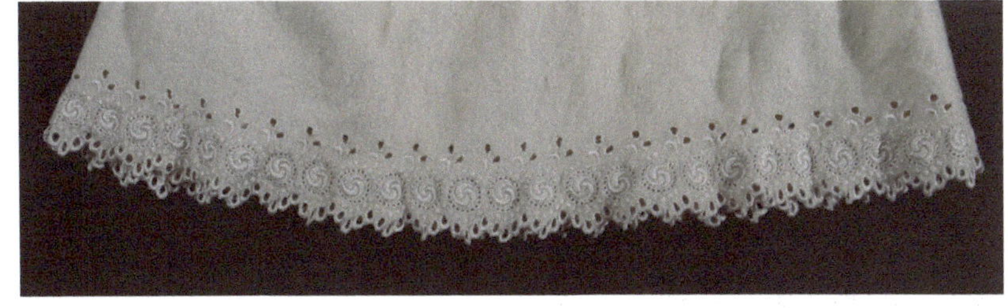

Crazy quilt, silks and velvet, embellished with paint and embroidery, 1876–1900

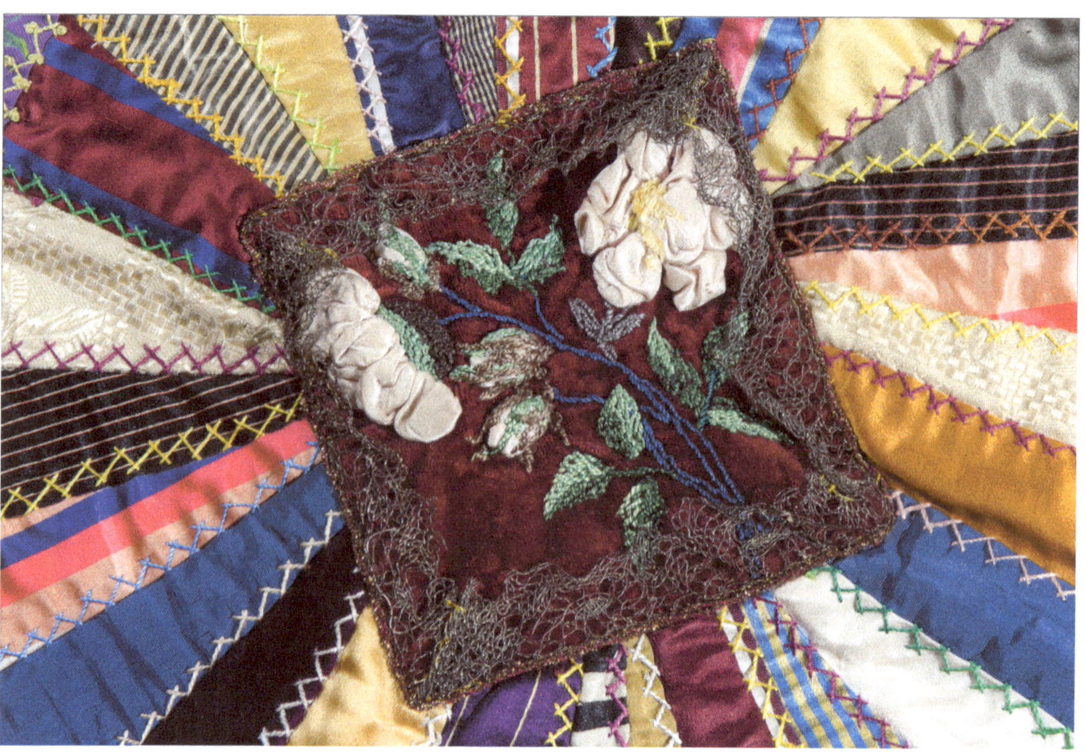

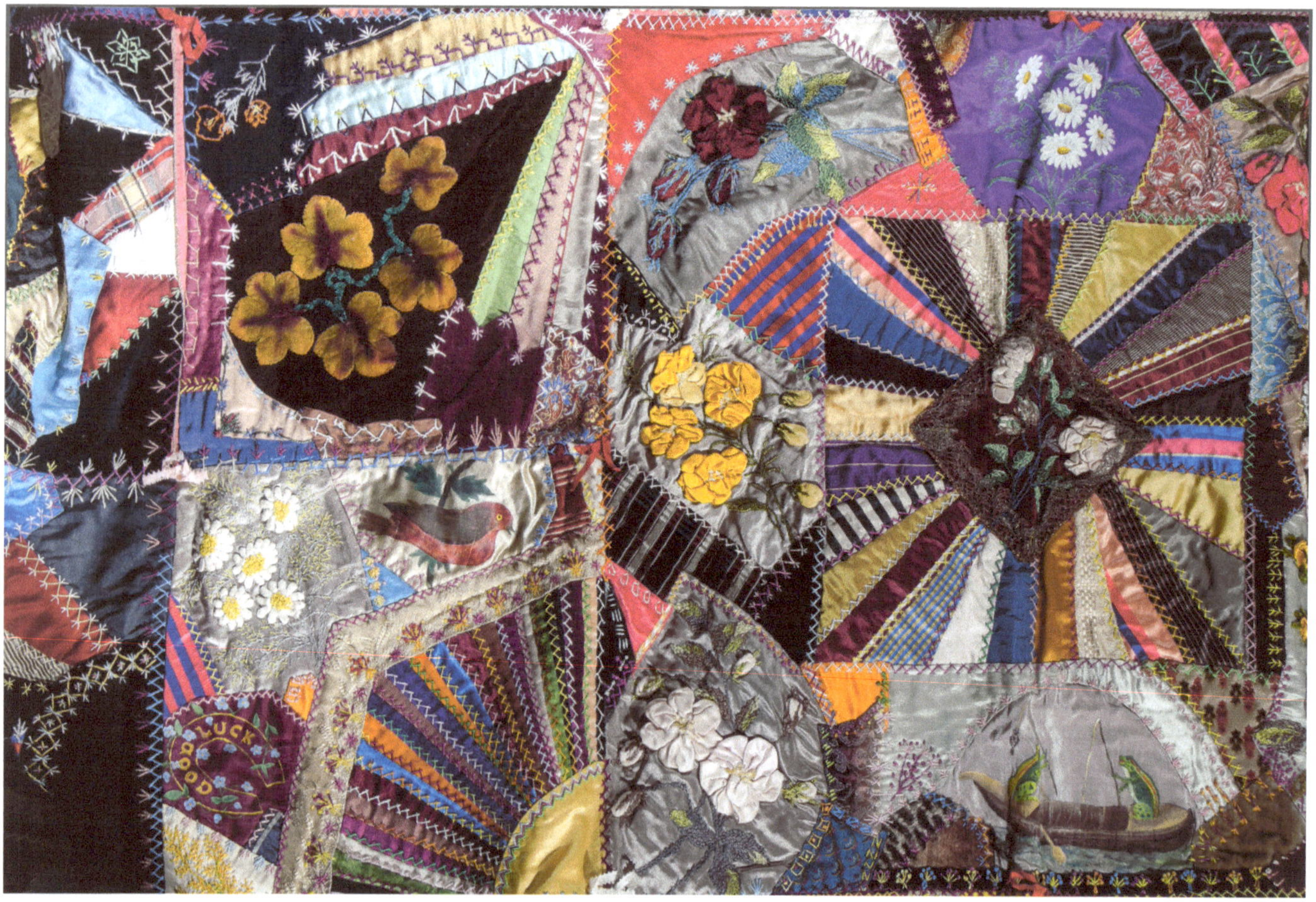

INDEX

www.ingramcontent.com/pod-product-compliance
Lightning Source LLC
LaVergne TN
LVHW070122110826
845147LV00002B/171

9781621371878